Better Homes and Gardens®

the *ultimate*
quick & healthy
book

More than **400** low-cal recipes with
15 grams of fat or less, ready in 30 minutes

Houghton Mifflin Harcourt
Boston • New York • 2014

Copyright © 2014 by Meredith Corporation, Des Moines, IA.

All rights reserved

Published by Houghton Mifflin Harcourt Publishing Company, New York, New York

Published simultaneously in Canada

For information about permission to reproduce selections from this book, write to Permissions, Houghton Mifflin Harcourt Publishing Company, 215 Park Avenue South, New York, New York 10003.

www.hmhco.com

Library of Congress Cataloging-in-Publication Data

The ultimate quick & healthy book : 400 low-cal recipes ready in 30 minutes / Better homes and gardens.

pages cm

Includes index.

ISBN 978-0-544-24579-2 (paperback); 978-0-544-24637-9 (ebk)

1. Low-calorie diet–Recipes. 2. Quick and easy cooking. I. Better homes and gardens. II. Title: Ultimate quick and healthy book.

RM222.2.U48 2014

641.5'635–dc23

2013042588

Meredith Corporation

Food and Nutrition Editor: Jan Miller

Contributing Project Manager: Lisa Kingsley, Waterbury Publications, Inc.

Art Director: Mary Pat Crowley

Cover Photographer: Jason Donnelly

Cover Food Stylist: Dianna Nolin

Houghton Mifflin Harcourt

Publisher: Natalie Chapman

Editorial Director: Cindy Kitchel

Executive Editor: Anne Ficklen

Associate Editor: Heather Dabah

Editorial Assistant: Molly Aronica

Managing Editor: Marina Padakis Lowry

Production Editor: Jacqueline Beach

Interior Design and Layout: Mary Pat Crowley

Production Director: Tom Hyland

Our seal assures you that every recipe in *The Ultimate Quick & Healthy Book* has been tested in the Better Homes and Gardens₈ Test Kitchen. This means that each recipe is practical and reliable and meets our high standards of taste appeal. We guarantee your satisfaction with this book for as long as you own it.

Printed in the United States of America

DOC 10 9 8 7 6 5 4 3 2 1

Cover photos:

Top row, from left: Raspberry-Citrus Swirly Smoothies, page 88, Shrimp Tacos with Lime Slaw, page 338, Lemon-Basil Pasta, page 289; middle row, from left: Creamy Carrot Soup, page 430, Chicken and Peaches with Green Beans and Orzo, page 324, Triple Chocolate Mint Sandwich Cookies, page 454; bottom row, from left: Tomato-Basil Turkey Burgers, page 120, Toasted Angel Food Cake with Fruit, page 449, Cornmeal Waffles with Blueberry Compote, page 28.

table of
contents

3

◀ *Recipes without meat or meat products*

◀ *Recipes ready to eat in 20 minutes or less*

◀ *No cooking required on stovetop or in oven*

Look for these tabs throughout to guide your recipe choices.

No time? No worries!

As a busy home cook, we know that you are most concerned with two things—the healthfulness of the food you feed your family and how fast you can get it on the table. Active families don't have much spare time, but nutritious, delicious, home-cooked meals can be part of everyday despite hectic schedules. *Better Homes and Gardens*® *The Ultimate Quick & Healthy Book* offers a solution to the hurry-up mealtime dilemma with more than 400 fast, fit, and flavorful recipes that can be made in 30 minutes or less.

A Cooking Basics chapter offers a variety of helpful information, including tips for stocking a healthful pantry, how-to's for making the quickest cuts of meat and poultry, as well as simple vinaigrette recipes for fast flavor.

Flip through the pages, find new favorites for breakfast, lunch, and dinner—and everything in between. *The Ultimate Quick & Healthy Book* ensures that good-for-you food is only minutes away!

nutrition
by the numbers

The recipes in this book aim for
a reasonable range of calories, fat,
cholesterol, and sodium. Here's
how the numbers stack up:

Entrées
Calories: 450 or less
Fat: 15 grams or less
Cholesterol: 130 mg or less
Sodium: Most recipes contain
750 mg or less*

Sides
Calories: 150 or less

Desserts
Calories: 250 or less

*If monitoring sodium is part of managing your
health, consider using salt-free items in place of
full or reduced sodium canned ingredients.

bas

1

Tap into these tips, tricks, and techniques for cooking fresh, fast, and healthful meals every night of the week.

ics

healthy pantry staples

When your pantry is stocked with healthful ingredients, you only need to add the fresh elements—lean proteins such as meat, poultry, and fish, plus fresh fruits and vegetables—to be able to whip up a satisfying, good-for-you meal in 30 minutes or less. Keep these basics on hand and you'll rise to the challenge of putting a dinner on the table you feel good about serving any day of the week.

A. HEALTHY OILS: Canola and olive oils are full of monounsaturated fat, which helps lower cholesterol and risk of heart disease. Drizzle lightly on a salad, mix with pasta, and use for stir-frying.

B. BALSAMIC VINEGAR: A fat-free alternative to creamy dressings that also can be used to marinate meat and flavor other dishes.

C. HONEY: The perfect natural sweetener for beverages, desserts, and even savory dishes.

H. WHOLE GRAIN PASTA: Choose a whole grain variety for a low-fat option that'll give quick energy.

I. SLICED BREAD: Choose whole wheat or whole grain for a dose of fiber, magnesium, B vitamins, and other important minerals.

L. WHOLE WHEAT AND ALL-PURPOSE FLOURS: The foundation of so many baked goods. Whenever possible, choose a whole wheat variety.

M. DRIED BREAD CRUMBS: For a good source of thiamin and manganese, use crumbs for stuffings or breading meat and vegetables. Whenever possible, choose a whole wheat variety.

D. REDUCED-SODIUM BROTH:
Beef, chicken, and vegetable broths
are useful for flavoring foods and
making soups.

E. APPLESAUCE: For a quick
snack or a fat replacement in
baking.

F. PEANUT BUTTER:
Offers protein, vitamin E, and
monounsaturated fats that help
regulate cholesterol.

G. CANNED TUNA: Add
to salads and casseroles to
get a healthy amount of
omega-3 fatty acids to boost
heart health.

J. LENTILS: A low-calorie, low-fat
way to get plenty of protein. Add
them to soups and sides. Red lentils,
in particular, cook quickly—usually
in just 15 to 20 minutes at the most.

K. FAVORITE WHOLE GRAINS: Some
options include wheat berries, quinoa, quick
brown rice, and bulgur—keep a variety for a
side dish or to add to casseroles, salads, and
soups. Most of these cook up in 30 minutes or
less. If not, you can cook them ahead of time
and simply reheat.

N. OATS: A tasty, hassle-
free meal or an ingredient
in baking that lowers
cholesterol and risk of
heart disease.

**O. DRIED HERBS AND
SPICES:** Keep the ones
you use most often on
hand for a flavor boost
without sodium or lots
of sugar.

P. LOW-SODIUM BEANS: For
a healthy dose of protein and fiber,
beans can be added to soups,
pastas, and served as a side. Keep
a variety on hand.

top 10 test-kitchen tips for healthful cooking

These tips, tricks, and techniques from the Better Homes and Gardens® Test Kitchen are simple enough to apply to your everyday meal prep—and they work!

2 cut carbs. Make sandwich wraps using lettuce or cabbage leaves instead of tortillas or pitas—you'll save about 150 calories and at least 5 g fat. Still craving carbs? Serve sandwiches open-face on half of a whole grain roll, English muffin, or bagel.

3 don't peel out. Leave the peels on all vegetables and fruits when you cook them. Not only does this save on prep time, you'll also add color and up the levels of vitamins C and B6, fiber, and other nutrients.

1 boost the fiber. Add fiber-packed foods such as chia seeds, flaxseeds, and wheat germ to your diet to help make you feel full longer. Stir them into casseroles, soups, meat loaf, and baked goods or sprinkle over salads, cereals, and yogurt.

8 reduce sodium. Rehydrate dried vegetables and fruits in hot water for 10 to 15 minutes. Use the resulting flavorful liquid to replace a portion of higher-sodium broth in recipes.

4 go for strong cheeses.

For the biggest cheese flavor, use sharp varieties such as Parmesan, Gorgonzola, and smoked Gouda. Small amounts satisfy taste buds without the excessive calories and fat of most milder cheeses.

6 swap the fats.

Replace fat in homemade salad dressings and vinaigrettes with nut oils, such as pecan oil, almond oil, hazelnut oil, and pistachio oil. These good-for-you fats amp up flavor and are high in heart-healthy mono- and polyunsaturated fats.

5 freshen up.

Instead of butter or sauces, try topping steamed veggies with a squirt of lemon or a dash of vinegar. You'll add a burst of fresh flavor with no added fat, calories, and sodium.

7 add creaminess without cream.

For added creaminess plus a fat-free protein boost, puree no-salt-added canned beans with a little fat-free milk and add to soups and stews. The same concept applies when blending tofu into a smoothie.

9 harness the heat.

Mimic the taste and feel of fried foods without adding any fat. Baking quick-cooking meats, such as boneless, skinless chicken breasts, thin cuts of pork and beef, shrimp, and fish fillets, at a high temp (450°F) for a short time keeps them moist on the inside and promotes browning on the outside.

10 chop, chop.

Finely chop nuts and chocolate when adding them to recipes and use a tablespoon or two less than the recipe calls for. Even though there will be fewer pieces overall, the flavor will be evenly distributed in every bite.

BROWN BAG IT

Start packing full-flavor breakfasts and lunches using simple (and smart!) formulas that combine whole grains, dairy, protein, fruit, and veggies to equal healthful take-along meals that will keep you satisfied and full of energy all day.

grab-and-go breakfasts

Starting your day with protein helps keep your appetite in check all day. Combine protein with high-fiber whole grains and nutrient-rich fruit, and you have a beautifully balanced breakfast.

+ WHOLE GRAIN

Whole wheat English muffin and 1 teaspoon light vegetable oil spread

2 slices reduced-calorie whole wheat bread, toasted, and 1 tablespoon low-sugar red raspberry preserves

1 cup high-fiber cereal

+ DAIRY/ PROTEIN

Vegetable sausage patty and ¾ ounce reduced-fat cheese

4-ounce container small curd low-fat cottage cheese

¾ cup fat-free milk

+ FRUIT

¾ cup blueberries

4-ounce container pineapple tidbits in 100% pineapple juice

½ cup strawberries, sliced

=

Sausage Breakfast Sandwich
339 cal., 10 g fat (4 g sat. fat), 15 mg chol., 681 mg sodium, 42 g carb., 7 g fiber, 21 g pro.

Toast with Pineapple and Cottage Cheese
265 cal., 3.5 g fat (2 g sat. fat), 15 mg chol., 590 mg sodium, 45 g carb., 5 g fiber, 17 g pro.

Strawberry-Topped Cereal
226 cal., 1 g fat (0 g sat. fat), 4 mg chol., 162 mg sodium, 45 g carb., 12 g fiber, 20 g pro.

smart lunches

+ WHOLE GRAIN

2 slices light-style extra-fiber bread and 1 tablespoon Dijonnaise-style mustard

1 low-carb, high-fiber whole wheat tortilla

+ DAIRY/ PROTEIN

3 ounces 50% less sodium turkey breast

1 light garlic-and-herb spreadable cheese wedge and ½ cup cooked black beans

+ FRUIT

1 large peach

1 large orange

+ VEGGIES

2 lettuce leaves, 2 tomato slices, 2 red onion slices, and 3 cucumber slices

1½ cups baby spinach leaves and 2 tablespoons salsa

=

Turkey Sandwich
299 cal., 5 g fat (0 g sat. fat),
30 mg chol., 933 mg sodium,
46 g carb., 9 g fiber, 24 g pro.

Southwestern Wrap
341 cal., 6 g fat (1 g sat. fat),
10 mg chol., 792 mg sodium,
67 g carb., 24 g fiber, 21 g pro.

1 whole wheat pita
bread half

⅓ cup cooked brown rice

1 90-calorie chocolate
chewy bar

3-ounce pouch light tuna salad
and 1 tablespoon plus 1 teaspoon
reduced-fat peanut butter

6-ounce carton nonfat Greek
yogurt and 2 tablespoons
shredded Parmesan cheese

3 ounces cooked chicken
breast

1 large apple

¾ cup fresh raspberries and
1 tablespoon honey

½ cup mandarin oranges

½ cup celery sticks for
peanut butter and ½ cup
chopped celery for pita

½ cup cooked mixed
vegetables

2 cups chopped romaine lettuce,
2 tablespoons shredded carrots,
2 tablespoons light Asian-style
sesame-ginger vinaigrette

Tuna-Stuffed Pita
373 cal., 12 g fat (2 g sat. fat),
30 mg chol., 705 mg sodium,
48 g carb., 10 g fiber, 22 g pro.

Rice and Veggie Bowl
375 cal., 4 g fat (2 g sat. fat),
7 mg chol., 272 mg sodium,
63 g carb., 11 g fiber, 24 g pro.

Asian Chicken Salad
331 cal., 7 g fat (2 g sat. fat),
72 mg chol., 532 mg sodium,
39 g carb., 9 g fiber, 30 g pro.

from thick to thin

It's no surprise that thinner cuts of lean meat and poultry cook more quickly than thicker ones do. Here's how to create a thin cut of meat from a thick one when time is short.

Pound: The most common method is to place the meat or poultry between two pieces of plastic wrap and pound it with the flat side of a meat mallet. Be sure to pound from the center out to ensure even thickness.

Halve: Thicker pieces of poultry—such as larger chicken breasts or turkey tenderloins—can be cut in half horizontally. Press down lightly on the top of the piece of poultry as you cut all of the way through.

Slice: Meats such as pork tenderloin can be sliced into medallions as thin or thick as you like. Cut them as evenly as possible so all of the slices cook in the same amount of time.

Butterfly: Cut into the piece of meat horizontally, but not all the way through. Open like a book. Flatten the center slightly by pressing on it with the palm of your hand, if necessary.

fast, fresh fish

For a healthful, light weeknight meal, try one of these simple fish dishes. The flavor-packed toppers are perfect with any whitefish.

1 Fish with Sugared Pecans

Thaw four 5-ounce tilapia or other whitefish fillets, if frozen. Rinse fish; pat dry with paper towels. Preheat oven to 450°F. Line a shallow baking pan with foil. Arrange fish in a single layer in prepared pan. Brush with 1 tablespoon melted butter; sprinkle with ¼ teaspoon salt and ⅛ teaspoon ground black pepper. In a small bowl stir together ½ cup chopped pecans, 4 teaspoons brown sugar, and 1 teaspoon snipped fresh thyme. Sprinkle over fish. Bake 10 to 12 minutes or until fish flakes easily when tested with a fork and topping is browned. Makes 4 servings.

per 1 fillet and 2 tablespoons topping: 274 cal., 15 g fat (3 g sat. fat), 79 mg chol., 246 mg sodium, 6 g carb., 1 g fiber, 30 g pro.

2 Fish with Spiced Mango Chutney

Thaw four 5-ounce tilapia or other whitefish fillets, if frozen. Rinse fish; pat dry with paper towels. Preheat oven to 450°F. Line a shallow baking pan with foil. Arrange fish in a single layer in prepared pan. Sprinkle with ½ teaspoon chili powder; drizzle with 1 tablespoon lime juice. Bake for 10 to 12 minutes or until fish flakes easily when tested with a fork. Meanwhile, for chutney, in a small bowl combine ¾ cup chopped fresh mango, 3 tablespoons golden raisins, 1 tablespoon cider vinegar, 1 teaspoon canola oil, ¼ teaspoon salt, and ⅛ teaspoon five-spice powder or ground cinnamon. Serve fish with chutney. Makes 4 servings.

per 1 fillet and ¼ cup chutney: 203 cal., 4 g fat (1 g sat. fat), 71 mg chol., 226 mg sodium, 14 g carb., 1 g fiber, 29 g pro.

3 Fish with Pickled Onion and Cucumber

Combine half of a cucumber, seeded and cut into thin bite-size strips; and half of a red onion, cut into thin slivers. In a saucepan combine ½ cup cider vinegar, ⅓ cup sugar, 1 teaspoon salt, and ½ teaspoon fennel seeds, crushed. Bring just to boiling, stirring to dissolve sugar. Pour over cucumber mixture; toss. Cover; chill for 8 hours. Thaw four 5-ounce tilapia or other whitefish fillets, if frozen. Rinse fish; pat dry with paper towels. Preheat oven to 450°F. Line a shallow baking pan with foil. Arrange fish in a single layer in prepared pan. Sprinkle with ¼ teaspoon salt and ⅛ teaspoon ground black pepper. Bake for 10 to 12 minutes or until fish flakes easily when tested with a fork. To serve, drain cucumber mixture; spoon over fish. Makes 4 servings.

per 1 fillet and ⅓ cup cucumber: 184 cal., 3 g fat (1 g sat. fat), 71 mg chol., 512 mg sodium, 11 g carb., 0 g fiber, 29 g pro.

4 Fish with Puttanesca Topping

Thaw four 5-ounce tilapia or other whitefish fillets, if frozen. Rinse fish; pat dry with paper towels. Preheat oven to 450°F. Line a shallow baking pan with foil. Arrange fish in a single layer in prepared pan. Sprinkle with ¼ teaspoon salt and ⅛ teaspoon ground black pepper. Bake for 10 to 12 minutes or until fish flakes easily when tested with a fork. For topping, in a bowl stir together 1 tablespoon no-salt-added tomato paste, 1 tablespoon lemon juice, 1 teaspoon anchovy paste (if desired), and 2 cloves garlic, minced. Stir in 1½ cups grape tomatoes, halved; ½ cup green olives, halved; and 4 teaspoons drained capers. Serve fish with topping. Makes 4 servings.

per 1 fillet and ½ cup topping: 179 cal., 5 g fat (1 g sat. fat), 71 mg chol., 556 mg sodium, 5 g carb., 2 g fiber, 30 g pro.

5 Fish with Panko and Dijon

Thaw four 5-ounce tilapia or other whitefish fillets, if frozen. Rinse fish; pat dry with paper towels. Preheat oven to 450°F. Line a shallow baking pan with foil. Arrange fish in a single layer in prepared pan. Spread 2 tablespoons Dijon-style honey mustard over fish. For topping, in a bowl stir together ¼ cup whole wheat panko (Japanese-style bread crumbs), 2 tablespoons melted butter, 1 tablespoon snipped fresh Italian (flat-leaf) parsley, ¼ teaspoon salt, and ⅛ teaspoon ground black pepper. Sprinkle evenly over fish. Bake for 10 to 12 minutes or until fish flakes easily when tested with a fork and topping is browned. If desired, garnish with fresh parsley sprigs. Makes 4 servings.

per 1 fillet and 1 tablespoon topping: 220 cal., 8 g fat (4 g sat. fat), 86 mg chol., 336 mg sodium, 5 g carb., 1 g fiber, 29 g pro.

6 Fish with Tomatillo-Pineapple Salsa

Thaw four 5-ounce tilapia or other whitefish fillets, if frozen. Rinse fish; pat dry with paper towels. Preheat oven to 450°F. Line a shallow baking pan with foil. Arrange fish in a single layer in prepared pan. Sprinkle with ¼ teaspoon salt and ⅛ teaspoon ground black pepper. Bake for 10 to 12 minutes or until fish flakes easily when tested with a fork. For salsa, in a bowl combine 1 cup chopped fresh tomatillos; half of a medium avocado, seeded, peeled, and chopped; ½ cup chopped fresh pineapple; ¼ cup finely chopped red sweet pepper; 2 tablespoons snipped fresh cilantro; 2 tablespoons lime juice; 1 tablespoon canola oil; and 1 teaspoon adobo sauce from canned chipotle peppers in adobo sauce. Spoon over fish. Makes 4 servings.

per 1 fillet and ½ cup salsa: 223 cal., 9 g fat (2 g sat. fat), 71 mg chol., 479 mg sodium, 7 g carb., 2 g fiber, 29 g pro.

dressed for dinner

These fresh homemade salad dressings beat the bottled stuff hands down. Tossed with fresh greens, they make a side salad special. Add some grilled chicken, shrimp, or steak, and dinner is done! Store any leftover dressing in the refrigerator for up to 1 week.

1 Basic Vinaigrette: On a cutting board, mash 1 garlic clove, peeled, with 3 pinches salt. Place garlic mixture in a screw-top jar. Add ⅓ to ½ cup red wine vinegar or fresh lemon juice, 1 teaspoon Dijon-style mustard, and salt and freshly ground black pepper to taste. Shake until well blended. Add 1 cup extra virgin olive oil. Cover; shake until smooth. Makes about 1⅓ cups.

2 Citrus Vinaigrette: In a screw-top jar combine ¾ cup grapefruit juice; ½ cup salad oil; 2 tablespoons honey; 1 tablespoon snipped fresh thyme or 1 teaspoon dried thyme, crushed; ¼ teaspoon salt; and ¼ teaspoon ground black pepper. Cover; shake well to mix. Makes about 1⅓ cups.

3 Herbed Balsamic Vinaigrette: In a screw-top jar combine ¼ cup olive oil; ¼ cup balsamic vinegar; 1 tablespoon sugar (optional); 1 teaspoon snipped fresh basil or ½ teaspoon dried basil, crushed; 1 teaspoon snipped fresh thyme or ½ teaspoon dried thyme, crushed; and ½ teaspoon snipped fresh marjoram or ¼ teaspoon dried marjoram, crushed. Cover; shake well. Makes about ½ cup.

4 Pancetta Vinaigrette: In a small skillet cook 2 ounces pancetta or 3 slices bacon, chopped, until crisp. Drain fat; set aside. In a small bowl stir together 3 tablespoons fresh lemon juice and 1 tablespoon red wine vinegar. Whisk in 1 tablespoon Dijon-style mustard. Gradually whisk in ⅔ cup olive oil until mixture is slightly thickened. Season to taste with salt and freshly ground black pepper. Stir in cooked pancetta. Makes about 1 cup.

5 Raspberry-Hazelnut Vinaigrette: In a screw-top jar combine ¼ cup hazelnut or walnut oil, ¼ cup raspberry vinegar, 1 tablespoon snipped fresh parsley, and 2 teaspoons honey. Cover; shake well. Makes about ⅔ cup.

6 Sesame-Soy Vinaigrette: In a screw-top jar combine 4 tablespoons salad oil,

4 tablespoons rice vinegar, 4 tablespoons soy sauce, 4 teaspoons toasted sesame oil, 1 teaspoon sugar, 1 teaspoon grated fresh ginger, and 1 teaspoon ground black pepper. Cover; shake well. Makes about ¾ cup.

7 Buttermilk-Garlic Dressing: In a screw-top jar combine ½ cup mayonnaise and 1 tablespoon cider vinegar. Cover; shake until well combined. Add 1 tablespoon snipped fresh parsley; 1 tablespoon snipped green onion; 1 small clove garlic, crushed; 1 teaspoon Dijon-style mustard; ½ teaspoon onion powder; ½ teaspoon salt; ¼ teaspoon ground black pepper; and ½ cup buttermilk. Cover; shake until combined. Makes about 1 cup.

8 Blue Cheese Dressing: In a blender or food processor combine ½ cup yogurt or sour cream, ¼ cup cottage cheese, ¼ cup mayonnaise, ¼ cup crumbled blue cheese, ¼ teaspoon salt, and ¼ teaspoon cracked black pepper. Cover; blend or process until smooth. Stir in 1 cup crumbled blue cheese.

If necessary, stir in 1 to 2 tablespoons milk to make dressing of desired consistency. Makes about 1¼ cups.

9 Pepper-Parmesan Dressing: In a medium bowl combine 1 cup mayonnaise, ¼ cup milk, 2 tablespoons grated Parmesan cheese, 1½ teaspoons cracked black pepper, 1½ teaspoons cider vinegar, ½ teaspoon onion powder, ½ teaspoon garlic powder, ¼ teaspoon lemon juice, a dash bottled hot pepper sauce, and a dash Worcestershire sauce. Whisk to combine. Cover; chill in refrigerator for at least 2 hours or up to 24 hours before serving. Makes about 1⅓ cups.

10 Thousand Island Dressing: In a small bowl combine 1 cup mayonnaise and ¼ cup bottled chili sauce. Stir in 2 tablespoons sweet pickle relish, 2 tablespoons finely chopped green or red sweet pepper, 2 tablespoons finely chopped onion, and 1 teaspoon Worcestershire sauce or prepared horseradish. Makes about 1½ cups.

label claims

When you're trying to eat healthfully, you read labels. But it's easy to be fooled by confusing claims on food labels—what do they mean? Here's a go-to guide for common label lingo.

❋ all natural

Consumer demand for natural foods is rising, prompting food companies to use the label "all natural" on as many products as possible. The Food and Drug Administration (FDA) hasn't defined "all natural," but it allows the label on foods that contain no added color, artificial flavors, or synthetic substances. However, the FDA does not regulate the term, so it can appear on products made with artificial sweeteners, genetically modified foods, and other not-so-natural ingredients. Remember, even if the product claims to have all natural ingredients, that doesn't necessarily mean it's nutritious.

❋ live & active cultures

As consumers learn more about probiotics, beneficial bacteria that promote digestive health, they want these live and active cultures in their yogurt. The National Yogurt Association created the Live & Active Cultures seal to help consumers identify products with these bacteria. Because scientists aren't sure how much of these cultures need to be eaten to benefit health, it's best not to assume that a container of yogurt with live and active cultures will really improve digestive health. However, yogurt is still a healthful food, especially yogurt without added sugars or artificial sweeteners.

❋ made with whole grains

The words "made with" are your clue that the product probably contains very little whole grains. Check the ingredients and you'll likely see just one whole grain listed along with refined white flour. The "made with" wording is a sneaky way to lead you to believe the product is made with 100% whole grains. To avoid being fooled, look for the word "whole" on all of the grains listed in the ingredient panel. And when possible, choose the product that clearly states "100% whole grain."

❋ 0 grams trans fat

Trans fats are considered worse for health than saturated fats, so many products no longer contain them. But check ingredient panels carefully to be sure. Even if the product claims to have zero grams of trans fats, it could still have small amounts. The FDA allows this claim on products having less than 0.5 gram trans fat per serving. To meet this rule, companies can shrink the serving size. If you eat several servings, then you're getting high levels of trans fats. To spot trans fats, look for the words "hydrogenated" or "partially hydrogenated" in the ingredient list and steer clear.

✳ rich in omega-3 fatty acids

Omega-3 fatty acids are healthy fats that are beneficial for the brain, nervous system, and heart health. These fats are now being added to orange juice, cereal, milk, eggs, and other foods. The omega-3 fats in fortified foods often come from flaxseeds, flaxseed oil, and other plant-base sources. Our bodies don't use plant sources of omega-3s as efficiently as omega-3s from animals (fatty fish, for example), so you're not getting a lot of these healthy fats from fortified foods. If you're trying to eat more omega-3 fats, choose salmon, tuna, or other fatty fish for omega-3s that are better absorbed.

✳ made with real fruit

This phrase is used on a variety of foods aimed at kids, including fruit drinks, fruit-flavor candies, and fruit-filled bars and cookies. Don't be fooled! There's no FDA regulation of this term. To use it, products don't have to contain a minimum amount of fruit. If you see this term on a product, check the ingredients—you may find little to no real fruit. Instead, you might see fruit flavors, added sugars, and artificial colors. If so, skip the fake fruit product and head to the produce department to buy the real deal.

✳ no sugar added

The key word here is "added." Products can make this claim if there were no sugars added during processing. That doesn't mean the product is sugar-free. It may contain ingredients that have naturally occurring sugars (such as lactose in ice cream) that were not added during processing. The product might also have artificial sweeteners or sugar alcohols. And "no added sugar" does not mean the product is low in calories or fat. Also beware of any products labeled "low sugar." This term is not defined by the FDA, so it's technically not allowed on packaging because it could be misleading.

✳ no high fructose corn syrup

With all of the negative media about high fructose corn syrup (HFCS), it's been taken out of many products. But when HFCS is removed, it's often replaced with another sweetener, such as sugar, artificial sweeteners, and/or agave syrup. Agave is promoted as a natural sweetener, but it's highly processed and has even more fructose than HFCS. To avoid the confusion of trying to choose which sweetener to use, pick foods that are naturally lower in sugar.

2

Start your day on the bright side with these hearty whole grain and hot egg dishes that will give you an energy boost that lasts until lunchtime.

break

maple-pecan breakfast porridge

fast

The mashed banana adds moistness to these indulgent-tasting pancakes and gives them a tender texture without having to add oil.

banana pancakes with chocolate bits and raspberries

start to finish: 25 minutes
makes: 4 servings

1¼ cups whole wheat flour
2 teaspoons baking powder
½ teaspoon salt
1 egg, lightly beaten
⅔ cup low-fat milk
½ cup mashed ripe banana
½ cup light maple-flavor syrup
2 ounces semisweet chocolate, finely chopped
Nonstick cooking spray
Light butter (optional)
1 cup fresh raspberries

1 In a medium bowl stir together whole wheat flour, baking powder, and salt. In a small bowl combine egg, milk, mashed banana, and 1 tablespoon of the syrup. Add egg mixture all at once to flour mixture. Stir just until moistened (batter should be slightly lumpy). Fold in chocolate.

2 Coat a nonstick griddle or heavy skillet with cooking spray; heat griddle over medium-low heat. For each pancake, pour ¼ cup of the batter onto hot griddle; spread if necessary. Cook about 2 minutes on each side or until pancakes are golden. Turn over when surfaces are bubbly and edges are slightly dry.

3 In a small saucepan heat the remaining syrup until warm. Serve warm pancakes with syrup and, if desired, butter. Top with raspberries.

nutrition facts per serving: 314 cal., 7 g total fat (3 g sat. fat), 49 mg chol., 606 mg sodium, 60 g carb., 8 g fiber, 9 g pro.

These breakfast cakes have lots of healthy fiber but still taste like a special treat.

buttermilk bran cakes with apple-walnut topping

start to finish: 30 minutes
makes: 4 servings

⅓ cup high-fiber wheat bran cereal, such as Kellogg's All-Bran Bran Buds
1¼ cups buttermilk or sour milk*
1 egg, lightly beaten
2 tablespoons packed brown sugar
2 teaspoons canola oil
1 cup all-purpose flour
1 teaspoon baking powder
½ teaspoon baking soda
¼ teaspoon salt
1 cup chopped apple
¼ cup coarsely chopped walnuts
1 tablespoon granulated sugar
¼ teaspoon ground cinnamon
⅓ cup vanilla low-fat yogurt
Nonstick cooking spray
Ground cinnamon (optional)

1 Place cereal in a medium bowl. Add buttermilk, egg, brown sugar, and oil; stir to mix well. Let stand for 10 minutes. Meanwhile, in a small bowl stir together flour, baking powder, baking soda, and salt; set aside.

2 For apple-walnut topping, in a small bowl combine apple and walnuts. Combine granulated sugar and the ¼ teaspoon cinnamon; toss with apple mixture. Stir yogurt until creamy; gently stir into apple mixture.

3 Add flour mixture to buttermilk mixture, stirring until combined. Coat a nonstick griddle or heavy skillet with cooking spray; heat griddle over medium-low heat. For each bran cake, pour ¼ cup of the batter onto hot griddle. Cook for 1 to 2 minutes or until bottom is golden. Flip bran cake; cook about 1 minute more or until golden. Transfer to a serving platter; keep warm while cooking the remaining bran cakes. Serve bran cakes with apple-walnut topping. If desired, sprinkle with additional cinnamon.

nutrition facts per serving: 319 cal., 10 g total fat (2 g sat. fat), 57 mg chol., 559 mg sodium, 52 g carb., 5 g fiber, 10 g pro.

✶tip: To make 1¼ cups sour milk, place 4 teaspoons lemon juice or vinegar in a glass measuring cup. Add enough milk to make 1¼ cups total liquid; stir. Let stand for 5 minutes before using.

Cornmeal adds a pleasant crunch to these waffles. Yellow or white cornmeal works equally well.

cornmeal waffles with blueberry compote

start to finish: 25 minutes
makes: 8 servings

¾ cup all-purpose flour
½ cup yellow or white cornmeal
2 tablespoons packed brown sugar
1 teaspoon baking powder
¼ teaspoon salt
1 cup buttermilk or sour milk*
½ cup fat-free milk
2 egg yolks
3 tablespoons canola oil
½ teaspoon vanilla
2 egg whites
Nonstick cooking spray
1 recipe Blueberry Compote
Fresh blueberries, raspberries, and/or strawberries (optional)

1 In a large bowl combine flour, cornmeal, brown sugar, baking powder, and salt.

2 In a medium bowl combine buttermilk, milk, egg yolks, oil, and vanilla. Whisk to combine. Whisk buttermilk mixture into flour mixture just until combined (do not overmix).

3 In a large bowl beat egg whites with an electric mixer on medium-high speed until soft peaks form. Fold egg whites gently into batter.

4 Coat a waffle baker with cooking spray; heat according to the manufacturer's directions. Pour about ¾ cup batter into grids of the waffle baker.** Close lid quickly; do not open until done. Bake according to manufacturer's directions. Repeat with remaining batter. Serve warm with Blueberry Compote, and if desired, fresh berries.

nutrition facts per serving: 204 cal., 7 g total fat (1 g sat. fat), 54 mg chol., 176 mg sodium, 31 g carb., 2 g fiber, 5 g pro.

nutrition note: Blueberries have one of the highest concentrations of antioxidants of any fruits or vegetables. Antioxidants may help prevent diseases such as cancer and Alzheimer's and may also be effective in holding off a number of age-related conditions. Some studies suggest antioxidants improve memory. Blueberries freeze beautifully, so stock up when they're in season.

Blueberry Compote: In a medium saucepan bring 1 cup apple juice and 1 tablespoon lemon juice to boiling; reduce heat. Simmer, uncovered, for 8 to 10 minutes or until reduced by half. Stir in 2 cups fresh blueberries, ½ teaspoon finely shredded lemon peel, and ⅛ teaspoon ground cinnamon. Return to boiling; reduce heat. Simmer, uncovered, for 5 minutes more.
makes: 1⅔ cups

*tip: To make 1 cup sour milk, place 1 tablespoon lemon juice or vinegar in a glass measuring cup. Add enough milk to make 1 cup total liquid; stir. Let stand for 5 minutes before using.

**tip: If using a 6-inch round waffle iron, use ½ cup batter per waffle and serve three-quarters of a round waffle per serving.

Put your waffle maker to a different sort of use with these ooey-gooey breakfast sandwiches.

strawberry and cream cheese waffle sandwiches

start to finish: 20 minutes
makes: 4 sandwiches

⅓   cup light cream
    cheese, softened
4   teaspoons honey
8   slices whole grain
    sandwich bread
1½ cups sliced fresh
    strawberries
¼   cup low-fat granola
2   tablespoons salted,
    roasted sunflower
    kernels
    Nonstick cooking
    spray
    Honey (optional)

1 In a small bowl stir together cream cheese and the 4 teaspoons honey. Spread one side of bread slices with cream cheese mixture. Top four of the bread slices with strawberries, granola, and sunflower kernels. Top with the remaining four bread slices, spread sides down.

2 Coat a waffle baker with cooking spray; heat according to the manufacturer's directions. Cook sandwiches, one at a time, in waffle baker about 2 minutes or until golden. When done, use a fork to lift sandwich off grid. Cut sandwiches into halves or quarters. If desired, serve with additional honey.

nutrition facts per sandwich: 274 cal., 8 g total fat (3 g sat. fat), 13 mg chol., 346 mg sodium, 40 g carb., 6 g fiber, 10 g pro.

Make these French toast strips (like those at the fast-food restaurant, only much better) ahead and store them in the freezer for an easy, eat-and-run hot breakfast on even the busiest mornings.

baked french toast strips with apricot dipping sauce

prep: 15 minutes   bake: 12 minutes at 450°F
makes: 6 servings

Nonstick cooking spray
- ¼ cup ground flaxseeds
- 2 tablespoons sugar
- ½ teaspoon ground cinnamon
- 2 eggs, lightly beaten
- 2 egg whites
- ½ cup fat-free milk
- 1 tablespoon sugar
- 1 teaspoon vanilla
- 8 ounces hearty whole wheat bread
- ¾ cup apricot spreadable fruit
- ¼ cup water
- 3 tablespoons maple-flavor syrup

1 Preheat oven to 450°F. Coat a large baking sheet with cooking spray; set aside. In a shallow dish combine ground flaxseeds, the 2 tablespoons sugar, and the cinnamon; set aside. In a medium bowl whisk together eggs, egg whites, milk, the 1 tablespoon sugar, and the vanilla.

2 Cut bread into twelve 1-inch-thick strips. Dip bread strips briefly in egg mixture, then roll in flaxseed mixture to coat. Place strips ½ inch apart on the prepared baking sheet. Bake for 12 to 15 minutes or until light brown and crisp.

3 Meanwhile, for sauce, in a small saucepan combine spreadable fruit, the water, and syrup. Bring to boiling; reduce heat. Simmer, uncovered, for 5 minutes. Cool slightly. Serve toast strips with sauce.

nutrition facts per serving: 288 cal., 5 g total fat (1 g sat. fat), 62 mg chol., 245 mg sodium, 51 g carb., 4 g fiber, 10 g pro.

make-ahead directions: Prepare as directed through Step 2, except cool toast strips completely. Place in an airtight container; cover. Freeze for up to 1 month. To serve, preheat oven to 450°F. Place frozen toast strips on an ungreased baking sheet. Bake about 6 minutes or until heated through, turning once. Or place four frozen toast strips on a microwave-safe plate. Microwave on 100 percent power (high) about 30 seconds or until heated through. Prepare sauce as directed; serve with toast strips.

The peanut butter and quinoa give this whole grain cereal a big protein boost.

peanut butter and fruit quinoa

prep: 10 minutes cook: 15 minutes
makes: 4 servings

2 cups water
1 cup uncooked quinoa, rinsed and drained
¼ cup apple juice
3 tablespoons reduced-fat creamy peanut butter
1 small banana, chopped
 Fat-free milk (optional)
2 tablespoons raspberry or strawberry spreadable fruit
4 teaspoons unsalted peanuts

1 In a medium saucepan bring the water to boiling; stir in quinoa. Return to boiling; reduce heat. Simmer, covered, about 15 minutes or until water is absorbed. Remove from heat. Stir in apple juice and peanut butter until combined. Stir in banana.

2 Divide quinoa mixture among serving bowls. If desired, pour milk over. Top with spreadable fruit and peanuts.

nutrition facts per serving: 290 cal., 9 g total fat (1 g sat. fat), 0 mg chol., 89 mg sodium, 44 g carb., 5 g fiber, 10 g pro.

Apples such as Rome Beauty, Jonathan, or Braeburn hold their shape against heat, so they don't turn to mush when cooked.

maple-pecan breakfast porridge

start to finish: 25 minutes
makes: 4 servings

2½ cups water
¼   teaspoon salt
1   cup cracked wheat
1   large cooking apple, such as Rome Beauty, Jonathan, or Braeburn; chopped
2   to 3 tablespoons pure maple syrup
1   teaspoon ground cinnamon
3   tablespoons chopped pecans, toasted*
    Vanilla low-fat yogurt (optional)
    Ground cinnamon (optional)

1 In a medium saucepan bring the water and salt to boiling; stir in cracked wheat. Return to boiling; reduce heat. Simmer, covered, for 10 minutes. Stir in apple. Return to boiling; reduce heat. Simmer, covered, for 2 to 5 minutes more or until cracked wheat is tender. Remove from heat. Let stand, covered, for 5 minutes.

2 Stir in maple syrup and the 1 teaspoon cinnamon. Divide mixture among serving bowls. Sprinkle with pecans. If desired, top with yogurt and sprinkle with additional cinnamon.

nutrition facts per serving: 234 cal., 4 g total fat (0 g sat. fat), 0 mg chol., 152 mg sodium, 46 g carb., 9 g fiber, 6 g pro.

*tip: To toast nuts, spread them in a shallow baking pan. Bake in a 350°F oven for 5 to 10 minutes or until light brown, shaking pan once or twice. Watch carefully so the nuts don't burn.

When the weather turns cool and you need a warm-up, try this spiced oatmeal flavored with a two fall fruits—pumpkin and apple.

pumpkin-apple quick oatmeal

start to finish: 15 minutes
makes: 4 servings

1⅓ cups water
⅔ cup apple juice or
    apple cider
½ cup canned pumpkin
⅓ cup snipped dried
    apples
1¼ cups quick-cooking
    rolled oats
1 tablespoon packed
    brown sugar
1 teaspoon ground
    cinnamon
¼ teaspoon ground
    nutmeg
½ cup plain fat-free
    yogurt
    Ground cinnamon
    (optional)
    Honey (optional)
    Pumpkin seeds
    (pepitas) (optional)

1 In a medium saucepan combine the water, apple juice, pumpkin, and dried apples. Bring to boiling. Meanwhile, in a small bowl stir together oats, brown sugar, the 1 teaspoon cinnamon, and the nutmeg. Stir oat mixture into boiling pumpkin mixture. Cook for 1 minute, stirring occasionally.

2 Divide mixture among four serving bowls. Top with yogurt. If desired, serve with additional cinnamon, honey, and pumpkin seeds.

nutrition facts per serving: 168 cal., 2 g total fat (0 g sat. fat), 1 mg chol., 30 mg sodium, 35 g carb., 4 g fiber, 5 g pro.

A savory Italian classic takes a sweet turn in this creamy breakfast dish. Here, instead of broth, the liquid is a combination of water and fat-free milk.

almond breakfast risotto with dried fruit

start to finish: 30 minutes
makes: 4 servings

1 cup water
⅔ cup Arborio rice
¼ teaspoon salt
⅓ cup dried cherries
¼ cup coarsely chopped dried apricots
3 cups fat-free milk
½ teaspoon ground cinnamon
½ teaspoon almond extract
¼ cup sliced almonds, toasted*

1 In a medium saucepan bring the water to boiling over medium-high heat. Stir in rice and salt. Cook, uncovered, for 5 to 6 minutes or until water is absorbed, stirring occasionally. Stir in dried cherries and apricots.

2 Meanwhile, pour milk into a 4-cup microwave-safe liquid measuring cup or medium bowl. Microwave on 100 percent power (high) for 2 minutes. Stir in cinnamon.

3 Add the hot milk mixture, ½ cup at a time, to the rice mixture, stirring until liquid is absorbed (this should take 20 to 25 minutes total). Remove from heat. Stir in almond extract. Sprinkle with toasted almonds.

nutrition facts per serving: 258 cal., 3 g total fat (0 g sat. fat), 4 mg chol., 227 mg sodium, 50 g carb., 2 g fiber, 10 g pro.

*tip: To toast nuts, spread them in a shallow baking pan. Bake in a 350°F oven for 5 to 10 minutes or until light brown, shaking pan once or twice. Watch carefully so the nuts don't burn.

This hearty, veggie-rich egg dish spiked with fresh chiles makes a great supper too.

spanish eggs

start to finish: 30 minutes
makes: 4 servings

1   tablespoon olive oil
½   cup chopped onion
      (1 medium)
1   small fresh Anaheim
      chile pepper,
      stemmed, seeded,
      and chopped*
1   clove garlic, minced
4   large tomatoes,
      chopped
1   small zucchini,
      halved lengthwise
      and thinly sliced
1   teaspoon dried
      savory or cilantro,
      crushed
½   teaspoon salt
4   eggs
½   cup crumbled queso
      fresco
      Fresh cilantro sprigs
      (optional)
      Corn tortillas,
      warmed (optional)

1 In a large skillet heat oil over medium heat. Add onion, chile pepper, and garlic; cook about 5 minutes or until tender. Add tomatoes, zucchini, savory, and salt; cook about 5 minutes or until tomatoes release their liquid and zucchini is tender.

2 Break one of the eggs into a custard cup. Carefully slide egg into the tomato mixture. Repeat with the remaining three eggs, allowing each egg an equal amount of space in the tomato mixture. Simmer, covered, over medium-low heat for 3 to 5 minutes or until whites are completely set and yolks begin to thicken but are not hard. Sprinkle with queso fresco. If desired, garnish with fresh cilantro and serve with warm corn tortillas.

nutrition facts per serving: 176 cal., 10 g total fat (3 g sat. fat), 191 mg chol., 395 mg sodium, 13 g carb., 3 g fiber, 11 g pro.

nutrition note: Eggs are a nutrient-dense food that are an excellent source of quality protein, only 75 calories, and are low in fat. One egg packs 6 grams of protein and 13 of the essential vitamins and minerals including vitamin D, selenium, riboflavin, phosphorus, and B_{12}. The American Heart Association recommends that you limit your average daily cholesterol intake to less than 300 milligrams. Balance out higher cholesterol meals with fruit and vegetables that have no cholesterol and are high in fiber, which help to lower cholesterol.

*tip: Because chile peppers contain volatile oils that can burn your skin and eyes, avoid direct contact with them as much as possible. When working with chile peppers, wear plastic or rubber gloves. If your bare hands do touch the peppers, wash your hands and nails well with soap and warm water.

Adding a little bit of vinegar to the water helps the edges of the egg coagulate quickly, which keeps a neat edge on your poached eggs.

ranchero eggs over polenta

start to finish: 30 minutes
makes: 4 servings

Nonstick cooking
  spray
1 16-ounce container
    refrigerated
    cooked polenta, cut
    crosswise into 8
    slices
1 10-ounce can diced
    tomatoes and green
    chiles, undrained
3 tablespoons tomato
    paste
¾ cup no-salt-added
    canned black beans
2 teaspoons vinegar
4 eggs
2 tablespoons snipped
    fresh cilantro
  Freshly ground black
    pepper (optional)

1 Coat a large nonstick skillet with cooking spray; heat over medium-high heat. Cook polenta slices in hot skillet about 6 minutes or until golden brown, turning once halfway through cooking time. Meanwhile, for sauce, in a microwave-safe medium bowl stir together tomatoes and tomato paste. Stir in black beans; cover. Microwave on 100 percent power (high) about 2 minutes or until hot; set aside.

2 Grease a large skillet; add 1½ to 2 inches of water to skillet. Bring water almost to boiling over medium-high heat. Stir in vinegar. Reduce heat until gently simmering. Break eggs, one at a time, into a small bowl or cup; gently slip each egg into the simmering water. Poach eggs for 4 to 6 minutes or until desired doneness, spooning water over eggs the last half of cooking time. Remove eggs with a slotted spoon.

3 To serve, place two slices of the fried polenta on each of four serving plates. Ladle one-fourth of the sauce over each serving. Top each with a poached egg and some of the cilantro. If desired, sprinkle with pepper.

nutrition facts per serving: 230 cal., 5 g total fat (2 g sat. fat), 212 mg chol., 897 mg sodium, 33 g carb., 6 g fiber, 13 g pro.

nutrition note: Eggs are a nutrient dense food that are an excellent source of quality protein, only 75 calories, and are low in fat. One egg packs 6 grams of protein and 13 of the essential vitamins and minerals including vitamin D, selenium, riboflavin, phosphorus, and B$_{12}$. The American Heart Association recommends that you limit your average daily cholesterol intake to less than 300 milligrams. Balance out higher cholesterol meals with fruit and vegetables that have no cholesterol and are high in fiber, which help to lower cholesterol.

In Switzerland, rösti (ROOSH-tee) means "crisp and golden." They are shredded-potato pancakes that are served as a main dish or as a hearty side dish with roasted meats.

bacon, cheddar, and tomato rösti

prep: 15 minutes   cook: 14 minutes
makes: 4 servings

breakfast

1   egg
1   egg white
1   medium zucchini, shredded (about 1½ cups)
2   slices packaged ready-to-serve cooked bacon, crumbled
1   teaspoon snipped fresh oregano
¼   teaspoon salt
¼   teaspoon ground black pepper
4   cups frozen shredded or diced hash brown potatoes with onions and peppers
2   teaspoons canola oil
½   cup shredded reduced-fat cheddar cheese (2 ounces)
1   cup halved cherry tomatoes
    Fresh oregano sprigs

1 In a large bowl beat together whole egg and egg white. Stir in zucchini, bacon, the 1 teaspoon oregano, the salt, and pepper. Stir in frozen hash brown potatoes.

2 In a large nonstick skillet heat oil over medium heat. Spread potato mixture evenly in skillet. Cook for 8 to 10 minutes or until bottom is browned. Using the edge of a nonmetal spatula, cut mixture into quarters. Carefully flip each quarter.* Sprinkle with cheddar cheese. Cook about 6 minutes more or until browned on bottom. Serve topped with tomatoes and additional oregano.

nutrition facts per serving: 208 cal., 7 g total fat (3 g sat. fat), 63 mg chol., 374 mg sodium, 26 g carb., 4 g fiber, 10 g pro.

*tip: If using diced potatoes, the mixture may fall apart when you try to flip the quarters. If desired, place the quarters on a baking sheet and broil 4 to 5 inches from the heat for 1 to 2 minutes or until tops are firm and starting to brown. Sprinkle with cheese; broil about 1 minute more or until cheese melts. Serve topped with tomatoes and additional oregano.

When you need a grab-and-go hot breakfast to take on your morning commute, these elegant egg sandwiches fill the bill.

mediterranean breakfast sandwiches

start to finish: 20 minutes
makes: 4 sandwiches

4   multigrain sandwich thins
4   teaspoons olive oil
1   tablespoon snipped fresh rosemary or ½ teaspoon dried rosemary, crushed
4   eggs
2   cups fresh baby spinach leaves
1   medium tomato, cut into 8 thin slices
4   tablespoons reduced-fat feta cheese
⅛   teaspoon kosher salt
    Freshly ground black pepper

1 Preheat oven to 375°F. Split sandwich thins; brush cut sides with 2 teaspoons of the olive oil. Place on baking sheet. Bake about 5 minutes or until edges are light brown and crisp.

2 Meanwhile, in a large skillet heat the remaining 2 teaspoons olive oil and the rosemary over medium-high heat. Break eggs, one at a time, into skillet. Cook about 1 minute or until whites are set but yolks are still runny. Break yolks with spatula. Flip eggs; cook on other side until done. Remove from heat.

3 Place the bottom halves of the toasted sandwich thins on four serving plates. Divide spinach among sandwich thins on plates. Top each with two of the tomato slices, an egg, and 1 tablespoon of the feta cheese. Sprinkle with salt and pepper. Top with the remaining sandwich thin halves.

nutrition facts per sandwich: 242 cal., 12 g total fat (3 g sat. fat), 214 mg chol., 501 mg sodium, 25 g carb., 6 g fiber, 13 g pro.

nutrition note: Eggs are a nutrient dense food that are an excellent source of quality protein, only 75 calories, and are low in fat. One egg packs 6 grams of protein and 13 of the essential vitamins and minerals including vitamin D, selenium, riboflavin, phosphorus, and B$_{12}$. The American Heart Association recommends that you limit your average daily cholesterol intake to less than 300 milligrams. Balance out higher cholesterol meals with fruit and vegetables that have no cholesterol and are high in fiber, which help to lower cholesterol.

With ripe, juicy tomatoes and green onions or herbs, this simple breakfast is a fresh way to start the day.

fried egg toast with tomatoes

start to finish: 20 minutes
makes: 4 servings

4   slices whole grain sandwich bread
2   teaspoons olive oil
4   eggs
¾   cup chopped tomatoes
2   teaspoons chopped green onions or snipped fresh parsley, oregano, and/or thyme (optional)
2   tablespoons finely shredded Parmesan cheese

1 Using a 2½-inch round cookie cutter, cut a hole from the center of each bread slice. In an extra-large nonstick skillet heat oil over medium-high heat. Add bread slices; cook about 1 minute or until lightly toasted. Turn bread over.

2 Break an egg into a cup, taking care not to break the yolk. Hold the lip of the cup as close to the hole in one of the bread slices as possible and slip egg into hole. Repeat with the remaining eggs and bread. Reduce heat to medium. Cook, covered, for 5 to 6 minutes or until whites are completely set and yolks begin to thicken.

3 Transfer egg toasts to serving plates. Top with tomatoes and, if desired, green onions. Sprinkle with Parmesan cheese.

nutrition facts per serving: 177 cal., 9 g total fat (3 g sat. fat), 188 mg chol., 225 mg sodium, 13 g carb., 2 g fiber, 11 g pro.

nutrition note: Eggs are a nutrient-dense food that are an excellent source of quality protein, only 75 calories, and are low in fat. One egg packs 6 grams of protein and 13 of the essential vitamins and minerals including vitamin D, selenium, riboflavin, phosphorus, and B12. The American Heart Association recommends that you limit your average daily cholesterol intake to less than 300 milligrams. Balance out higher cholesterol meals with fruit and vegetables that have no cholesterol and are high in fiber, which help to lower cholesterol.

nutrition note: Farm-fresh or pastured eggs are the best choice for quality and animal health. (Pastured eggs are produced by chickens that roam and forage for their natural diet of seeds and insects.) Find them at farmer's markets, co-ops, natural-food stores, or direct from the producer. If you can't find them, make the best choice possible from the supermarket. Options usually include the following:
Cage-free: Hens are tightly packed but uncaged in warehouses. No restrictions on diet.
Certified organic: Hens are fed an all-vegetarian diet free of antibiotics and pesticides.
Free-range: Hens are tightly packed but uncaged in warehouses. They have some outdoor access. No restrictions on diet.
Natural: No artificial ingredients or color is added to the eggs and they undergo minimal processing.

Kale is currently the queen of greens—and for good reason. One cup of cooked kale has more than three times the daily value for vitamin A, nearly all of the recommended daily value for vitamin C—and more than 1300 percent of the recommended daily dose of vitamin K, which can help you have healthy blood and strong bones.

greens and bacon omelet wraps

start to finish: 25 minutes
makes: 4 wraps

Nonstick cooking
  spray
2 slices turkey bacon
⅓ cup chopped red
  sweet pepper
¼ cup sliced green
  onions (2)
2 cups coarsely
  chopped, stemmed
  fresh kale
1½ cups refrigerated egg
  product
½ cup low-fat cottage
  cheese
½ teaspoon dried Italian
  seasoning, crushed
¼ teaspoon freshly
  ground black
  pepper
4 10-inch low-fat,
  high-fiber whole
  grain flour tortillas,
  such as LaTortilla
  Factory Low Carb,
  High Fiber tortillas,
  warmed

1 Coat a large skillet with cooking spray. Cook bacon in skillet until crisp. Remove bacon from skillet. Cool and chop; set aside.

2 Coat the same skillet again with cooking spray; heat skillet over medium heat. Add sweet pepper and green onions; cook about 2 minutes or until tender, stirring occasionally. Add kale; cook and stir for 2 to 3 minutes more or until kale begins to wilt.

3 In a medium bowl combine refrigerated egg product, cottage cheese, Italian seasoning, black pepper, and the chopped bacon. Pour egg mixture over vegetables in skillet. Cook over medium heat. As mixture sets, run a spatula around edges of skillet, lifting egg mixture so the uncooked portion flows underneath. Continue cooking and lifting edges just until egg mixture is set. Slide egg mixture from skillet onto a cutting board; cut into quarters.

4 For each wrap, place one egg portion in the center of each tortilla. Fold in opposite sides; roll up. If desired, secure with wooden skewers.

nutrition facts per wrap: 181 cal., 4 g total fat (0 g sat. fat), 6 mg chol., 669 mg sodium, 25 g carb., 13 g fiber, 23 g pro.

With a well-stocked pantry that includes quinoa, salsa, multigrain tortillas, and canned green chiles, these tasty breakfast burritos can be made on the spur of the moment with refrigerated staples such as eggs, milk, and cheese.

chile-quinoa breakfast burritos

start to finish: 30 minutes
makes: 4 burritos

43

1	cup water
½	cup uncooked quinoa, rinsed and drained
¼	cup salsa
2	eggs
2	egg whites
2	tablespoons low-fat milk
⅛	teaspoon salt
	Nonstick cooking spray
¼	cup shredded reduced-fat Mexican-style four cheese blend (1 ounce)
4	10-inch multigrain tortillas
1	7-ounce can whole green chile peppers, drained
	Chopped fresh tomato (optional)
	Snipped fresh cilantro (optional)

1 In a small saucepan combine the water and quinoa. Bring to boiling; reduce heat to medium low. Cook, covered, for 10 to 15 minutes or until water is absorbed. Remove from heat. Stir in salsa.

2 Meanwhile, in a small bowl use a fork to beat together whole eggs and egg whites. Beat in milk and salt. Coat a medium nonstick skillet with cooking spray; heat skillet over medium heat. Pour egg mixture into hot skillet. As eggs begin to set, fold mixture over on itself, continuing to fold until fully cooked. Cut egg mixture into four portions in skillet; top each with 1 tablespoon of the cheese. Remove from heat.

3 Place a tortilla on each of four serving plates. Lay chile peppers to cover half of each tortilla. Spread chile peppers with quinoa mixture. Top with eggs. If desired, garnish with tomatoes and/or cilantro. Roll up tortillas. If desired, toast burritos in a large dry skillet over medium heat until light brown and crisp.

nutrition facts per burrito: 342 cal., 10 g total fat (2 g sat. fat), 106 mg chol., 1042 mg sodium, 51 g carb., 9 g fiber, 17 g pro.

Homemade taco shells have all of the great crispy texture of the store-bought variety, but with less fat and calories.

hearty breakfast tacos

prep: 20 minutes   bake: 7 minutes at 375°F
makes: 8 tacos

8   6-inch corn tortillas
1   teaspoon vegetable
    oil
¼   teaspoon salt
    Nonstick cooking
    spray
1   cup frozen shredded
    hash brown
    potatoes
2   tablespoons chopped
    green sweet pepper
1½ cups refrigerated egg
    product
5   tablespoons salsa
½   cup canned reduced-
    sodium black beans,
    drained and rinsed
¼   cup shredded
    reduced-fat cheddar
    cheese (1 ounce)
    Lime wedges
    (optional)
    Salsa (optional)

1 Position oven rack in center of oven. Preheat oven to 375°F. Stack tortillas and wrap in damp paper towels. Microwave on 100 percent power (high) about 40 seconds or until warm and softened. Lightly brush both sides of tortillas with oil; sprinkle with salt. Slide oven rack out slightly. Carefully drape each tortilla over two bars of oven rack, forming shells with flat bottoms (sides will drape farther as they bake). Bake about 7 minutes or until crisp. Using tongs, transfer warm shells to a plate.

2 Meanwhile, lightly coat a large nonstick skillet with cooking spray; heat skillet over medium-high heat. Add hash brown potatoes and sweet pepper; cook for 2 to 3 minutes or until potatoes are light brown, stirring occasionally. Reduce heat to medium. In a small bowl combine refrigerated egg product and 1 tablespoon of the salsa. Pour egg mixture over potato mixture in skillet. Cook, without stirring, until mixture begins to set on the bottom and around edges. Using a spatula or large spoon, lift and fold the partially cooked egg mixture so the uncooked portion flows underneath. Continue cooking over medium heat for 2 to 3 minutes or until egg mixture is cooked through, but is still glossy and moist. Immediately remove from heat.

3 Spoon egg mixture into tortilla shells. Top with beans and the remaining 4 tablespoons salsa; sprinkle with cheddar cheese. If desired, serve with lime wedges and additional salsa.

nutrition facts per 2 tacos: 203 cal., 4 g total fat (1 g sat. fat), 5 mg chol., 593 mg sodium, 29 g carb., 3 g fiber, 15 g pro.

make-ahead directions: Prepare as directed in Step 1, except cool shells completely on oven rack. Wrap in foil and store at room temperature for up to 24 hours. Continue as directed.

Kids will love these beautiful, berry-topped breakfast pizzas. They feel like a special treat but are simple to make and healthy to boot.

berry breakfast pizzas

start to finish: 25 minutes
makes: 4 pizzas

¼ cup granulated sugar
4 teaspoons cornstarch
Dash salt
½ cup water
2 cups mixed fresh
   berries, such
   as blueberries,
   raspberries, and/or
   blackberries
1 teaspoon butter
1 teaspoon finely
   shredded orange
   peel
4 ounces reduced-
   fat cream cheese
   (Neufchâtel),
   softened
2 tablespoons orange
   marmalade
2 teaspoons granulated
   sugar
¼ teaspoon ground
   cardamom
2 pita bread rounds,
   split
2 tablespoons butter,
   melted
   Powdered sugar
   (optional)

1 For berry topping, in a medium saucepan combine the ¼ cup granulated sugar, the cornstarch, and salt. Stir in the water. Stir in ½ cup of the berries. Cook and stir over medium heat until thickened. Remove from heat. Add an additional 1 cup of the berries and the 1 teaspoon butter, stirring until butter is melted. Gently stir in orange peel.

2 In a medium bowl combine cream cheese and orange marmalade; beat with an electric mixer on low to medium speed until smooth. In a small bowl stir together the 2 teaspoons granulated sugar and the cardamom.

3 Toast the split pita rounds. Brush pita rounds with the 2 tablespoons melted butter; sprinkle with the sugar-cardamom mixture. Spread cream cheese mixture over split pita rounds. Spread berry topping over cream cheese mixture. Top with the remaining ½ cup berries. If desired, sprinkle with powdered sugar.

nutrition facts per pizza: 343 cal., 14 g total fat (8 g sat. fat), 39 mg chol., 359 mg sodium, 51 g carb., 4 g fiber, 6 g pro.

make-ahead directions: Prepare the berry topping as directed in Step 1 and cool completely. Cover and chill for 2 to 8 hours.

crab-fennel salad

lun

3

Whether you're at home, work, or school for the midday meal, these sandwiches, salads, wraps, and calzones will make your look forward to your lunch break.

ch

These tasty Mexican-style wraps can be whipped up in just 25 minutes—faster than you can get in your car and go through a drive-through for a decidedly less healthful lunch.

beef and black bean wraps

start to finish: 25 minutes
makes: 6 wraps

8   ounces lean ground beef
1   cup chopped onion (1 large)
2   cloves garlic, minced
1½   teaspoons ground cumin
1   teaspoon chili powder
½   teaspoon ground coriander
1   15-ounce can black beans, rinsed and drained
1   cup chopped tomatoes (2 medium)
¼   teaspoon salt
¼   teaspoon ground black pepper
6   8-inch whole wheat flour tortillas
1½   cups shredded lettuce
1 to   1½ cups shredded cheddar or Monterey Jack cheese (4 to 6 ounces)
     Salsa (optional)

1 In a large skillet cook ground beef, onion, and garlic for 5 minutes or until meat is brown, using a wooden spoon to break up meat as it cooks. Drain off fat.

2 Stir cumin, chili powder, and coriander into meat mixture in skillet. Cook and stir for 1 minute. Stir in black beans, tomatoes, salt, and black pepper. Cook, covered, for 5 minutes more, stirring occasionally.

3 To serve, spoon beef mixture down the center of each tortilla. Sprinkle with lettuce and cheddar cheese. Roll up. If desired, serve with salsa.

nutrition facts per wrap: 267 cal., 10 g total fat (5 g sat. fat), 44 mg chol., 593 mg sodium, 27 g carb., 14 g fiber, 19 g pro.

High in protein and packed with veggies, chef salad is a crunchy lunch that really satisfies. This handheld version makes it totable too.

all-wrapped-up chef salad

start to finish: 20 minutes
makes: 2 wraps

2 8-inch whole grain, whole wheat, or plain flour tortillas
¾ cup torn romaine lettuce
4 ounces thinly sliced deli roast beef and/ or turkey breast
½ of an avocado, seeded, peeled, and sliced
¼ of a cucumber, seeded and thinly sliced
¼ cup shredded Monterey Jack cheese with jalapeño peppers (1 ounce)
   Bottled Thousand Island or ranch salad dressing (optional)

1 Layer tortillas with romaine, roast beef, avocado, cucumber, and Monterey Jack cheese. Roll up tortillas. If desired, cut tortilla rolls in half diagonally.

2 Serve immediately or wrap each tortilla tightly in plastic wrap. Chill for up to 6 hours. If desired, serve with dressing.

nutrition facts per wrap: 351 cal., 15 g total fat (5 g sat. fat), 39 mg chol., 1081 mg sodium, 33 g carb., 6 g fiber, 20 g pro.

tip: To transport for lunch, place wrap and, if desired, dressing in an insulated container with ice packs. Do not hold longer than 6 hours or avocado may darken.

kitchen tip: Toting your own lunch to work means you can eat more healthfully and inexpensively than buying lunch out. If you don't have a refrigerator at your workplace, be sure to keep cold foods cold—40°F or below—to keep them safe for eating. The best way to do this is to pack your lunch in an insulated lunch tote with refreezable cold packs. When you get home from work, wash and dry the packs, then put them immediately back into the freezer so they're ready for the next day.

Canned salmon that still contains the bones (that are easily removed before eating, of course) is a very good source of calcium.

salmon and asparagus wraps

start to finish: 20 minutes
makes: 2 wraps

6   thin fresh asparagus spears
¼   cup tub-style fat-free cream cheese
1   teaspoon finely shredded lemon peel
1   tablespoon lemon juice
     Dash cayenne pepper
3   ounces smoked salmon, coarsely flaked and skin and bones removed
2   tablespoons snipped fresh basil or 1 teaspoon dried basil, crushed
2   6- to 7-inch whole wheat flour tortillas
¼   red sweet pepper, cut into thin bite-size strips

1 Snap off and discard woody bases from asparagus. In a covered large saucepan cook asparagus spears in a small amount of boiling lightly salted water for 3 to 5 minutes or until crisp-tender. Drain asparagus and immediately plunge into ice water to cool quickly. Drain again; pat dry with paper towels. Set asparagus aside.

2 In a small bowl stir together cream cheese, lemon peel, lemon juice, and cayenne pepper. Fold in flaked salmon and basil. Spread on tortillas. Top with asparagus spears and sweet pepper. Roll up tortillas. If necessary, secure with toothpicks. Serve immediately or wrap individually in plastic wrap and chill overnight.

nutrition facts per wrap: 160 cal., 3 g total fat (1 g sat. fat), 12 mg chol., 555 mg sodium, 20 g carb., 3 g fiber, 13 g pro.

tip: To transport for lunch, chill wraps for at least 2 hours or up to 24 hours. Pack chilled wraps in insulated lunch boxes with ice packs.

If you like your lunch lip-tingling, try to find Thai chiles. These blazing-hot chiles can be red or green. They are small and slender with a very pointed tip.

thai tuna wraps

start to finish: 25 minutes
makes: 6 wraps

¼ pound dried
   cappellini pasta
   (thin spaghetti)
5 tablespoons fresh
   lime juice
3 tablespoons Thai fish
   sauce (nam pla)
4 teaspoons sugar
1 tablespoon reduced-
   sodium soy sauce
1 tablespoon rice wine
   vinegar
¼ teaspoon salt
¼ cup chopped fresh
   cilantro
1 Thai or jalapeño chile
   pepper, seeded and
   finely chopped*
1 12-ounce can solid
   white tuna packed
   in water, drained
   and coarsely flaked
6 6- to 7-inch flour
   tortillas
2 cups coarsely
   chopped romaine
   leaves
   Orange slices
   (optional)
   Green onions
   (optional)

1 Cook pasta according to package directions.

2 Meanwhile, for the Thai dressing, in a large bowl combine lime juice, fish sauce, sugar, soy sauce, rice wine vinegar, and salt. Stir in cilantro and chile pepper. Gently fold in tuna.

3 Drain pasta. Rinse under cold water until cool; drain well. Stir into tuna mixture.

4 Stack tortillas and wrap in damp paper towels. Microwave on 100 percent power (high) for 1 minute or until tortillas are heated through.

5 Arrange ⅓ cup romaine down center of one tortilla. Spoon about ½ cup of the tuna mixture on the romaine; roll up. Repeat with remaining tortillas and tuna mixture. If desired, garnish with orange slices and green onions.

nutrition facts per wrap: 233 cal., 3 g total fat (1 g sat. fat), 18 mg chol., 865 mg sodium, 35 g carb., 2 g fiber, 16 g pro.

✱tip: Because chile peppers contain volatile oils that can burn your skin and eyes, avoid direct contact with them as much as possible. When working with chile peppers, wear plastic or rubber gloves. If your bare hands do touch the peppers, wash your hands and nails well with soap and warm water.

Store-bought hummus is convenient, but homemade hummus is so simple to make—and a lot more economical. Chickpeas, garlic, olive oil, lemon juice, and tahini (sesame butter) are the main ingredients. Make some on the weekend (see recipe for Creamy Hummus, page 78) to enjoy all week.

tuna and hummus wrap

start to finish: 20 minutes
makes: 4 wraps

1 6-ounce can very low sodium chunk white tuna (water pack), drained
1 small cucumber, peeled, seeded, and finely chopped
1 small tomato, seeded and chopped
2 tablespoons olive oil
1 tablespoon snipped fresh dill or 1 teaspoon dried dill, crushed
¼ teaspoon ground black pepper
⅓ cup refrigerated cucumber-dill hummus
4 8-inch whole wheat tortillas
4 cups torn packaged lettuce (such as hearts of romaine, European blend, or Mediterranean blend)

1 In a medium bowl stir together tuna, cucumber, tomato, oil, dill, and pepper.

2 Spread hummus on one side of each tortilla. Toss tuna mixture with lettuce. Divide evenly among the tortillas. Roll up.

nutrition facts per wrap: 280 cal., 11 g total fat (1 g sat. fat), 19 mg chol., 482 mg sodium, 32 g carb., 4 g fiber, 16 g pro.

This super-fresh vegetarian wrap packed with carrot, cucumber, and sweet pepper takes just minutes to make in the morning before you dash out the door.

crunch-time veggie wrap

start to finish: 15 minutes
makes: 1 wrap

¼   of a medium peeled, seeded avocado
⅛   teaspoon lime juice
1   light flatbread original wrap, such as Flatout brand
1   medium carrot, cut into thin bite-size strips
¼   small cucumber, cut into thin bite-size strips
¼   small red sweet pepper, seeded and cut into thin bite-size strips
1   tablespoon crumbled feta cheese

1 Place avocado in a small bowl; mash with a fork. Stir in lime juice. Spread avocado mixture over the wrap.

2 Arrange carrot, cucumber, and red pepper strips on top of the avocado mixture, leaving about 2 inches of space at each end of the wrap. Sprinkle with feta cheese; roll up.

3 Serve wrap immediately or cover and chill for up to 4 hours. If desired, cut in half diagonally.

nutrition facts per wrap: 211 cal., 10 g total fat (2 g sat. fat), 8 mg chol., 471 mg sodium, 28 g carb., 14 g fiber, 12 g pro.

This Greek-style sandwich offers up the flavors of a traditional gyro—with a lot less fat, calories, and sodium.

cucumber chicken pita sandwiches

start to finish: 15 minutes
makes: 4 sandwiches

1 For dressing, in a small bowl stir together yogurt, cucumber, dill, and mint; set aside.

½ cup plain yogurt
¼ cup finely chopped cucumber
½ teaspoon dried dill
¼ teaspoon dried mint, crushed
4 large pita bread rounds
4 lettuce leaves
6 ounces thinly sliced fully cooked chicken breast
1 small tomato, thinly sliced
⅓ cup crumbled feta cheese

2 Place pita bread rounds on plates. Top with lettuce, chicken, tomato, and feta cheese. Spoon dressing on top. Roll up pita bread. Secure with wooden toothpicks. Serve immediately.

nutrition facts per sandwich: 377 cal., 14 g total fat (5 g sat. fat), 55 mg chol., 793 mg sodium, 43 g carb., 1 g fiber, 18 g pro.

kitchen tip: Cooked boneless, skinless chicken breast is a helpful thing to have on hand in a household that is looking to cook quick and healthy. It's great on sandwiches and in wraps or tossed on top of some greens for a hearty main-dish salad. The simplest way to cook boneless chicken breast is to poach it, which helps keep it moist. Simply place 3 to 4 chicken breasts in a large skillet and add 1 to 2 cups water. Bring to a boil. Cover and reduce heat and cook for about 10 to 12 minutes or until an instant-read thermometer reads 170°F. Remove to a plate and let cool 15 to 20 minutes. Wrap each breast tightly in plastic wrap, then place in a resealable plastic bag. Store in the refrigerator for up to 3 days.

Here's a tip for keeping avocadoes from bruising before you use them. Buy them green, when very firm, and then let them sit on the counter for a couple of days until they are ripe—they yield gently when pressed with a finger.

chicken club sandwiches with avocado spread

start to finish: 15 minutes
makes: 4 sandwiches

1   ripe avocado
1   tablespoon lime juice
    Salt
    Ground black pepper
4   potato rolls, ciabatta
    buns, or hamburger
    buns, split and
    toasted if desired
1   6-ounce package
    refrigerated
    Southwestern
    cooked chicken
    breast strips*
8   slices packaged
    ready-to-serve
    cooked bacon
1   tomato, thinly sliced

1 Halve, seed, and peel avocado. Place avocado halves in a medium bowl; mash with a fork or the back of a wooden spoon. Stir in lime juice. Season with salt and pepper.

2 On bottom halves of rolls layer chicken, bacon, and tomato. Spread avocado mixture over cut sides of roll tops. Place roll tops on sandwiches, spread sides down.

nutrition facts per sandwich: 280 cal., 12 g total fat (3 g sat. fat), 38 mg chol., 892 mg sodium, 27 g carb., 5 g fiber, 17 g pro.

nutrition note: Avocado adds a creamy texture and rich taste—and a shot of heart-healthy unsaturated fats—to sandwiches and wraps. Avocados are a good source of fiber, potassium, folate, and vitamins C, K, and B6. Half of an avocado has about 160 calories.

*tip: For a warm sandwich, heat chicken strips according to package directions. Assemble sandwiches as directed.

If you can find daikon, try the crisp, sweet Japanese radish in this curried chicken salad. It is long and slender—like a very large carrot—with creamy white skin and white flesh.

cashew-curry chicken salad sandwiches

start to finish: 30 minutes
makes: 6 sandwiches

3 cups shredded cooked chicken (1 pound)
¾ cup red seedless grapes, quartered
½ cup finely chopped red onion (1 medium)
¼ cup finely chopped radish or daikon
¼ cup shredded coconut
1 5- to 6-ounce carton piña colada or pineapple low-fat yogurt
⅓ cup mango chutney, chopped
1 tablespoon curry powder
½ cup dry roasted cashews, coarsely chopped
1 cup fresh basil leaves
12 slices whole grain bread, toasted

1 In a large bowl combine chicken, grapes, onion, radish, and coconut; toss to combine. Set aside.

2 In a small bowl stir together yogurt, chutney, and curry powder. Stir into chicken mixture. If desired, cover and chill for up to 24 hours.

3 Stir cashews into chicken mixture. Divide basil leaves among 6 of the bread slices. Spread chicken mixture over basil; top with remaining bread slices.

nutrition facts per sandwich: 410 cal., 14 g total fat (4 g sat. fat), 63 mg chol., 501 mg sodium, 41 g carb., 5 g fiber, 30 g pro.

Most Cajun seasoning mixes are high in sodium, so if you are watching your sodium intake, seek out a salt-free variety—or make your own (see recipe, below).

cajun-spiced turkey sandwiches

start to finish: 15 minutes
makes: 4 sandwiches

⅓   cup light mayonnaise
1   teaspoon purchased
    salt-free Cajun
    seasoning or
    Homemade
    Salt-Free Cajun
    Seasoning
1   clove garlic, minced
8   thin slices firm-
    texture whole
    wheat bread,
    toasted if desired
1   cup fresh spinach
    leaves
8   ounces reduced-
    sodium cooked
    turkey breast, sliced
4   slices tomato
1   green sweet pepper
    or poblano chile
    pepper, seeded
    and sliced*

1 In a small bowl stir together mayonnaise, Cajun seasoning, and garlic. Spread one side of the bread slices with the mayonnaise mixture.

2 On four of the bread slices layer spinach, turkey, tomato, and pepper slices. Top with the remaining bread slices, spread sides down.

nutrition facts per sandwich: 210 cal., 9 g total fat (1 g sat. fat), 37 mg chol., 635 mg sodium, 19 g carb., 3 g fiber, 16 g pro.

∗tip: Because chile peppers contain volatile oils that can burn your skin and eyes, avoid direct contact with them as much as possible. When working with chile peppers, wear plastic or rubber gloves. If your bare hands do touch the peppers, wash your hands and nails well with soap and warm water.

Homemade Salt-Free Cajun Seasoning:
In a small bowl stir together ¼ teaspoon ground white pepper, ¼ teaspoon garlic powder, ¼ teaspoon onion powder, ¼ teaspoon paprika, ¼ teaspoon ground black pepper, and ⅛ to ¼ teaspoon cayenne pepper.

Pressing the tofu before mixing it with the other ingredients keeps this "eggless salad" creamy and prevents it from watering out.

the mighty eggless salad sandwich

start to finish: 30 minutes
makes: 4 sandwiches

1   pound firm tofu
¼   cup chopped celery
¼   cup light mayonnaise
2   tablespoons finely
      chopped onion
4   teaspoons fresh
      lemon juice
2   teaspoons dry
      mustard
1   teaspoon turmeric
½   teaspoon salt
8   slices whole wheat
      bread
1   cup watercress
      leaves

1 To drain the tofu, press on it to remove excess liquid. Slice tofu in half horizontally into two 1-inch-thick pieces. Invert a dinner plate onto a jelly-roll pan and cover with plastic wrap. Arrange tofu pieces side by side in the center of the plate. Cover tofu with plastic wrap, then top with another plate. Weigh the plate down with a can. Let stand for 25 minutes, until tofu is firm and most of the water has drained out.

2 In a medium bowl combine tofu, celery, mayonnaise, onion, lemon juice, mustard, turmeric, and salt. Using a fork, mash tofu mixture until smooth. If desired, cover and chill for 1 hour, for flavors to blend.

3 Spread tofu mixture on 4 of the bread slices. Top with watercress and the remaining 4 bread slices.

nutrition facts per sandwich: 285 cal., 13 g total fat (3 g sat. fat), 5 mg chol., 722 mg sodium, 31 g carb., 6 g fiber, 15 g pro.

kitchen tip: Tofu comes in three basic types: **Extra-firm and firm:** This variety is dense and keeps its shape. It's best for slicing or cubing. **Soft**: Ideal for whipping, blending, or crumbling. **Silken:** Sold in shelf-stable packages, this type has a much finer consistency than other forms. It comes in extra-firm, firm, soft, and reduced-fat varieties.

   Look for tofu in the produce section or deli or dairy departments of your grocery store. Check the "sell by" date for maximum freshness. Store in the refrigerator (unless it comes in an aseptic package). Once opened, refrigerate tofu covered in water for up to 1 week, changing the water daily. Tofu can be frozen for up to 5 months.

The elements of that classic and cooling Spanish soup—tomatoes, cucumber, onions, olive oil, and vinegar—are present in this super-quick lunch, but in a handy to-go "container" made of crisp French baguette. They can be made up to 24 hours ahead.

gazpacho sandwich to go

start to finish: 20 minutes
makes: 2 sandwiches

½ of an 8-ounce
    baguette-style
    French bread
¾ cup yellow pear,
    cherry, and/or grape
    tomatoes, quartered
¼ cup coarsely chopped
    cucumber
2 thin slices red onion,
    separated into rings
2 ounces fresh
    mozzarella cheese,
    cubed
1 tablespoon snipped
    fresh mint
1 tablespoon red wine
    vinegar
1 teaspoon olive oil
¼ teaspoon salt
⅛ teaspoon ground
    white pepper
½ cup basil leaves

1 Slice half baguette vertically through the center. (You should have two 2-ounce mini baguettes.) Cut a thin horizontal slice from the top of each portion. Use a knife to carefully remove bread from center of mini-baguettes, leaving ¼-inch shells; set aside. Reserve the center pieces of baguette for another use.

2 In a medium bowl combine tomatoes, cucumber, onion, mozzarella cheese, mint, vinegar, oil, salt, and pepper. Line bottoms of baguettes with basil leaves. Fill lined baguettes with tomato mixture. Replace tops. Serve immediately or wrap each sandwich in plastic wrap and chill for up to 24 hours.

nutrition facts per sandwich: 237 cal., 8 g total fat (3 g sat. fat), 16 mg chol., 691 mg sodium, 29 g carb., 3 g fiber, 12 g pro.

tip: To transport sandwiches for lunch, chill sandwiches for at least 2 hours or up to 24 hours. Pack chilled sandwiches in insulated lunch boxes with ice packs.

Watercress or arugula—both of which are pleasantly peppery greens—spike the mashed-bean filling with color and flavor.

lemony garbanzo bean sandwich

start to finish: 20 minutes
makes: 4 sandwiches

1 15-ounce can no-salt-added garbanzo beans (chickpeas),* rinsed and drained
3 tablespoons snipped fresh parsley
1 teaspoon finely shredded lemon peel
2 tablespoons lemon juice
1 tablespoon finely chopped red onion
1 tablespoon olive oil
⅛ teaspoon ground black pepper
1 cup quartered and sliced peeled cucumber
½ cup torn watercress or arugula
⅓ cup bottled roasted red sweet pepper strips
1 1-pound loaf focaccia bread, quartered

1 In a medium bowl combine beans, parsley, lemon peel, lemon juice, red onion, oil, and black pepper. Using a potato masher or fork, coarsely mash bean mixture. Stir in cucumber, watercress, and roasted red pepper.

2 Split each portion of focaccia. Fill with garbanzo bean mixture.

nutrition facts per sandwich: 401 cal., 8 g total fat (0 g sat. fat), 10 mg chol., 472 mg sodium, 71 g carb., 5 g fiber, 16 g pro.

*tip: If desired, substitute 1¾ cups cooked dried garbanzo beans for the canned beans.

Make a double batch of these Reubenesque calzones, then cool and freeze them. Thaw, then briefly reheat in a microwave to serve.

corned beef and cabbage calzone

prep: 15 minutes   bake: 12 minutes at 400°F
makes: 4 calzones

1   teaspoon caraway seeds, lightly crushed
6   ounces cooked corned beef, finely chopped
½   of a medium red onion, thinly sliced
1   14- to 16-ounce package shredded cabbage with carrot (coleslaw mix)
½   teaspoon ground black pepper
1   13.8-ounce package refrigerated pizza dough
     Bottled Thousand Island salad dressing (optional)

1 Preheat oven to 400°F. Lightly grease 2 baking sheets; set aside.

2 For filling, in a very large skillet cook caraway seeds over medium-high heat until lightly toasted. Add corned beef and onion; cook and stir for 2 minutes. Add shredded cabbage with carrot and pepper; cook for 5 to 7 minutes or until cabbage is wilted. Remove from heat. Cover and set aside.

3 On a lightly floured surface unroll pizza dough. Roll dough into a 16-inch square. Using a pizza cutter or kitchen scissors, cut dough into four 8-inch squares. If necessary, drain filling to remove excess liquid. Place one-fourth of the filling on each dough piece. Brush edges with water and fold dough over filling to form a rectangle. Roll edges up. Press edges with a fork to seal. Place on the prepared baking sheets.

4 Bake for 12 to 14 minutes or until golden brown, rotating sheets halfway through baking time. Using a large metal spatula, transfer calzones to a wire rack. Cool for 1 minute. If desired, serve with Thousand Island dressing.

nutrition facts per calzone: 380 cal., 11 g total fat (3 g sat. fat), 42 mg chol., 1206 mg sodium, 54 g carb., 4 g fiber, 17 g pro.

tip: Another time, substitute diced cooked ham or turkey for the corned beef and broccoli slaw for the shredded cabbage and carrot. If you like, serve with bottled ranch salad dressing instead of the Thousand Island.

Celery adds crunch to the filling for these classic calzones. They make a great lunch—or a perfect handheld munch for movie night at home.

chicken and olive calzones

prep: 20 minutes bake: 10 minutes at 425°F
makes: 6 calzones

1½ cups chopped cooked chicken (8 ounces)
½ cup shredded Monterey Jack cheese
¼ cup chopped celery
¼ cup chopped pitted ripe olives
½ teaspoon dried basil, crushed
¼ teaspoon dried oregano, crushed
⅛ teaspoon garlic powder
⅛ teaspoon ground black pepper
⅓ cup tub-style cream cheese with chives and onion
1 10-ounce package refrigerated pizza dough
1 egg, lightly beaten
1 tablespoon water
Grated Parmesan cheese (optional)
Tomato-base pasta sauce, warmed (optional)

1 Preheat oven to 425°F. For filling, in a medium bowl combine chicken, Monterey Jack cheese, celery, olives, basil, oregano, garlic powder, and pepper. Stir in cream cheese; set aside.

2 On a lightly floured surface, unroll pizza dough. Roll dough into a 15×10-inch rectangle. Using a pizza cutter or kitchen scissors, cut dough into six 5-inch squares. Divide chicken filling among the squares. Brush edges with water. Lift one corner and stretch dough over to the opposite corner. Press edges of dough well with a fork to seal. Arrange calzones on a greased baking sheet. Prick tops with a fork. In a small bowl combine egg and the water; brush over the calzones. If desired, sprinkle with Parmesan cheese.

3 Bake for 10 to 12 minutes or until golden brown. If desired, serve with pasta sauce.

nutrition facts per calzone: 268 cal., 13 g total fat (5 g sat. fat), 90 mg chol., 320 mg sodium, 19 g carb., 18 g pro.

Crab, fennel, and fresh fruit all have a natural sweetness that takes beautifully to the spices contained in curry powder—turmeric, cinnamon, cardamom, cloves, coriander, and a bit of heat from ground chiles.

crab-fennel salad

start to finish: 20 minutes
makes: 3 servings

⅓ cup plain low-fat yogurt
2 tablespoons mayonnaise
2 tablespoons milk
½ teaspoon curry powder
2 cups coarsely chopped fresh fruit, such as cantaloupe, strawberries, honeydew melon, and/or pineapple
1 6- to 8-ounce package chunk-style imitation crabmeat or lobster
¾ cup sliced fennel
4 cups torn mixed salad greens

1 For dressing, in a small bowl stir together yogurt, mayonnaise, milk, and curry powder. If desired, thin dressing with additional milk.

2 In a large bowl combine fresh fruit, crabmeat, and fennel. Add dressing and gently toss to coat; set aside. Divide salad greens among three salad plates. Top with crabmeat mixture.

nutrition facts per serving: 176 cal., 5 g total fat (1 g sat. fat), 16 mg chol., 601 mg sodium, 24 g carb., 3 g fiber, 10 g pro.

Some people have a sensitivity to sulfur dioxide, the preservative used on dried apricots to help them retain their bright color and softness. If you do, look for unsulfured apricots in the health-food section of your supermarket. They won't be as pretty—they will be brown—but they will taste just as good.

moroccan couscous salad with apricots

start to finish: 20 minutes
makes: 6 servings

1½   cups chicken or
        vegetable broth
        Dash ground nutmeg
  1   cup couscous
  ½   cup raisins
  ¼   cup chopped dried
        apricots
  1   15-ounce can
        garbanzo beans
        (chickpeas), rinsed
        and drained
  3   tablespoons olive or
        canola oil
  ½   teaspoon finely
        shredded lemon
        peel
  3   tablespoons fresh
        lemon juice
  ½   teaspoon salt
  ¼   teaspoon freshly
        ground black
        pepper

1 In a medium saucepan combine broth and nutmeg. Bring to boiling; remove from heat. Stir in couscous, raisins, and apricots. Cover and let stand for 5 minutes.

2 Fluff couscous with fork. In a large bowl combine couscous and garbanzo beans.

3 For dressing, in a small bowl whisk together oil, lemon peel, lemon juice, salt, and pepper. Pour over couscous mixture; toss to combine. Serve at room temperature.

nutrition facts per serving: 277 cal., 8 g total fat (1 g sat. fat), 1 mg chol., 581 mg sodium, 45 g carb., 5 g fiber, 8 g pro.

The elements of the classic Italian caprese salad—mozzarella, tomatoes, and basil—are combined with multigrain pasta, and sweet peppers to make a hearty main-dish pasta salad.

caprese pasta salad

start to finish: 30 minutes
makes: 6 servings

8 ounces dried multigrain penne pasta
2 cups cherry or grape tomatoes, halved
4 ounces fresh mozzarella bocconcini or chopped fresh mozzarella cheese (1 cup)
¾ cup coarsely chopped yellow sweet pepper (1 medium)
½ cup fresh basil, torn
2 tablespoons balsamic vinegar
2 tablespoons olive oil
1 teaspoon Dijon-style mustard
2 cloves garlic, minced
½ teaspoon salt
¼ teaspoon ground black pepper

1 Cook pasta according to package directions. Rinse under cold running water to cool; drain well.

2 In a serving bowl combine pasta, tomatoes, mozzarella cheese, sweet pepper, and basil. In a screw-top jar combine vinegar, oil, mustard, garlic, salt, and black pepper. Cover and shake well to combine. Pour over salad and toss to combine.

nutrition facts per serving: 251 cal., 9 g total fat (3 g sat. fat), 13 mg chol., 292 mg sodium, 30 g carb., 4 g fiber, 11 g pro.

tip: To tote for lunch, chill salad overnight. Transport a serving of the salad in a container in an insulated lunch box with ice packs; refrigerate within 1 hour. Hold in the refrigerator for up to 5 hours.

4

When you need a nibble or something special to sip, these tasty bites can add life to a party—or tide you over to the next meal.

snacks, smoothies &
bever

creamy hummus

ages

70

A small amount of pungent blue cheese—just ¼ cup for 16 appetizers—adds a lot of flavor to the cheese spread without adding a lot of calories. Each sweet-savory bite has just 30 calories and 2 grams of fat.

blue cheese–apricot bites

start to finish: 25 minutes
makes: 16 appetizers

1   teaspoon canola oil
2   tablespoons finely
      chopped walnuts
2   teaspoons sugar
½   teaspoon snipped
      fresh rosemary or
      ¼ teaspoon dried
      rosemary, finely
      crushed
¼   cup crumbled blue
      cheese (1 ounce)
1   ounce reduced-fat
      cream cheese
      (Neufchâtel)
16   dried apricots
      Fresh rosemary
      (optional)

1 In a small skillet heat oil over medium heat. Add walnuts and sugar; cook and stir for 2 to 3 minutes or until walnuts are lightly toasted. Stir in ½ teaspoon fresh or ¼ teaspoon dried rosemary. Cook and stir for 30 seconds more. Transfer nuts to a baking sheet lined with foil; cool.

2 Meanwhile, in a small bowl combine blue cheese and cream cheese. Beat with an electric mixer on medium speed until smooth.

3 Spoon about ¾ teaspoon of the blue cheese mixture on top of each dried apricot. Sprinkle with nuts. If desired, garnish with additional fresh rosemary.

nutrition facts per appetizer: 30 cal., 2 g total fat (1 g sat. fat), 3 mg chol., 31 mg sodium, 3 g carb., 0 g fiber, 1 g pro.

The simplest way to chop dried tomatoes that are not packed in oil is to snip them in small pieces with clean kitchen scissors.

two tomato bruschetta

prep: 10 minutes   **bake:** 5 minutes at 350°F
makes: 4 servings

⅓ cup crumbled feta cheese with tomato and basil
⅓ cup dried tomatoes (not oil-packed), chopped
2 tablespoons snipped fresh basil
2 tablespoons snipped fresh Italian (flat-leaf) parsley
2 tablespoons olive oil
¼ teaspoon freshly ground black pepper
1 clove garlic, minced
8 to 10 slices whole grain baguette (each about ½ inch thick)
2 roma tomatoes, thinly sliced

1 Preheat oven to 350°F. In a small bowl combine feta cheese, dried tomatoes, basil, and parsley; set aside.

2 In another small bowl stir together oil, pepper, and garlic. Brush oil mixture evenly over bread slices. Place bread slices on a large baking sheet.

3 Bake about 5 minutes or until lightly toasted. Remove from oven. Top with tomato slices. Spoon feta cheese mixture on top of tomato slices. Serve immediately or broil 3 to 4 inches from the heat for 1 to 2 minutes or until cheese is slightly melted.

nutrition facts per 2 bruschetta: 181 cal., 11 g total fat (2 g sat. fat), 8 mg chol., 344 mg sodium, 18 g carb., 2 g fiber, 6 g pro.

Thin slices of skillet-toasted garlic pack a powerful flavor punch in the creamy green puree that tops these toasts.

edamame and ricotta toasts

start to finish: 25 minutes
makes: 8 servings

⅔ cup frozen peas
½ cup frozen shelled
    sweet soybeans
    (edamame)
3 tablespoons lemon
    juice
½ teaspoon kosher salt
½ teaspoon freshly
    ground black
    pepper
1 tablespoon olive oil
6 cloves garlic, sliced
⅓ cup snipped fresh
    basil or mint
24 whole grain
    baguette-style
    French bread slices,
    ¼ to ½ inch thick,
    toasted
½ cup part-skim ricotta
    cheese
⅛ teaspoon kosher salt
⅛ teaspoon freshly
    ground black
    pepper

1 Preheat broiler. In a small saucepan cook peas and edamame in boiling water about 10 minutes or until very tender; drain. Transfer to a food processor. Add lemon juice, the ½ teaspoon salt, and the ½ teaspoon pepper. Cover and process until smooth, stopping and scraping down sides as necessary. Transfer mixture to a small bowl.

2 In the same saucepan heat oil over medium heat. Add garlic; cook and stir about 1 minute or until tender. Stir garlic and basil into pureed edamame mixture.

3 To assemble, spread toasted baguette slices with ricotta cheese. Arrange on a baking sheet. Broil about 4 inches from the heat for 1 to 2 minutes or until ricotta is warm. Sprinkle with the ⅛ teaspoon salt and the ⅛ teaspoon pepper. Serve ricotta toasts with pureed edamame mixture.

nutrition facts per 3 appetizers: 133 cal., 4 g total fat (1 g sat. fat), 5 mg chol., 372 mg sodium, 20 g carb., 3 g fiber, 7 g pro.

One of these mini pizzas is a satisfying snack. Enjoy two of them as a light lunch, along with a piece of fruit.

arugula blt pizzas

start to finish: 15 minutes
makes: 4 mini pizzas

¼ cup marinara sauce
2 whole grain English muffins, split and toasted
½ cup arugula leaves
¼ cup chopped, seeded tomato
1 slice turkey bacon, crisp-cooked and chopped
½ cup shredded part-skim mozzarella cheese (2 ounces)

1 Preheat broiler. Spread marinara sauce evenly over English muffin halves. Top with arugula, tomato, and bacon. Sprinkle with mozzarella cheese.

2 Broil 3 to 4 inches from the heat for 1 to 2 minutes or until cheese is melted.

nutrition facts per mini pizza: 128 cal., 4 g total fat (2 g sat. fat), 13 mg chol., 354 mg sodium, 16 g carb., 3 g fiber, 7 g pro.

nutrition note: The Academy of Nutrition and Dietetics (AND) recommends maximizing the health benefits of snacking by including at least two different food groups in each snack. Keep snacks to 200 calories and eat a healthy snack once or twice a day.

In order for these breadsticks to have the proper texture, be sure you use spread that is at least 60 to 70 percent vegetable oil. Anything that contains less than that—in other words, more water—will yield tough breadsticks.

tomato-bacon breadsticks

prep: 20 minutes **bake:** 8 minutes at 425°F
makes: 16 breadsticks

4   slices turkey bacon
¼   cup dried tomatoes
     (not oil-packed)
     Boiling water
1   cup all-purpose flour
½   cup whole wheat
     pastry flour or
     whole wheat flour
2   teaspoons baking
     powder
½   teaspoon salt
¼   teaspoon cream of
     tartar
2   tablespoons chopped
     green onion tops
⅓   cup 60 to 70 percent
     vegetable oil
     spread, chilled
1   tablespoon butter
½   cup fat-free milk
     Nonstick cooking
     spray
¼   cup grated Parmesan
     cheese (1 ounce)

1 Preheat oven to 425°F. Cook bacon according to package directions; cool slightly and crumble or chop bacon. Set aside. Place dried tomatoes in a small bowl. Add enough boiling water to cover; let stand for 5 minutes. Drain tomatoes, discarding the liquid. Finely chop tomatoes; set aside.

2 In a medium bowl stir together all-purpose flour, whole wheat pastry flour, baking powder, salt, and cream of tartar. Stir in green onion. Using a pastry blender, cut in vegetable oil spread and butter until mixture resembles coarse crumbs. Stir in crumbled bacon and chopped dried tomatoes. Make a well in the center of the flour mixture. Add milk all at once; stir just until dough clings together.

3 Turn out dough onto a lightly floured surface. Knead by folding and gently pressing dough for four to six strokes or until nearly smooth. Roll dough into an 8-inch square. Cut into 1-inch-wide strips; cut each strip in half crosswise. If desired, twist each strip.

4 Place strips 1 inch apart on an ungreased baking sheet. Coat with cooking spray; sprinkle with Parmesan cheese. Bake for 8 to 10 minutes or until tops are golden brown. Serve warm.

nutrition facts per breadstick: 94 cal., 5 g total fat (2 g sat. fat), 6 mg chol., 251 mg sodium, 9 g carb., 1 g fiber, 3 g pro.

A healthy snack is in the bag—and not the potato-chip bag—with these colorful and crisp veggie chips. A combination of different vegetables makes for the most eye-catching snack.

baked root vegetable chips

prep: 10 minutes **bake:** 14 minutes at 375°F
stand: 5 minutes **makes:** 4 servings

Nonstick cooking
spray
2 sweet potatoes,
purple beets, or
golden beets,*
peeled
¼ teaspoon salt
¼ teaspoon ground
black pepper

make-ahead directions:
Store cooled chips in an airtight container for up to 24 hours. If necessary, re-crisp the chips by baking them in a 325°F oven for 3 to 4 minutes.

1 Preheat oven to 375°F. Lightly coat two large baking sheets with cooking spray.

2 Using a mandoline, slice vegetables ¹/₁₆-inch thick. If using beets, sandwich slices between layers of paper towels and press firmly to remove excess liquid. Arrange vegetable slices in a single layer on the prepared baking sheets. Coat the tops of the vegetable slices with cooking spray; sprinkle with salt and pepper.

3 Bake for 10 minutes. Remove baking sheets from oven; let stand for 5 minutes. Return baking sheets to oven. Bake for 4 to 8 minutes more, removing baking sheets to check for doneness every minute after 4 minutes. Chips are done when the center of each chip no longer looks wet. Transfer chips to paper towels. Let cool for 5 minutes to crisp the chips.

nutrition facts per serving: 56 cal., 0 g total fat (0 g sat. fat), 0 mg chol., 181 mg sodium, 13 g carb., 2 g fiber, 1 g pro.

*tip: For a change, try a combination of these vegetables. To avoid burning, check the doneness frequently and remove each type of chip when done.

A little bit of olive oil and some heat from the oven transform this highly nutritious, leafy green vegetable into a crispy snack you don't have to feel guilty about devouring.

peppered kale chips

prep: 8 minutes **bake:** 22 minutes at 300°F
makes: 4 servings

1 bunch (12 ounces) fresh kale
1 tablespoon olive oil
¼ teaspoon salt
¼ teaspoon coarsely ground black pepper
⅛ teaspoon cayenne pepper (optional)

1 Preheat oven to 300°F. Line two large baking sheets with parchment paper; set aside.

2 Remove and discard thick stems from kale. Tear leaves into bite-size pieces. Rinse and dry in a salad spinner or pat dry with paper towels.

3 In a large bowl combine kale, oil, salt, black pepper, and, if desired, cayenne pepper, rubbing kale with your hands to thoroughly coat. Arrange in a single layer on the prepared baking sheets.

4 Bake for 20 minutes. Stir gently. Bake for 2 to 4 minutes more or until completely dry and crisp, watching carefully so chips don't burn.

nutrition facts per serving: 73 cal., 4 g total fat (1 g sat. fat), 0 mg chol., 182 mg sodium, 9 g carb., 2 g fiber, 3 g pro.

nutrition note: Kale is a darling of the nutrition world. A single cup of chopped kale contains only 33 calories but more than 200 percent of the recommended dose of vitamin A; more than 130 percent of the recommended vitamin C; and nearly 700 percent of cancer-fighting vitamin K. It's also a great source of calcium and iron. It's incredibly versatile, too. Sauté in olive oil and garlic for a quick and delicious side dish—or try these crispy chips as the ultimate feel-good snack.

make-ahead directions: Place cooled chips in an airtight container and store at room temperature for up to 24 hours. If necessary, re-crisp the chips by warming them in a 325°F oven for 3 to 4 minutes.

These are nice to have on hand for eating alone or for pairing with yogurt- or bean-based dips or salsas.

savory baked pita chips

prep: 10 minutes   **bake:** 12 minutes at 350°F
makes: 24 chips

Nonstick cooking
    spray
2 6-inch pita bread
    rounds
4 teaspoons olive oil
½ teaspoon garlic
    powder
¼ teaspoon salt
⅛ teaspoon chili
    powder
⅛ teaspoon cayenne
    pepper (optional)

1 Preheat oven to 350°F. Lightly coat a large baking sheet with cooking spray; set aside. Split pita bread rounds in half horizontally; cut each half into six wedges (24 wedges total). Brush pita wedges with oil.

2 In a small bowl combine garlic powder, salt, chili powder, and, if desired, cayenne pepper. Sprinkle garlic powder mixture over pita wedges. Place pita wedges on prepared baking sheet. Bake about 12 minutes or until golden brown and toasted.

nutrition facts per 4 chips: 82 cal., 3 g total fat (0 g sat. fat), 0 mg chol., 205 mg sodium, 11 g carb., 0 g fiber, 2 g pro.

Sweet Baked Pita Chips: Omit garlic powder, salt, chili powder, and cayenne pepper. Prepare as directed in Step 1. In a small bowl combine 2 teaspoons packed brown sugar and 1 teaspoon ground cinnamon. Sprinkle brown sugar mixture over pita wedges. Place pita wedges on baking sheet; bake as directed.

Look for tahini at the supermarket in the aisle with the olives and capers. If you can't find it at your local market, look at a Middle Eastern grocery store or specialty food shop. Once opened, store it in the refrigerator. If it separates, give it a good stir before using.

creamy hummus

start to finish: 15 minutes
makes: 12 servings (1¾ cups)

1   15-ounce can
    garbanzo beans
    (chickpeas), rinsed
    and drained
¼   cup tahini (sesame
    seed paste)
½   teaspoon finely
    shredded lemon
    peel
3   tablespoons lemon
    juice
4   cloves garlic, peeled
¼   teaspoon salt
⅛   to ¼ teaspoon
    cayenne pepper
¼   to ½ cup water
    Halved or quartered
    grape tomatoes
    (optional)
    Fresh chives
    (optional)
    Extra virgin olive oil
    (optional)
    Cayenne pepper
    (optional)
    Dippers: cracker
    bread, Belgian
    endive or baby bok
    choy leaves, bias-
    sliced cucumber

1 In a food processor combine garbanzo beans, tahini, lemon peel, lemon juice, garlic, salt, and the cayenne pepper. Cover and process until smooth, adding enough of the water to reach desired consistency. Spoon into serving bowl.

2 Cover and chill for up to 48 hours. To serve, if desired, top hummus with tomatoes and/or chives, a drizzle of olive oil, and/or additional cayenne pepper. Serve with dippers.

nutrition facts per 2 tablespoons: 75 cal., 3 g total fat (0 g sat. fat), 0 mg chol., 158 mg sodium, 10 g carb., 2 g fiber, 3 g pro.

Try a sprinkle of smoked paprika on top of this beautiful green dip for great flavor and a splash of complementary color.

edamame hummus

start to finish: 20 minutes
makes: 16 servings (2 cups)

1 **Cook edamame until tender according to package directions; drain.**

2 **In a food processor combine edamame, parsley, lemon juice, the water, tahini, salt, cumin, and garlic. Cover and process until smooth. With food processor running, slowly add oil in a thin steady stream, processing until smooth. Add additional water if necessary to reach desired consistency. If desired, sprinkle with paprika. Serve with vegetable dippers.**

1   10-ounce package
    frozen sweet
    soybeans
    (edamame)
½   cup snipped fresh
    Italian (flat-leaf)
    parsley
¼   cup lemon juice
¼   cup water
1   tablespoon tahini
    (sesame seed paste)
½   teaspoon salt
½   teaspoon ground
    cumin
3   cloves garlic, peeled
    and quartered
⅓   cup olive oil
⅛   teaspoon paprika
    (optional)
8   cups assorted
    vegetable dippers,
    such as sweet
    pepper pieces,
    cucumber slices,
    baby carrots, snow
    pea pods, and/or
    celery sticks

nutrition facts per 2 tablespoons: 81 cal., 6 g total fat (1 g sat. fat), 0 mg chol., 78 mg sodium, 5 g carb., 1 g fiber, 3 g pro.

Real maple syrup is pricey, but if you use it in small amounts to add flavor to foods rather than soaking your pancakes with it, it's well worth having a bottle in the refrigerator.

apples with maple-cinnamon dip

start to finish: 10 minutes
makes: 4 servings

4 ounces reduced-fat cream cheese (Neufchâtel)
2 tablespoons pure maple syrup
¾ teaspoon ground cinnamon
¼ cup chopped walnuts or pecans, toasted* (optional)
2 cups thinly sliced apples (2 medium)

1 In a food processor combine cream cheese, maple syrup, and cinnamon. Cover and process until smooth. Transfer mixture to a serving bowl. If desired, sprinkle with toasted walnuts. Serve dip with apple slices.

nutrition facts per 3 tablespoons dip + ½ cup apple slices: 146 cal., 7 g total fat (4 g sat. fat), 21 mg chol., 97 mg sodium, 21 g carb., 2 g fiber, 3 g pro.

*tip: To toast nuts, spread them in a shallow baking pan. Bake in a 350°F oven for 5 to 10 minutes or until light brown, shaking pan once or twice. Watch carefully so the nuts don't burn.

Spanish smoked paprika (also called pimentón) comes in two basic types—sweet (dulce) and hot (picante). You can use either type in this recipe, depending on what you like.

sweet and smoky nuts

prep: 5 minutes   **bake:** 25 minutes at 350°F
makes: 16 servings (4 cups)

1   egg white
1   cup dry-roasted peanuts
1   cup whole almonds or hazelnuts (filberts)
1   cup pecan or walnut halves
⅓   cup packed brown sugar
1½   teaspoons smoked paprika
1   teaspoon kosher salt
¼   teaspoon ground cinnamon
¼   teaspoon ground allspice

1 Preheat oven to 350°F. Line a 15×10×1-inch baking pan with foil or parchment paper; set aside.

2 In a large bowl whisk egg white until foamy. Add peanuts, almonds, and pecans; toss gently to coat. Stir in brown sugar, paprika, salt, cinnamon, and allspice. Spread nuts in prepared baking pan.

3 Bake for 25 to 30 minutes or until nuts are toasted and appear dry, stirring twice. Remove from the oven and stir again. Cool completely in the baking pan. Break up any large clusters.

nutrition facts per ¼ cup: 165 cal., 13 g total fat (1 g sat. fat), 0 mg chol., 126 mg sodium, 9 g carb., 2 g fiber, 5 g pro.

make-ahead directions: Prepare as directed. Place nut clusters in an airtight container. Cover and store at room temperature for up to 2 weeks.

Sweet—with a little heat—this herbed blend of almonds, walnuts, and pumpkin seeds works equally well as a late-afternoon hunger-pang killer and as an elegant nibble with a glass of wine on Friday night with friends.

rosemary roasted nuts

prep: 15 minutes bake: 12 minutes at 375°F
makes: 30 servings (about 5½ cups)

3   cups whole
      unblanched
      almonds
1½ cups walnuts
1   cup raw pumpkin
      seeds (pepitas)
2   tablespoons finely
      snipped fresh
      rosemary
2   teaspoons packed
      brown sugar
1   teaspoon sea salt
½   teaspoon cayenne
      pepper
2   tablespoons butter,
      melted

1 Preheat oven to 375°F. In a 15×10×1-inch baking pan combine almonds, walnuts, and pumpkin seeds. Bake about 12 minutes or until toasted, stirring once.

2 In a small bowl combine rosemary, brown sugar, salt, and cayenne pepper. Stir in butter. Drizzle butter mixture over nuts, tossing gently to coat. Serve warm or cooled to room temperature.

nutrition facts per 3-tablespoon serving: 177 cal., 15 g total fat (2 g sat. fat), 2 mg chol., 60 mg sodium, 5 g carb., 2 g fiber, 6 g pro.

make-ahead directions: Cool nuts to room temperature. Place cooled nuts in an airtight container. Store at room temperature for up to 3 days.

84

Curry powder comes in several heat levels. Madras curry powder tends to be a little hotter than just straight-up curry powder. If you really want to spice things up, look for curry powder that's labeled "hot."

curried snack mix

prep: 10 minutes bake: 20 minutes at 300°F
makes: 12 servings (6 cups)

3 plain rice cakes, broken into bite-size pieces
1 3-ounce can chow mein noodles
2 cups bite-size square corn cereal or oyster crackers
1 cup salted roasted soy nuts
⅓ cup butter
2 teaspoons soy sauce
1 to 1½ teaspoons curry powder

1 Preheat oven to 300°F. In a 13×9×2-inch baking pan gently stir together rice cakes, chow mein noodles, cereal, and soy nuts.

2 In a small saucepan combine butter, soy sauce, and curry powder. Cook and stir over low heat until butter is melted. Drizzle butter mixture over rice cake mixture; toss gently to coat.

3 Bake for 20 minutes, stirring once or twice. Let cool.

nutrition facts per ½-cup serving: 144 cal., 8 g total fat (4 g sat. fat), 14 mg chol., 236 mg sodium, 13 g carb., 2 g fiber, 5 g pro.

make-ahead directions: Prepare as directed. Place mix in an airtight container. Cover and store at room temperature for up to 5 days.

Snacks that contain nuts do have a higher fat content than some other kinds of snacks, but you can take comfort in knowing that they are the heart-healthy unsaturated fats that can actually help lower your cholestersol.

spicy-savory snack mix

prep: 10 minutes **bake:** 20 minutes at 375°F
makes: 16 servings (4 cups)

1 **Preheat oven to 375°F. In a 15×10×1-inch baking pan evenly spread almonds, pecans, and hazelnuts. Bake about 8 minutes or until nuts are lightly toasted, stirring once or twice.**

1   cup whole almonds or peanuts
¾   cup pecan halves
¼   cup hazelnuts (filberts)
2   tablespoons butter
2   tablespoons finely snipped fresh rosemary or 1 teaspoon dried rosemary, crushed
2   tablespoons packed brown sugar
2   teaspoons soy sauce
½   to 1 teaspoon crushed red pepper
3   cups pretzel nuggets

2 **Meanwhile, in a large saucepan melt butter over medium heat. Remove from heat. Stir in rosemary, brown sugar, soy sauce, and crushed red pepper. Add nuts and pretzels to butter mixture; toss gently to coat. Spread mixture in the baking pan; let cool.**

nutrition facts per ¼-cup serving: 162 cal., 11 g total fat (2 g sat. fat), 4 mg chol., 146 mg sodium, 14 g carb., 2 g fiber, 4 g pro.

make-ahead directions: Prepare mix as directed. Place in an airtight container. Cover and store in the refrigerator for up to 1 month or in the freezer for up to 3 months.

At farmer's markets and outdoor food festivals, the line at the kettle-corn stand is usually one of the longest. This recipe brings the fabulous sweet-salty (and spicy!) flavor of this favorite snack into your kitchen.

chipotle kettle corn

start to finish: 15 minutes
makes: 16 servings (16 cups)

1   cup sugar
2   teaspoons salt
2   teaspoons ground
     cumin
1   teaspoon ground
     chipotle chile
     pepper
⅓   cup canola oil
⅔   cup popcorn kernels

1 In a small bowl combine sugar, salt, cumin, and chipotle pepper; set aside.

2 Heat the oil in an 8-quart pan over medium-high heat. Add the popcorn and cook for 2 minutes, shaking pan occasionally. Add ½ cup of the sugar mixture. Cover and cook until popcorn begins to pop, shaking pan often. Shake continuously until the popping slows. Immediately remove pan from heat and carefully pour into a large serving bowl (popcorn will be very hot).

3 Place remaining sugar mixture in a shaker jar; sprinkle some on the popped corn. Pass remaining sugar mixture.

nutrition facts per 1 cup: 78 cal., 3 g total fat (0 g sat. fat), 0 mg chol., 266 mg sodium, 15 g carb., 1 g fiber, 1 g pro.

microwave directions: Prepare sugar mixture as above. One at a time, pop two 3.3-ounce bags microwave kettle corn. Immediately after popping, pour popcorn into a very large bowl and toss with 2 tablespoons of the sugar mixture. Repeat with remaining bag of popcorn and 2 more tablespoons of sugar mixture. Pass remaining sugar mixture as above.

Keep a bag of peeled, cut up bananas in your freezer to make quick and creamy smoothies whenever the mood strikes. It's a great way to use up bananas that are on the verge of being overripe.

raspberry-citrus swirly smoothie

start to finish: 15 minutes
makes: 2 (10-ounce) servings

½ cup frozen
    unsweetened
    raspberries
½ cup orange juice
2 6-ounce cartons
    vanilla yogurt
1 ripe banana, peeled,
    cut up, and frozen
2 tablespoons honey
½ teaspoon vanilla

1 In a blender combine raspberries and orange juice. Cover and blend until smooth. Divide between two glasses.

2 Wash the blender container with warm, soapy water. In the blender combine yogurt, banana, honey, and vanilla. Cover and blend until smooth. Pour over raspberry mixture in glasses. Swirl with a spoon.

nutrition facts per 10 ounces: 335 cal., 2 g total fat (1 g sat. fat), 10 mg chol., 87 mg sodium, 74 g carb., 3 g fiber, 6 g pro.

If you want a special treat, look for the bags of wild blueberries that are sold in the frozen-fruit section of your supermarket. The tiny berries are packed with flavor and nutrients.

blueberry swirly smoothie

start to finish: 10 minutes
makes: 3 (8-ounce) servings

2 cups frozen
    blueberries
½ cup apple juice
1 6-ounce carton plain
    fat-free yogurt
1 ripe banana, peeled,
    cut up, and frozen
2 to 3 teaspoons honey

1 In a blender combine blueberries and apple juice. Cover and blend until smooth. Divide among three glasses.

2 Wash the blender container with warm, soapy water. In the blender combine yogurt, banana, and honey. Cover and blend until smooth. Spoon over the blueberry mixture in glasses. Swirl with a spoon.

nutrition facts per 8 ounces: 148 cal., 1 g total fat (0 g sat. fat), 1 mg chol., 41 mg sodium, 34 g carb., 4 g fiber, 4 g pro.

Use a spoon to scrape off the woody outer peel of fresh gingerroot— then use a Microplane to grate the peeled root.

ginger-mango smoothie

start to finish: 10 minutes
makes: 2 (8-ounce) servings

½ cup plain Greek
 yogurt
½ cup mango slices
¼ cup mango nectar
½ of a banana
¼ cup milk
1 tablespoon honey
½ teaspoon grated fresh
 ginger

1 In a blender combine yogurt, mango, mango nectar, banana, milk, honey, and ginger. Cover and blend until nearly smooth.

nutrition facts per 8 ounces: 202 cal., 2 g total fat (1 g sat. fat), 10 mg chol., 56 mg sodium, 37 g carb., 2 g fiber, 11 g pro.

kitchen tip: To pit, peel, and slice a mango, hold the mango upright on a flat surface. Use a sharp chef's knife to cut down as close as possible to the pit on all four "sides" of the mango. Use a paring knife to peel the skin from the pieces. Slice as desired. For cubed mango, place one of the large pieces of mango round side down on a cutting board. Use a paring knife to score a series of crisscross lines in the flesh. Gently invert the mango so that the scored cubes pop up off of the skin. Slip a knife between the flesh and skin to cut the cubes free from the skin.

Blitz this creamy melange of Greek yogurt, pomegranate juice, and frozen berries and banana in your blender any time of day for a refreshing pick-me-up.

mixed berry smoothie

start to finish: 10 minutes
makes: 2 (8-ounce) servings

½ cup plain Greek yogurt
½ cup pomegranate juice
½ cup frozen mixed berries
1 ripe banana, peeled, cut up, and frozen
1 tablespoon honey
1 tablespoon lime juice

1 In a blender combine yogurt, pomegranate juice, berries, banana, honey, and lime juice. Cover and blend until nearly smooth.

nutrition facts per 8 ounces: 203 cal., 2 g total fat (1 g sat. fat), 7 mg chol., 44 mg sodium, 39 g carb., 3 g fiber, 10 g pro.

Kids will love this drinkable version of a favorite sandwich.

pb&j smoothie

start to finish: 10 minutes
makes: 2 (8-ounce) servings

½ cup plain Greek yogurt
½ cup milk
1 banana
2 tablespoons grape jelly
2 to 3 tablespoons creamy peanut butter

1 In a blender combine yogurt, milk, banana, jelly, and peanut butter. Cover and blend until nearly smooth.

nutrition facts per 8 ounces: 293 cal., 11 g total fat (3 g sat. fat), 12 mg chol., 146 mg sodium, 38 g carb., 3 g fiber, 15 g pro.

For ease and speed, use frozen sweet cherries—which are already pitted—in this almond-milk smoothie.

cherry-almond smoothie

start to finish: 10 minutes
makes: 2 (8-ounce) servings

½   cup plain Greek
      yogurt
½   cup plain almond
      milk
½   cup dark sweet
      cherries, pitted
1   tablespoon honey
½   teaspoon almond
      extract

1 In a blender combine yogurt, almond milk, cherries, honey, and almond extract. Cover and blend until nearly smooth.

nutrition facts per 8 ounces: 122 cal., 2 g total fat (1 g sat. fat), 3 mg chol., 56 mg sodium, 20 g carb., 1 g fiber, 6 g pro.

There's a double dose of nutrition hidden inside this smoothie—in the form of heart-healthy, fiber-rich flaxseed meal and high-protein tofu.

ultimate berry smoothie

start to finish: 15 minutes
makes: 4 (12-ounce) servings

4   cups fresh or frozen
      mixed berries
1   12.3-ounce package
      silken-style tofu
      (fresh bean curd)
      (1½ cups)
1   cup unsweetened
      cranberry-raspberry
      juice
¼   cup flaxseed meal
3   tablespoons honey
      Fresh raspberries
        and/or blueberries
        (optional)

1 In a blender combine the frozen berries, tofu, juice, flaxseed meal, and honey. Cover and blend until smooth. If desired, garnish with fresh raspberries and/or blueberries.

nutrition facts per 12 ounces: 242 cal., 5 g total fat (1 g sat. fat), 0 mg chol., 50 mg sodium, 42 g carb., 7 g fiber, 9 g pro.

92

In some of the hottest areas of the world—Mexico, Central America, and the Caribbean—agua frescas ("fresh waters") cool and refresh with a combination of cold water, pureed fruits, lime juice, and honey.

watermelon agua fresca

start to finish: 25 minutes
makes: 8 (8-ounce) servings

1   7- to 8-pound
     seedless
     watermelon
2   cups cold water
2   tablespoons lime
     juice
2   tablespoons honey
     Ice cubes
     Lime wedges
     Additional honey
     (optional)

1 Cut the rind from the whole watermelon and discard. Cut 13 cups of 2-inch cubes from the watermelon flesh; cut the remaining watermelon into slices and reserve for garnish.

2 In a blender combine about one-third of the watermelon cubes and ²/₃ cup of the water. Cover and blend until smooth. Strain through a fine-mesh sieve into a pitcher or large glass jar. Discard solids. Repeat twice, using remaining watermelon and remaining water.

3 Stir lime juice and 2 tablespoons honey into strained watermelon mixture. Serve immediately or chill until ready to serve.

4 Serve in ice-filled glasses. Garnish with lime wedges and watermelon slices. If desired, serve with additional honey.

nutrition facts per 8 ounces: 73 cal., 0 g total fat (0 g sat. fat), 0 mg chol., 2 mg sodium, 19 g carb., 1 g fiber, 1 g pro.

Melon-Berry Agua Fresca: Increase water to 3 cups and add 3 cups fresh blueberries. Cut watermelon as directed in Step 1. In a blender combine one-third of the watermelon cubes, 1 cup of the water, and 1 cup of the blueberries. Cover and blend until smooth. Strain through a fine-mesh sieve into a very large pitcher or glass jar. Discard solids. Repeat twice. Continue as directed. Garnish with watermelon slices, lime wedges, and additional blueberries.
makes: 12 (8-ounce) servings

nutrition facts per 8 ounces: 77 cal., 1 g total fat (0 g sat. fat), 0 mg chol., 4 mg sodium, 20 g carb., 2 g fiber, 1 g pro.

This is not your ordinary lemonade. The refreshing, licoricey flavor of basil infuses this bubbly concoction, while slices of fresh jalapeño give it just a bit of heat.

sparkling basil lemonade

prep: 20 minutes **freeze:** 10 minutes
makes: 16 (8-ounce) servings

4   cups water
3   cups sugar
2   cups fresh basil
     leaves (about 1½
     ounces)
2   1-liter bottles club
     soda, chilled
2   cups lemon juice
     Ice cubes
1   fresh jalapeño chile
     pepper, sliced*
     Fresh basil leaves

1 For basil syrup, in a large saucepan combine the water, sugar, and the 2 cups basil. Bring to boiling over medium-high heat. Reduce heat. Simmer, uncovered, for 20 minutes. Strain syrup and discard leaves. Cover syrup and place in freezer for 10 minutes or chill for 2 to 24 hours.

2 For lemonade, in a very large punch bowl combine chilled syrup, club soda, and lemon juice. Serve over ice. Garnish with chile pepper slices and fresh basil leaves.

nutrition facts per 8 ounces: 155 cal., 0 g total fat (0 g sat. fat), 0 mg chol., 29 mg sodium, 40 g carb., 0 g fiber, 0 g pro.

∗tip: Because hot chile peppers contain volatile oils that can burn skin and eyes, avoid direct contact with them as much as possible. When working with chile peppers, wear plastic or rubber gloves. If your bare hands do touch the peppers, wash your hands and nails well with soap and warm water.

There is a whole (small) sweet potato in just one serving of this warming coffee drink. It's a great way to get a shot of vitamins B6, C, and D—as well as magnesium, which is a relaxation and antistress mineral.

sweet potato latte

start to finish: 25 minutes
makes: 1 serving (1½ cups)

1 small sweet potato
1¼ cups unsweetened almond milk
1 tablespoon packed brown sugar
½ teaspoon instant coffee crystals (optional)
⅛ to ¼ teaspoon ground cinnamon
Ground cinnamon (optional)
Cinnamon stick (optional)

1 Prick sweet potato several times with a fork. Wrap potato in damp paper towels. Microwave on 100 percent power (high) for 3 minutes. Turn potato over. Microwave for 2 to 3 minutes more or until tender. Cool slightly. Remove and discard peel. Mash potato with a fork; measure 1/3 cup.

2 In a blender combine the 1/3 cup mashed sweet potato, almond milk, brown sugar, coffee crystals (if desired), and ground cinnamon. Cover and blend on high for 1 minute. Strain through a fine-mesh sieve into a small saucepan. Cook and stir over medium-low heat until heated through. Transfer to a heat-proof mug. If desired, sprinkle with additional ground cinnamon and garnish with a cinnamon stick.

nutrition facts per serving: 110 cal., 3 g total fat (0 g sat. fat), 0 mg chol., 152 mg sodium, 19 g carb., 2 g fiber, 2 g pro.

The cranberry, orange, and cinnamon-spice flavors make this a fitting drink to serve during the winter holidays.

cranberry-orange tea sipper

start to finish: 15 minutes
makes: 6 (6-ounce) servings

3 cups light cranberry-raspberry juice
1 cup water
4 bags orange-spice-flavor tea
½ cup orange juice
¼ cup vodka or water
6 cinnamon sticks (optional)

1 In a medium saucepan combine cranberry-raspberry juice and the 1 cup water. Bring just to boiling. Add tea bags. Remove from heat. Cover and let stand for 4 minutes.

2 Remove tea bags and discard. Stir in orange juice; heat through. Stir in vodka. Serve warm. If desired, garnish with cinnamon sticks.

nutrition facts per 6 ounces: 30 cal., 0 g total fat (0 g sat. fat), 0 mg chol., 40 mg sodium, 7 g carb., 0 g fiber, 0 g pro.

tip: Chill any leftover sipper. To reheat, place ¾ cup of the sipper in a microwave-safe tea cup. Microwave on 50 percent power (medium) about 1½ minutes or until hot.

*Star anise is a star-shaped brown pod native to China that contains
a pea-size seed in each of its eight segments. The ground pods are
one of the spices in five-spice powder, which is used frequently in
Asian cooking.*

spiced black tea

prep: 10 minutes stand: 10 minutes
makes: 8 (8-ounce) servings

7 cups water
1 cup sugar
1 3-inch piece stick
   cinnamon
1 1-inch piece peeled
   fresh ginger
3 whole cloves
1 star anise pod
   (optional)
4 black tea bags
1 cup pomegranate
   juice
¼ cup lemon juice
   Lemon slices
   (optional)
   Cinnamon sticks
   (optional)

1 In a large saucepan combine the water,
sugar, the 3-inch piece stick cinnamon, the
ginger, cloves, and, if desired, star anise. Bring
to boiling, stirring to dissolve sugar. Boil for
1 minute. Remove from heat and strain. Return
mixture to saucepan.

2 Add tea bags. Steep for 10 minutes. Remove
tea bags. Stir in pomegranate juice and
lemon juice; heat through. If desired, serve with
lemon slices and additional cinnamon sticks.

nutrition facts per 8 ounces: 122 cal., 0 g total fat (0 g
sat. fat), 0 mg chol., 11 mg sodium, 32 g carb., 0 g fiber, 0 g pro.

greek feta burgers

sandwiches, burgers &
piz

5

This fork-free fare is perfect for casual dining any day of the week—or for game night or movie night with family and friends.

zzas

Classic Italian beef takes hours to prepare. This version jazzes up refrigerated herbed Italian-style beef with a little vinegar, sugar, and salt. Serve it topped with pickled hot peppers, if you like—or the spicy pickled vegetable relish called giardiniera.

open-face italian beef sandwiches

start to finish: 20 minutes
makes: 4 open-face sandwiches

¼ cup white wine or
    cider vinegar
1 teaspoon sugar
½ teaspoon salt
½ teaspoon ground
    black pepper
1 17-ounce package
    refrigerated cooked
    herb-rubbed Italian-
    style beef roast
    au jus
1 cup sliced baby
    or regular sweet
    peppers
2 square whole grain
    ciabatta rolls or
    whole grain buns
4 1-ounce slices
    provolone cheese
2 tablespoons snipped
    fresh Italian (flat-
    leaf) parsley
  Snipped fresh Italian
    (flat-leaf) parsley
    (optional)

1 Preheat broiler. In a large microwave-safe bowl combine vinegar, sugar, salt, and black pepper. Stir in undrained beef and sweet peppers. Cover with vented plastic wrap. Microwave on 100 percent power (high) for 4 minutes. Using two forks, shred meat.

2 Meanwhile, split rolls. Place rolls, cut sides up, on baking sheet. Broil 3 to 4 inches from heat for 1 minute or until lightly toasted. Top cut sides of rolls with a slice of provolone cheese. Broil 1 to 2 minutes more or until cheese is melted.

3 Stir the 2 tablespoons parsley into meat mixture. With a slotted spoon, spoon beef mixture over toasted rolls. If desired, sprinkle with additional snipped parsley. Serve with any remaining cooking liquid.

nutrition facts per open-face sandwich: 341 cal., 15 g total fat (8 g sat. fat), 78 mg chol., 774 mg sodium, 22 g carb., 2 g fiber, 31 g pro.

If you have time, follow the grilling directions for this hearty pub-style sandwich. The meat will get a nice smoky flavor from the grill—particularly if you use charcoal. It's nearly as good made under the broiler, however.

garlic-mustard steak sandwiches

start to finish: 30 minutes
makes: 4 sandwiches

8   ½-inch slices French bread
1   tablespoon honey mustard
½   teaspoon dried marjoram or thyme, crushed
¼   teaspoon coarsely ground black pepper
2   cloves garlic, minced
12 ounces beef flank steak
1   large red onion, cut into ½-inch slices
2   tablespoons light sour cream
2   ounces thinly sliced reduced-fat Swiss cheese

1 Preheat broiler. Place bread on the unheated rack of a broiler pan. Broil 4 to 5 inches from heat for 2 to 4 minutes or until toasted, turning once. Transfer to a wire rack and set aside. In a small bowl stir together honey mustard, marjoram, pepper, and garlic; set aside.

2 Trim fat from the steak. Score both sides of steak in a diamond pattern by making shallow diagonal cuts at 1-inch intervals. Place steak on one side of the broiler pan. Spoon half of the mustard mixture onto steak; spread evenly. Place onion slices beside steak on broiler pan.

3 Broil 4 to 5 inches from heat for 15 to 18 minutes or until steak is medium doneness (160°F) and onion is crisp-tender, turning onion slices once (do not turn steak).

4 In a small bowl stir together sour cream and the remaining mustard mixture. Spread sour cream mixture on one side of each half of the bread slices; set aside. Transfer steak to a cutting board; thinly slice steak across the grain. Separate onion slices into rings. Arrange steak strips, onion rings, and Swiss cheese on the bread slices spread with the sour cream mixture. Place on the broiler pan. Broil about 1 minute or until cheese is melted. Top with the remaining bread slices.

nutrition facts per sandwich: 334 cal., 9 g total fat (4 g sat. fat), 38 mg chol., 425 mg sodium, 35 g carb., 2 g fiber, 30 g pro.

grilling directions: For a charcoal or gas grill, grill bread on the rack directly over medium heat for 2 to 4 minutes or until toasted, turning once halfway through grilling. Place steak and onion slices on the grill rack directly over medium heat. Cover and grill for 17 to 21 minutes or until steak is medium doneness (160°F) and onion is crisp-tender, turning steak and onion slices once halfway through grilling.

There are so many great flavors melding in this autumnal sandwich—sourdough bread salty-smoky ham, rich and creamy Brie cheese, and sweet-tartness from both the apples and the cranberry sauce.

apple, ham, and brie panini

start to finish: 20 minutes
makes: 4 sandwiches

8   ½-inch slices
     sourdough bread
2   ounces low-fat,
     reduced-sodium
     sliced cooked ham,
     cut into bite-size
     strips
1½ ounces brie cheese,
     sliced
2   medium tart apples,
     cored and thinly
     sliced
½   cup whole cranberry
     sauce
2   tablespoons olive oil

1 On four of the bread slices layer ham, brie cheese, and apples. Spread the remaining four bread slices with cranberry sauce; place on top of the apples, cranberry sides down. Brush outsides of sandwiches with oil.

2 Preheat a covered indoor grill, panini press, grill pan, or large skillet. Place sandwiches, half at a time if necessary, in grill or panini press. Cover and cook about 6 minutes or until golden brown and cheese is melted. (If using a grill pan or skillet, place sandwiches on grill pan or skillet. Weigh sandwiches down with a heavy skillet; add food cans for more weight and cook for 2 minutes. Turn sandwiches over, weigh down, and cook about 2 minutes more or until golden brown and cheese is melted.)

nutrition facts per sandwich: 333 cal., 11 g total fat (3 g sat. fat), 18 mg chol., 505 mg sodium, 49 g carb., 3 g fiber, 10 g pro.

Here's a great trick for quickly cooking bacon with the least amount of mess possible—and for eliminating as much fat as possible: Line a large microwave plate with several layers of paper towels. Lay down a single layer of bacon. Lay down several layers of paper towels over the bacon. Cook to desired doneness on high, in 1-minute increments, checking and changing the paper towels after 2 to 3 minutes for maximum fat absorption. Allow bacon to cool completely.

avocado blt sandwiches

start to finish: 25 minutes
makes: 4 sandwiches

1   ripe avocado
2   tablespoons light
      mayonnaise or
      salad dressing
1   teaspoon lemon juice
1   clove garlic, minced
4   slices bacon, crisp-
      cooked and halved
      crosswise
4   leaves romaine
      lettuce
1   medium tomato,
      thinly sliced
8   slices whole wheat
      bread, toasted

1 Halve, seed, and peel avocado. Transfer one of the avocado halves to a small bowl; mash with a potato masher or the back of a wooden spoon. Stir in mayonnaise, lemon juice, and garlic; set aside. Thinly slice the remaining avocado half.

2 Arrange avocado slices, bacon, lettuce, and tomato on four of the bread slices. Spread the mashed avocado mixture over the remaining four bread slices; place on top of the filled bread slices, spread sides down.

nutrition facts per sandwich: 257 cal., 14 g total fat (2 g sat. fat), 10 mg chol., 432 mg sodium, 27 g carb., 7 g fiber, 9 g pro.

These sliders offer a fabulous combination of flavors and textures in every bite—sweet and chewy raisins, piquant onion, soy and ginger—and crisp, cool slices of cucumber.

ginger pork rolls

start to finish: 30 minutes
makes: 8 mini sandwiches

1   cup water
⅔   cup golden raisins
½   cup coarsely chopped
        red onion
        (1 medium)
3   tablespoons reduced-
        sodium soy sauce
2   teaspoons ground
        ginger
¼   teaspoon ground
        black pepper
1   pound pork loin,
        thinly sliced
8   mini hamburger buns
        or dinner rolls, split
1   small cucumber,
        thinly sliced

1 In a large skillet combine the water, raisins, onion, soy sauce, and ginger. Bring to boiling; reduce heat. Simmer, covered, for 5 to 6 minutes or until raisins are plump and onion is tender. Using a slotted spoon, remove raisins and onion reserving liquid in skillet. Place raisin and onions in a small bowl. Stir in pepper; set aside.

2 Add sliced pork to cooking liquid in skillet. Return to boiling; reduce heat. Simmer, uncovered, for 7 to 8 minutes or until pork is cooked through (just a trace of pink remains), turning once. Using the slotted spoon, remove pork slices.

3 Serve pork in buns with cucumber slices, raisins, and onion.

nutrition facts per 2 mini sandwiches: 433 cal., 9 g total fat (2 g sat. fat), 74 mg chol., 797 mg sodium, 57 g carb., 3 g fiber, 34 g pro.

This knife-and-fork sandwich is built with layers of basil cream cheese, a "filling" of chopped chicken, tomatoes—and more basil—and a topping of Parmesan cheese that gets toasty under the broiler.

open-face chicken and basil sandwiches

start to finish: 30 minutes
makes: 8 open-face sandwiches

1   8-ounce container
     whipped cream
     cheese
½   cup snipped fresh
     basil
3   tablespoons bottled
     ranch salad
     dressing
2   6-ounce packages
     refrigerated
     chopped cooked
     chicken breast
1   cup chopped roma
     tomatoes
     (3 medium)
2   tablespoons snipped
     fresh basil
8   ½-inch slices French
     or Italian bread,
     toasted
½   cup finely shredded
     Parmesan cheese
     (2 ounces)

1 Preheat broiler. In a small bowl combine cream cheese, the ½ cup basil, and salad dressing; set aside.

2 In a medium bowl combine chicken, tomatoes, and the 2 tablespoons basil.

3 Spread cream cheese mixture over bread slices. Place on a baking sheet. Top with chicken mixture; sprinkle with Parmesan cheese. Broil 3 to 4 inches from the heat for 1 to 2 minutes or until heated through and cheese is melted.

nutrition facts per open-face sandwich: 268 cal., 15 g total fat (7 g sat. fat), 62 mg chol., 795 mg sodium, 17 g carb., 1 g fiber, 17 g pro.

kitchen tip: Fresh basil, with its spicy licorice undertones, is intensely fragrant and flavorful. There are several ways to prep the leaves for recipes, including:
Shredded: To shred basil, stack several leaves on top of one another, lining them up end to end. Starting at the top, roll them into a tube. Cut the tube into thin slices with a sharp chef's knife.
Snipped: To snip basil, use kitchen scissors to cut leaves into small pieces.
Torn: To tear basil, simply use your fingers to rip leaves into smaller pieces.

Americans have enthusiastically embraced the Vietnamese sandwiches called banh mi in the last few years. The meat fillings are flavored with Asian ingredients such as soy, chili sauce, and cilantro—but the bread is always a crisp French baguette.

rotisserie chicken banh mi

prep: 25 minutes   bake: 5 minutes at 425°F
makes: 4 sandwiches

⅓ cup white vinegar
¼ cup sugar
⅛ teaspoon salt
1 cup shredded carrots (2 medium)
¼ cup light mayonnaise or salad dressing
1 to 2 teaspoons Asian chili sauce (Sriracha sauce)
½ teaspoon reduced-sodium soy sauce
⅛ teaspoon sugar
1 8-ounce loaf baguette-style French bread, split horizontally
8 ounces sliced purchased roasted chicken breast
⅓ of a long seedless cucumber, thinly sliced (about 3 ounces)
1 fresh jalapeño chile pepper, thinly sliced* (optional)
⅓ cup fresh cilantro leaves

1 Preheat oven to 425°F. In a small bowl combine vinegar, the ¼ cup sugar, and salt, stirring until sugar is dissolved. Add carrots; toss gently to coat. Let stand for 15 minutes.

2 Meanwhile, in another small bowl combine mayonnaise, Asian chili sauce, soy sauce, and the ⅛ teaspoon sugar.

3 Place bread halves, cut sides up, on rack in oven. Bake about 5 minutes or just until warm and lightly toasted. Spread mayonnaise mixture on cut sides of bread; top with chicken. Drain carrots; pat dry with paper towels. Arrange carrots on chicken. Top with cucumber and, if desired, chile pepper. Sprinkle with cilantro leaves. Cut into four portions.

nutrition facts per sandwich: 358 cal., 8 g total fat (2 g sat. fat), 49 mg chol., 840 mg sodium, 51 g carb., 2 g fiber, 21 g pro.

✱tip: Because chile peppers contain volatile oils that can burn your skin and eyes, avoid direct contact with them as much as possible. When working with chile peppers, wear plastic or rubber gloves. If your bare hands do touch the peppers, wash your hands and nails well with soap and warm water.

Pressing a hot sandwich as it grills helps the ingredients become more cohesive—and the sandwich easier to eat when it comes off the press.

chicken panini

start to finish: 20 minutes
makes: 4 sandwiches

8   ½-inch slices crusty country multigrain bread
¼   cup light mayonnaise or salad dressing
1   cup lightly packed fresh basil leaves
1½ cups sliced or shredded roasted chicken breast (8 ounces)
½   cup roasted red sweet pepper strips
2   tablespoons olive oil

1 Preheat a covered indoor electric grill, panini press, grill pan, or skillet to medium. To assemble sandwiches, spread one side of bread slices with mayonnaise. On four of the bread slices layer basil, chicken, and roasted pepper strips. Top with the remaining four bread slices, spread sides down. Brush outsides of sandwiches with oil.

2 Place sandwiches, half at a time if necessary, in grill or panini press. Cover and cook about 6 minutes or until golden and heated through. (If using a grill pan or skillet, place sandwiches on grill pan or skillet. Weigh sandwiches down with a heavy skillet; add food cans for more weight and cook for 2 minutes. Turn sandwiches over, weigh down, and cook about 2 minutes more or until golden and heated through.)

nutrition facts per sandwich: 218 cal., 14 g total fat (2 g sat. fat), 53 mg chol., 152 mg sodium, 4 g carb., 1 g fiber, 18 g pro.

A creamy and cooling condiment provides a nice contrast to the hot, tomato-sauced turkey filling in these nontraditional "sloppy" sandwiches.

sloppy turkey and veggie sandwiches

start to finish: 25 minutes
makes: 6 sandwiches

8   ounces uncooked ground turkey breast
2   cups chopped fresh cremini or button mushrooms
¾   cup chopped yellow or green sweet pepper (1 medium)
½   cup chopped onion (1 medium)
1   14.5-ounce can no-salt-added diced tomatoes with basil, garlic, and oregano, undrained
6   whole wheat hamburger buns, split and toasted
1   recipe Goat Cheese–Yogurt Sauce

1 In a large nonstick skillet cook turkey, mushrooms, sweet pepper, and onion over medium heat until turkey is brown and vegetables are tender, using a wooden spoon to break up meat as it cooks. Stir in tomatoes. Cook over medium-low heat for 5 minutes to blend flavors, stirring occasionally.

2 Place bun bottoms on serving plates. Divide meat mixture among bun bottoms. Spoon Goat Cheese–Yogurt Sauce over meat mixture. Top with bun tops.

nutrition facts per sandwich: 263 cal., 5 g total fat (3 g sat. fat), 27 mg chol., 392 mg sodium, 32 g carb., 7 g fiber, 21 g pro.

nutrition note: Knowing the fat content of ground meats can help you make the best choices for both the recipe you are preparing and for your family's nutritional needs. The fat content of ground beef is usually printed clearly on the package. Ground chuck is 80 to 85 percent lean; ground round is 85 percent to 90 percent lean; and ground sirloin is 90 to 92 percent lean. Regular ground turkey—made from light and dark meat, as well as skin—can contain up to 15 percent fat. The most common type is 93 percent lean. Ground turkey breast is 99 percent lean.

Goat Cheese–Yogurt Sauce: In a small bowl combine 4 ounces goat cheese (chèvre), softened; ¼ cup snipped fresh chives; 1 clove garlic, minced; ⅛ teaspoon salt; and ⅛ teaspoon ground black pepper. Gradually stir in one 6-ounce container plain fat-free Greek yogurt until smooth. makes: about 1¼ cups

Tarragon has a distinctively strong licorice flavor. If you'd like something a little milder, use fresh basil intead.

pita with figs, caramelized onions, and ricotta

start to finish: 30 minutes
makes: 4 open-face sandwiches

1 tablespoon butter
1 tablespoon olive oil
1 large sweet onion, such as Vidalia or Maui, halved lengthwise and thinly sliced
1 teaspoon sugar
¼ teaspoon salt
⅛ teaspoon ground black pepper
1 tablespoon balsamic vinegar
½ cup part-skim ricotta cheese
1 tablespoon snipped fresh tarragon
2 whole wheat pita bread rounds
6 to 8 fresh figs, quartered
¼ cup chopped walnuts, toasted* (optional)
¼ cup honey

1 For caramelized onions, in a large skillet heat butter and oil over medium-low heat. Add onion; cook, covered, for 13 to 15 minutes or until onion is tender, stirring occasionally. Uncover; stir in sugar, salt, and pepper. Cook and stir over medium-high heat for 3 to 5 minutes or until golden brown. Add balsamic vinegar, stirring to scrape up any brown bits from the bottom of the skillet. Remove from heat.

2 In a small bowl stir together ricotta cheese and tarragon; set aside.

3 Cut pita bread rounds in half crosswise; wrap in microwave-safe paper towels. Microwave on 100 percent power (high) for 10 to 20 seconds or just until warm.

4 Divide ricotta mixture among pita halves, spreading evenly. Layer with caramelized onions, figs, and, if desired, walnuts. Drizzle with honey.

nutrition facts per open-face sandwich: 318 cal., 10 g total fat (4 g sat. fat), 17 mg chol., 383 mg sodium, 55 g carb., 5 g fiber, 8 g pro.

✱tip: To toast nuts, spread them in a shallow baking pan. Bake in a 350°F oven for 5 to 10 minutes or until light brown, shaking pan once or twice. Watch carefully so the nuts don't burn.

make-ahead directions: Prepare caramelized onions and combine ricotta and tarragon. Cover and chill for up to 24 hours. Reheat caramelized onions in the microwave on 100 percent power (high) for 1 minute.

The meaty texture of eggplant—breaded with crushed seasoned croutons—makes a fine substitute for high-fat, high-sodium deli meats usually found between the buns in this classic Italian-American sandwich.

eggplant-parmesan heros

prep: 15 minutes bake: 15 minutes at 400°F
makes: 4 sandwiches

Nonstick cooking
   spray
1 medium eggplant
   (about 1 pound)
1 cup seasoned
   croutons
⅓ cup shredded
   Parmesan cheese
1 cup purchased
   marinara sauce
4 bratwurst buns, split
   Fresh basil leaves
   (optional)

1 Preheat oven to 400°F. Lightly coat a baking sheet with cooking spray. If desired, peel eggplant. Slice eggplant about ¼ inch thick.

2 Place croutons in a plastic bag. Use a rolling pin to crush croutons. In a shallow dish combine crushed croutons and ¼ cup of the Parmesan cheese. Place marinara sauce in another shallow dish. Dip eggplant slices into marinara sauce and then into croutons, pressing lightly to coat. Place on the prepared baking sheet. Lightly coat eggplant with cooking spray.

3 Bake for 15 minutes or until coating is browned and eggplant is tender. Remove eggplant from oven. If desired, place buns, cut sides up, on a baking sheet; bake or broil buns for 2 minutes or until toasted.

4 Meanwhile, heat the remaining sauce in a small saucepan or in a small microwave-safe bowl in the microwave oven on high for 30 seconds.

5 Place eggplant slices on buns and top with remaining sauce and cheese. If desired, garnish with fresh basil.

nutrition facts per sandwich: 423 cal., 9 g total fat (3 g sat. fat), 7 mg chol., 1011 mg sodium, 73 g carb., 9 g fiber, 13 g pro.

There are just a few simple ingredients in this sandwich, so try to make each one as high quality as possible. Use dense, chewy Italian-style whole grain bread and ripe, juicy, in-season tomatoes, if possible.

111

caprese panini

start to finish: 25 minutes
makes: 4 sandwiches

8   slices whole wheat bread
    Nonstick olive oil cooking spray
2   medium tomatoes, thinly sliced
4   ounces fresh mozzarella cheese, cut into 4 slices
½   cup fresh basil leaves
    Balsamic vinegar (optional)

1 Coat one side of each bread slice with cooking spray. Place bread slices on a work surface, coated sides down. Arrange tomatoes, mozzarella cheese, and basil on four of the bread slices. Cover with the remaining four bread slices, coated sides up; press together gently.

2 Preheat a covered indoor grill, panini press, grill pan, or large skillet. Place sandwiches, half at a time if necessary, in grill or panini press. Cover and cook for 3 to 4 minutes or until brown and cheese is melted. (If using a grill pan or skillet, place sandwiches on grill pan or skillet. Weigh sandwiches down with a heavy skillet; add food cans for more weight, and cook for 2 to 3 minutes or until bread is toasted. Turn sandwiches over, weigh down, and cook about 2 minutes more or until browned and cheese is melted.) If desired, serve with balsamic vinegar for dipping.

nutrition facts per sandwich: 216 cal., 8 g total fat (4 g sat. fat), 20 mg chol., 324 mg sodium, 23 g carb., 4 g fiber, 12 g pro.

Bagged baby spinach is a terrific convenience product for health- and time-conscious cooks because it doesn't have to be washed or stemmed before using.

veggie grilled cheese

start to finish: 20 minutes
makes: 4 sandwiches

2 cups purchased pickled mixed vegetables (giardiniera)
3 cups packed fresh baby spinach
6 ounces fresh mozzarella cheese, chopped
½ cup oil-packed dried tomatoes, snipped
½ teaspoon ground black pepper
2 cloves garlic, minced, or 1 teaspoon bottled minced garlic
12 slices whole grain bread, toasted

1 Rinse and drain the pickled vegetables well. In a large microwave-safe bowl combine the pickled vegetables, spinach, mozzarella cheese, tomatoes, pepper, and garlic.

2 Microwave on 100 percent power (high), uncovered, about 2 minutes or just until the mixture is warm, the spinach is wilted, and the cheese is beginning to melt.

3 To assemble sandwiches, layer half of the cheese and vegetable mixture on four slices of bread. Add another slice of bread and top with the remaining cheese and vegetable mixture and another slice of bread. Cut sandwiches diagonally into halves.

nutrition facts per sandwich: 359 cal., 14 g total fat (7 g sat. fat), 30 mg chol., 782 mg sodium, 42 g carb., 7 g fiber, 17 g pro.

Diced fresh mango adds an unexpected burst of sweetness, freshness, and color to these hearty beef tacos.

fajita-style beef tacos

start to finish: 30 minutes
makes: 8 tacos

12   ounces boneless beef
       sirloin steak, cut
       ¾ inch thick
⅛   teaspoon salt
⅛   teaspoon ground
       black pepper
⅛   teaspoon cayenne
       pepper
1   tablespoon canola oil
2   large sweet onions,
       such as Vadalia or
       Maui, halved and
       thinly sliced
1   mango, seeded,
       peeled, and
       chopped
8   6-inch corn tortillas,
       warmed
¼   cup snipped fresh
       cilantro
       Lime wedges

1 Preheat broiler. Trim fat from steak. In a small bowl combine salt, black pepper, and cayenne pepper; sprinkle evenly over steak. Place steak on the unheated rack of a broiler pan. Broil steaks 3 to 4 inches from the heat for 8 to 12 minutes for medium rare or until desired doneness, turning once. Cover with foil; let steak stand for 5 minutes.

2 Meanwhile, in a large skillet heat oil over medium heat. Add onions; cook, covered, about 12 minutes or until very tender and brown, stirring occasionally. Turn heat to medium low if onions start to get too brown.

3 Thinly slice steak across the grain. Divide steak, onions, and mango among tortillas. Sprinkle with cilantro and serve with lime wedges. Serve immediately.

nutrition facts per 2 tacos: 377 cal., 15 g total fat (5 g sat. fat), 39 mg chol., 140 mg sodium, 41 g carb., 6 g fiber, 22 g pro.

To seed the cucumber for the Cucumber Sauce, peel the cucumber and then cut it in half horizontally. Use a spoon to drag down the center of each cucumber half, scooping the seeds out as you go.

greek feta burgers

prep: 20 minutes cook: 8 minutes
makes: 2 burgers

8 ounces lean ground beef
1 tablespoon crumbled reduced-fat feta cheese
1½ teaspoons snipped fresh Italian (flat-leaf) parsley
⅛ teaspoon ground black pepper
1 clove garlic, minced
2 whole wheat hamburger buns, split and toasted
½ cup fresh spinach leaves
2 tomato slices
1 recipe Cucumber Sauce
   Thin slivers red onion (optional)

1 In a medium bowl combine ground beef, feta cheese, parsley, pepper, and garlic. Shape mixture into two ½-inch-thick patties.

2 In a large nonstick skillet cook patties over medium-high heat for 8 to 10 minutes or until an instant-read thermometer inserted into sides of patties registers 160°F,* turning once.

3 Line cut sides of bun halves with spinach. Top with burgers, tomato slices, and Cucumber Sauce. If desired, garnish with red onion.

nutrition facts per burger: 312 cal., 15 g total fat (6 g sat. fat), 79 mg chol., 424 mg sodium, 18 g carb., 3 g fiber, 27 g pro.

*tip: The internal color of a burger is not a reliable doneness indicator. A beef or pork patty cooked to 160°F is safe, regardless of color. To measure the doneness of a patty, insert an instant-read thermometer through the side of the patty to a depth of 2 to 3 inches.

Cucumber Sauce: In a small bowl combine 3 tablespoons chopped, seeded cucumber; 2 tablespoons light sour cream; 1 clove garlic, minced; ½ teaspoon snipped fresh Italian (flat-leaf) parsley; ¼ teaspoon snipped fresh mint; and ⅛ teaspoon sea salt. makes: about ¼ cup

These beef burgers served on slices of toasted whole-wheat baguette are so packed with vegetables—inside and out—it's like eating a salad simultaneously with your sandwich.

garden beef burgers

prep: 15 minutes grill: 14 minutes
makes: 4 burgers

1   egg white, lightly beaten
½   cup shredded carrot (1 medium)
¼   cup thinly sliced green onions (2)
¼   cup shredded zucchini
2   cloves garlic, minced
⅛   teaspoon ground black pepper
12 ounces lean ground beef
8   ½-inch slices whole wheat baguette-style French bread, toasted
¾   cup fresh spinach
1   medium tomato, thinly sliced
½   cup thinly shaved zucchini**

1 In a large bowl combine egg white, carrot, green onions, shredded zucchini, garlic, and pepper. Add ground beef; mix well. Shape meat mixture into four ¾-inch-thick patties.

2 For a charcoal or gas grill, place patties on the grill rack directly over medium heat. Cover and grill for 14 to 18 minutes or until patties are done (160°F),* turning once.

3 Line 4 slices toasted bread with spinach and tomato. Top with burger and shaved zucchini. Top with remaining 4 slices toasted bread.

nutrition facts per burger: 258 cal., 10 g total fat (3 g sat. fat), 55 mg chol., 229 mg sodium, 19 g carb., 3 g fiber, 21 g pro.

nutrition note: Mild-flavored zucchini is a no-fail secret weapon against the perennial picky eater. When finely shredded or chopped, this veggie can be seamlessly incorporated into sauces, casseroles, burgers, meat loaves and soups, adding valuable nutrients without detection. The result: a healthy shot of veggies in each bite!

＊tip: The internal color of a burger is not a reliable doneness indicator. A beef or pork patty cooked to 160°F is safe, regardless of color. To measure the doneness of a patty, insert an instant-read thermometer through the side of the patty to a depth of 2 to 3 inches.

＊＊tip: To make zucchini ribbons, use a vegetable peeler to thinly shave the zucchini.

sandwiches, **burgers & pizzas**

Here's a combination of two of the country's favorite foods—pizza and hamburgers—but lightened up considerably on both counts.

turkey pizza burgers

prep: 15 minutes   grill: 14 minutes
makes: 4 burgers

1   egg, lightly beaten, or ¼ cup refrigerated or frozen egg product, thawed
¼   cup quick-cooking rolled oats
4   teaspoons snipped fresh oregano
⅛   teaspoon salt
⅛   teaspoon ground black pepper
1   pound uncooked ground turkey breast
4   ½-ounce slices provolone cheese
½   cup low-sodium tomato pasta sauce
4   whole wheat hamburger buns, toasted

1 In a medium bowl combine egg, rolled oats, 2 teaspoons of the oregano, the salt, and pepper. Add ground turkey breast; mix well. Shape turkey mixture into four ¾-inch-thick patties.

2 For a charcoal or gas grill, place patties on the grill rack directly over medium coals. Cover and grill for 14 to 18 minutes or until done (165°F),* turning once halfway through grilling and topping each burger with a provolone cheese slice for the last minute of grilling.

3 Meanwhile, in a small saucepan cook pasta sauce until heated though.

4 Place burgers on the bottom halves of buns. Top with pasta sauce, the remaining 2 teaspoons oregano, and the bun tops.

nutrition facts per burger: 351 cal., 9 g total fat (3 g sat. fat), 127 mg chol., 487 mg sodium, 28 g carb., 3 g fiber, 38 g pro.

* tip: The internal color of a burger is not a reliable doneness indicator. A turkey or chicken patty cooked to 165°F is safe, regardless of color. To check the doneness of a patty, insert an instant-read thermometer through the side of the patty to a depth of 2 to 3 inches.

Finely shredded lemon peel adds a burst of freshness to bottled light Caesar dressing in this 20-minute dinner burger.

caesar salad burgers

start to finish: 20 minutes
makes: 4 burgers

1 pound uncooked ground turkey breast

2 tablespoons Worcestershire-style marinade for chicken

¼ to ½ teaspoon ground black pepper

⅓ cup bottled light Caesar salad dressing

1 teaspoon finely shredded lemon peel

4 whole grain ciabatta buns, split and toasted

2 leaves romaine lettuce, trimmed and torn into 8 pieces

4 thin slices red onion (optional)

4 slices tomato (optional)

1 In a large bowl combine ground turkey, Worcestershire-style marinade, and pepper. Shape mixture into four ½-inch-thick patties. Heat a lightly greased grill pan over medium-high heat. Place patties in hot pan. Cook for 10 to 12 minutes or until done (165°F),* turning once halfway through cooking. If patties brown too quickly, reduce heat to medium.

2 Meanwhile, in a small bowl combine salad dressing and lemon peel. Spread about half of the dressing mixture on bottoms of buns. Add lettuce, onion (if desired), tomato (if desired), and burgers. Spoon the remaining dressing mixture over burgers. Top with bun tops.

nutrition facts per burger: 368 cal., 14 g total fat (3 g sat. fat), 87 mg chol., 797 mg sodium, 33 g carb., 2 g fiber, 26 g pro.

* tip: The internal color of a burger is not a reliable doneness indicator. A chicken or turkey patty cooked to 165°F is safe, regardless of color. To check the doneness of a patty, insert an instant-read thermometer through the side of the patty to a depth of 2 to 3 inches.

Serve these Greek-inspired burgers with iced mint tea.

greek-style turkey burgers

prep: 15 minutes   grill: 14 minutes
makes: 4 burgers

1   egg white, lightly beaten
⅓   cup fine dry whole wheat bread crumbs*
1   tablespoon plain low-fat yogurt
1   teaspoon snipped fresh rosemary or ½ teaspoon dried rosemary, crushed
1   teaspoon snipped fresh oregano or ½ teaspoon dried oregano, crushed
1   tablespoon crumbled feta cheese
⅛   teaspoon ground black pepper
1   pound uncooked ground turkey breast or chicken breast
    Mixed torn greens (optional)
1   recipe Olive-Tomato Salsa
¼   cup crumbled feta cheese (1 ounce)
    Plain low-fat yogurt (optional)
2   whole wheat pita bread rounds, halved and lightly toasted

1 In a medium bowl combine egg white, bread crumbs, the 1 tablespoon yogurt, rosemary, oregano, the 1 tablespoon feta cheese, and pepper. Add turkey; mix well. Shape turkey mixture into four ¾-inch-thick patties.

2 For a charcoal or gas grill, grill patties on the rack of a covered grill directly over medium heat for 14 to 18 minutes or until no longer pink (165°F),** turning once halfway through grilling.

3 If desired, divide greens among four serving plates; top with burgers. Top burgers evenly with Olive-Tomato Salsa, the ¼ cup feta cheese, and, if desired, additional yogurt. Serve burgers with pita bread.

nutrition facts per burger: 275 cal., 6 g total fat (2 g sat. fat), 53 mg chol., 507 mg sodium, 23 g carb., 4 g fiber, 35 g pro.

*tip: For fine dry whole wheat bread crumbs, place 1 slice whole wheat bread, toasted, in a food processor. Cover and process until fine crumbs form.
makes: ⅓ cup

**tip: The internal color of a burger is not a reliable doneness indicator. A chicken or turkey patty cooked to 165°F is safe, regardless of color. To check the doneness of a patty, insert an instant-read thermometer through the side of the patty to a depth of 2 to 3 inches.

Olive-Tomato Salsa: In a small bowl stir together 1 cup chopped, seeded tomato; ¼ cup chopped, seeded cucumber; ¼ cup chopped pitted Kalamata or other ripe olives; ½ teaspoon snipped fresh rosemary or ¼ teaspoon dried rosemary, crushed; and ½ teaspoon snipped fresh oregano or ¼ teaspoon dried oregano, crushed.
makes: about 1½ cups

If you can find it, smoked mozzarella really does add special flavor to these Mediterranean-style burgers.

tomato-basil turkey burgers

start to finish: 30 minutes
makes: 8 burgers

sandwiches, **burgers & pizzas**

2 pounds uncooked ground turkey breast
2 tablespoons finely chopped oil-packed dried tomatoes
2 tablespoons snipped fresh basil
1 teaspoon sea salt
½ teaspoon freshly ground black pepper
4 ounces smoked or fresh mozzarella cheese, thinly sliced
2 cups lightly packed arugula or watercress
8 sourdough or other hamburger buns, split and toasted
1 yellow sweet pepper, roasted** and cut into strips, or ¾ cup bottled roasted red sweet pepper strips (optional)
Pesto Mayonnaise (optional)

Pesto Mayonnaise: In a small bowl stir together ½ cup reduced-fat mayonnaise and 2 to 4 tablespoons purchased pesto.

1 In a large bowl combine ground turkey, dried tomato, basil, salt, and black pepper; mix well. Shape turkey mixture into eight ½-inch-thick patties.

2 For a charcoal or gas grill, place patties on the rack of a covered grill directly over medium heat. Cover and grill for 10 to 13 minutes or until no longer pink (165°F),* turning once and adding mozzarella cheese for the last 1 to 2 minutes of grilling.

3 Place arugula on bottoms of toasted buns; add burgers. If desired, top with roasted pepper strips and Pesto Mayonnaise. Top with bun tops.

nutrition facts per burger: 328 cal., 5 g total fat (2 g sat. fat), 65 mg chol., 700 mg sodium, 33 g carb., 2 g fiber, 35 g pro.

*tip: The internal color of a burger is not a reliable doneness indicator. A beef or pork patty cooked to 160°F is safe, regardless of color. To measure the doneness of a patty, insert an instant-read thermometer through the side of the patty to a depth of 2 to 3 inches.

**tip: To roast sweet peppers on the grill, quarter pepper lengthwise; remove stems, seeds, and membranes. For a charcoal or gas grill, place pepper quarters, skin sides down, on grill rack. Cover and grill about 10 minutes or until blistered. Wrap peppers in foil; let stand about 15 minutes or until cool enough to handle. Using a sharp knife, loosen edges of skins; gently pull off skins and discard.

To seed a tomato, cut it in half horizontally, then use the tip of a small spoon to scoop out the seeds from each segment of the tomato.

cheesy eggplant burgers

prep: 15 minutes   grill: 6 minutes
makes: 6 burgers

1 teaspoon garlic powder

½ teaspoon ground black pepper

⅛ teaspoon salt

½ cup chopped, seeded tomato

2 tablespoons olive oil

1 tablespoon snipped fresh oregano

2 teaspoons snipped fresh thyme

2 teaspoons cider vinegar

6 ½-inch-thick slices eggplant

6 ¾-ounce slices smoked gouda cheese

6 ½-inch slices whole grain baguette-style bread, toasted

1 In a small bowl combine garlic powder, pepper, and salt. In another small bowl combine half of the garlic powder mixture, the tomato, 1 tablespoon of the oil, the oregano, thyme, and vinegar; set aside.

2 Brush eggplant slices with the remaining 1 tablespoon oil and sprinkle with the remaining garlic powder mixture.

3 For a charcoal or gas grill, place eggplant slices on the rack of an uncovered grill directly over medium heat. Cover and grill for 6 to 8 minutes or just until tender and golden brown, turning once halfway through grilling and topping with the gouda cheese slices for the last 2 minutes of grilling.

4 Place eggplant slices on top of toasted bread slices. Top with tomato mixture.

nutrition facts per burger: 201 cal., 11 g total fat (4 g sat. fat), 17 mg chol., 506 mg sodium, 19 g carb., 4 g fiber, 7 g pro.

There are a multitude of meatless burgers on the market—spicy black bean, barbecue-flavor, veggie medley, vegan, flame-grilled— and the list goes on. Pick one you like—they're all delicious crusted with toasted cumin and topped with pineapple salsa.

cumin-crusted veggie burgers with pineapple salsa

start to finish: 20 minutes
makes: 4 burgers

122

2   teaspoons cumin
    seeds
4   refrigerated or frozen
    meatless burger
    patties, thawed
    Olive oil
6   slices fresh or canned
    pineapple
4   pita bread rounds or
    flatbreads
1   tablespoon bottled
    pepper and onion
    relish
    Fresh basil leaves
    (optional)
    Chopped peanuts
    (optional)

1 In a medium skillet heat cumin seeds over medium heat for 3 to 4 minutes or until fragrant and starting to brown. Crush seeds using a mortar and pestle or rolling pin.

2 Brush burger patties with oil; coat with crushed cumin seeds. Blot excess moisture from pineapple slices and lightly coat with oil.

3 For a charcoal or gas grill, grill pineapple slices on the rack of a covered grill directly over medium-high heat for 6 to 8 minutes or until heated through, turning once halfway through grilling. Transfer to a cutting board; set aside. Add meatless patties to grill rack; grill about 8 minutes or until heated through, turning patties and adding pita bread after 4 minutes of grilling. Cover and keep warm.

4 For pineapple salsa, chop pineapple and place in a bowl. Stir in relish.

5 Serve veggie burgers on pita bread with pineapple salsa. If desired, top with fresh basil and chopped peanuts.

nutrition facts per burger: 316 cal., 5 g total fat (1 g sat. fat), 0 mg chol., 619 mg sodium, 52 g carb., 6 g fiber, 19 g pro.

Barbecued chicken pizza might have come first, but barbecued pork pizza is a natural. Spice it up with shredded Pepper Jack cheese, if you like.

easy barbecued pork pizza

prep: 15 minutes   bake: 12 minutes at 425°F
makes: 8 servings

1   17- to 18-ounce tub refrigerated barbecue sauce with shredded pork (2 cups)
1   tablespoon canola oil
2   medium red and/ or yellow sweet peppers, cut into thin strips
1   medium onion, cut into thin wedges
1   12-inch packaged prebaked pizza crust
½   8-ounce package shredded Monterey Jack cheese (1 cup)

1 Preheat oven to 425°F. Heat shredded pork according to package directions.

2 Meanwhile, in a large skillet heat oil over medium-high heat. Add sweet peppers and onion; cook about 5 minutes or until crisp-tender.

3 Place pizza crust on an ungreased baking sheet. Spoon shredded pork over crust, spreading evenly. Top with sweet peppers and onion. Sprinkle with Monterey Jack cheese.

4 Bake about 12 minutes or until cheese melts and crust edge turns light brown.

nutrition facts per serving: 319 cal., 11 g total fat (3 g sat. fat), 33 mg chol., 862 mg sodium, 39 g carb., 1 g fiber, 17 g pro.

Celery can get limp in the refrigerator in just a few days. To crisp it up before eating or cooking with it, trim and cut each stalk into halves or thirds. Rinse well and place in a bowl of ice water. Let stand for 10 to 15 minutes. The porous stalks will soak up the water and get crunchy again!

buffalo chicken pizzas

prep: 10 minutes bake: 10 minutes at 450°F
makes: 4 individual pizzas

4 pita bread rounds
¼ cup bottled blue
    cheese salad
    dressing
1 9-ounce package
    refrigerated
    Southwest-flavor
    cooked chicken
    breast strips, cut
    into bite-size pieces
2 stalks celery, cut into
    thin strips
4 tablespoons blue
    cheese crumbles
    Bottled hot pepper
    sauce or buffalo
    wing sauce
    (optional)

1 Preheat oven to 450°F. Place pita rounds on a baking sheet. Brush with blue cheese dressing. Top with chicken and celery strips.

2 Bake, uncovered, about 10 minutes or until heated through and pitas are crisp. Transfer to plates. Sprinkle with blue cheese crumbles. If desired, pass hot pepper sauce.

nutrition facts per individual pizza: 353 cal., 13 g total fat (4 g sat. fat), 52 mg chol., 1171 mg sodium, 36 g carb., 2 g fiber, 22 g pro.

To save even more time, you can use the breast meat from a rotisserie chicken instead of starting with raw chicken. Just stir in the 2 tablespoons of the peanut butter mixture into the cut-up chicken and heat gently in the microwave to help the sauce coat the chicken.

thai chicken pizza

prep: 20 minutes   bake: 10 minutes at 475°F
makes: 8 servings

⅓ cup natural creamy
    peanut butter
¼ cup warm water
2 teaspoons sugar
2 teaspoons rice
    vinegar
¼ to ½ teaspoon
    crushed red pepper
2 teaspoons canola oil
12 ounces skinless
    boneless chicken
    breast, cut into bite-
    size pieces
½ cup thinly sliced
    green onions (4)
2 cloves garlic, minced
    Nonstick cooking
    spray
1 16-ounce loaf frozen
    whole wheat bread
    dough, thawed
1 cup thin red sweet
    pepper strips
½ cup shredded part-
    skim mozzarella
    cheese (2 ounces)
½ cup snipped fresh
    cilantro

1 Preheat oven to 475°F. In a small bowl combine peanut butter, the warm water, sugar, vinegar, and crushed red pepper; set aside.

2 In a medium skillet heat oil over medium heat. Add chicken; cook and stir until no longer pink. Add green onions and garlic; cook and stir for 1 minute more. Stir in 2 tablespoons of the peanut butter mixture. Cook and stir over low heat until chicken is coated. Remove from heat.

3 Coat a 12- to 14-inch pizza pan, large baking sheet, or pizza screen with cooking spray; set aside. On a lightly floured surface, roll bread dough into an 11- to 13-inch circle. Transfer to the prepared pizza pan. Spread dough with the remaining peanut butter mixture, adding water if necessary to make it of spreading consistency. Top with chicken mixture, sweet pepper, and mozzarella cheese.

4 Bake for 10 to 12 minutes or until cheese is melted and crust is lightly browned. Sprinkle with cilantro.

nutrition facts per serving: 306 cal., 10 g total fat (2 g sat. fat), 29 mg chol., 430 mg sodium, 32 g carb., 4 g fiber, 21 g pro.

Whew! At just 13 minutes start to finish, this is your go-to recipe when you don't have a minute to spare. Serve these toasty pizzas with a dressing-included bagged salad and you'll be in and out of the kitchen in less than 30 minutes.

chicken parmesan pita pizzas

prep: 5 minutes broil: 8 minutes
makes: 12 mini pizzas

2 teaspoons olive oil
¼ teaspoon salt
2 cloves garlic, minced
1 pound chicken breast tenderloins
6 6-inch pita breads
¾ cup prepared tomato sauce or pizza sauce
⅓ cup grated Parmesan cheese
1 cup shredded reduced-fat mozzarella cheese (4 ounces)

1 Preheat broiler. In a shallow dish combine oil, salt, and garlic. Add chicken; turn to thoroughly coat the chicken. Arrange the chicken in a single layer on the unheated rack of a broiler pan.

2 Broil chicken 3 to 4 inches from the heat about 5 minutes or until no longer pink, turning once. Cool chicken slightly; thinly slice.

3 For crusts, split pita bread to make 12 rounds. Arrange pita rounds, cut sides up, on two large baking sheets. Broil pita rounds for 30 to 45 seconds or until lightly toasted.

4 Spread a generous 1 tablespoon tomato sauce over each crust. Top with chicken, Parmesan cheese, and mozzarella cheese. Broil the pizzas about 1 minute or just until mozzarella melts.

nutrition facts per 2 mini pizzas: 345 cal., 8 g total fat (3 g sat. fat), 55 mg chol., 935 mg sodium, 38 g carb., 2 g fiber, 29 g pro.

Frozen cooked and peeled shrimp is handy to have in the freezer. It thaws very quickly and can be used in a variety of ways—on top of pizza or salad greens, or tossed last-minute into a pasta dish.

grilled shrimp and pepperoni pizza

prep: 15 minutes   grill: 15 minutes
makes: 6 servings

1   cup broccoli florets
1   small zucchini, quartered lengthwise and sliced
1   13.8-ounce package refrigerated pizza dough
¾   cup pizza sauce or ⅓ cup purchased pesto
12   ounces peeled, cooked shrimp
½   3.5-ounce package sliced pepperoni
1½   cups shredded mozzarella cheese (6 ounces)

1 In a medium saucepan cook broccoli and zucchini in enough boiling water to cover for 2 minutes. Drain and rinse immediately in cold water; set aside.

2 Lightly grease an 11- to 13-inch pizza pan. Unroll pizza dough and transfer to prepared pan, pressing out dough with your hands. Build up edges slightly. Prick generously with a fork.

3 For a gas or charcoal grill, place pizza pan on the grill rack directly over medium heat. Cover grill and grill for 5 minutes. Carefully remove pan from grill.

4 Spread pizza sauce over hot crust. Top with cooked vegetables, shrimp, and pepperoni. Sprinkle with mozzarella cheese. Return pizza to grill rack. Grill, covered, about 10 minutes more or until cheese melts and pizza is heated through, checking occasionally to make sure crust doesn't overbrown.

nutrition facts per serving: 289 cal., 11 g total fat (4 g sat. fat), 127 mg chol., 726 mg sodium, 23 g carb., 24 g pro.

A little advance planning is required for this recipe. To thaw the bread at room temperature, set it out 2 to 3 hours before using. Or, you can thaw in the refrigerator for 10 to 12 hours.

roasted pepper and chèvre pizzas

prep: 20 minutes bake: 10 minutes at 450°F
makes: 8 individual pizzas

128

1	16-ounce loaf frozen whole wheat or white bread dough
2	tablespoons yellow cornmeal
3	medium red, yellow, and/or green sweet peppers, roasted (see tip, page 120)
2	tablespoons olive oil
¼	teaspoon crushed red pepper
1	medium red onion, cut into thin wedges and separated into strips
4	ounces semisoft goat cheese (chèvre) or feta cheese, crumbled or cut up (¾ cup)
10	ripe olives, pitted and quartered lengthwise
4	roma tomatoes, sliced
1½	cups shredded part-skim mozzarella cheese (6 ounces)
3	to 4 tablespoons fresh oregano leaves or snipped fresh basil*

1 For pizza crusts, thaw bread dough. Preheat oven to 450°F. On a lightly floured surface, divide dough into eight pieces. Cover; let dough rest for 10 minutes. Pat or roll each piece into a 6-inch circle. Grease two extra-large baking sheets; sprinkle with cornmeal. Transfer dough circles to baking sheets.

2 Bake pizza crusts for 5 minutes. Remove baking sheets from the oven; place on wire racks to cool, leaving the dough on the baking sheets.

3 Meanwhile, cut roasted peppers into 1-inch-wide strips. Stir together oil and crushed red pepper. Brush the mixture onto pizza crusts. Top with roasted peppers, onion, goat cheese, olives, and tomatoes. Sprinkle with mozzarella cheese.

4 Bake for 5 to 7 minutes or until mozzarella is golden brown and crusts are crisp. Before serving, sprinkle with fresh oregano.

nutrition facts per individual pizza: 329 cal., 14 g total fat (6 g sat. fat), 25 mg chol., 565 mg sodium, 37 g carb., 4 g fiber, 16 g pro.

*tip: You can substitute 1 tablespoon dried oregano or basil, crushed, for the fresh herbs. Instead of sprinkling it on top of the pizzas, stir the dried herb into the oil mixture before brushing it onto the crust.

Serve this pizza with your favorite salsa—fresh or jarred—for topping after it's baked, if you like.

spicy tex-mex pizza

prep: 5 minutes bake: 20 minutes at 425°F stand: 5 minutes
makes: 6 servings

1 12-inch thin-crust Italian bread shell (10-ounce Boboli) or Italian flatbread (12.5-ounce focaccia)

2 cups shredded Monterey Jack cheese with jalapeño peppers or Monterey Jack cheese (8 ounces)

1 15-ounce can black beans, rinsed and drained

1 11-ounce can whole kernel corn with red and green peppers, drained

2 to 4 tablespoons chopped pickled jalapeño peppers (optional)

1 Preheat oven to 425°F. Place bread shell on an ungreased pizza pan or baking sheet. Top with 1 cup of the Monterey Jack cheese, the black beans, corn, and, if desired, jalapeño peppers. Sprinkle with the remaining 1 cup cheese.

2 Bake about 20 minutes or until heated through and cheese is melted. Let cool for 5 minutes.

nutrition facts per serving: 373 cal., 14 g total fat (8 g sat. fat), 36 mg chol., 942 mg sodium, 41 g carb., 4 g fiber, 16 g pro.

6

A flash in the pan can be a very good thing! These dishes that go from stovetop to tabletop in 30 minutes or less maximize efficiency to make terrific one-pot meals.

skillet dinners &

stir-

chicken with cherry-ginger chutney

fries

To partially freeze the beef, place it—thoroughly wrapped—in the freezer for about 30 minutes before slicing.

sweet and spicy edamame-beef stir-fry

prep: 20 minutes   **cook:** 10 minutes
makes: 4 servings

8   ounces beef sirloin
     steak
4   teaspoons canola oil
2   teaspoons finely
     chopped fresh
     ginger
2   cups fresh broccoli
     florets
1   cup red and/or yellow
     sweet pepper strips
     (1 large)
1   cup frozen shelled
     sweet soybeans
     (edamame)
3   tablespoons hoisin
     sauce
2   tablespoons rice
     vinegar
1   teaspoon red chili
     paste
2   cups hot cooked
     brown or white rice

1 If desired, partially freeze beef for easier slicing. Trim fat from meat. Thinly slice meat across the grain into bite-size strips. Set beef aside.

2 In a nonstick wok or large skillet heat 2 teaspoons of the oil over medium-high heat. Add ginger; cook and stir for 15 seconds. Add broccoli and sweet pepper; cook and stir about 4 minutes or until crisp-tender. Remove vegetables from wok.

3 Add the remaining 2 teaspoons oil to wok. Add beef and edamame; cook and stir about 2 minutes or until beef is desired doneness. Return vegetables to wok.

4 In a small bowl combine hoisin, vinegar, and chili paste. Add to beef mixture; toss to coat. Heat through. Serve over rice.

nutrition facts per serving: 340 cal., 11 g total fat (2 g sat. fat), 24 mg chol., 262 mg sodium, 38 g carb., 6 g fiber, 22 g pro.

nutrition note: Fiber- and protein-rich edamame is a natural source of antioxidants and isoflavones, which may help reduce the risk of breast cancer and heart disease.

"Blistering" simply means cooking vegetables such as green beans, zucchini, or tomatoes at a very high temperature so they get speckled with deliciously flavorful spots where the natural sugars have caramelized and turned the skin of the vegetable crisp. Yum!

soy-glazed flank steak with blistered green beans

start to finish: 30 minutes
makes: 4 servings

1 pound fresh green beans
1 pound beef flank steak
6 cloves garlic, minced
1 tablespoon grated fresh ginger
2 tablespoons soy sauce
1 teaspoon packed brown sugar
5 teaspoons peanut oil
4 green onions, white parts only, thinly sliced
2 tablespoons sweet rice wine (mirin)
1 teaspoon red chili paste (sambal oelek)
Sesame seeds, toasted* (optional)
Hot cooked jasmine rice (optional)

1 Trim and diagonally halve green beans; set aside. Trim fat from beef. Thinly slice meat across the grain into bite-size strips. Set beef aside. In a small bowl combine garlic and ginger; set aside. In another small bowl combine soy sauce and brown sugar; set aside.

2 In a wok or very large skillet heat 3 teaspoons of the oil over medium-high heat. Add green beans; cook and stir for 7 to 8 minutes or until beans are blistered and brown in spots. Transfer beans to paper towels to drain. Add the remaining 2 teaspoons oil to wok.

3 Add garlic mixture to the wok; cook and stir for 30 seconds. Add half of the beef strips; cook and stir about 3 minutes or until meat is slightly pink in the center. Using a slotted spoon, transfer meat to a medium bowl. Repeat with the remaining beef. Return all beef to skillet. Stir in green onions, rice wine, chili paste, and the soy sauce mixture. Cook and stir for 1 minute. Add green beans; cook and stir about 2 minutes more or until heated through.

4 If desired, sprinkle with sesame seeds and serve with hot cooked rice.

nutrition facts per serving: 294 cal., 14 g total fat (5 g sat. fat), 50 mg chol., 668 mg sodium, 16 g carb., 4 g fiber, 26 g pro.

*tip: To toast sesame seeds, scatter them in a dry small skillet and heat over medium heat just until golden. Stir frequently so they don't burn.

Brown rice takes more time than white rice to cook—usually 45 to 55 minutes. You can cook it ahead of time and store, covered, in the refrigerator. Simply reheat in the microwave with a little bit of water before serving. Or, you can use packaged precooked brown rice.

sesame ginger beef stir-fry

start to finish: 30 minutes
makes: 4 servings

12	ounces boneless beef sirloin steak
1	cup reduced-sodium chicken broth
1	tablespoon cornstarch
1	tablespoon grated fresh ginger or 1 teaspoon ground ginger
1	teaspoon ground coriander
⅛	to ¼ teaspoon crushed red pepper
2	cloves garlic, minced
2	teaspoons sesame oil
1	medium onion, halved and sliced
2	cups broccoli florets
1	medium red sweet pepper, seeded and cut into bite-size strips
1	to 2 teaspoons canola oil (optional)
1⅓	cups hot cooked brown rice
1	teaspoon sesame seeds, toasted* (optional)

1 If desired, partially freeze beef for easier slicing. Trim fat from meat. Thinly slice meat across the grain into bite-size strips. Set beef aside.

2 For sauce, in a small bowl stir together broth, cornstarch, ginger, coriander, crushed red pepper, and garlic; set aside.

3 In a nonstick wok or large skillet heat sesame oil over medium-high heat. Add onion; cook and stir for 2 minutes. Add broccoli and sweet pepper; cook and stir for 1 to 2 minutes more or until vegetables are crisp-tender. Remove vegetables from wok.

4 Add beef strips to hot wok. (Add canola oil to skillet if necessary.) Cook and stir for 2 to 3 minutes or until meat is slightly pink in center. Push meat from center of wok.

5 Stir sauce. Add sauce to center of wok; cook and stir until thickened and bubbly. Return cooked vegetables to wok; stir to coat all ingredients with sauce. Cook and stir for 1 to 2 minutes more or until heated through. Serve with rice. If desired, sprinkle with sesame seeds.

nutrition facts per serving: 255 cal., 7 g total fat (2 g sat. fat), 36 mg chol., 212 mg sodium, 25 g carb., 4 g fiber, 23 g pro.

*tip: To toast sesame seeds, scatter them in a dry small skillet and heat over medium heat just until golden. Stir frequently so they don't burn.

If you're really pressed for time, buy the prepared butternut squash found in the produce section that is already peeled, seeded, and cubed.

mexican beef and veggies

start to finish: 30 minutes
makes: 4 servings

1   1¼-pound butternut
    squash, peeled,
    seeded, and cubed
    (about 3 cups)
12 ounces lean ground
    beef
1   teaspoon ground
    cumin
½   teaspoon salt
⅛   teaspoon ground
    cinnamon
2   cloves garlic, minced
1   14.5-ounce can
    diced tomatoes,
    undrained
1   medium zucchini,
    halved lengthwise
    and cut into ¼-inch
    slices
¼   cup water
¼   cup snipped fresh
    cilantro
2   to 3 cups hot cooked
    white or brown rice
    Bottled hot pepper
    sauce (optional)

1 In a large skillet cook butternut squash, ground beef, cumin, salt, cinnamon, and garlic over medium heat until meat is brown, using a wooden spoon to break up meat as it cooks. Drain off fat.

2 Stir tomatoes into meat mixture. Bring to boiling; reduce heat. Simmer, covered, about 8 minutes or just until butternut squash is tender. Stir in zucchini and the water. Return to boiling; reduce heat. Simmer, covered, about 4 minutes more or until zucchini is tender. Stir in cilantro. Serve over hot cooked rice. If desired, season with bottled hot pepper sauce.

nutrition facts per serving: 313 cal., 9 g total fat (3 g sat. fat), 54 mg chol., 504 mg sodium, 39 g carb., 3 g fiber, 20 g pro.

This really is a complete one-dish meal packed with veggies, meat, and pasta. Just a little bit of ground lamb—2 ounces per serving—gives it great Greek flavor.

greek skillet supper

start to finish: 30 minutes
makes: 4 servings

8 ounces lean ground lamb or ground beef
¾ cup chopped onion
2 cloves garlic, minced
1 14.5-ounce can beef broth
1½ cups dried medium shell macaroni
2 cups frozen mixed vegetables
1 14.5-ounce can diced tomatoes, undrained
2 tablespoons tomato paste
2 teaspoons snipped fresh marjoram or 1 teaspoon dried marjoram, crushed
⅛ teaspoon ground cinnamon
⅛ teaspoon ground nutmeg
½ cup crumbled feta cheese (2 ounces)
Snipped fresh marjoram (optional)

1 In a large skillet cook ground meat, onion, and garlic over medium-high heat until meat is brown, using a wooden spoon to break up meat as it cooks. Drain off fat.

2 Add broth and macaroni to meat mixture in skillet. Bring to boiling; reduce heat. Simmer, covered, for 10 minutes.

3 Stir frozen vegetables, tomatoes, tomato paste, dried marjoram (if using), cinnamon, and nutmeg into meat mixture in skillet. Return to boiling; reduce heat. Simmer, uncovered, for 5 to 10 minutes or until vegetables are tender. Stir in 2 teaspoons fresh marjoram (if using). Sprinkle with feta cheese and, if desired, additional fresh marjoram.

nutrition facts per serving: 400 cal., 12 g total fat (6 g sat. fat), 50 mg chol., 783 mg sodium, 51 g carb., 3 g fiber, 22 g pro.

Broccoli raab—also called rapini—is most delicious when young and slender. Avoid buying overgrown broccoli raab, as it can be bitter. Look for bunches with large, dark green leaves with no yellowing or wilting.

pork medallions with broccoli raab

start to finish: 25 minutes
makes: 4 servings

2 tablespoons butter
2 cups sliced fresh mushrooms
2 cups chopped broccoli raab, small broccoli florets, or chopped broccolini
12 ounces pork tenderloin, cut into ½-inch slices
Salt
Ground black pepper
2 ounces prosciutto or thinly sliced ham, cut into bite-size strips
¼ cup balsamic vinegar
1 tablespoon packed brown sugar

1 In a large skillet melt 1 tablespoon of the butter over medium-high heat. Add mushrooms and broccoli raab; cook about 3 minutes or until crisp-tender, stirring occasionally. Remove vegetables from skillet; set aside.

2 Sprinkle pork with salt and pepper. Melt the remaining 1 tablespoon butter in the skillet. Add pork slices; cook for 4 to 6 minutes or until juices run clear, turning once.

3 Add prosciutto, vinegar, and brown sugar to skillet. Return vegetables to skillet; heat through.

nutrition facts per serving: 238 cal., 10 g total fat (5 g sat. fat), 80 mg chol., 559 mg sodium, 10 g carb., 0 g fiber, 25 g pro.

This is a perfect dish for fall, when both parsnips and pears are in season. Serve it with a green salad of watercress, crisp apples, and a sprinkling of blue cheese.

pork loin with parsnips and pears

start to finish: 25 minutes
makes: 4 servings

1½   pounds boneless
       pork loin
       Salt
       Ground black pepper
3   tablespoons
       Pickapeppa sauce
       or Worcestershire
       sauce
1   tablespoon olive oil
3   to 4 small parsnips,
       peeled and sliced
2   medium pears, cored
       and sliced and/or
       chopped
½   cup pear nectar or
       apple juice
       Snipped fresh Italian
       (flat-leaf) parsley
       (optional)

1 Trim fat from pork; cut pork into ½-inch slices. Sprinkle pork lightly with salt and pepper. Brush with some of the Pickapeppa sauce.

2 In a very large skillet heat oil over medium heat. Add pork to skillet; cook until browned on each side. Transfer pork to a plate. Add parsnips and pears to skillet; cook about 5 minutes or until parsnips are crisp-tender, stirring occasionally. Stir in pear nectar and any remaining Pickapeppa sauce. Return pork to skillet. Cook, uncovered, about 5 minutes more or until pork is slightly pink in centers (160°F). Using a slotted spoon, transfer pork, parsnips, and pears to a platter.

3 For sauce, bring liquid remaining in skillet to boiling; reduce heat. Simmer, uncovered, until slightly thickened. Spoon sauce over pork, parsnips, and pears. If desired, sprinkle with parsley.

nutrition facts per serving: 399 cal., 15 g total fat (4 g sat. fat), 94 mg chol., 318 mg sodium, 28 g carb., 4 g fiber, 38 g pro.

Apricot season is short and sweet. Look for these luscious fruits in early summer—and try them in this gorgeous dish.

apricot pork with garlic green beans

start to finish: 20 minutes
makes: 4 servings

4   pork rib chops, cut
       ½ inch thick
     Salt
     Ground black pepper
1   tablespoon olive oil
4   apricots, pitted and
       cut in wedges
2   tablespoons honey
3   cloves garlic, sliced
1   pound green beans,
       trimmed, if desired
¼   cup of water

1 Trim fat from chops. Lightly sprinkle chops with salt and pepper. In a very large nonstick skillet heat oil over medium-high heat; reduce heat to medium. Add chops; cook for 5 minutes, turning once. Add apricots, honey, and garlic; cook, covered, for 5 to 7 minutes or until apricots are tender and pork is slightly pink in center and juices run clear (160°F).

2 Meanwhile, in a 2-quart microwave-safe bowl combine beans and the ¼ cup water. Cover with vented plastic wrap. Microwave on 100 percent power (high) for 6 minutes, stirring once; drain.

3 Serve pork and apricots with green beans. Spoon cooking juices from skillet over all.

nutrition facts per serving: 295 cal., 14 g total fat (4 g sat. fat), 57 mg chol., 207 mg sodium, 20 g carb., 4 g fiber, 22 g pro.

Cellophane noodles—also called glass noodles—are made from mung bean starch and are available at most Asian markets. They have a delightfully chewy texture.

ginger pork stir-fry

start to finish: 30 minutes
makes: 4 servings

1 tablespoon canola oil
1 medium onion, cut into thin wedges
2 cloves garlic, minced
8 ounces boneless pork loin, cut into bite-size strips, or cubed firm tofu (fresh bean curd)
1 cup thinly bias-sliced carrots (2 medium)
1½ cups fresh snow pea pods
1 tablespoon sesame seeds
2 tablespoons reduced-sodium soy sauce
1 tablespoon grated fresh ginger
1 teaspoon toasted sesame oil
¼ to ½ teaspoon crushed red pepper
¼ cup bottled plum sauce
¼ cup water
2 to 3 cups hot cooked cellophane noodles, rice vermicelli, or rice
Snipped fresh cilantro and/or chopped roasted cashews (optional)

1 In a wok or large skillet heat oil over medium-high heat. Add onion and garlic; cook for 2 minutes. Add pork and carrots; cook for 2 minutes more. Add pea pods and sesame seeds; cook and stir for 3 minutes. Add soy sauce, ginger, sesame oil, and crushed red pepper; cook and stir for 1 minute more. Stir in plum sauce and the water; heat through.

2 Serve over hot cooked noodles. If desired, top with cilantro and/or cashews.

nutrition facts per serving: 326 cal., 13 g total fat (3 g sat. fat), 34 mg chol., 418 mg sodium, 37 g carb., 3 g fiber, 14 g pro.

The trick to making this dish so quick to fix is cutting the pork into very thin (½-inch-thick) slices. The slices cook in a flash to seal in the juices—and the veggies are also cooked quickly, just until crisp-tender, to retain their flavor and nutrients.

cornmeal-crusted pork

start to finish: 20 minutes
makes: 4 servings

½ cup yellow cornmeal
½ teaspoon salt
½ teaspoon ground
   black pepper
1 egg, lightly beaten
1 tablespoon water
1 pound pork
   tenderloin, cut into
   ½-inch slices
2 tablespoons olive oil
   or canola oil
12 ounces fresh green
   beans, trimmed
2 medium zucchini
   and/or yellow
   summer squash,
   thinly bias-sliced
   Snipped fresh
   oregano and/or
   oregano sprigs
   (optional)

1 In a shallow dish combine cornmeal, ¼ teaspoon of the salt, and ¼ teaspoon of the pepper. In another shallow dish combine egg and the water. Dip pork slices into egg mixture and then into cornmeal mixture, coating both sides.

2 In a very large skillet heat oil over medium-high heat. Add pork slices in a single layer; cook for 4 to 6 minutes or until slightly pink in center and juices run clear (160°F), turning once. Transfer pork to serving platter.

3 Add green beans and zucchini to the skillet; cook and stir for 6 to 8 minutes or until crisp-tender. Sprinkle with the remaining ¼ teaspoon salt and ¼ teaspoon pepper; toss. Serve with pork. If desired, garnish with oregano.

nutrition facts per serving: 288 cal., 9 g total fat (2 g sat. fat), 120 mg chol., 381 mg sodium, 22 g carb., 4 g fiber, 29 g pro.

Mustard is a bit magical. It adds so much flavor and texture (if it's whole grain) to dishes with just a small spoonful or two. Keep a couple of good-quality mustards in your refrigerator—a smooth Dijon and a coarse-ground variety as well.

skillet pork chops with apples

start to finish: 25 minutes
makes: 4 servings

4   boneless pork loin chops, cut ¾ inch thick (about 1¼ pounds total)
    Salt
    Ground black pepper
2   tablespoons canola oil
2   medium onions, sliced and separated into rings
1   teaspoon dried marjoram, crushed
2   to 4 teaspoons coarse-grain brown mustard or Dijon-style mustard
2   medium red and/ or green cooking apples, cored and cut into thin wedges

1 Sprinkle pork chops with salt and pepper. In a large skillet heat oil over medium-high heat. Add chops; cook for 4 minutes, turning once. Remove chops from skillet, reserving drippings in skillet.

2 Add onion rings to reserved drippings in skillet; cook over medium heat for 4 to 5 minutes or until crisp-tender, stirring occasionally. Reduce heat to medium low. Sprinkle onions with ½ teaspoon of the marjoram.

3 Place chops on onions in skillet. Spread mustard over chops. Arrange apple wedges around and on top of chops; sprinkle chops and apples with the remaining ½ teaspoon marjoram. Cook, covered, for 5 to 8 minutes or until chops are slightly pink in centers and juices run clear. Spoon apples, onions, and cooking juices over chops to serve.

nutrition facts per serving: 313 cal., 12 g total fat (2 g sat. fat), 94 mg chol., 278 mg sodium, 18 g carb., 3 g fiber, 33 g pro.

kitchen tip: Cast-iron skillets are both versatile and durable. They cook evenly and can go from searing on the stovetop to finishing in the oven. Properly cared for (scrubbed immediately after use with hot water only—no soap—and thoroughly dried), a cast-iron skillet can last a lifetime. With use, cast-iron skillets build up a nonstick surface, which reduces the need for additional cooking fats and oils. This process is called seasoning. Most cast-iron skillets come preseasoned from the factory. If your skillet isn't preseasoned, coat the inside of the skillet with vegetable oil and bake in a 350°F oven for 1 hour.

Slicing on a bias, as is done to the fresh green beans in this recipe, simply means slicing on an angle. Bias slicing makes the vegetables prettier and it takes no additional effort to do.

thai pork and vegetable curry

start to finish: 30 minutes
makes: 4 servings

1 cup uncooked jasmine rice (about 9 ounces)
12 ounces pork tenderloin or lean boneless pork
Salt
Ground black pepper
4 teaspoons canola oil
8 ounces green beans,* bias-sliced into 1½-inch pieces (2 cups)
1 medium red sweet pepper, cut into thin bite-size strips
2 green onions, bias-sliced into ¼-inch pieces
1 14-ounce can unsweetened light coconut milk
4 teaspoons bottled curry paste
1 teaspoon sugar
⅛ teaspoon crushed red pepper
1 lime, cut into wedges

1 Cook rice according to package directions; drain. Keep warm.

2 Meanwhile, thinly cut pork into bite-size pieces. Sprinkle with salt and black pepper. In a large nonstick skillet heat 2 teaspoons of the oil over medium-high heat. Add pork; cook and stir about 4 minutes or until brown. Remove pork from skillet.

3 Add the remaining 2 teaspoons oil to skillet. Add green beans; cook and stir for 3 minutes. Add sweet pepper and green onions; cook and stir about 2 minutes more or until vegetables are crisp-tender. Remove from skillet. Add coconut milk, curry paste, sugar, and crushed red pepper to skillet. Bring to boiling; reduce heat. Simmer, uncovered, about 2 minutes or until mixture is slightly thickened. Stir in pork and vegetables; heat through. Serve over hot cooked rice with lime wedges.

nutrition facts per serving: 402 cal., 13 g total fat (6 g sat. fat), 55 mg chol., 464 mg sodium, 50 g carb., 4 g fiber, 22 g pro.

✻tip: A 9-ounce package of frozen cut green beans, thawed, may be substituted for the fresh beans. Add them to the skillet along with the sweet pepper and onions; cook as directed.

Butterflying a cut of meat is a way to make it cook more quickly. Once you've cut three-quarters of the way down through each piece, turn your knife parallel to the meat and then cut almost through each side, opening it like a book.

garlic pork and sweet potato hash

start to finish: 30 minutes
makes: 4 servings

4   cups chopped sweet
      potatoes (3 small)
1½ pounds pork
      tenderloin, cut into
      1-inch slices
2   tablespoons reduced-
      sodium soy sauce
      Ground black pepper
2½ tablespoons canola
      oil
8   cloves garlic, peeled
      and thinly sliced
¼   cup sliced green
      onions (2)
2   tablespoons honey
2   tablespoons water

1 Place sweet potatoes in a microwave-safe bowl. Cover with vented plastic wrap. Microwave on 100 percent power (high) for 8 minutes, stirring once. Carefully remove plastic wrap; set sweet potatoes aside.

2 Meanwhile, to butterfly pork slices, cut three-quarters through each; open and flatten slightly. Brush with 1 tablespoon of the soy sauce; lightly sprinkle with pepper.

3 In a very large skillet heat 1 tablespoon of the oil over medium-high heat. Add garlic; cook just until it begins to turn golden.* Remove garlic; set aside. Add pork to the skillet; cook for 4 to 6 minutes or until slightly pink in centers and juices run clear (160°F), turning once. Transfer pork to a platter; cover to keep warm.

4 Add remaining 1½ tablespoons oil to skillet. For hash, add partially cooked sweet potatoes to the skillet; cook until potatoes begin to crisp, stirring occasionally. Add green onions; cook for 1 minute. Spoon hash onto plates; top with pork and garlic.

5 For sauce, in the hot skillet whisk together honey, the water, and the remaining 1 tablespoon soy sauce; cook just until bubbly. Drizzle sauce over pork.

nutrition facts per serving: 432 cal., 14 g total fat (3 g sat. fat), 105 mg chol., 448 mg sodium, 39 g carb., 4 g fiber, 37 g pro.

*tip: Cook the garlic just until golden but not too brown. If it burns, it will taste bitter.

To remove the strings from snow peas before cooking, use a paring knife to cut one end of the flatter side of each pod, then pull down the length of the pod.

asian pork and noodle skillet

start to finish: 20 minutes
makes: 4 servings

2 tablespoons canola oil
12 ounces boneless pork, trimmed of fat and cut into bite-size strips
1½ cups water
1 3-ounce package oriental- or pork-flavor ramen noodles, broken
2 cups fresh snow pea pods
2 orange, red, and/or yellow sweet peppers, cut into bite-size strips
2 tablespoons hoisin sauce
Ground black pepper

1 In a large skillet heat oil over medium-high heat. Add pork; cook and stir about 2 minutes or until lightly browned.

2 Add the water to skillet; bring to boiling. Add noodles and seasoning packet, snow peas, sweet peppers, and hoisin sauce. Return to boiling; reduce heat. Simmer, covered, for 5 minutes. Season with black pepper.

nutrition facts per serving: 312 cal., 15 g total fat (2 g sat. fat), 54 mg chol., 646 mg sodium, 21 g carb., 2 g fiber, 23 g pro.

To get the most juice from a lemon, warm it in the microwave for 10 seconds (no longer!), then roll it under your hand on the counter. The rolling motion breaks the lemon down and makes it easier to juice.

lickety-split lemon chicken

start to finish: 30 minutes
makes: 4 servings

2   tablespoons butter
12   ounces chicken
     breast tenderloins
1   8-ounce package
     sliced fresh
     mushrooms
1   medium red sweet
     pepper, cut into
     bite-size strips
2   tablespoons all-
     purpose flour
1   14.5-ounce can
     chicken broth
1   teaspoon finely
     shredded lemon
     peel
2   tablespoons lemon
     juice
1   teaspoon dried
     thyme, crushed
     Salt
     Ground black pepper
1   8.8-ounce package
     cooked long grain
     white rice
     Lemon wedges
     (optional)

1 In a very large skillet melt butter over medium heat. Add chicken; cook for 6 to 8 minutes or until no longer pink (170°F), adding mushrooms and sweet pepper for the last 5 minutes of cooking time. Stir in flour. Cook and stir for 1 minute more. Add broth, lemon peel, lemon juice, and thyme; cook and stir until thickened and bubbly. Cook and stir for 2 minutes more. Season with salt and black pepper.

2 Meanwhile, prepare rice according to package directions. Serve chicken mixture over rice. If desired, serve with lemon wedges.

nutrition facts per serving: 361 cal., 10 g total fat (4 g sat. fat), 66 mg chol., 643 mg sodium, 41 g carb., 2 g fiber, 25 g pro.

Jarred curry paste—red, green, or yellow—is a busy cook's dream. Just the tiniest bit infuses a dish with complex flavor. It's powerful stuff, though. Use the higher amount if you like your food spicy, the lesser amount if you like it on the mild side.

chicken curry skillet with rice noodles

start to finish: 30 minutes
makes: 6 servings

148

8 ounces wide rice noodles, broken
2 tablespoons canola oil
1½ pounds skinless, boneless chicken breast, cut into 1-inch pieces
1 16-ounce package frozen green bean or sugar snap pea stir-fry vegetables, thawed
1 14-ounce can unsweetened light coconut milk
½ cup water
1 tablespoon sugar
1 tablespoon fish sauce
½ to 1 teaspoon red curry paste
¼ teaspoon salt
¼ teaspoon ground black pepper
¼ cup snipped fresh basil

1 Soak rice noodles according to package directions; drain.

2 Meanwhile, in a very large skillet heat oil over medium-high heat. Add chicken; cook and stir for 8 to 10 minutes or until chicken is no longer pink, adding stir-fry vegetables for the last 4 minutes of cooking. Remove chicken mixture from skillet.

3 In the same skillet combine coconut milk, the water, sugar, fish sauce, curry paste, salt, and pepper. Bring to boiling. Stir in rice noodles and chicken mixture. Return to boiling; reduce heat. Simmer, uncovered, about 2 minutes or until noodles are tender but still firm and sauce is thickened. Sprinkle with basil.

nutrition facts per serving: 386 cal., 10 g total fat (3 g sat. fat), 66 mg chol., 529 mg sodium, 42 g carb., 2 g fiber, 28 g pro.

Shred the cabbage on the large-holed side of a box grater, in a food processor—or simply by cutting the cabbage into quarters and slicing very thinly with a chef's knife.

nutty chicken stir-fry

start to finish: 30 minutes
makes: 6 servings

2½ cups shredded cabbage

1¼ cups sliced zucchini (1 medium)

¾ cup red sweet pepper strips (1 medium)

½ cup sliced onion (1 medium)

½ cup sliced carrot (1 medium)

1 tablespoon canola oil

12 ounces skinless, boneless chicken breast, cut into 1-inch pieces

½ cup bottled stir-fry sauce

½ teaspoon ground ginger

3 to 4 cups hot cooked white or brown rice

¾ cup chopped peanuts or cashews

1 In a large bowl combine cabbage, zucchini, sweet pepper, onion, and carrot. In a wok or large nonstick skillet heat oil over medium-high heat. Add half of the vegetable mixture; cook and stir about 2 minutes or until crisp-tender. Remove cooked vegetables from wok. Repeat with the remaining vegetable mixture, adding more oil if necessary.

2 If necessary, add more oil to wok. Add chicken; cook and stir for 3 to 5 minutes or until tender and no longer pink. Push chicken from the center of the wok. Add stir-fry sauce and ginger to center of wok; cook and stir until bubbly. Return vegetables to wok; cook and stir about 1 minute or until heated through. Serve over rice. Sprinkle with peanuts.

nutrition facts per serving: 355 cal., 14 g total fat (2 g sat. fat), 33 mg chol., 816 mg sodium, 37 g carb., 5 g fiber, 22 g pro.

The little bit of acid in the fresh-tomato topping cuts through the creaminess of this dish in a most pleasant way.

range-top chicken, macaroni, and cheese

start to finish: 30 minutes
makes: 5 servings

1½ cups dried multigrain or regular elbow macaroni (6 ounces)
    Nonstick cooking spray
12 ounces skinless, boneless chicken breast, cut into 1-inch pieces
¼ cup finely chopped onion
1 6.5-ounce package light semisoft cheese with garlic and herb
1⅔ cups fat-free milk
1 tablespoon all-purpose flour
¾ cup shredded reduced-fat cheddar cheese (3 ounces)
2 cups baby spinach
1 cup cherry tomatoes, quartered

1 In a medium saucepan cook macaroni according to package directions, except do not add salt to the water; drain.

2 Meanwhile, coat a large nonstick skillet with cooking spray; heat skillet over medium-high heat. Add chicken and onion; cook for 4 to 6 minutes or until chicken is no longer pink and onion is tender, stirring frequently. (If onion browns too quickly, reduce heat to medium.) Remove skillet from heat. Add semisoft cheese; stir until melted.

3 In a medium bowl whisk together milk and flour until smooth. Add all at once to chicken mixture; cook and stir over medium heat until thickened and bubbly. Reduce heat to low. Add cheddar cheese, stirring until melted. Add cooked macaroni; cook and stir for 1 to 2 minutes or until heated through. Stir in spinach. Top with cherry tomatoes. Serve immediately.

nutrition facts per serving: 369 cal., 12 g total fat (7 g sat. fat), 85 mg chol., 393 mg sodium, 33 g carb., 4 g fiber, 33 g pro.

For a bit of additional flavor in this expeditious version of the classic Spanish dish, substitute a can of fire-roasted diced tomatoes for the regular tomatoes.

arroz con pollo

start to finish: 25 minutes
makes: 4 servings

1   purchased roasted chicken
1   14.5-ounce can diced tomatoes, undrained
1   4-ounce can diced green chiles, undrained
1   cup frozen peas
⅓   cup pitted green olives, sliced
1   8.8-ounce pouch cooked Spanish-style rice
⅓   cup shredded Monterey Jack cheese

1 Remove chicken meat from bones, discarding skin and bones. Tear chicken into large pieces. Measure 3 cups of the chicken; save remaining chicken for another use.

2 In a large skillet combine tomatoes, green chiles, peas, and olives. Bring to boiling. Stir in rice and the 3 cups chicken; heat through. Top each serving with Monterey Jack cheese.

nutrition facts per serving: 399 cal., 14 g total fat (4 g sat. fat), 102 mg chol., 939 mg sodium, 29 g carb., 4 g fiber, 37 g pro.

nutrition note: When it comes to vegetables, the mantra that "fresh is best" is nearly always true. One exception is garden peas. Peas get starchy and lose their nutrients almost immediately after being picked, so it's actually best to freeze them right after picking. They're sweeter and more nutritious that way. Keep a bag of peas in your freezer for a quick side dish or stir-in to a main dish such as this one.

Butterhead lettuce—also called Boston lettuce—has tender, buttery-textured leaves (hence, its name). Here, the flavorful chicken mixture is simply served on top of the leaves, as a salad, but they are ideal for wrapping up fillings and eating out of hand as well.

sesame and ginger chicken

start to finish: 20 minutes
makes: 4 servings

1   pound skinless, boneless chicken breast, cut into bite-size strips
    Salt
    Ground black pepper
    Nonstick cooking spray
2   cups packaged julienned carrots
¼   cup bottled light Asian-style salad dressing with sesame and ginger
⅛   teaspoon crushed red pepper
1   head butterhead lettuce, leaves separated
¼   cup coarsely chopped honey-roasted peanuts
    Lime wedges

1 Lightly sprinkle chicken with salt and black pepper. Lightly coat a large skillet with cooking spray; heat skillet over medium-high heat. Add chicken to hot skillet; cook and stir about 3 minutes or until brown. Add carrots and 1 tablespoon of the dressing to the skillet; cook and stir for 2 to 3 minutes or until carrots are crisp-tender and chicken is no longer pink. Stir in crushed red pepper.

2 On a large platter arrange four stacks of lettuce leaves. Spoon the chicken mixture on top of the lettuce stacks. Sprinkle with peanuts. Serve with the remaining dressing and lime wedges.

nutrition facts per serving: 231 cal., 7 g total fat (1 g sat. fat), 66 mg chol., 436 mg sodium, 12 g carb., 3 g fiber, 29 g pro.

If you don't have lemon-pepper seasoning, you can use ½ teaspoon of finely shredded lemon peel and ½ teaspoon freshly ground black pepper.

rosemary chicken with vegetables

start to finish: 30 minutes
makes: 4 servings

4   medium skinless, boneless chicken breast halves (1 to 1¼ pounds total)
½   teaspoon lemon-pepper seasoning
2   tablespoons olive oil
4   ounces refrigerated spinach or plain linguine
2   cloves garlic, minced
2   medium zucchini and/or yellow summer squash, cut into ¼-inch slices
½   cup apple juice
2   teaspoons snipped fresh rosemary or ½ teaspoon dried rosemary, crushed
¼   teaspoon salt
2   tablespoons dry white wine or chicken broth
2   teaspoons cornstarch
1   cup halved cherry or grape tomatoes
     Fresh rosemary sprigs (optional)

1 Sprinkle chicken with lemon-pepper seasoning. In a large skillet heat oil over medium-high heat. Add chicken; cook for 8 to 10 minutes or until no longer pink (165°F), turning once. Transfer chicken to a platter; cover and keep warm.

2 Meanwhile, cook pasta according to package directions; drain and keep warm.

3 Add garlic to drippings in skillet; cook and stir for 15 seconds. Add zucchini, apple juice, the 2 teaspoons fresh or ½ teaspoon dried rosemary, and salt. Bring to boiling; reduce heat. Simmer, covered, for 2 minutes.

4 In a small bowl stir together wine and cornstarch. Add to skillet; cook and stir until thickened and bubbly. Cook and stir for 2 minutes more. Stir in tomatoes. Serve vegetables and pasta with chicken. If desired, garnish with rosemary sprigs.

nutrition facts per serving: 324 cal., 11 g total fat (2 g sat. fat), 93 mg chol., 339 mg sodium, 26 g carb., 2 g fiber, 29 g pro.

An apple corer (the kind that just removes the core but doesn't segment the apple) makes super-quick work of preparing the apple for slicing.

chicken with cherry-ginger chutney

start to finish: 20 minutes
makes: 4 servings

4   medium skinless, boneless chicken breast halves, each cut into 4 pieces
Salt
Ground black pepper
½   teaspoon ground ginger
1   tablespoon olive oil
1   large apple, thinly sliced across fruit and seeded
½   cup dried tart red cherries
⅓   cup coarsely chopped walnuts
¼   cup water
3   tablespoons cider vinegar
4   teaspoons packed brown sugar

1 Lightly sprinkle chicken with salt, pepper, and ¼ teaspoon of the ginger.

2 In a large skillet heat oil over medium-high heat. Add chicken; cook for 10 to 12 minutes or until no longer pink, turning once. Transfer to serving platter; cover to keep warm.

3 For cherry-ginger chutney, add apple, cherries, and walnuts to drippings in skillet; cook for 2 minutes, stirring frequently. In a small bowl stir together the water, vinegar, brown sugar, and the remaining ¼ teaspoon ginger. Add to skillet; cook and stir for 30 seconds. Serve chutney with chicken.

nutrition facts per serving: 364 cal., 12 g total fat (2 g sat. fat), 82 mg chol., 249 mg sodium, 30 g carb., 3 g fiber, 35 g pro.

Look in the produce section for prepared fresh pineapple that has already been peeled and cored.

jerk chicken and slaw

start to finish: 20 minutes
makes: 4 servings

3   heads baby bok choy, trimmed and thinly sliced
2   cups shredded red cabbage
½   of a peeled, cored fresh pineapple, chopped
2   tablespoons cider vinegar
4   teaspoons packed brown sugar
2   teaspoons all-purpose flour
2   teaspoons jerk seasoning
    Nonstick cooking spray
4   small skinless, boneless chicken breast halves

1 For slaw, in a very large bowl combine bok choy, cabbage, and pineapple. Combine vinegar and 2 teaspoons of the brown sugar. Drizzle over bok choy mixture; toss to coat. Set aside.

2 In a large, resealable plastic bag combine the remaining 2 teaspoons of the brown sugar, the flour, and jerk seasoning. Add chicken; shake well to coat. Lightly coat a very large nonstick skillet or grill pan with cooking spray; heat skillet over medium heat. Add chicken to hot skillet; cook for 6 to 8 minutes, turning once, until no pink remains (170°F). Remove chicken to cutting board.

3 Slice chicken. Serve chicken with pineapple slaw.

nutrition facts per serving: 205 cal., 2 g total fat (0 g sat. fat), 66 mg chol., 318 mg sodium, 19 g carb., 3 g fiber, 29 g pro.

To prepare fresh lemongrass for cooking, cut off and discard the lower bulb and peel off the tough outer leaves, which are very woody. Cut the stalk in half horizontally, then thinly slice.

thai green chicken curry

start to finish: 30 minutes
makes: 4 servings

skillet dinners & **stir-fries**

12 ounces skinless, boneless chicken thighs
1   cup canned unsweetened light coconut milk
¼   cup reduced-sodium chicken broth
2   to 3 tablespoons bottled green curry paste
2   teaspoons cornstarch
2   teaspoons finely chopped fresh lemongrass or 1 teaspoon finely shredded lemon peel
    Nonstick cooking spray
1   medium green sweet pepper, seeded and cut into thin bite-size strips (1 cup)
1   medium onion, halved and thinly sliced
¾   cup packaged shredded fresh carrots
3   cloves garlic, minced
2   teaspoons canola oil
2   cups hot cooked brown basmati rice or regular brown rice
¼   cup flaked coconut, toasted*
    Snipped fresh cilantro

1 Trim fat from chicken. Cut chicken into thin bite-size strips; set aside. For sauce, in a medium bowl whisk together coconut milk, broth, curry paste, cornstarch, and lemon peel (if using); set aside.

2 Coat a wok or large nonstick skillet with cooking spray; heat wok over medium-high heat. Add sweet pepper and onion; cook and stir for 3 minutes. Add carrots, garlic, and lemongrass (if using); cook and stir about 2 minutes more or until vegetables are crisp-tender. Remove vegetables from wok.

3 Add oil to wok. Add chicken; cook and stir over medium-high heat for 3 to 5 minutes or until chicken is no longer pink. Push chicken from center of wok.

4 Stir sauce. Add to center of wok; cook and stir until slightly thickened and bubbly. Return vegetables to wok. Stir all ingredients together to coat with sauce. Cook and stir about 2 minutes or until heated through.

5 Serve chicken mixture over rice. Sprinkle with toasted coconut and cilantro.

nutrition facts per serving: 344 cal., 13 g total fat (5 g sat. fat), 81 mg chol., 445 mg sodium, 37 g carb., 4 g fiber, 21 g pro.

*tip: To toast coconut, spread the coconut in a shallow baking pan. Bake in 350°F oven about 5 minutes or until golden, shaking pan once or twice. Watch carefully so coconut doesn't burn.

Use your favorite blue cheese here—Roquefort, Gorgonzola, Danish blue, or one simply labeled "blue cheese."

turkey steaks with spinach, pears, and blue cheese

start to finish: 20 minutes
makes: 4 servings

2   turkey breast tenderloins (1 to 1¼ pounds total)
1   teaspoon dried sage, crushed
     Salt
     Freshly ground black pepper
2   tablespoons butter
1   6-ounce package fresh baby spinach
1   large pear, cored and thinly sliced
¼   cup crumbled blue cheese (1 ounce)

1 Horizontally split turkey tenderloins to make four ½-inch-thick steaks. Rub turkey with sage; sprinkle with salt and pepper.

2 In a very large skillet melt 1 tablespoon of the butter over medium-high heat. Add turkey steaks; cook for 14 to 16 minutes or until no longer pink (170°F), turning once. (Reduce heat to medium if turkey browns too quickly.) Remove turkey from skillet; cover to keep warm. Add spinach to skillet; cook and stir just until wilted.

3 Meanwhile, in a small skillet melt the remaining 1 tablespoon butter over medium heat. Add pear slices; cook about 5 minutes or until tender and lightly browned, stirring occasionally.

4 Serve turkey with spinach and pears. Sprinkle with blue cheese.

nutrition facts per serving: 240 cal., 9 g total fat (5 g sat. fat), 92 mg chol., 380 mg sodium, 8 g carb., 2 g fiber, 31 g pro.

158

Be sure the shrimp is only warmed through. Because it is already cooked, it can get tough if exposed to the heat for too long.

ginger shrimp and rice

start to finish: 15 minutes
makes: 4 servings

1 small bunch green onions
1 1-inch piece fresh ginger
1 tablespoon olive oil
¼ cup water
1 tablespoon reduced-sodium soy sauce
2 8.8-ounce packages cooked long grain rice
12 ounces peeled and deveined cooked medium shrimp
¼ cup mango chutney

1 Slice green onions. Set aside ¼ cup of the onions for garnish. Peel the ginger. Finely grate ginger using the smallest openings on a box or flat grater.

2 In a very large skillet heat oil over medium heat. Add the remaining green onions and the grated ginger; cook for 1 to 2 minutes or until onions are tender. Add the water and soy sauce. Bring to boiling. Add rice and shrimp; return to boiling. Cook, covered, until most of the liquid is absorbed and shrimp are heated through.

3 Divide among four shallow bowls. Top with chutney and reserved green onions.

nutrition facts per serving: 335 cal., 7 g total fat (1 g sat. fat), 107 mg chol., 702 mg sodium, 53 g carb., 3 g fiber, 15 g pro.

Haricots verts can be a little hard to find, but worth the few extra pennies if you do. They are especially slender, sweet, and flavorful.

shrimp and tomato piccata

start to finish: 30 minutes
makes: 4 servings

1 pound fresh or frozen
     medium shrimp in
     shells
3 tablespoons olive oil
8 ounces fresh French
     string beans
     (haricots verts)
     or other small,
     thin green beans,
     trimmed
3 medium tomatoes,
     cut into wedges
1 teaspoon finely
     shredded lemon
     peel
3 tablespoons lemon
     juice
1 tablespoon capers,
     drained
2 cups hot cooked
     pasta (optional)

1 Thaw shrimp, if frozen. Peel and devein shrimp, leaving tails intact if desired. Rinse shrimp; pat dry with paper towels. Set aside.

2 In a very large skillet heat 1 tablespoon of the oil over medium-high heat. Add green beans; cook and stir for 3 minutes. Add shrimp; cook and stir about 3 minutes or until shrimp are opaque. Add tomatoes; cook for 1 minute more.

3 For sauce, in a small bowl whisk together the remaining 2 tablespoons oil, the lemon peel, lemon juice, and capers.

4 If desired, serve shrimp mixture over hot cooked pasta. Drizzle sauce over shrimp and vegetables.

nutrition facts per serving: 187 cal., 11 g total fat (2 g sat. fat), 107 mg chol., 477 mg sodium, 9 g carb., 3 g fiber, 14 g pro.

If you'd like, use mirin—a sweetened Japanese rice wine—in this dish. It is widely available in the Asian sections of most supermarkets.

stir-fried shrimp with snow peas

start to finish: 25 minutes
makes: 4 servings

12 ounces fresh or frozen medium shrimp in shells
1 tablespoon minced fresh ginger
2 teaspoons sherry or rice wine
2 teaspoons cornstarch
⅛ to ¼ teaspoon crushed red pepper (optional)
1 tablespoon canola oil
1 walnut-size piece fresh ginger, smashed*
1 large clove garlic, smashed*
6 ounces fresh snow peas,** strings removed
3 green onions, cut into 1-inch pieces
½ of a small onion, sliced
½ cup chicken broth
2 cups hot cooked brown rice

1 Thaw shrimp if frozen. Peel and devein shrimp. Rinse shrimp; pat dry with paper towels. Place shrimp in a large bowl. In a small bowl stir together the 1 tablespoon minced ginger, the sherry, cornstarch, and, if desired, crushed red pepper.

2 In a wok or large skillet heat oil over medium-high heat. Add the smashed ginger and garlic; cook for 1 minute. Add snow peas, green onions, and the sliced onion; cook and stir about 2 minutes or until the snow peas turn bright green. Add the shrimp and broth; cook and stir for 1 to 2 minutes or until the shrimp are opaque. Serve over brown rice.

nutrition facts per serving: 237 cal., 5 g total fat (1 g sat. fat), 108 mg chol., 744 mg sodium, 30 g carb., 3 g fiber, 16 g pro.

✳**tip:** Smashing the ginger and garlic releases their aromatic oils, lending a mellow richness to the dish. Simply crush them with the flat side of a knife.

✳✳**tip:** Sugar snap peas, Chinese long beans, or Chinese broccoli can be used in place of the snow peas.

The "red" in this dish comes from chili powder. There is fresh chile in it as well. The Anaheim chile is relatively mild, with a crisp texture and fresh taste—and just a little bit of heat.

red cumin-lime shrimp on jicama rice

start to finish: 30 minutes
makes: 4 servings

12	ounces fresh or frozen peeled and deveined medium shrimp
3	teaspoons olive oil
1½	cups chopped onions (3 medium)
1	medium fresh Anaheim chile pepper, seeded and sliced*
1½	tablespoons chili powder
1½	teaspoons ground cumin
1	cup hot cooked brown rice
1½	cups peeled jicama cut into thin bite-size strips
2	tablespoons lime juice
2	tablespoons 60 to 70 percent vegetable oil spread
¼	teaspoon salt
⅓	cup snipped fresh cilantro
	Lime wedges (optional)

1 Thaw shrimp, if frozen. Rinse shrimp; pat dry with paper towels. Set shrimp aside. In a large nonstick skillet heat 1 teaspoon of the oil over medium-high heat. Tilt and swirl skillet to coat bottom lightly. Add onions and chile pepper; cook about 3 minutes or until tender, stirring frequently. Stir in shrimp, chili powder, and cumin. Cook for 3 to 4 minutes or until shrimp are opaque.

2 Meanwhile, spoon hot rice into a serving bowl. Stir jicama into rice. Cover and let stand until ready to serve.

3 Remove skillet from heat; stir in the remaining 2 teaspoons oil, the lime juice, vegetable oil spread, and salt. Cover and let stand for 5 minutes to allow flavors to absorb and vegetable oil spread to melt.

4 Stir cilantro into rice mixture. Serve shrimp mixture over rice mixture. If desired, pass lime wedges.

nutrition facts per serving: 284 cal., 11 g total fat (2 g sat. fat), 129 mg chol., 350 mg sodium, 26 g carb., 6 g fiber, 21 g pro.

*tip: Because chile peppers contain volatile oils that can burn your skin and eyes, avoid direct contact with them as much as possible. When working with chile peppers, wear plastic or rubber gloves. If your bare hands do touch the peppers, wash your hands and nails well with soap and warm water.

This dish reflects the flavors of The Big Easy—and the attitude, too! Quick-cooking couscous subs for more traditional rice.

shrimp and couscous jambalaya

start to finish: 25 minutes
makes: 4 servings

12 ounces fresh or frozen cooked, peeled, and deveined medium shrimp
2 tablespoons olive oil or canola oil
1 cup sliced celery (2 stalks)
¾ cup chopped green sweet pepper (1 medium)
½ cup chopped onion (1 medium)
½ teaspoon Cajun seasoning
¼ teaspoon dried oregano, crushed
1 14.5-ounce can reduced-sodium chicken broth
1 cup quick-cooking couscous
⅔ cup chopped tomato (1 medium)
   Bottled hot pepper sauce (optional)
   Lemon wedges (optional)

1 Thaw shrimp, if frozen; set aside. In a large skillet heat oil over medium heat. Add celery, sweet pepper, onion, Cajun seasoning, and oregano; cook until vegetables are tender.

2 Carefully add broth to vegetables in skillet. Bring to boiling. Stir in couscous, tomato, and the shrimp. Remove skillet from heat. Cover and let stand for 5 minutes.

3 Before serving, fluff shrimp mixture with a fork. If desired, serve with hot pepper sauce and lemon wedges.

nutrition facts per serving: 357 cal., 9 g total fat (1 g sat. fat), 129 mg chol., 440 mg sodium, 43 g carb., 4 g fiber, 25 g pro.

To prepare leeks for cooking, trim off the green leaves and the root end. Cut the white part in half horizontally, then rinse each half under running water, fanning the layers, to remove any grit or sand. Shake dry, then thinly slice.

greek leeks and shrimp stir-fry

start to finish: 30 minutes
makes: 4 servings

1   pound fresh or frozen
      peeled, deveined
      medium shrimp
⅔   cup water
⅓   cup lemon juice
1   tablespoon
      cornstarch
¾   teaspoon bouquet
      garni seasoning
      or dried oregano,
      crushed
1   cup quick-cooking
      couscous
1½   cups boiling water
1   tablespoon olive oil
1⅓   cups thinly sliced
      leeks
½   cup crumbled feta
      cheese (2 ounces)

1 Thaw shrimp, if frozen. Rinse shrimp; pat dry with paper towels. Set shrimp aside.

2 In a small bowl combine the ⅔ cup water, lemon juice, cornstarch, and ¼ teaspoon of the bouquet garni seasoning; set aside.

3 In a small bowl combine couscous and the remaining ½ teaspoon bouquet garni seasoning. Pour boiling water over couscous. Cover and let stand for 5 minutes.

4 Meanwhile, in a wok or very large skillet heat oil over medium heat. Add leeks; cook and stir for 2 to 3 minutes or until tender. Remove leeks from wok; set aside. Stir lemon juice mixture; add to wok. Bring to boiling. Add shrimp; cook for 2 to 3 minutes or until shrimp are opaque. Stir in cooked leeks and ¼ cup of the feta cheese.

5 To serve, fluff couscous mixture with a fork. Transfer couscous mixture to a serving platter. Spoon shrimp mixture over couscous. Sprinkle with the remaining ¼ cup feta cheese.

nutrition facts per serving: 364 cal., 9 g total fat (3 g sat. fat), 160 mg chol., 770 mg sodium, 45 g carb., 3 g fiber, 25 g pro.

nutrition note: With 20 grams of protein and only 84 calories per 3 ounces, shrimp are an excellent source of protein. Shrimp also provide selenium, vitamin D, and Vitamin B-12.

The American Heart Association recommends that you limit your average daily cholesterol intake to less than 300 milligrams. Balance out higher cholesterol meals with fruit and vegetables that have no cholesterol and are high in fiber, which help to lower cholesterol.

Precooked bacon is available in the supermarket, but it's pricey. When you have some time, cook up a pound of bacon, then drain well and cool. Wrap in clean paper towels and store for 2 to 3 days in a tightly sealed plastic bag in the refrigerator. When you want to use it, wrap a few slices in a clean paper towel and heat in the microwave for 30 seconds or so.

pan-seared scallops with bacon and spinach

start to finish: 20 minutes
makes: 4 servings

1 pound fresh or frozen
sea scallops*
2 tablespoons all-
purpose flour
1 to 2 teaspoons
blackened steak
seasoning or Cajun
seasoning
1 tablespoon canola oil
1 10-ounce package
fresh spinach
1 tablespoon water
2 tablespoons balsamic
vinegar
¼ cup cooked bacon
pieces

1 Thaw scallops, if frozen. Rinse scallops; pat very dry with paper towels. Remove the small muscles if still attached. In a self-sealing plastic bag combine flour and blackened seasoning. Add scallops to bag; toss to coat.

2 In a large skillet heat oil over medium-high heat. When oil is very hot, add scallops; cook for 2 minutes without stirring or turning (the scallops should be well seared). Turn scallops; cook for 1 to 2 minutes more or just until scallops are opaque in the center. Remove scallops from skillet; set aside.

3 Add spinach to the skillet; sprinkle with the water. Cook, covered, over medium-high heat about 2 minutes or until spinach is wilted. Add vinegar; toss to coat spinach. Return scallops to skillet; heat through. Sprinkle with bacon.

nutrition facts per serving: 195 cal., 7 g total fat (0 g sat. fat), 43 mg chol., 538 mg sodium, 10 g carb., 2 g fiber, 23 g pro.

*tip: Sea scallops are the larger of the two most widely available varieties of scallops. Bay scallops are smaller. Scallops should be firm, sweet smelling, and free of excess cloudy liquid. Store scallops covered with their own liquid in a covered container and use within 2 days.

Jewel-like pomegranate seeds, also called arils, contain all of the fruit and juice in a pomegranate.

seared scallops and baby spinach with spiced pomegranate glaze

start to finish: 30 minutes
makes: 4 servings

12 large fresh or frozen
    sea scallops (about
    1¼ pounds total)
¾   cup 100 percent
    pomegranate juice
2   tablespoons honey
½   teaspoon ground
    coriander
⅛   teaspoon ground
    cinnamon
1   tablespoon lemon
    juice
¾   teaspoon cornstarch
3   teaspoons canola oil
¼   teaspoon sugar
¼   teaspoon ground
    black pepper
1   10-ounce package
    fresh baby spinach
    Dash salt
¼   cup pomegranate
    seeds*

1 Thaw scallops, if frozen. Rinse scallops; pat very dry with paper towels. Remove the small muscles if still attached; set scallops aside.

2 For sauce, in a medium saucepan combine pomegranate juice, honey, coriander, and cinnamon. Bring to boiling over medium-high heat. In a small bowl combine lemon juice and cornstarch; stir into boiling juice mixture. Gently boil, uncovered, about 10 minutes or until reduced and slightly syrupy; set aside.

3 Meanwhile, in a very large nonstick skillet heat 1 teaspoon of the oil over medium-high heat, brushing to coat the skillet. Sprinkle scallops with the sugar and ⅛ teaspoon of the pepper. When skillet is very hot, add scallops; cook for 2 minutes without stirring or turning (the scallops should be well seared). Turn scallops; cook for 1 to 2 minutes more or just until scallops are opaque in the center. Transfer to a plate.

4 Wipe skillet clean; add the remaining 2 teaspoons oil. Add spinach in batches; toss for 1 to 2 minutes or just until slightly wilted. Season with the dash salt and the remaining ⅛ teaspoon pepper.

5 Arrange scallops and spinach on four serving plates; drizzle with sauce. Sprinkle with pomegranate seeds.

nutrition facts per serving: 214 cal., 4 g total fat (0 g sat. fat), 34 mg chol., 651 mg sodium, 25 g carb., 2 g fiber, 19 g pro.

✳tip: Look for packages of fresh pomegranate seeds in your grocer's produce or freezer section.

Cod is a meaty, mild-tasting white fish that easily takes to a whole host of flavors—Asian, Mediterranean, and Scandinavian among them. Keep a bag of fillets in your freezer for last-minute dinners like this one.

lemon-ginger fish

start to finish: 20 minutes
makes: 4 servings

1 pound fresh or frozen cod or other firm white fish fillets
2 small lemons
1 tablespoon grated fresh ginger
2 teaspoons sugar
¼ cup butter
2 5-ounce packages fresh baby spinach
2 tablespoons water
¼ teaspoon salt
¼ teaspoon ground black pepper

1 Thaw fish, if frozen. Rinse fish; pat dry with paper towels. Cut fish into 4 pieces; set fish aside. Thinly slice one lemon; set aside. Finely shred peel from the remaining lemon; juice the lemon. In a small bowl combine the lemon peel and juice, ginger, and sugar; set aside.

2 In a large skillet melt butter over medium heat. Add fish to skillet; cook for 1 to 2 minutes or until browned. Turn fish. Add lemon juice mixture to skillet; cover and cook for 2 to 3 minutes or until fish flakes when tested with a fork. Using a slotted spatula, transfer fish to platter; cover to keep warm.

3 Add lemon slices to the skillet; cook about 2 minutes or until lemon slices are softened and liquid is slightly thickened.

4 Meanwhile, place spinach in a very large microwave-safe bowl. Sprinkle with the water. Microwave on 100 percent power (high) about 2 minutes or just until wilted, tossing once after 1 minute.

5 To serve, divide spinach among four shallow serving bowls. Top with fish. Spoon lemon slices and cooking liquid over fish and spinach. Sprinkle with salt and pepper.

nutrition facts per serving: 228 cal., 12 g total fat (7 g sat. fat), 79 mg chol., 344 mg sodium, 9 g carb., 3 g fiber, 22 g pro.

Orange Pepper Salmon: Prepare as directed, except substitute salmon for the cod and 2 small oranges for the lemons. Omit ginger; add ¼ teaspoon crushed red pepper to the juice mixture.

Much of the catfish and tilapia sold in this country is raised in China, but for the best-tasting and best-textured fish, look for those farmed in the U.S. It may cost a little more, but it is worth the price.

chile-lime catfish with corn sauté

start to finish: 30 minutes
makes: 4 servings

4   4- to 5-ounce fresh or frozen skinless catfish, sole, or tilapia fillets
1   tablespoon lime juice
1   teaspoon ground ancho chile pepper or chili powder
¼   teaspoon salt
1   tablespoon canola oil
2⅔   cups frozen whole kernel corn, thawed
¼   cup finely chopped red onion
2   teaspoons finely chopped seeded fresh jalapeño pepper*
2   cloves garlic, minced
1   tablespoon snipped fresh cilantro
    Lime wedges (optional)

1 Thaw fish, if frozen. Rinse fish; pat dry with paper towels. Measure thickness of fish. In a small bowl stir together lime juice, ancho chile pepper, and salt. Brush mixture evenly over both sides of each fish fillet.

2 In a large nonstick skillet heat 2 teaspoons of the oil over medium-high heat. Add fish fillets; cook for 4 to 6 minutes per ½-inch thickness or until fish flakes easily when tested with a fork, turning once. Remove fish from skillet. Cover and keep warm.

3 In the same skillet heat the remaining 1 teaspoon oil. Add corn, onion, jalapeño pepper, and garlic; cook about 2 minutes or until vegetables are heated through and just starting to soften, stirring occasionally. Remove from heat. Stir in cilantro.

4 To serve, divide corn mixture among serving plates. Top with fish. If desired, serve with lime wedges.

nutrition facts per serving: 350 cal., 6 g total fat (1 g sat. fat), 0 mg chol., 711 mg sodium, 65 g carb., 10 g fiber, 11 g pro.

＊tip: Because chile peppers contain volatile oils that can burn your skin and eyes, avoid direct contact with them as much as possible. When working with chile peppers, wear plastic or rubber gloves. If your bare hands do touch the peppers, wash your hands and nails well with soap and warm water.

Sugar snap peas and summer squash add a fresh twist to this 15-minute pantry meal.

twisty tuna noodles

start to finish: 15 minutes
makes: 4 servings

1   10-ounce container
    refrigerated light
    Alfredo pasta sauce
1   cup water
2   3-ounce packages
    ramen noodles (any
    flavor)
2   6-ounce cans very-
    low-sodium chunk
    light tuna, drained
2   medium yellow
    summer squash,
    halved lengthwise
    and sliced (2 cups)
1   cup fresh sugar
    snap peas, halved
    diagonally
    Ground black pepper

1 In a large skillet combine Alfredo sauce and the water; bring to boiling. Meanwhile, break up noodles; discard seasoning packet.

2 Stir noodles, tuna, squash, and sugar snap peas into skillet. Return to boiling; reduce heat. Simmer, covered, for 5 minutes. Season with pepper.

nutrition facts per serving: 396 cal., 14 g total fat (8 g sat. fat), 70 mg chol., 751 mg sodium, 35 g carb., 2 g fiber, 31 g pro.

This dish, featuring cheesy ravioli, is a great way to get kids to eat their vegetables.

ravioli and zucchini skillet

start to finish: 20 minutes
makes: 4 servings

1   14.5-ounce can Italian-style stewed tomatoes, undrained
½   cup water
2   zucchini and/or yellow summer squash, halved lengthwise and cut into ½-inch pieces (about 2½ cups)
1   9-ounce package refrigerated whole wheat four-cheese ravioli
1   15-ounce can cannellini beans (white kidney beans) or navy beans, rinsed and drained
2   tablespoons finely shredded or grated Parmesan cheese
2   tablespoons snipped fresh basil or parsley

1 In a very large skillet combine tomatoes and the water. Bring to boiling. Stir in zucchini and ravioli. Return to boiling; reduce heat. Boil gently, covered, for 6 to 7 minutes or until ravioli are tender, stirring gently once or twice.

2 Stir beans into ravioli mixture; heat through. Sprinkle with Parmesan cheese and basil.

nutrition facts per serving: 305 cal., 8 g total fat (4 g sat. fat), 44 mg chol., 986 mg sodium, 49 g carb., 11 g fiber, 18 g pro.

This inspired twist on rice and beans has it all—fruit, vegetables, legumes, rice—and fresh flavors that will make it a family favorite.

asian-style fried rice and beans

start to finish: 30 minutes
makes: 4 servings

½ of a purchased peeled pineapple, cored and sliced, or one 8-ounce can pineapple slices (juice pack), drained
1 tablespoon canola oil
1 cup thinly biased-sliced carrots (2 medium)
4 cloves garlic, minced
2 teaspoons grated fresh ginger*
2 cups cooked brown rice**
1 15-ounce can garbanzo beans (chickpeas), rinsed and drained
1 cup frozen peas, thawed
3 tablespoons reduced-sodium soy sauce
⅓ cup snipped fresh cilantro
1 lime, halved
Fresh cilantro leaves (optional)

1 Quarter pineapple slices. In a very large nonstick skillet heat 2 teaspoons of the oil over medium heat. Add pineapple; cook about 4 minutes or until golden brown, turning once. Remove from skillet; set aside.

2 Add the remaining 1 teaspoon oil to hot skillet. Add carrots; cook for 5 minutes or just until tender, stirring frequently. Add garlic and ginger; cook for 30 seconds.

3 Stir in rice, garbanzo beans, peas, and soy sauce. Cook and stir about 4 minutes or until heated through. Stir in the ⅓ cup cilantro. Return pineapple to skillet; heat through.

4 To serve, squeeze lime over pineapple mixture. If desired, sprinkle with cilantro leaves.

nutrition facts per serving: 350 cal., 6 g total fat (1 g sat. fat), 0 mg chol., 711 mg sodium, 65 g carb., 10 g fiber, 11 g pro.

*tip: Store fresh ginger in the freezer. Place unpeeled ginger in a freezer bag. When a recipe calls for fresh ginger, peel and grate in its frozen state, no thawing required.

**tip: Leftover or quick-cooking microwaveable rice also works well in this recipe.

Sweet potatoes are very easy and quick to cook in the microwave— and they add so much flavor, nutrition, and color to a dish. Here, they are just partially cooked in the microwave, then finished in a skillet until browned and crispy.

sweet potato hash

start to finish: 25 minutes
makes: 4 servings

2 medium sweet potatoes, peeled and quartered (about 1 pound)
Salt
1 tablespoon canola oil
1 11-ounce can Southwestern-style corn with black beans and peppers, rinsed and drained
½ cup light sour cream
2 tablespoons chipotle salsa
1 medium avocado, peeled, seeded, and sliced
Fresh cilantro leaves (optional)
Chili powder (optional)

1 Place sweet potatoes in a microwave-safe dish; cover with vented plastic wrap. Microwave on 100 percent power (high) for 5 to 8 minutes or just until tender enough to chop. Cool slightly; cut into chunks. Sprinkle lightly with salt.

2 In a large skillet heat oil over medium heat. Add sweet potatoes; cook about 3 minutes or until browned and crisp-tender. Add drained corn to sweet potatoes in skillet. Cook about 3 minutes more or until sweet potatoes are tender.

3 Meanwhile, for sauce, in a small bowl stir together sour cream and chipotle salsa.

4 To serve, divide sweet potato mixture among four plates. Top with avocado slices and serve with sauce. If desired, top with fresh cilantro and sprinkle with chili powder.

nutrition facts per serving: 246 cal., 14 g total fat (4 g sat. fat), 12 mg chol., 463 mg sodium, 29 g carb., 5 g fiber, 4 g pro.

pork tenderloin with cucumber-mango salad

oven-baked &
broi

Lean proteins and veggies get the
high-heat treatment in these dishes
that roast or broil in mere minutes.

174

For a quick herbed mayonnaise, blend ½ cup mayonnaise, ½ cup sour cream, 3 tablespoons snipped fresh dill, 2 tablespoons snipped fresh basil, and 1 tablespoon snipped chives. Cover and chill until ready to use.

herbed steaks with horseradish

start to finish: 20 minutes
makes: 4 servings

2   12- to 14-ounce beef
    top loin steaks, cut
    1 inch thick
    Salt
    Ground black pepper
2   tablespoons prepared
    horseradish
1   tablespoon Dijon-
    style mustard
2   teaspoons snipped
    fresh Italian (flat-
    leaf) parsley
1   teaspoon snipped
    fresh thyme
    Broiled cherry
    tomatoes (optional)
    Broiled sweet pepper
    strips (optional)
    Herbed mayonnaise
    (optional)

1 Preheat broiler. Trim fat from steaks. Lightly sprinkle steaks with salt and pepper. Place steaks on the unheated rack of a broiler pan. Broil 4 to 5 inches from heat for 7 minutes.

2 Meanwhile, in a small bowl stir together horseradish, mustard, parsley, and thyme.

3 Turn steaks. Broil for 8 to 9 minutes more for medium (160°F). The last 1 minute of broiling, spread horseradish mixture over steaks. If desired, serve with tomatoes, peppers, and herbed mayonnaise.

nutrition facts per serving: 284 cal., 15 g total fat (6 g sat. fat), 84 mg chol., 351 mg sodium, 1 g carb., 0 g fiber, 33 g pro.

There are two types of sesame oil. The toasted version—which has a nutty taste and a deep brown color—is used mostly in small amounts to add flavor to foods. The untoasted, light yellow variety is used only as cooking oil.

glazed teriyaki pork chops with potatoes

prep: 20 minutes broil: 9 minutes
makes: 4 servings

4	boneless pork loin chops, cut ¾ inch thick
¼	cup bottled teriyaki glaze
12	ounces tiny new potatoes, quartered
1	tablespoon olive oil
1	tablespoon toasted sesame oil
¼	teaspoon salt
⅛	teaspoon ground black pepper
1	cup fresh pea pods, halved lengthwise
	Bottled teriyaki glaze (optional)

1 Preheat broiler. Brush both sides of chops with the ¼ cup teriyaki glaze. Arrange chops on half of the unheated rack of a broiler pan; set aside.

2 Place potatoes in a large bowl. Sprinkle potatoes with olive oil, sesame oil, salt, and pepper; toss to coat. Arrange potatoes in a single layer on the rack next to chops.

3 Broil 3 to 4 inches from heat for 9 to 11 minutes or until chops are done (160°F) and potatoes are tender, turning pork and potatoes once.

4 Place pea pods in a large bowl. Add potatoes; toss to combine. Serve pork with potatoes and pea pods. If desired, pass additional teriyaki glaze.

nutrition facts per serving: 394 cal., 15 g total fat (4 g sat. fat), 86 mg chol., 626 mg sodium, 23 g carb., 2 g fiber, 38 g pro.

Five-spice powder is used frequently in Asian and Arabic cooking. It adds complex flavor to a dish with just a teaspoon or two. The five spices are star anise, cloves, cinnamon, Szeuchan pepper, and fennel.

pork tenderloin with cucumber-mango salad

prep: 5 minutes   roast: 20 minutes at 425°F   stand: 5 minutes
makes: 4 servings

2   tablespoons packed brown sugar
2   teaspoons five-spice powder
½   teaspoon salt
1½ pounds pork tenderloin
4   green onions
1   mango, peeled, seeded, and chopped
1   small English cucumber, sliced and/or chopped
1   jalapeño pepper, seeded and sliced* (optional)

1 Preheat oven to 425°F. In a small bowl combine brown sugar, five-spice powder, and salt; set aside 1 teaspoon brown sugar mixture to use in salad. Rub the remaining brown sugar mixture onto pork tenderloin. Place tenderloin in a foil-lined baking pan.

2 Roast, uncovered, about 20 minutes or until a meat thermometer registers 155°F. Cover with foil and let stand for 5 minutes (meat temperature will rise to 160°F).

3 Meanwhile, for cucumber-mango salad, slice the green portion of green onions into thin strips; chop the white portion. In a medium bowl combine green onions, mango, cucumber, jalapeño pepper (if desired), and the reserved brown sugar mixture.

4 Slice pork and serve with cucumber-mango salad.

nutrition facts per serving: 258 cal., 3 g total fat (1 g sat. fat), 110 mg chol., 370 mg sodium, 19 g carb., 2 g fiber, 37 g pro.

*tip: Because hot chile peppers, such as jalapeños, contain volatile oils that can burn your skin and eyes, avoid direct contact with chiles as much as possible. When working with chile peppers, wear plastic or rubber gloves. If your bare hands do touch chile peppers, wash your hands well with soap and warm water.

If you use fresh tomatillos, remove the papery outer skin. The flesh underneath will be a little bit sticky. Just rinse it under cool water and pat dry. Then use a paring knife to remove the core, similarly to a tomato.

jamaican pork kabobs

prep: 15 minutes broil: 12 minutes
makes: 4 servings

2 fresh ears corn, husked and cleaned
1 12- to 14-ounce pork tenderloin
1 small red onion, cut into ½-inch-thick wedges
16 baby pattypan squash, about 1 inch in diameter, or 4 tomatillos, quartered
¼ cup mango chutney, finely chopped
3 tablespoons Pickapeppa sauce
1 tablespoon vegetable oil
1 tablespoon water

1 Preheat broiler. Cut corn crosswise into 1-inch pieces. In medium saucepan cook corn pieces in small amount of boiling water for 3 minutes; drain and rinse with cold water. Meanwhile, cut tenderloin into 1-inch slices.

2 For kabobs, on long metal skewers alternately thread pork, onion, squash, and corn. In a small bowl combine chutney, Pickapeppa sauce, oil, and water; set aside.

3 Place kabobs on the unheated rack of broiler pan. Broil 4 to 5 inches from the heat for 12 to 14 minutes or until pork is slightly pink in center, juices run clear, and vegetables are tender, turning once and brushing with the chutney mixture during the last 5 minutes of broiling. Serve with rice, if desired.

nutrition facts per serving: 252 cal., 7 g total fat (2 g sat. fat), 60 mg chol., 127 mg sodium, 27 g carb., 3 g fiber, 21 g pro.

make-ahead directions: Cook corn as directed. Drain and chill for up to 24 hours. To serve, assemble kabobs and continue as directed.

With just a few minutes and a few ingredients, you can easily put together this pretty dish. Serve it with steamed baby red potatoes.

zucchini-wrapped pork

prep: 12 minutes   roast: 18 minutes at 450°F
makes: 4 servings

1   small zucchini
1   12-ounce pork
      tenderloin
      Olive oil
      Salt
      Ground black pepper
⅓   cup purchased basil
      pesto
      Small fresh basil
      leaves
      Watercress or arugula
      (optional)

1 Preheat oven to 450°F. Line a 15×10×1-inch baking pan with foil; set aside. With a sharp knife or vegetable peeler, cut zucchini lengthwise into thin slices (you'll need 8 slices). Cut pork tenderloin crosswise into 4 equal portions. Press meat with the palm of your hand to flatten slightly.

2 Wrap each tenderloin portion with two zucchini slices (reserve remaining zucchini for another use). Place in prepared pan. Lightly brush with oil; sprinkle with salt and pepper.

3 Roast, uncovered, for 18 to 20 minutes or until an instant-read meat thermometer inserted in center of meat registers 160°F. Spoon some of the pesto over meat and sprinkle with basil leaves. Serve with the remaining pesto and, if desired, watercress.

nutrition facts per serving: 203 cal., 11 g total fat (2 g sat. fat), 62 mg chol., 382 mg sodium, 4 g carb., 1 g fiber, 21 g pro.

Sweet and heat come together in this quick chicken dish featuring fruit and chile peppers. The chicken bakes while you make the salsa.

chipotle chile chicken with blueberry pepper salsa

prep: 15 minutes   bake: 15 minutes at 400°F
makes: 4 servings

Nonstick cooking
   spray
2   tablespoons honey
1   tablespoon butter,
   melted
2   teaspoons finely
   chopped canned
   chipotle chile
   pepper in adobo
   sauce
1   teaspoon dried
   oregano, crushed
½   teaspoon salt
4   small skinless,
   boneless chicken
   breast halves (1 to
   1¼ pounds total)
1½   cups frozen
   blueberries, thawed
   and drained
1   11-ounce can
   mandarin orange
   sections, drained
3   tablespoons finely
   chopped red onion
1   teaspoon finely
   shredded lime peel
2   teaspoons lime juice

1 Preheat oven to 400°F. Coat a 13×9×2-inch baking pan with cooking spray; set aside.

2 In a small bowl stir together 1 tablespoon of the honey, the melted butter, 1 teaspoon of the chile pepper, the oregano, and salt. Brush both sides of each chicken breast half with the honey mixture. Arrange chicken in prepared pan. Bake for 15 to 20 minutes or until tender and no longer pink (170°F).

3 Meanwhile, for blueberry pepper salsa, in a medium bowl combine blueberries, orange sections, red onion, lime peel, lime juice, the remaining 1 tablespoon honey, and the remaining 1 teaspoon chipotle chile. Serve salsa with chicken.

nutrition facts per serving: 279 cal., 5 g total fat (2 g sat. fat), 90 mg chol., 420 mg sodium, 25 g carb., 2 g fiber, 34 g pro.

A crisp, oven-baked coating makes this chicken taste fried—but with only 6 grams of fat, it is decidedly not. Toasted pecans add a nice crunch to the finished dish.

crusted chicken with winter squash

prep: 15 minutes bake: 9 minutes at 450°F
makes: 4 servings

Nonstick cooking
    spray
14 to 16 ounces chicken
    breast tenderloins
    Salt
    Ground black pepper
¾ cup packaged
    cornflake crumbs
3 tablespoons pure
    maple syrup or
    maple-flavor syrup
1 10- to 12-ounce
    package frozen
    cooked winter
    squash
¼ cup pecan pieces

1 Preheat oven to 450°F. Line a baking sheet with foil; lightly coat foil with cooking spray. Set baking sheet aside.

2 Sprinkle chicken lightly with salt and pepper. Place cornflake crumbs in a shallow dish. Brush chicken on both sides with 1 tablespoon of the syrup. Coat chicken with cornflake crumbs, turning to coat evenly. Place chicken on the prepared baking sheet. Bake for 9 to 11 minutes or until tender and no longer pink (170°F).

3 Meanwhile, place squash in a 1½-quart microwave-safe casserole. Microwave, uncovered, on 100 percent power (high) for 5 to 6 minutes or until heated through, stirring twice. Stir in 1 tablespoon of the syrup. Season with salt and pepper.

4 In a small skillet heat pecans over medium-high heat for 2 to 3 minutes or until lightly toasted, stirring frequently. To serve, divide squash mixture among four plates. Drizzle with the remaining 1 tablespoon syrup; sprinkle with the pecans.

nutrition facts per serving: 296 cal., 6 g total fat (1 g sat. fat), 58 mg chol., 333 mg sodium, 35 g carb., 2 g fiber, 26 g pro.

If you can find quick-cooking or instant polenta, you can substitute it for the regular cornmeal. Make it according to the package directions.

mediterranean chicken and polenta

prep: 20 minutes bake: 10 minutes at 375°F

makes: 4 servings

½ 6.5-ounce jar oil-packed dried tomatoes with Italian herbs

4 small skinless, boneless chicken breast halves (1 to 1¼ pounds total)

Salt

Ground black pepper

1 cup assorted olives, drained

½ cup dry white wine or reduced-sodium chicken broth

4 small bay leaves (optional)

3 cups water

1 cup cornmeal

1 cup cold water

1 teaspoon salt

1 Preheat oven to 375°F. Drain tomatoes, reserving the oil. Season chicken with salt and pepper. In a large ovenproof skillet heat the reserved oil over medium-high heat. Add chicken; cook about 6 minutes or until browned, turning once. Add tomatoes, olives, wine, and, if desired, bay leaves. Place skillet in oven. Bake, uncovered, for 10 to 15 minutes or until chicken is tender and no longer pink (170°F).

2 Meanwhile, for polenta, in a large saucepan bring the 3 cups water to boiling. In a medium bowl combine cornmeal, the 1 cup cold water, and the 1 teaspoon salt; gradually stir into boiling water. Cook and stir until thickened and bubbly. Reduce heat; stir occasionally.

3 Remove chicken from oven; discard bay leaves (if using). Serve chicken with polenta and tomatoes and olives.

nutrition facts per serving: 370 cal., 8 g total fat (1 g sat. fat), 66 mg chol., 575 mg sodium, 46 g carb., 3 g fiber, 30 g pro.

oven-baked & broiled

For directions on how to peel and seed a mango, see the recipe for Ginger-Mango Smoothie, page 89.

quick coconut chicken

prep: 20 minutes   bake: 10 minutes at 450°F
makes: 4 servings

¾ cup panko (Japanese-
    style bread crumbs)
⅓ cup shredded coconut
½ cup mango chutney
2 tablespoons butter,
    melted
¼ teaspoon salt
¼ teaspoon ground
    black pepper
14 to 16 ounces chicken
    breast tenderloins
1 fresh mango

1 Preheat oven to 450°F. Line a baking sheet with foil; set aside. In small bowl combine panko and coconut; set aside.

2 Place chutney in another small bowl. Snip any large fruit pieces in chutney. Stir in butter, salt, and pepper. Using tongs, dip each chicken piece into the chutney mixture. Dip into panko mixture, turning to coat. Arrange chicken on the prepared baking sheet. Sprinkle any remaining panko mixture over chicken.

3 Bake for 10 to 12 minutes or until coating is golden and chicken is tender and no longer pink (170°F).

4 Meanwhile, seed, peel, and chop mango. Transfer chicken to a serving platter. Sprinkle with mango.

nutrition facts per serving: 339 cal., 10 g total fat (6 g sat. fat), 73 mg chol., 545 mg sodium, 35 g carb., 2 g fiber, 25 g pro.

Mashed cauliflower is a healthier (lower carb, lower calorie) alternative to mashed potatoes. If you like, toss in a peeled smashed garlic clove into the casserole before you cook the cauliflower for additional flavor.

parmesan-crusted turkey with mashed cauliflower

start to finish: 25 minutes
makes: 4 servings

3   cups cauliflower (½ of a medium head)
¼   cup water
2   8-ounce turkey breast tenderloins, halved horizontally
    Salt
    Ground black pepper
⅓   cup light mayonnaise
⅓   cup finely shredded Parmesan cheese
3   tablespoons fine dry bread crumbs
2   tablespoons butter
    Snipped fresh Italian (flat-leaf) parsley and/or paprika (optional)

1 Preheat broiler. In a microwave-safe 1½-quart casserole combine cauliflower and the water; cover. Microwave on 100 percent power (high) for 12 to 15 minutes or until very tender, stirring once.

2 Meanwhile, lightly sprinkle turkey with salt and pepper. Place on the unheated rack of a broiler pan. Broil 4 to 5 inches from the heat for 5 minutes. Turn turkey steaks over; broil for 4 minutes more.

3 Meanwhile, in a small bowl stir together mayonnaise, ¼ cup of the Parmesan cheese, and the bread crumbs. Spread over turkey. Broil for 2 to 3 minutes more or until topping is golden and turkey is no longer pink (170°F).

4 Add butter and the remaining Parmesan cheese to cauliflower; mash until smooth. If desired, sprinkle with parsley and/or paprika. Serve cauliflower with turkey.

nutrition facts per serving: 310 cal., 15 g total fat (6 g sat. fat), 97 mg chol., 574 mg sodium, 10 g carb., 2 g fiber, 33 g pro.

Yes, you can make meat loaf in 30 minutes or less! Golden raisins add a touch of sweetness to this deliciously spiced, slightly exotic loaf. Serve it with saffron rice.

moroccan meat loaf with tomato chutney

prep: 10 minutes   bake: 20 minutes at 425°F
makes: 4 servings

1¼   cups golden raisins
⅓   cup chopped red
     onion (1 small)
½   cup couscous
1   teaspoon salt
1   teaspoon curry
     powder
1   teaspoon ground
     cinnamon
¾   cup boiling water
1   pound uncooked
     ground turkey
1   egg, lightly beaten
2   cups grape tomatoes
¼   cup water

1 Preheat oven to 425°F. Adjust oven rack to upper third of the oven. Line an 8×8×2-inch baking pan with foil, overlapping sides of pan with foil; grease foil. Set pan aside. In a large mixing bowl combine 1 cup of the raisins, half of the red onion, the couscous, salt, curry powder, and ½ teaspoon of the cinnamon. Pour the ¾ cup boiling water over the mixture. Cover and let stand for 2 minutes. Add turkey and egg; mix well. Pat mixture into the prepared pan.

2 Bake meat loaf in the top third of the oven about 20 minutes or until done (165°F).

3 Meanwhile, for tomato chutney, in a medium saucepan combine the remaining ¼ cup raisins, remaining half of the red onion, remaining ½ teaspoon cinnamon, the tomatoes, and the ¼ cup water. Cook, covered, over medium-high heat until tomatoes pop, stirring occasionally. Cover and keep warm.

4 Lift meat loaf from pan with foil. Slice meat loaf and serve with tomato chutney.

nutrition facts per serving: 454 cal., 11 g total fat (3 g sat. fat), 125 mg chol., 679 mg sodium, 65 g carb., 5 g fiber, 30 g pro.

These personal-sized casseroles are a great way to use up leftover roast chicken or turkey. Instead of being topped with fat-laden pastry, the casseroles are covered with thin slices of fresh apple seasoned with nutmeg and black pepper.

turkey-vegetable casseroles

prep: 15 minutes   bake: 10 minutes at 450°F
makes: 4 servings

1   16-ounce bag frozen
    stew vegetables
    (potatoes, carrots,
    onion, and celery)
1   18-ounce jar home-
    style gravy
    (1¾ cups)
1   teaspoon finely
    snipped fresh sage
    or ½ teaspoon
    ground sage
2   cups cut-up cooked
    turkey or chicken
1   medium cooking
    apple, thinly sliced
    Fresh sage leaves
    (optional)
2   tablespoons butter,
    melted
¼   teaspoon ground
    nutmeg
¼   teaspoon ground
    black pepper

1 Preheat oven to 450°F. In a large microwave-safe bowl combine vegetables, gravy, and the 1 teaspoon sage. Cover with vented plastic wrap. Microwave on 100 percent power (high) for 5 minutes. Add turkey; cover. Microwave for 4 to 6 minutes more or until heated through and vegetables are tender, stirring occasionally.

2 Spoon turkey mixture into four 14- to 16-ounce casseroles. Top with apple and, if desired, fresh sage leaves. Drizzle with melted butter. In a small bowl stir together nutmeg and pepper; sprinkle over casseroles.

3 Bake, uncovered, about 10 minutes or until bubbly and apple slices begin to brown.

nutrition facts per serving: 297 cal., 12 g total fat (5 g sat. fat), 71 mg chol., 753 mg sodium, 23 g carb., 3 g fiber, 24 g pro.

The fat content in this dish may appear high, but keep in mind that there are only 3 grams of saturated fat. Salmon is rich in heart-healthy omega-3 fatty acids that help reduce cholesterol.

peanut-crusted salmon

prep: 20 minutes bake: 8 minutes at 450°F
makes: 6 servings

6   5- to 6-ounce fresh
    or frozen skinless
    salmon fillets, about
    1 inch thick
2   to 3 tablespoons
    orange juice
¼   teaspoon salt
⅛   teaspoon coarse
    ground black
    pepper
1   cup whole wheat
    panko (Japanese-
    style bread crumbs)
⅓   cup peanuts, toasted*
    and finely chopped
2   tablespoons finely
    snipped fresh
    parsley
2   tablespoons olive oil
2   cloves garlic, minced
2   teaspoons finely
    shredded orange
    peel
½   cup dry white wine
    or chicken broth

1 Preheat oven to 450°F. Thaw fish, if frozen. Rinse fish; pat dry with paper towels. Drizzle fish with orange juice. Sprinkle with salt and pepper.

2 In a shallow dish combine panko, peanuts, parsley, oil, garlic, and orange peel. Dip fish into peanut mixture, turning and pressing to coat.

3 Place fish in a single layer in an ungreased 3-quart rectangular baking dish. Add wine to dish.

4 Bake, uncovered, for 8 to 12 minutes or until fish flakes easily when tested with a fork.

nutrition facts per serving: 356 cal., 18 g total fat (3 g sat. fat), 78 mg chol., 177 mg sodium, 13 g carb., 2 g fiber, 32 g pro.

*tip: To toast nuts, spread them in a shallow baking pan. Bake in a 350°F oven for 5 to 10 minutes or until light brown, shaking pan once or twice. Watch carefully so the nuts don't burn.

Here's how to section a grapefruit (or an orange): Cut a slice off of the top and the bottom of the fruit, then cut the peel off in strips, from the top to the bottom. Take a sharp knife and cut toward the center of the fruit on either side of each section. Pop the section out—it should be clean, with no bitter white pith attached.

citrus salsa salmon

start to finish: 20 minutes
makes: 4 servings

4	4- to 5-ounce fresh or frozen skinless salmon fillets, ¾ to 1 inch thick
¼	teaspoon salt
⅛	teaspoon ground black pepper
¼	cup red jalapeño jelly
2	medium oranges, peeled, seeded, and coarsely chopped
1	medium grapefruit, peeled and sectioned
1	cup grape or cherry tomatoes, halved
	Salad greens (optional)

1 Thaw fish, if frozen. Rinse fish; pat dry with paper towels. Preheat broiler. Sprinkle fish with salt and pepper. In a small saucepan melt the jelly over low heat. Brush 2 tablespoons of the melted jelly over the fish. Set remaining jelly aside.

2 Place salmon on the unheated rack of broiler pan. Broil 4 inches from the heat for 8 to 10 minutes or until fish flakes easily when tested with a fork.

3 Meanwhile, for fresh citrus salsa, in a medium bowl combine oranges, grapefruit, tomatoes, and the remaining 2 tablespoons melted jelly. Season with salt and pepper. Serve salmon with citrus salsa and, if desired, salad greens.

nutrition facts per serving: 357 cal., 15 g total fat (3 g sat. fat), 62 mg chol., 221 mg sodium, 31 g carb., 3 g fiber, 25 g pro.

Miso—an essential flavoring in Japanese cooking—is made from fermented soybeans. The most common types are white, yellow, or red. White is the mildest in flavor of the three. Look for it at Asian markets and whole-foods stores.

miso and maple-glazed salmon

start to finish: 30 minutes
makes: 4 servings

4   5- to 6-ounce fresh or
     frozen salmon fillets
¼   teaspoon freshly
     ground black
     pepper
2   tablespoons white
     miso paste
2   tablespoons pure
     maple syrup
2   teaspoons rice wine
     vinegar
1   teaspoon black
     sesame seeds
1   recipe Asian Broccoli
     Slaw

1 Thaw fish, if frozen. Rinse fish; pat dry with paper towels. Preheat broiler. Line a 15×10×1-inch baking pan with foil. Arrange fish, skin sides down, in the prepared pan. Sprinkle with pepper.

2 Broil 4 to 5 inches from the heat for 5 minutes. Meanwhile, for glaze, in a small bowl whisk together miso paste, maple syrup, and vinegar until smooth.

3 Brush some of the glaze over each piece of fish. Broil 4 to 5 minutes more or until fish flakes easily when tested with a fork.

4 To serve, use a wide spatula to lift fish from skin. Transfer salmon to four serving plates; sprinkle with sesame seeds. Serve with Asian Broccoli Slaw.

nutrition facts per serving: 330 cal., 12 g total fat (2 g sat. fat), 78 mg chol., 562 mg sodium, 23 g carb., 3 g fiber, 31 g pro.

nutrition note: Wild-caught salmon is much leaner than farm-raised salmon. The diet and low-activity level of commercially raised salmon contributes to additional fat content. Although both types contain heart-healthy omega-3 fatty acids, additional fat means more calories. Omega-3 fatty acids boost your levels of leptin—a hormone that plays a key role in energy intake and expenditure. Higher levels of leptin can translate into a higher metabolism, which helps you burn fat more quickly.

Asian Broccoli Slaw: In a large bowl toss together 3 cups packaged shredded broccoli (broccoli slaw mix); one 11-ounce can mandarin orange sections, drained; and ¼ cup light Asian sesame salad dressing. Toss to coat.

If you're buying fresh salmon, have the fishmonger remove the skin for you. He likely can do it much easier than you can—and it saves you a step when it's time to cook.

salmon with roasted vegetables

prep: 15 minutes   bake: 4 minutes to 6 minutes per ½-inch thickness at 450°F
makes: 4 servings

189

4   4- to 5-ounce fresh
      or frozen skinless
      salmon fillets, about
      1 inch thick
      Nonstick cooking
      spray
1   tablespoon snipped
      fresh dill
½   teaspoon salt
¼   teaspoon ground
      black pepper
2   medium zucchini
      and/or yellow
      summer squash, cut
      into ¼-inch slices
      (about 2½ cups)
1   cup grape or cherry
      tomatoes, halved
4   green onions, cut into
      1-inch pieces
1   tablespoon Dijon-
      style mustard

1 Preheat oven to 450°F. Thaw fish, if frozen. Rinse fish; pat dry with paper towels. Set fish aside. Line a 15×10×1-inch baking pan with foil; lightly coat foil with cooking spray. Set pan aside.

2 In a small bowl combine dill, salt, and pepper; set aside. In a large bowl combine zucchini, tomatoes, and green onions. Generously coat vegetables with cooking spray. Sprinkle half of the dill mixture over vegetables; toss to coat evenly. Spread vegetable mixture in one side of the prepared baking pan.

3 Place fish in the other side of the pan; tuck under thin edges to make even thickness. Stir mustard into the remaining dill mixture; spread evenly over fish. Measure thickness of fish.

4 Bake, uncovered, for 4 to 6 minutes per ½-inch thickness of fish or until fish begins to flake easily when tested with a fork and zucchini is crisp-tender.

nutrition facts per serving: 239 cal., 12 g total fat (3 g sat. fat), 66 mg chol., 463 mg sodium, 6 g carb., 2 g fiber, 24 g pro.

Panko bread crumbs are made from crustless bread. The resulting large, airy crumbs give foods a light, crunchy coating that stays crispier than regular bread crumbs because panko don't absorb as much grease.

parmesan-crusted cod

start to finish: 20 minutes
makes: 4 servings

4   fresh or frozen
     skinless cod fillets
     (1½ pounds total)
     Nonstick cooking
     spray
¼   teaspoon salt
⅛   teaspoon ground
     black pepper
⅓   cup panko (Japanese-
     style bread crumbs)
¼   cup finely shredded
     Parmesan cheese
½   cup water
1   10-ounce package
     julienned or
     shredded fresh
     carrots (3 cups)
1   tablespoon butter
¾   teaspoon ground
     ginger
     Mixed fresh salad
     greens (optional)

1 Thaw fish, if frozen. Preheat oven to 450°F. Lightly coat a baking sheet with cooking spray. Rinse fish; pat dry with paper towels. Arrange fish on the prepared baking sheet. Sprinkle fish with the salt and pepper. In a small bowl stir together panko and Parmesan cheese; sprinkle over fish.

2 Bake, uncovered, for 4 to 6 minutes per ½-inch thickness of fish or until crumbs are golden brown and fish flakes easily when tested with a fork.

3 Meanwhile, in a large skillet bring the water to boiling; add carrots. Reduce heat. Cook, covered, over medium heat for 5 minutes. Uncover and cook about 2 minutes more or until water evaporates. Add butter and ginger; toss until butter melts and carrots are coated. Serve fish with carrot mixture and, if desired, salad greens.

nutrition facts per serving: 233 cal., 6 g total fat (3 g sat. fat), 84 mg chol., 407 mg sodium, 11 g carb., 2 g fiber, 34 g pro.

The Olive Relish can be enjoyed with nearly any kind of fish—or roasted or grilled chicken. Or, toss it with chopped fresh tomatoes and hot cooked pasta for a quick meatless meal.

baked mediterranean cod with olive relish

prep: 15 minutes   bake: 12 minutes at 475°F
makes: 4 servings

4   fresh or frozen
    skinless cod fillets
    (about 1½ pounds
    total)
2   tablespoons olive oil
    Salt
    Ground black pepper
1   pound asparagus,
    trimmed
1   recipe Olive Relish

1 Thaw fish, if frozen. Preheat oven to 475°F. Lightly coat a 15×10×1-inch baking pan with some of the oil. Rinse fish; pat dry with paper towels. On one side of the pan arrange fish, tucking under any thin portions to make an even thickness. Brush fish with some of the remaining oil. Sprinkle with salt and pepper. Bake for 5 minutes. Place asparagus in opposite side of pan; brush with the remaining oil; sprinkle with salt and pepper.

2 Bake for 7 to 10 minutes more or until fish flakes easily when tested with a fork. Serve fish with Olive Relish and asparagus.

nutrition facts per serving: 220 cal., 9 g total fat (1 g sat. fat), 73 mg chol., 309 mg sodium, 3 g carb., 2 g fiber, 32 g pro.

Olive Relish: In a small bowl combine ¼ cup chopped, pitted Kalamata or ripe olives; ¼ cup chopped French green olives with herbes de Provence, French green Picholine olives, or pimiento-stuffed green olives; ¼ cup chopped pepperoncini peppers (stems removed); 2 tablespoons chopped red onion; 1 tablespoon olive oil; 1 tablespoon red wine vinegar; 1 tablespoon drained capers; ½ teaspoon snipped fresh oregano or ¼ teaspoon dried oregano, crushed; and ⅛ teaspoon freshly ground black pepper. Cover and chill for up to 24 hours.
makes: about 1 cup

Any firm white fish works well on these crunchy and flavorful tostadas.

fish tostadas with chili-lime cream

start to finish: 20 minutes
makes: 4 servings

1   pound fresh or frozen tilapia or cod fillets
½   teaspoon chili powder
¼   teaspoon salt
1   lime, halved
½   cup sour cream
½   teaspoon garlic powder
8   6-inch tostada shells
2   cups shredded cabbage mix
1   avocado, halved, seeded, peeled, and sliced (optional)
1   cup cherry tomatoes, quartered
    Bottled hot pepper sauce (optional)

1 Thaw fish, if frozen. Rinse fish; pat dry with paper towels. Sprinkle fish with ¼ teaspoon of the chili powder and the salt; set aside. Preheat broiler. For chili-lime cream, in a small bowl squeeze 2 teaspoons juice from half the lime. Stir in sour cream, garlic powder, and the remaining ¼ teaspoon chili powder; set aside. Cut the remaining lime half into wedges for serving.

2 Place fish on the unheated greased rack of a broiler pan; tuck under thin edges to make fish an even thickness. Measure thickness. Place tostada shells on a baking sheet. Place in oven on the lowest rack. Broil fish 4 inches from heat for 4 to 6 minutes per ½-inch thickness or until fish flakes easily when tested with a fork. Break fish into chunks. Top tostada shells with fish, chili-lime cream, cabbage mix, avocado (if desired), tomatoes, and, if desired, hot pepper sauce. Serve with lime wedges.

nutrition facts per serving: 278 cal., 14 g total fat (5 g sat. fat), 67 mg chol., 303 mg sodium, 17 g carb., 2 g fiber, 25 g pro.

194

When buying melon, look for firm, unblemished flesh. Press gently on the stem end—it should give just a bit. It should also smell slightly fragrant. Let the melon sit on the counter for a few days to fully ripen and reach maximum sweetness and juiciness.

tilapia on melon

start to finish: 20 minutes
makes: 4 servings

1   pound fresh or frozen tilapia fillets
1   tablespoon olive oil
1½   teaspoons lemon-pepper seasoning
⅓   cup plain low-fat yogurt
1   tablespoon honey
½   of a small cantaloupe, peeled and thinly sliced
1   medium cucumber, thinly sliced

1 Thaw fish, if frozen. Preheat broiler. Rinse fish; pat dry with paper towels. If necessary, cut fish into 4 serving-size pieces. Measure fish at its thickest point. Brush fish with oil; sprinkle with ¾ teaspoon of the lemon-pepper seasoning.

2 Place fish on the rack of an unheated broiler pan. Broil fish 3 to 4 inches from the heat for 4 to 6 minutes per ½-inch thickness or until fish flakes easily when tested with a fork.

3 Meanwhile, for sauce, in a small bowl combine yogurt, honey, and the remaining ¾ teaspoon lemon-pepper seasoning. Arrange cantaloupe and cucumber on a large platter. Top with fish. Serve with sauce.

nutrition facts per serving: 204 cal., 6 g total fat (2 g sat. fat), 58 mg chol., 493 mg sodium, 14 g carb., 1 g fiber, 25 g pro.

kitchen tip: Fresh whitefish, such as tilapia, packs a lot of lean protein without many calories. Because it's so low in fat, it cooks quickly and can dry out before you even realize it's done. Be sure to follow the recipe directions carefully, measuring fish fillets at their thickest point and the distance between the fish and the broiler. When done, the fish will be opaque and will flake easily when tested with a fork at its thickest point.

Quick-pickled cucumbers add sweetness and crunchiness to this ethereally light fish dish.

ginger tilapia

start to finish: 20 minutes
makes: 4 servings

4   4- to 5-ounce fresh or
     frozen tilapia fillets,
     ½ to ¾ inch thick
½   cup cider vinegar
¼   cup packed brown
     sugar
2   teaspoons grated
     fresh ginger
¼   teaspoon salt
2   medium cucumbers,
     sliced (about
     3½ cups)
     Nonstick cooking
     spray
1   6-ounce carton plain
     yogurt
2   tablespoons snipped
     fresh mint
     Fresh mint leaves
     (optional)
     Lemon peel strips
     (optional)
     Lemon wedges
     (optional)
     Cracked black pepper

1 Thaw fish, if frozen. Preheat broiler. In a medium bowl combine vinegar, brown sugar, ginger, and salt; stir until sugar dissolves. Set aside ¼ cup. Add cucumbers to the remaining vinegar mixture; toss to coat. Set aside.

2 Rinse fish; pat dry with paper towels. Lightly coat the rack of an unheated broiler pan with cooking spray; place fish on rack of broiler pan. Brush the reserved ¼ cup vinegar mixture over the fish. Broil 4 inches from the heat for 4 to 6 minutes or until fish flakes easily when tested with a fork.

3 Meanwhile, in a small bowl combine yogurt and the 2 tablespoons snipped mint.

4 Using a slotted spoon, divide cucumber among four plates. Top with fish and yogurt mixture. If desired, garnish with mint leaves, lemon peel, and lemon wedges. Sprinkle with cracked pepper.

nutrition facts per serving: 210 cal., 3 g total fat (1 g sat. fat), 59 mg chol., 388 mg sodium, 23 g carb., 0 g fiber, 26 g pro.

kitchen tip: To peel fresh ginger, use a metal spoon to gently scrape away the thin outer coating, then finely chop the yellow flesh with a sharp chef's knife or grate it with a Microplane or box grater. Preserve any remaining ginger by thinly slicing it and freezing in a resealable plastic bag.

A splash of malt vinegar at the table gives these crisp-coated fish fillets authentic pub-food flavor.

catfish 'n' chips

prep: 15 minutes   bake: 4 to 6 minutes per ½-inch thickness at 450°F
makes: 4 servings

1 pound fresh or frozen skinless catfish fillets
   Nonstick cooking spray
1 teaspoon chili powder or paprika
½ teaspoon salt
¼ teaspoon dried dill
¼ teaspoon ground black pepper
2 small sweet potatoes (10 ounces)
1 medium Yukon gold potato
1 tablespoon canola oil
⅓ cup buttermilk
⅔ cup panko (Japanese-style bread crumbs)
2 cloves garlic, minced
   Fresh dill sprigs (optional)
   Malt vinegar (optional)

1 Thaw fish, if frozen. Rinse fish; pat dry with paper towels. Cut fish into four serving-size pieces. Set fish aside. Preheat oven to 450°F. Line two baking sheets with foil; lightly coat with cooking spray. In a small bowl combine chili powder, salt, dill, and pepper; set aside.

2 Scrub sweet and Yukon gold potatoes. Cut potatoes into ½-inch-thick wedges and place in large bowl. Sprinkle potatoes with oil and ½ teaspoon of the chili powder mixture; toss to coat. Arrange potatoes in single layer on one prepared baking sheet. Bake for 10 minutes.

3 Meanwhile, pour buttermilk in shallow dish. In another shallow dish combine panko, garlic, and the remaining chili powder mixture. Dip fish in buttermilk, turning to coat and allowing excess to drip off. Dip in panko mixture, coating both sides. Place fish on second baking sheet. Lightly coat with cooking spray. Measure thickness of fish.

4 Bake for 4 to 6 minutes per ½-inch thickness of fish or until fish flakes easily when tested with fork and potatoes are tender. If desired, sprinkle fish with fresh dill and serve with vinegar.

nutrition facts per serving: 317 cal., 13 g total fat (2 g sat. fat), 54 mg chol., 449 mg sodium, 28 g carb., 3 g fiber, 22 g pro.

Shrimp is labeled with a set of numbers that indicate how many shrimp make a pound and therefore indicate the size of the individual shrimp. The smaller the numbers, the larger the shrimp. For example, shrimp labeled 36/45 will have an average of 40 shrimp per pound. Shrimp labeled 16/20—between 16 and 20 per pound—are considered extra-large.

coconut shrimp with mango rice pilaf

prep: 20 minutes   bake: 8 minutes at 450°F
makes: 4 servings

1 pound fresh or frozen extra-large shrimp in shells
  Nonstick cooking spray
¼ cup refrigerated or frozen egg product, thawed, or 2 egg whites, lightly beaten
¾ cup finely crushed reduced-fat or reduced-sodium shredded wheat crackers
⅓ cup shredded coconut
¼ teaspoon ground ginger
¼ teaspoon ground black pepper
1 8.8-ounce pouch cooked brown rice
½ cup chopped fresh mango or chopped jarred mango, rinsed and drained
⅓ cup sliced green onions
2 tablespoons snipped fresh cilantro

1 Thaw shrimp, if frozen. Peel and devein shrimp, leaving tails intact. Rinse shrimp; pat dry with paper towels. Set shrimp aside. Preheat oven to 450°F. Lightly coat a large baking sheet with cooking spray; set aside.

2 Place egg product in a shallow dish. In another shallow dish combine crushed crackers, coconut, ginger, and pepper. Dip shrimp into egg, turning to coat. Dip into coconut mixture, pressing to coat except leaving tail uncoated. Arrange shrimp in a single layer on the prepared baking sheet.

3 Bake for 8 to 10 minutes or until shrimp are opaque and coating is lightly browned.

4 Meanwhile, for pilaf, heat rice according to package directions. Transfer to a serving bowl. Stir in mango and green onions. Serve shrimp with pilaf; sprinkle with cilantro.

nutrition facts per serving: 303 cal., 7 g total fat (2 g sat. fat), 129 mg chol., 249 mg sodium, 36 g carb., 3 g fiber, 23 g pro.

Mexican crema is similar to French crème fraîche—a tangy, thickened sour cream. This recipe calls for fat-free sour cream, but if you can find Mexican crema—and it's widely available these days, even in the dairy department of some big-box stores—try it here. It will add a few more calories per serving, but not many.

edamame, black bean, and corn quesadillas with lime crema

prep: 20 minutes   bake: 8 minutes at 425°F
makes: 4 quesadillas

Nonstick cooking spray
⅔   cup fat-free sour cream
1   teaspoon finely shredded lime peel
3   teaspoons lime juice
½   teaspoon honey
    Dash salt
1   cup frozen sweet soybeans (edamame), thawed
½   cup canned no-salt-added black beans, rinsed and drained
1   cup frozen whole kernel corn, thawed
⅓   cup chopped green onion
1   teaspoon ground cumin
    Dash ground black pepper
4   8-inch fat-free flour tortillas
¾   cup shredded reduced-fat Monterey Jack or cheddar cheese (3 ounces)
⅓   cup snipped fresh cilantro
    Nonstick cooking spray

1 Preheat oven to 425°F. Lightly coat a large baking sheet with cooking spray; set aside. For crema, in a small bowl combine sour cream, the 1 teaspoon lime peel, 2 teaspoons of the lime juice, the honey, and salt. Set crema aside.

2 In a medium bowl combine edamame and black beans. Using a potato masher, coarsely mash the beans, leaving some whole. Add half of the crema, the corn, green onion, cumin, pepper, and the remaining 1 teaspoon lime juice.

3 Arrange tortillas on a work surface. Sprinkle Monterey Jack cheese over half of each tortilla. Top cheese with corn-bean mixture. Sprinkle evenly with cilantro; fold unfilled halves of tortillas over filled halves, making half moon shapes.

4 Arrange quesadillas on prepared baking sheet. Lightly coat tops of quesadillas with cooking spray. Bake about 8 minutes or until lightly golden. Transfer to a cutting board. Cut each quesadilla into three wedges. Serve with the remaining crema.

nutrition facts per quesadilla: 341 cal., 8 g total fat (3 g sat. fat), 19 mg chol., 603 mg sodium, 51 g carb., 6 g fiber, 18 g pro.

nutrition note: Fiber- and protein-rich edamame are a natural source of antioxidants and isoflavones, which may help reduce the risk of breast cancer and heart disease, as well as ease menopausal symptoms.

Get the tofu as dry as possible before dipping in the egg mixture and panko mixture to help the coating adhere better.

coconut-crusted tofu with black bean slaw

prep: 15 minutes   bake: 10 minutes at 450°F
makes: 4 servings

Nonstick cooking
   spray
¾ cup panko (Japanese-
   style bread crumbs)
½ cup shredded or
   flaked coconut
1 egg
¼ cup unsweetened
   light coconut milk
2 teaspoons ground
   coriander
1 teaspoon salt
1 18-ounce package
   firm, tub-style tofu
   (fresh bean curd)
2½ cups packaged
   shredded broccoli
   (broccoli slaw mix)
1 15-ounce can no-salt-
   added black beans,
   rinsed and drained
1 8.25-ounce can
   mandarin orange
   sections, undrained
¼ cup rice vinegar
2 tablespoons
   unsweetened light
   coconut milk
¼ teaspoon crushed red
   pepper

1 Preheat oven to 450°F. Line a baking sheet with foil; coat foil with cooking spray. Set baking sheet aside. In a food processor or blender combine panko and coconut. Cover and process or blend until coconut is finely chopped. Transfer to a shallow dish. In another shallow dish whisk together egg, the ¼ cup coconut milk, coriander, and salt.

2 Drain tofu; cut crosswise into four slices. Cut each slice in half diagonally to make two triangles. Pat dry with paper towels. Dip tofu triangles into egg mixture, then into panko mixture, turning to coat all sides. Place on the prepared baking sheet. Coat tops of tofu with cooking spray. Bake about 10 minutes or until golden and heated through.

3 Meanwhile, for slaw, in a large bowl combine shredded broccoli and black beans. Drain mandarin oranges, reserving 2 tablespoons juice. Add the reserved juice, rice vinegar, the 2 tablespoons coconut milk, and crushed red pepper to broccoli mixture; toss to coat. Gently stir in mandarin oranges.

4 Divide slaw among serving plates. Top with tofu triangles.

nutrition facts per serving: 328 cal., 11 g total fat (5 g sat. fat), 47 mg chol., 711 mg sodium, 39 g carb., 9 g fiber, 21 g pro.

escarole and poached egg salad

main-dish
sal

Toss together combinations of crisp greens, veggies or fruits, and flavorful meats, poultry, or fish for a fresh and fast meal that fills you up.

8

ads

The Cilantro Dressing does double-duty here, as both a marinade for the steak and as a dressing for the finished salads.

grilled flank steak salad

start to finish: 30 minutes
makes: 2 servings

1 recipe Cilantro
   Dressing
8 ounces beef flank
   steak
2 small yellow and/or
   red sweet peppers,
   seeded and halved
1 fresh ear corn,
   husked and silks
   removed
2 green onions,
   trimmed
   Nonstick cooking
   spray
2 cups torn romaine
   lettuce
4 cherry tomatoes,
   halved
¼ of a small avocado,
   halved, seeded,
   peeled, and cut up
   (optional)

1 Prepare Cilantro Dressing and divide it into two portions.

2 Trim fat from steak. Score both sides of steak in a diamond pattern by making shallow diagonal cuts at 1-inch intervals. Place steak in a resealable plastic bag set in a shallow dish. Pour one portion of the Cilantro Dressing over steak in bag; set aside remaining dressing portion. Seal bag; turn to coat steak. Marinate in refrigerator for 15 to 30 minutes.

3 Coat sweet peppers, corn, and green onions with cooking spray.

4 For a charcoal or gas grill, place steak and corn on the grill rack directly over medium heat. Grill, covered, for 15 to 18 minutes or until steak is medium rare (145°F), turning once. For corn, allow 15 to 20 minutes. Add sweet pepper halves to the grill for the last 8 minutes of grilling and green onions for the last 4 minutes grilling, turning frequently.

5 Thinly slice steak against the grain. Coarsely chop sweet peppers and green onions; cut corn from cob. Divide romaine lettuce between two salad plates. Arrange sliced steak, grilled vegetables, tomatoes, and, if desired, avocado on lettuce. Drizzle salads with the remaining portion of the Cilantro Dressing.

nutrition facts per serving: 357 cal., 15 g total fat (4 g sat. fat), 47 mg chol., 376 mg sodium, 31 g carb., 5 g fiber, 29 g pro.

Cilantro Dressing: In a blender or small food processor combine 3 tablespoons lime juice; 2 tablespoons chopped shallot; 2 tablespoons snipped fresh cilantro; 1 tablespoon olive oil; 1 tablespoon water; 2 teaspoons honey; 1 large clove garlic, peeled and quartered; ¼ teaspoon chili powder; ¼ teaspoon salt; and ¼ teaspoon ground cumin. Cover and blend or process until combined.

For directions on how to section an orange, see the recipe for Citrus Salsa Salmon on page 187.

spinach and basil salad with beef

start to finish: 25 minutes
makes: 2 servings

½   of a small very ripe pear, cored and peeled
1   tablespoon white wine vinegar or cider vinegar
¼   teaspoon Worcestershire-style marinade for chicken or Worcestershire sauce
    Dash ground black pepper
2   cups lightly packed torn fresh spinach
1   cup sliced fresh mushrooms
½   cup lightly packed fresh basil leaves
6   ounces sliced cooked beef, cut into thin strips (about 1 cup)
2   small oranges, peeled and sectioned, or one 11-ounce can mandarin orange sections, drained

1 For dressing, in a food processor or blender combine the pear, vinegar, Worcestershire-style marinade, and pepper. Cover and process or blend until smooth. Set dressing aside.

2 In a large bowl toss together the spinach, mushrooms, and basil leaves. Add the beef strips and orange sections. Toss lightly to mix. Add the dressing; toss to coat. Divide salad mixture between two bowls or plates.

nutrition facts per serving: 301 cal., 10 g total fat (2 g sat. fat), 75 mg chol., 67 mg sodium, 26 g carb., 7 g fiber, 29 g pro.

nutrition note: The bold but sweet flavor of spinach makes it a favorite for a wide variety of dishes. Since it can be eaten raw or cooked in a variety of ways, it's easy to fit this excellent source of fiber and iron into your diet.

For the thinnest, most delicate slices of steak, partially freeze the meat for about 30 minutes before slicing.

gingered beef and broccoli salad bowl

start to finish: 20 minutes
makes: 4 servings

12 ounces boneless beef sirloin steak
⅔ cup bottled ginger vinaigrette salad dressing
3 cups fresh broccoli florets
8 cups mixed spring greens or baby salad greens
1 medium red sweet pepper, cut into bite-size strips

1 Trim fat from beef; thinly slice meat across the grain into bite-size strips. Set aside.

2 In a wok or large skillet heat 2 tablespoons of the salad dressing over medium-high heat. Add broccoli; cook and stir for 3 minutes. Add meat to wok; cook and stir for 2 to 3 minutes more or until meat is slightly pink in center. Remove beef and broccoli from wok.

3 In a large bowl toss together meat, broccoli, greens, and sweet pepper. Drizzle with remaining salad dressing; toss to coat.

nutrition facts per serving: 237 cal., 9 g total fat (2 g sat. fat), 60 mg chol., 468 mg sodium, 17 g carb., 4 g fiber, 22 g pro.

The corn in this salad is served uncooked and fresh off the cob for a crunchy texture and very sweet flavor. To keep it in planks, be sure you cut it fairly close to the cob.

beefy pasta salad

start to finish: 30 minutes
makes: 4 servings

1 cup dried multigrain penne pasta (about 3½ ounces)
2 fresh ears corn, husks and silks removed
Nonstick cooking spray
12 ounces boneless beef sirloin steak, trimmed of fat and cut into thin bite-size strips*
1 cup cherry tomatoes, halved
¼ cup shredded fresh basil
2 tablespoons finely shredded Parmesan cheese
3 tablespoons white wine vinegar
2 tablespoons olive oil
¼ teaspoon salt
⅛ teaspoon ground black pepper
1 clove garlic, minced
Finely shredded Parmesan cheese (optional)

1 In a 4- to 6-quart Dutch oven cook pasta according to package directions, adding corn for the last 3 minutes of cooking time. Using tongs, transfer corn to a large cutting board. Drain pasta. Rinse in cold water and drain again; set aside. Cool corn until easy to handle.

2 Meanwhile, coat an unheated large nonstick skillet with cooking spray. Preheat skillet over medium-high heat. Add beef strips; cook for 4 to 6 minutes or until slightly pink in the center, stirring occasionally. Remove from heat and cool slightly.

3 On a cutting board place an ear of corn pointed end down. While holding corn firmly at stem end to keep in place, use a sharp knife to cut corn from cobs, leaving corn in planks; rotate cob as needed to cut corn from all sides. Repeat with the remaining ear of corn. In a large bowl combine pasta, beef, tomatoes, basil, and the 2 tablespoons Parmesan cheese.

4 For dressing, in a screw-top jar combine vinegar, oil, salt, pepper, and garlic. Cover and shake well. Pour dressing over pasta mixture; toss gently to coat. Gently fold in corn planks or place corn planks on top of individual servings. Serve immediately. If desired, sprinkle with additional Parmesan cheese.

nutrition facts per serving: 322 cal., 12 g total fat (3 g sat. fat), 38 mg chol., 256 mg sodium, 27 g carb., 4 g fiber, 26 g pro.

✱tip: If you have leftover beef pot roast, use it instead of the steak in this pasta salad. Simply shred the meat and use 2 cups of it in the salad.

Use a mix of apples and pears for more interest on the plate and palate.

pork and apple salad with blue cheese dressing

prep: 20 minutes broil: 9 minutes
makes: 4 servings

206

⅓ cup buttermilk

2 tablespoons light mayonnaise

2 tablespoons crumbled blue cheese

2 tablespoons thinly sliced green onion (1)

12 ounces boneless pork top loin chops, cut ¾ inch thick

2 teaspoons snipped fresh thyme or 1 teaspoon dried thyme, crushed

¼ teaspoon ground black pepper

8 cups torn mixed salad greens

2 cups thinly sliced apples and/or pears (2 medium)

¼ cup coarsely chopped walnuts, toasted* (optional)

Cracked black pepper (optional)

1 Preheat broiler. For dressing, in a small bowl whisk together buttermilk and mayonnaise until smooth. Stir in blue cheese and green onion; set aside.

2 Trim fat from chops. Sprinkle thyme and the ¼ teaspoon ground pepper evenly over both sides of chops; rub in with your fingers. Place chops on the unheated rack of a broiler pan. Broil 3 to 4 inches from the heat for 9 to 11 minutes or until meat is slightly pink in center and juices run clear (160°F), turning once halfway.

3 Divide salad greens and apples among dinner plates. Slice chops; arrange on top of greens mixture. Drizzle with dressing. If desired, sprinkle with walnuts and cracked pepper.

nutrition facts per serving: 234 cal., 11 g total fat (4 g sat. fat), 61 mg chol., 203 mg sodium, 14 g carb., 3 g fiber, 21 g pro.

*tip: To toast nuts, spread them in a shallow baking pan. Bake in a 350°F oven for 5 to 10 minutes or until light brown, shaking pan once or twice. Watch carefully so the nuts don't burn.

A sprinkling of sunflower seeds adds a pleasant crunch to these creamy stuffed peppers.

ham salad stuffed peppers

start to finish: 20 minutes
makes: 4 servings

3 cups packaged shredded broccoli (broccoli slaw mix)
1 cup cubed cooked ham (5 ounces)
¼ cup bottled Parmesan ranch or peppercorn ranch salad dressing
4 small yellow, orange, red, and/or green sweet peppers
2 tablespoons sunflower kernels

1 In a Dutch oven bring a large amount of water to boiling. Meanwhile, for slaw, in a medium bowl combine shredded broccoli and ham. Drizzle with dressing; toss gently to coat.

2 Cut tops off sweet peppers; remove and discard seeds and membranes. Add the pepper bottoms and tops to the boiling water; reduce heat. Simmer, covered, for 3 minutes; drain in a colander. Rinse with cold running water until cool; drain well.

3 Place pepper bottoms, cut sides up, on dinner plates. Mound slaw in pepper bottoms, allowing any extra to overflow onto plates. Sprinkle with sunflower kernels. Replace pepper tops.

nutrition facts per serving: 190 cal., 13 g total fat (3 g sat. fat), 24 mg chol., 597 mg sodium, 13 g carb., 4 g fiber, 9 g pro.

If whole fresh mangoes are intimidating or will take a little too much time to prep, look for the jarred fresh mango in the refrigerated section of the produce section.

mango chicken salad

start to finish: 30 minutes
makes: 4 servings

3 skinless, boneless
    chicken breast
    halves (12 to
    16 ounces total)
2 limes
1 cup unsweetened
    coconut milk
1 tablespoon soy sauce
½ teaspoon crushed red
    pepper
½ cup flaked
    unsweetened
    coconut
2 mangoes, seeded,
    peeled, and
    chopped
    Lettuce leaves

1 Preheat oven to 350°F. Cut chicken into bite-size pieces. Squeeze juice from 1 lime; set juice aside. Cut the remaining lime into wedges; set aside.

2 In a large saucepan stir together the lime juice, the coconut milk, soy sauce, and crushed red pepper. Add chicken. Bring to boiling; reduce heat. Cook, covered, for 12 to 15 minutes or until chicken is tender and no longer pink, stirring occasionally.

3 Meanwhile, spread coconut in a shallow baking pan. Bake, uncovered, for 4 to 5 minutes or until golden, stirring once.

4 Transfer chicken and cooking liquid to a large bowl. Add mangoes; toss to coat. Arrange lettuce leaves on serving plates; top with chicken mixture. Sprinkle with toasted coconut and serve with lime wedges.

nutrition facts per serving: 302 cal., 10 g total fat (7 g sat. fat), 62 mg chol., 381 mg sodium, 29 g carb., 4 g fiber, 27 g pro.

Look for the pomegranate seeds—also called arils—in small containers in the refrigerated case in the produce section of your supermarket. If you can't find them, check at a whole-foods or specialty-foods market.

wilted chicken salad with pomegranate dressing

start to finish: 30 minutes
makes: 4 servings

¾ cup pomegranate juice
2 tablespoons olive oil
1 14- to 16-ounce package chicken tenderloins
½ medium red onion, cut lengthwise into thin wedges
1 tablespoon snipped fresh oregano or ½ teaspoon dried oregano, crushed
¾ teaspoon coarsely ground black pepper
½ teaspoon salt
2 tablespoons red wine vinegar
2 6-ounce packages fresh baby spinach
½ cup pomegranate seeds
¼ cup slivered almonds, toasted*

1 In a small saucepan bring pomegranate juice to boiling; boil gently, uncovered, for 5 to 8 minutes or until reduced to ¼ cup. Remove from heat; set aside. Meanwhile, in a very large skillet heat 1 tablespoon of the oil over medium-high heat. Add chicken and cook for 6 to 8 minutes or until chicken is tender and no longer pink (170°F), turning occasionally. Remove chicken from skillet. Keep warm.

2 Add the remaining 1 tablespoon oil, the onion, dried oregano (if using), pepper, and salt to skillet; cook for 3 to 5 minutes or just until onion is tender, stirring occasionally. Stir in reduced pomegranate juice and vinegar; bring to boiling. Boil 1 minute. Remove skillet from heat. Stir in fresh oregano (if using). Gradually add spinach, tossing just until spinach is wilted.

3 Transfer spinach mixture to a large shallow dish. Top with chicken, pomegranate seeds, and almonds. Serve immediately.

nutrition facts per serving: 292 cal., 11 g total fat (2 g sat. fat), 58 mg chol., 425 mg sodium, 21 g carb., 4 g fiber, 27 g pro.

*tip: To toast almonds, spread nuts, in a shallow baking pan. Bake in a 350°F oven for 5 to 10 minutes or until light golden brown, stirring once or twice. Watch carefully so the nuts don't burn.

Poaching is a wonderful, low-fat way to cook and add flavor to foods at the same time. There is no added oil—and, in fact, it infuses the poultry, fish, or seafood with additional moisture.

poached lemon chicken salad

start to finish: 25 minutes
makes: 4 servings

1 lemon
1 pound skinless, boneless chicken breast halves
1 cup chicken broth
¼ teaspoon ground black pepper
2 cloves garlic, minced
4 cups thinly sliced vegetables, such as cucumber, radishes, and carrots
6 cups torn mixed salad greens
3 tablespoons olive oil
Salt
Ground black pepper

1 Using a vegetable peeler, remove yellow peel from lemon. Halve the lemon and set aside. Cut chicken into 2-inch pieces.

2 In a medium saucepan combine the lemon peel, the chicken, broth, the ¼ teaspoon pepper, and garlic. Bring to boiling; reduce heat. Simmer, covered, about 7 minutes or until chicken is tender and no longer pink. Drain, discarding liquid and lemon peel. Cool chicken slightly (about 5 minutes).

3 Using two forks, coarsely shred chicken. In a large bowl combine chicken and vegetables; toss to combine.

4 Divide chicken mixture among serving plates. Top with mixed greens. Drizzle with olive oil; squeeze lemon halves over salads. Season with salt and additional pepper.

nutrition facts per serving: 255 cal., 12 g total fat (2 g sat. fat), 66 mg chol., 495 mg sodium, 10 g carb., 4 g fiber, 29 g pro.

The normally high-fat blue cheese in anything labeled "Buffalo" is substituted here for light blue cheese wedges and fat-free blue cheese salad dressing. Same great tang, far fewer fat grams and calories.

buffalo chicken salad

start to finish: 15 minutes
makes: 4 servings

2   hearts romaine,
      sliced
3   cups coarsely
      chopped cooked
      chicken breast
½   cup Buffalo wing
      sauce, such as Wing
      Time brand
4   21-gram wedges light
      blue cheese, such
      as Laughing Cow
      brand, crumbled
1   teaspoon cracked
      black pepper
¼   cup bottled fat-free
      blue cheese salad
      dressing
4   teaspoons fat-free
      milk
4   stalks celery, each cut
      into 4 sticks

1 Divide romaine among four serving plates or bowls.

2 In a medium microwave-safe bowl combine chicken and wing sauce. Microwave on 100 percent power (high) about 60 seconds or until heated through. Evenly divide chicken mixture and spoon over romaine. Top with blue cheese and pepper.

3 In a small bowl combine salad dressing and milk; drizzle over salads. Serve with celery sticks.

nutrition facts per serving: 297 cal., 10 g total fat (3 g sat. fat), 99 mg chol., 596 mg sodium, 13 g carb., 3 g fiber, 37 g pro.

*Although there's no legal or medical definition of a "superfood,"
it is generally accepted to be a food that is a nutrient powerhouse
and that contributes to your overall health and well-being.
The superfoods in this recipe include strawberries, blueberries,
spinach, and walnuts.*

superfoods salad

start to finish: 25 minutes
makes: 4 servings

⅓ cup raspberry
vinegar
2 tablespoons snipped
fresh mint
2 tablespoons honey
1 tablespoon canola oil
¼ teaspoon salt
4 cups packaged fresh
baby spinach leaves
2 cups chopped cooked
chicken breast
(10 ounces)
2 cups fresh
strawberries, hulled
and sliced
½ cup fresh blueberries
¼ cup coarsely chopped
walnuts, toasted*
1 ounce semisoft goat
cheese, crumbled
½ teaspoon freshly
ground black
pepper

1 For vinaigrette, in a screw-top jar combine
vinegar, mint, honey, oil, and salt. Cover and
shake well.

2 In a large bowl toss together spinach,
chicken, strawberries, blueberries, walnuts,
and goat cheese. Transfer to salad plates. Drizzle
with vinaigrette and sprinkle with pepper.

nutrition facts per serving: 303 cal., 13 g total fat
(2 g sat. fat), 63 mg chol., 249 mg sodium, 22 g carb., 3 g fiber,
26 g pro.

✻tip: To toast nuts, spread them in a shallow
baking pan. Bake in a 350°F oven for 5 to
10 minutes or until light brown, shaking pan
once or twice. Watch carefully so the nuts
don't burn.

Serve this sweet-savory salad with crusty multigrain rolls or bread.

turkey salad with oranges

start to finish: 30 minutes
makes: 4 servings

1   5-ounce package
    arugula or baby
    spinach
2½ cups shredded
    cooked turkey or
    chicken (12 ounces)
1   large red sweet
    pepper, cut into
    strips (1 cup)
¼   cup snipped fresh
    cilantro
3   tablespoons orange
    juice
2   tablespoons peanut
    oil or canola oil
1   tablespoon honey
2   teaspoons lemon
    juice
2   teaspoons Dijon-style
    mustard
¼   teaspoon ground
    cumin
¼   teaspoon salt
¼   teaspoon ground
    black pepper
4   oranges, peeled and
    sectioned

1 In a large bowl toss together arugula, turkey, sweet pepper, and cilantro; set aside.

2 For vinaigrette, in a small bowl whisk together orange juice, oil, honey, lemon juice, mustard, cumin, salt, and black pepper. Drizzle vinaigrette over salad; toss gently to coat. Add orange sections to salad.

nutrition facts per serving: 281 cal., 8 g fat (1 g sat. fat), 71 mg chol., 263 mg sodium, 25 g carb., 5 g fiber, 28 g pro.

kitchen tip: Bagged greens labeled as "Ready to Eat" really are ready to eat! In fact, washing produce that has already been double- or triple-washed can actually increase the risk of cross-contamination. Whether you are buying whole heads of lettuce or bagged greens, look for the same qualities: Greens should be crisp, brightly colored, and free from blemishes. Look for greens that are not wilted or discolored.

The smoky flavor from the bacon and turkey is a delicious complement to the sweetness of the sugar snap peas in this crunchy salad.

smoked turkey and bacon salad

start to finish: 20 minutes
makes: 4 servings

5   slices low-sodium bacon
2   cups sugar snap peas
½   cup light mayonnaise
1   tablespoon Dijon-style mustard
1   tablespoon cider vinegar
1   tablespoon snipped fresh dill
1   small head romaine, torn
8   ounces smoked turkey breast, cut into bite-size strips

1 Line a 9-inch microwave-safe pie plate with paper towels. Arrange bacon slices in a single layer on top of paper towels. Cover with additional paper towels. Microwave on 100 percent power (high) for 4 to 5 minutes or until bacon is crisp. Carefully remove the pie plate from the microwave. Set cooked bacon slices aside to cool.

2 Meanwhile, in a covered medium saucepan cook the sugar snap peas in a small amount of boiling salted water for 2 to 4 minutes or until crisp-tender; drain. Crumble one bacon slice; set aside. Break remaining bacon slices into 1-inch pieces.

3 For dressing, in a small bowl combine mayonnaise, mustard, vinegar, and dill. Stir in crumbled bacon.

4 Divide romaine among four plates. Top with sugar snap peas, turkey, and bacon pieces. Serve with dressing.

nutrition facts per serving: 258 cal., 14 g total fat (3 g sat. fat), 68 mg chol., 601 mg sodium, 9 g carb., 3 g fiber, 23 g pro.

Serve this elegant Provençal-style salad with a glass of chilled white wine or rosé and crusty French bread.

fast niçoise salad

start to finish: 20 minutes
makes: 4 servings

2 teaspoons butter
2 cups refrigerated red
   potato wedges
6 cups mixed salad
   greens
3 2.6-ounce pouches
   lemon-pepper
   chunk light tuna*
1 cup cherry tomatoes
2 hard-cooked eggs,
   sliced
2 tablespoons white
   wine vinegar
2 tablespoons olive oil
½ teaspoon Dijon-style
   mustard
⅛ teaspoon ground
   black pepper

1 In a large skillet melt butter over medium heat. Add potatoes; cook, covered, about 15 minutes or until golden brown, stirring occasionally.

2 Meanwhile, divide greens among four plates. Top with tuna, tomatoes, egg slices, and potatoes.

3 For dressing, in a small bowl whisk together vinegar, oil, mustard, and pepper. Drizzle dressing over salads.

nutrition facts per serving: 247 cal., 12 g total fat (3 g sat. fat), 125 mg chol., 543 mg sodium, 14 g carb., 4 g fiber, 20 g pro.

*tip: If you can't find lemon-pepper tuna, use any herb-seasoned tuna.

Purchased pesto is a great convenience, but homemade is better—and it's easily stored. When you have an abundance of basil and time, make a batch and freeze it in small portions in an ice cube tray. When the pesto has frozen, pop the pesto cubes out of the tray into a resealable plastic bag. Place the bag back in the freezer for perfect portions of pesto whenever they're needed.

salmon, rice, and pesto salad

start to finish: 25 minutes
makes: 4 servings

1½ cups fresh sugar snap peas or 1-inch pieces fresh asparagus

1 8.8-ounce pouch cooked long grain and wild rice

¼ cup purchased basil or dried tomato pesto

¼ cup light mayonnaise

1 8-ounce piece smoked salmon, flaked and skin and bones removed

1 cup cherry tomatoes, halved

⅓ cup thinly sliced radishes

Lettuce leaves

1 In a medium saucepan cook sugar snap peas in a small amount of boiling lightly salted water for 2 minutes; drain. Place peas in a bowl of ice water to chill; drain.

2 In a large bowl combine cooked rice, pesto, and mayonnaise. Gently stir in sugar snap peas, smoked salmon, tomatoes, and radishes. Divide lettuce among four plates. Spoon salad over lettuce.

nutrition facts per serving: 312 cal., 14 g total fat (3 g sat. fat), 23 mg chol., 892 mg sodium, 28 g carb., 3 g fiber, 16 g pro.

Try a blend of greens here—arugula, watercress, and baby spinach— for the best flavor.

citrus salad with poached cod

start to finish: 25 minutes
makes: 4 servings

1 pound fresh or
frozen skinless
cod, haddock, or
salmon fillets, about
1 inch thick
3 limes
5 oranges
½ cup water
¼ cup olive oil
1 teaspoon sugar
Salt
Ground black pepper
4 cups arugula, fresh
baby spinach, and/
or watercress,
trimmed
Orange pieces
(optional)

1 Thaw fish, if frozen. Rinse fish; pat dry with paper towels. Finely shred 1 teaspoon peel from one of the limes; squeeze juice from lime. Squeeze juice from two of the oranges. In a small bowl combine lime juice and orange juice. Remove ¼ cup of the juices to use for dressing.

2 Pour the remaining juices into a large nonstick skillet; add shredded lime peel and the water. Bring to boiling. Add fish; reduce heat to medium. Simmer, covered, for 8 to 12 minutes or until fish flakes easily when tested with a fork.

3 Meanwhile, for dressing, in a small bowl whisk together the reserved ¼ cup juices, the oil, and sugar. Season with salt and pepper.

4 Thinly slice the remaining two limes and the remaining three oranges. Stack the citrus slices on dinner plates. Divide fish and arugula among citrus stacks. Whisk dressing; drizzle over salads. If desired, garnish with additional orange pieces.

nutrition facts per serving: 314 cal., 15 g total fat (2 g sat. fat), 49 mg chol., 141 mg sodium, 26 g carb., 6 g fiber, 23 g pro.

The saltiness of the feta cheese tastes terrific with the sweet, juicy watermelon in this whisper-light, summery salad.

shrimp and watermelon salad

start to finish: 20 minutes
makes: 4 servings

12 ounces fresh or frozen peeled, deveined medium shrimp

2 tablespoons olive oil

2 teaspoons snipped fresh thyme

4 cups sliced bok choy or napa cabbage

1 cup grape tomatoes, halved

Salt

Ground black pepper

2 1-inch slices seedless watermelon, halved

Small limes, halved

Fresh thyme sprigs

Feta cheese (optional)

1 Thaw shrimp, if frozen. Rinse shrimp; pat dry with paper towels. In a large skillet heat 1 tablespoon of the oil over medium-high heat. Add shrimp; cook and stir for 3 to 4 minutes or until shrimp are opaque. Transfer shrimp to a bowl; stir in snipped thyme.

2 Add the remaining 1 tablespoon oil, the bok choy, and tomatoes to skillet; cook and stir for 1 minute. Return shrimp to skillet; cook and stir for 1 minute more. Season with salt and pepper.

3 Serve shrimp and vegetables with watermelon. Squeeze lime juice on salads; sprinkle with thyme sprigs and, if desired, feta cheese.

nutrition facts per serving: 163 cal., 8 g total fat (1 g sat. fat), 107 mg chol., 477 mg sodium, 11 g carb., 2 g fiber, 14 g pro.

Serve these hearty salads with steak knives for carving the wedges down to size.

iceberg wedges with shrimp and blue cheese dressing

start to finish: 35 minutes
makes: 6 servings

1½ pounds fresh or frozen large shrimp in shells
3 tablespoons lemon juice
¼ teaspoon ground black pepper
½ cup light mayonnaise
¼ to ½ teaspoon bottled hot pepper sauce
2 tablespoons crumbled blue cheese
3 to 4 tablespoons fat-free milk
Nonstick cooking spray
1 large head iceberg lettuce, cut into 12 wedges
1 large tomato, chopped
⅓ cup thinly sliced, quartered red onion
2 slices turkey bacon, cooked and crumbled

1 Thaw shrimp, if frozen. Peel and devein shrimp, leaving tails intact if desired. Rinse shrimp; pat dry with paper towels. In a medium bowl combine shrimp, 2 tablespoons of the lemon juice, and ⅛ teaspoon of the black pepper. Toss to coat; set aside.

2 For dressing, in a small bowl combine the remaining 1 tablespoon lemon juice, the remaining ⅛ teaspoon black pepper, the mayonnaise, and hot pepper sauce. Stir in blue cheese. Stir in enough of the milk to make desired consistency.

3 Coat an unheated grill pan with cooking spray. Preheat grill pan over medium-high heat. Thread shrimp onto six 10- to 12-inch-long skewers.* Place skewers on grill pan. Cook for 3 to 5 minutes or until shrimp are opaque, turning once. (If necessary, cook shrimp skewers half at a time.)

4 Place two of the lettuce wedges on each of six serving plates. Top with shrimp, tomato, red onion, and bacon. Serve with dressing.

nutrition facts per serving: 190 cal., 10 g total fat (2 g sat. fat), 129 mg chol., 360 mg sodium, 8 g carb., 1 g fiber, 18 g pro.

＊tip: If using wooden skewers, soak skewers in enough water to cover for at least 30 minutes before using.

English cucumbers are longer and thinner than standard slicing cucumbers. They are considered seedless (or they have nearly indetectable seeds) and are usually found in the produce section wrapped in plastic.

gazpacho shrimp salad

start to finish: 30 minutes
makes: 6 servings

1½ pounds fresh or frozen extra-large or jumbo shrimp, unpeeled
1 recipe Red Pepper–Tomato Dressing
5 ripe large tomatoes, chopped
¾ cup chopped green sweet pepper, chopped
1 medium red onion, chopped
1 English cucumber, chopped
  Salt
  Ground black pepper
2 cups purchased crushed croutons
  Italian (flat-leaf) parsley

1 Thaw shrimp, if frozen. Peel and devein shrimp. Rinse shrimp; pat dry with paper towels. Fill a large skillet half full with lightly salted water; bring to boiling. Add shrimp; cook, uncovered, for 1 minute. Remove skillet from heat. Let shrimp stand in water for 1 to 2 minutes or until opaque. Remove with slotted spoon; set aside to cool.

2 Prepare Red Pepper–Tomato Dressing. In a large bowl toss together tomatoes, sweet pepper, onion, and cucumber. Season with salt and black pepper.

3 Divide dressing among 6 bowls. Top with vegetables, shrimp, croutons, and parsley.

nutrition facts per serving: 285 cal., 14 g total fat (2 g sat. fat), 115 mg chol., 371 mg sodium, 21 g carb., 4 g fiber, 19 g pro.

Red Pepper–Tomato Dressing: Drain one 12-ounce jar roasted red sweet peppers; discard liquid. In a blender combine the peppers; 2 ripe large tomatoes, quartered; ⅓ cup olive oil; 1 tablespoon vinegar; 1 clove garlic, minced; and 1 teaspoon smoked paprika. Cover and blend until very smooth. Stir in1 tablespoon vinegar. Season with salt and black pepper.

Escarole is a dark, leafy green that is loaded with nutrients. It is an excellent and hearty salad green when eaten raw. It is also delicious sauteed in olive oil and garlic and served as a hot vegetable side dish.

escarole and poached egg salad

start to finish: 20 minutes
makes: 4 servings

8 cups torn escarole or arugula
1 large tomato, halved
½ cup frozen peas, thawed
4 eggs
1 recipe Red Wine Vinaigrette
¼ cup finely shredded Parmesan cheese (1 ounce)
4 slices whole grain country-style bread, toasted

1 On a serving platter combine escarole, tomato, and peas; set aside.

2 In a deep large skillet add enough water to fill halfway. Bring water to simmer. Break eggs, one at a time, into a small cup and slide eggs into water. Cook eggs in simmering water for 4 to 5 minutes or until whites are firm and yolks begin to thicken. Remove eggs with slotted spoon; drain on paper towels.

3 Place eggs on top of salad. Drizzle with Red Wine Vinaigrette. Sprinkle with Parmesan cheese. Serve with toast.

nutrition facts per serving: 242 cal., 11 g total fat (2 g sat. fat), 186 mg chol., 333 mg sodium, 23 g carb., 8 g fiber, 13 g pro.

nutrition note: Eggs are a nutrient-dense food that are an excellent source of quality protein, only 75 calories, and are low in fat. One egg packs 6 grams of protein and 13 of the essential vitamins and minerals including vitamin D, selenium, riboflavin, phosphorus, and B$_{12}$. The American Heart Association recommends that you limit your average daily cholesterol intake to less than 300 milligrams. Balance out higher cholesterol meals with fruit and vegetables that have no cholesterol and are high in fiber, which help to lower cholesterol.

Red Wine Vinaigrette: In a screw-top jar combine 2 tablespoons red wine vinegar; 4 teaspoons olive oil; 1 teaspoon snipped fresh oregano or ½ teaspoon dried oregano, crushed; ½ teaspoon Dijon-style mustard; ¼ teaspoon cracked black pepper; and ⅛ teaspoon salt. Cover and shake well to combine.

tip: If you have trouble keeping your poached eggs intact, add a teaspoon or so of vinegar to the boiling water, then slip in the eggs. Vinegar helps the eggs keep their shape by quickly firming up and congealing the edges.

It's very important when preparing kale for eating raw or cooked that you cut out the center rib and discard it. It is very tough and not pleasant to eat.

southwest kale salad

start to finish: 30 minutes
makes: 6 servings

2 slices turkey bacon, cut crosswise into thin strips
1 cup fresh or frozen corn kernels
2 to 3 tablespoons water
2 tablespoons finely chopped shallot (1 medium)
½ teaspoon finely shredded lime peel
¼ cup lime juice
2 tablespoons olive oil
1 teaspoon honey
½ teaspoon salt
½ teaspoon ground ancho chile pepper
½ teaspoon ground coriander
⅛ teaspoon ground cumin
Dash cayenne pepper
1 bunch Tuscan or dinosaur kale* (about 12 ounces)
½ cup finely shredded carrot (1 medium)
½ cup roasted red sweet pepper, drained and chopped
⅓ cup dried cranberries
¼ cup pumpkin seeds (pepitas), toasted**

1 In a medium nonstick skillet cook bacon over medium heat until crisp. Using a slotted spoon, remove bacon and drain on paper towels. Discard drippings. In the same skillet combine corn, the water, and shallot. Cook, covered, over medium heat for 3 to 4 minutes or until corn is heated through; drain.

2 Meanwhile, for dressing, in a large bowl whisk together lime peel, lime juice, oil, honey, salt, ancho chile pepper, coriander, cumin, and cayenne pepper.

3 Remove and discard thick stems from kale. Coarsely chop leaves (you should have about 8 cups). On a serving platter arrange bacon, corn mixture, kale, carrot, roasted pepper, cranberries, and pumpkin seeds. Drizzle with dressing. Serve at room temperature.

nutrition facts per serving: 199 cal., 11 g total fat (2 g sat. fat), 4 mg chol., 309 mg sodium, 22 g carb., 3 g fiber, 7 g pro.

*tip: Tuscan kale has many different names—cavolo nero, black cabbage, lacinato, or dinosaur—to name a few. It has a better texture for raw preparations than the curly leaf variety.

**tip: To toast pumpkin seeds, scatter them in a dry small skillet and heat over medium heat just until golden. Stir frequently so they don't burn.

ham and vegetable soup

soups &
ste

9

These soul-soothing bowls of comfort taste like they simmered all day—but didn't. Packed with good-for-you ingredients, this is good-mood food.

WS

Combine refrigerated cooked beef tips in gravy with fresh vegetables and herbs, and you've got a comforting stew that tastes like Mom's long-simmered version in a fraction of the time.

sunday dinner stew

start to finish: 25 minutes
makes: 4 servings

1 pound small new potatoes
3 large carrots, halved lengthwise and cut up
1 17-ounce package refrigerated cooked beef tips in gravy
1¼ cups water
1 bunch green onions, chopped
Fresh thyme leaves (optional)

1 Scrub potatoes. Halve or quarter large potatoes so all pieces are about the same size. Place potatoes in a large microwave-safe bowl. Cover with vented plastic wrap. Microwave on 100 percent power (high) for 5 minutes. Add carrots; cover. Microwave for 5 to 7 minutes or just until potatoes and carrots are tender.

2 In a 4-quart Dutch oven combine potatoes and carrots, beef tips in gravy, and the water. Cook over medium-high heat just until bubbly around edges. Add green onions; cover and cook about 5 minutes more or until heated through. Ladle into bowls. If desired, sprinkle with thyme.

nutrition facts per serving: 302 cal., 9 g total fat (3 g sat. fat), 52 mg chol., 686 mg sodium, 36 g carb., 6 g fiber, 22 g pro.

Sunday Dinner Sweet Potato and Kale Stew: Prepare as directed, except substitute 1 pound sweet potatoes, peeled and cut up, for the new potatoes. Add 1 cup chopped kale with the green onions.

This dish is for the garlic-lovers in your life. Six whole cloves go into mashed potatoes that are topped with veggie-rich beef stew.

beef stew with garlic mash

start to finish: 25 minutes
makes: 4 servings

1   1-pound package frozen vegetable blend (carrots, peas, and onions)
½   cup water
1   17-ounce package refrigerated cooked beef tips in gravy
2   teaspoons Worcestershire sauce
6   cloves garlic
2   tablespoons water
1   pound Yukon gold or red potatoes, halved
2   tablespoons olive oil
¼   teaspoon salt
¼   teaspoon ground black pepper
2   tablespoons fresh oregano leaves

1 In a 4-quart Dutch oven combine frozen vegetables and the ½ cup water. Bring to boiling. Meanwhile, microwave beef tips according to package directions. Add beef and Worcestershire sauce to vegetables in Dutch oven. Reduce heat to low. Cook, covered, for 5 minutes or until vegetables are tender.

2 In a small microwave-safe bowl combine garlic and the 2 tablespoons water. Cover with vented plastic wrap. Microwave on 100 percent power (high) for 1 minute; set aside. In a large microwave-safe bowl microwave potatoes on 100 percent power (high) for 8 to 10 minutes, stirring once.

3 Peel and mash garlic. Add garlic, olive oil, salt, and pepper to potatoes. Mash with a potato masher or beat with an electric mixer on low speed. Divide potatoes among four dishes; top with stew and sprinkle with oregano.

nutrition facts per serving: 368 cal., 14 g total fat (3 g sat. fat), 47 mg chol., 888 mg sodium, 47 g carb., 8 g fiber, 24 g pro.

This old-fashioned soup made with ground beef will bring back memories for the older set—and create memories for the younger ones. Serve it with warm whole grain dinner rolls or crackers.

beefy vegetable soup

start to finish: 30 minutes
makes: 6 servings

1½ pounds lean ground beef
1 cup chopped onion (1 large)
1 cup sliced celery (2 stalks)
2 14-ounce cans lower-sodium beef broth
1 28-ounce can diced tomatoes, undrained
1 10-ounce package frozen mixed vegetables
2 tablespoons steak sauce
2 teaspoons Worcestershire sauce
¼ teaspoon salt
¼ teaspoon ground black pepper
¼ cup all-purpose flour

1 In a 4-quart Dutch oven cook ground beef, onion, and celery over medium-high heat until meat is brown, using a wooden spoon to break up meat as it cooks. Drain off fat.

2 Stir in 1 can of the broth, the tomatoes, frozen vegetables, steak sauce, Worcestershire sauce, salt, and pepper. Bring to boiling; reduce heat. Simmer, covered, for 15 to 20 minutes or until vegetables are tender.

3 In a medium bowl whisk together the remaining can of broth and the flour; stir into meat mixture. Cook and stir until thickened and bubbly. Cook and stir for 1 minute more.

nutrition facts per serving: 306 cal., 12 g total fat (5 g sat. fat), 74 mg chol., 747 mg sodium, 21 g carb., 4 g fiber, 27 g pro.

Top this lightning-fast chili with sour cream, shredded cheese, sliced green onions, or diced yellow onion, if you like.

easy texas-style chili

start to finish: 20 minutes
makes: 6 servings

12   ounces lean ground
        beef
 1   15-ounce can pinto
        beans, undrained
 1   cup bottled salsa
 ½   cup beef broth
 1   teaspoon chili
        powder
 ½   teaspoon ground
        cumin
        Light sour cream
        (optional)

1 In a large skillet cook meat over medium heat until brown, using a wooden spoon to break up meat as it cooks. Drain off fat.

2 Stir undrained beans, salsa, broth, chili powder, and cumin into meat. Bring to boiling; reduce heat. Simmer, covered, for 10 minutes. If desired, serve with sour cream.

nutrition facts per serving: 178 cal., 8 g total fat (3 g sat. fat), 36 mg chol., 442 mg sodium, 12 g carb., 4 g fiber, 15 g pro.

A single can of chipotle chile peppers in adobo sauce is usually too big for any one recipe. Divide the remainder of the can in 1- to 2-tablespoon portions and freeze in small plastic bags for future use.

chipotle chili with beans

start to finish: 25 minutes
makes: 4 servings

Nonstick cooking
   spray
8 ounces lean ground
   beef, uncooked
   ground chicken
   breast, or uncooked
   ground turkey
   breast
1 cup chopped onion
   (1 large)
1½ teaspoons ground
   cumin
2 14.5-ounce cans
   stewed tomatoes,
   undrained and cut
   up
1 15-ounce can red
   beans, rinsed and
   drained
1½ cups coarsely
   chopped red and/
   or yellow sweet
   peppers (2 medium)
½ cup water
2 to 3 teaspoons
   chopped canned
   chipotle peppers in
   adobo sauce
1 tablespoon snipped
   fresh oregano
¼ cup shredded
   reduced-fat cheddar
   cheese (1 ounce)
Lime wedges
   (optional)
Baked tortilla chips
   (optional)

1 Lightly coat a large saucepan with cooking spray; heat saucepan over medium-high heat. Add ground beef and onion; cook until meat is brown, using a wooden spoon to break up meat as it cooks. If necessary, drain off fat.

2 Stir in cumin. Cook and stir for 1 minute. Stir in tomatoes, beans, sweet peppers, the water, and chipotle peppers. Bring to boiling; reduce heat. Simmer, covered, for 5 minutes. Stir in oregano.

3 Sprinkle each serving with cheddar cheese. If desired, serve with lime wedges and tortilla chips.

nutrition facts per serving: 398 cal., 14 g total fat (6 g sat. fat), 57 mg chol., 1030 mg sodium, 40 g carb., 10 g fiber, 27 g pro.

A package of pureed vegetables in garlic-herb sauce provides the foundation for the liquid in this healthful Mexican-style pork stew.

green chile pork stew

start to finish: 30 minutes
makes: 4 servings

1   1-pound pork
     tenderloin
     Salt
     Ground black pepper
1   tablespoon olive oil
3   7-ounce packages
     frozen yellow
     carrots, spinach,
     and white bean
     medley in garlic-
     herb sauce,*
     thawed
1   4.5-ounce can diced
     green chiles,
     undrained
1   teaspoon ground
     cumin
1   cup water
     Fresh cilantro
     (optional)
     Lime wedges
     (optional)

1 Cut pork into ¾-inch pieces; sprinkle lightly with salt and pepper. In a 4-quart Dutch oven heat oil over medium-high heat. Add pork; cook for 4 to 5 minutes or until browned. Stir in two of the packages of thawed vegetables, the chiles, and the cumin.

2 In a food processor or blender combine the remaining package thawed vegetables and the water. Cover and process or blend until smooth.

3 Add pureed vegetables to pork mixure in Dutch oven. Bring to boiling; reduce heat. Simmer, covered, about 15 minutes or until pork is cooked through, stirring occasionally.

4 Ladle into soup bowls. If desired, top with cilantro and serve with lime wedges.

nutrition facts per serving: 297 cal., 11 g total fat (2 g sat. fat), 74 mg chol., 823 mg sodium, 21 g carb., 7 g fiber, 30 g pro.

*tip: If you can't find the frozen vegetable blend, in a medium bowl stir together one 15-ounce can navy beans, rinsed and drained; 1 cup frozen sliced carrots, thawed; half of a 10-ounce package frozen chopped spinach, thawed and well drained; and ¼ cup bottled Italian vinaigrette salad dressing. Stir 2 cups of the mixture into the pork with the chiles and cumin and blend the remaining 1 cup with the water. Continue as directed in Step 3.

Put a little reggae music on and make this a passport meal. Take a trip to the islands in just 30 minutes and be back in time for evening activities!

caribbean-style pork stew

start to finish: 30 minutes
makes: 6 servings

232

1 15-ounce can black beans, rinsed and drained
1 14.5-ounce can beef broth
1¾ cups water
12 ounces cooked lean pork, cut into bite-size strips
3 plantains, peeled and cubed
½ of a 16-ounce package (2 cups) frozen pepper stir-fry vegetables (yellow, green, and red sweet peppers and onion)
1 cup chopped tomatoes (2 medium)
1 tablespoon grated fresh ginger
1 teaspoon ground cumin
¼ teaspoon salt
¼ teaspoon crushed red pepper
3 cups hot cooked brown rice
   Crushed red pepper (optional)
   Fresh pineapple slices (optional)

1 In a 4-quart Dutch oven combine black beans, broth, and the water. Bring to boiling. Stir in pork, plantains, frozen vegetables, tomatoes, ginger, cumin, salt, and the ¼ teaspoon crushed red pepper.

2 Return to boiling; reduce heat. Simmer, covered, about 10 minutes or until plantains are tender. Serve stew with rice. If desired, sprinkle with additional crushed red pepper and garnish with pineapple slices.

nutrition facts per serving: 425 cal., 9 g total fat (3 g sat. fat), 52 mg chol., 547 mg sodium, 66 g carb., 6 g fiber, 26 g pro.

kitchen tip: Plantains are related to bananas, but they are higher in starch and lower in sugar than bananas. They are popular in African and Caribbean cooking and are used much like potatoes are used—always eaten cooked, never raw. Their skin turns from green to black as they ripen but the flesh stays creamy-white. They can be eaten at any stage of ripeness but are best cooked by different methods at different stages. For this stew, they are best used when green.

Light and brothy, but with a hearty touch from the ham, this soup is delicious served with warm corn bread.

ham and vegetable soup

start to finish: 30 minutes
makes: 4 servings

2 teaspoons canola oil
1 cup cubed low-fat, reduced-sodium cooked ham (5 ounces)
2 cups water
1 14.5-ounce can reduced-sodium chicken broth
12 ounces fresh peas or one 10-ounce package frozen baby peas
1 cup sliced carrots (2 medium)
1 cup sliced celery (2 stalks)
⅓ cup diagonally sliced green onions
1 tablespoon snipped fresh tarragon or ½ teaspoon dried tarragon, crushed
Lemon wedges
½ of a 6-ounce carton plain fat-free yogurt

1 In a large saucepan heat oil over medium heat. Add ham; cook, without stirring, over medium heat for 3 minutes. Stir ham; cook for 2 to 3 minutes more or until browned.

2 Add the water, broth, peas, carrots, celery, green onions, and tarragon. Bring to boiling; reduce heat. Simmer, covered, for 5 to 10 minutes or until peas and carrots are tender. Serve with lemon wedges and yogurt.

nutrition facts per serving: 176 cal., 4 g total fat (1 g sat. fat), 19 mg chol., 586 mg sodium, 21 g carb., 6 g fiber, 14 g pro.

soups & **stews**

This soup employs a smart trick for making a soup taste rich and creamy without the fat and calories contributed by heavy cream: evaporated milk.

creamy asparagus and bacon soup

prep: 15 minutes   cook: 15 minutes
makes: 4 servings

1¼   pounds fresh
      asparagus spears,
      trimmed
   1 12-ounce can
      evaporated milk
1¼   cups water
1¼   pounds potatoes,
      peeled and cut into
      ½-inch pieces
   ½ teaspoon salt
   ½ teaspoon ground
      black pepper
   6 slices bacon
   1 tablespoon honey
      Desired toppings,
      such as finely
      shredded lemon
      peel, snipped fresh
      Italian (flat-leaf)
      parsley, coarse
      salt, and/or freshly
      ground black
      pepper

1 Set aside about one-third of the asparagus. In a large saucepan combine the remaining asparagus, evaporated milk, the water, potatoes, the ½ teaspoon salt, and the ½ teaspoon pepper. Bring to boiling; reduce heat. Simmer, covered, about 10 minutes or until potatoes are tender. Cool slightly.

2 Transfer potato mixture, half at a time, to a food processor or blender. Cover and process or blend until smooth.

3 Meanwhile, in a large skillet cook bacon over medium heat until crisp. Remove bacon and drain on paper towels, reserving 1 tablespoon drippings in skillet. Crumble bacon; set aside. Add the reserved asparagus to the reserved drippings; cook for 5 to 6 minutes or until asparagus is crisp-tender, stirring occasionally.

4 Before serving, place crumbled bacon in a microwave-safe pie plate. Drizzle with honey. Cover with vented plastic wrap. Microwave on 100 percent power (high) for 30 seconds.

5 Top each serving with the reserved asparagus, honey-drizzled bacon, and your choice of toppings.

nutrition facts per serving: 356 cal., 15 g total fat (7 g sat. fat), 41 mg chol., 673 mg sodium, 43 g carb., 4 g fiber, 15 g pro.

To keep the spinach or other greens as vibrant and tasty as possible, stir them in right before serving so they are barely wilted.

chicken soup with spinach and orzo

start to finish: 20 minutes
makes: 6 servings

4	14.5-ounce cans reduced-sodium chicken broth
1	cup dried orzo pasta (rosamarina)
12	ounces fresh asparagus spears, trimmed and cut diagonally into 1½-inch pieces
3	cups chopped fresh spinach, Swiss chard, or kale or one 10-ounce package frozen chopped spinach, thawed and well drained
1½	cups chopped tomatoes (3 medium)
1½	cups shredded cooked chicken (8 ounces)
⅓	cup cubed cooked ham
	Salt
	Ground black pepper
	Snipped fresh chives and/or parsley (optional)

1 Pour broth into a 5- to 6-quart Dutch oven. Bring to boiling. Stir in pasta. Return to boiling; reduce heat. Simmer, uncovered, for 6 minutes. Stir in asparagus. Simmer, uncovered, about 2 minutes more or until pasta is tender and asparagus is crisp-tender.

2 Stir in spinach, tomatoes, chicken, and ham; heat through. Season with salt and pepper. If desired, sprinkle each serving with chives and/or parsley.

nutrition facts per serving: 221 cal., 4 g total fat (1 g sat. fat), 35 mg chol., 837 mg sodium, 28 g carb., 3 g fiber, 20 g pro.

kitchen tip: Fill your freezer with healthful, wholesome homemade soups. Here are a few things to keep in mind for best results:
Pasta, potatoes, and rice may soften when frozen and reheated. Undercook these ingredients by a minute or two when making soups for freezing.
Allow hot soup to cool in the refrigerator overnight before freezing to avoid the formation of large ice crystals, which can make the soup mushy.
Freeze soup in portion-size containers—either rigid plastic or zip-top plastic bags.
Label soups with recipe name and date of freezing.
For best results, allow frozen soup to thaw 24 hours in the refrigerator. If you're in a hurry, place the frozen soup in a saucepan with about 1 inch water. Cover the pan and bring water to boiling. Reduce heat to simmer, covered, for about 10 minutes, stirring occasionally.

The bok choy steams on top of the stew as it simmers so that it stays crisp-tender and clean-tasting.

spring chicken stew

start to finish: 30 minutes
makes: 4 servings

1   lemon
1¼ pounds skinless,
     boneless chicken
     thighs
     Salt
     Ground black pepper
1   tablespoon olive oil
1½ cups water
1   12-ounce jar chicken
     gravy
8   ounces baby carrots,
     halved lengthwise
1   tablespoon Dijon-
     style mustard
2   heads baby bok choy,
     quartered
     Snipped fresh lemon
     thyme (optional)

1 Finely shred peel from lemon; set peel aside. Juice lemon; set juice aside. Sprinkle chicken lightly with salt and pepper.

2 In a 4-quart Dutch oven heat oil over medium-high heat. Add chicken; cook for 2 to 3 minutes or until chicken is brown, turning occasionally.

3 Add the water, gravy, carrots, and mustard to chicken in Dutch oven. Bring to boiling; place bok choy on top. Reduce heat; simmer, covered, about 10 minutes or until chicken is no longer pink and vegetables are tender. Add lemon juice to taste.

4 Ladle stew into bowls. Top with lemon peel and, if desired, lemon thyme.

nutrition facts per serving: 273 cal., 12 g total fat (2 g sat. fat), 117 mg chol., 909 mg sodium, 13 g carb., 3 g fiber, 31 g pro.

Tiny grains of orzo pasta add a chewy bite to this soup. An added benefit: The pasta leaches starch into the soup as it simmers to help thicken the broth slightly and give it body.

chicken-pasta soup with pesto

start to finish: 25 minutes
makes: 4 servings

2   14.5-ounce cans reduced-sodium chicken broth
1   pound skinless, boneless chicken breast halves or thighs, cubed
1   14.5-ounce can diced tomatoes with basil, garlic, and oregano, undrained
½   cup dried orzo pasta (rosamarina)
1   cup chopped zucchini (1 small)
1   teaspoon finely shredded lemon peel
1   tablespoon lemon juice
    Ground black pepper
4   to 6 tablespoons purchased basil pesto

1 In a large saucepan combine broth, chicken, tomatoes, and uncooked orzo. Bring to boiling; reduce heat. Simmer, covered, for 6 minutes.

2 Add zucchini, lemon peel, and lemon juice. Return to boiling; reduce heat. Simmer, uncovered, for 3 to 4 minutes or until orzo and zucchini are tender and chicken is no longer pink. Season with pepper. Top each serving with pesto.

nutrition facts per serving: 371 cal., 12 g total fat (0 g sat. fat), 68 mg chol., 1180 mg sodium, 30 g carb., 1 g fiber, 35 g pro.

When you're sick—and even when you feel great—this comforting soup will make you feel better.

easy chicken noodle soup

start to finish: 30 minutes
makes: 6 servings

238

3 14.5-ounce cans
    reduced-sodium
    chicken broth
1 cup chopped onion
    (1 large)
1 cup sliced carrots
    (2 medium)
1 cup sliced celery
    (2 stalks)
1 cup water
2 teaspoons dried
    Italian seasoning,
    crushed
½ teaspoon ground
    black pepper
1 bay leaf
1 16-ounce package
    frozen egg noodles
2 cups chopped cooked
    chicken or turkey*
    (10 ounces)
2 tablespoons snipped
    fresh parsley
    (optional)

1 In a 3-quart saucepan combine broth, onion, carrots, celery, the water, Italian seasoning, pepper, and bay leaf. Bring to boiling; reduce heat. Simmer, covered, for 5 minutes. Stir in frozen noodles. Return to boiling; reduce heat. Simmer, covered, for 10 to 12 minutes or until noodles are tender but still firm and vegetables are crisp-tender.

2 Stir in chicken; heat through. Discard bay leaf. To serve, ladle soup into bowls. If desired, sprinkle with parsley.

nutrition facts per serving: 339 cal., 6 g total fat (2 g sat. fat), 130 mg chol., 554 mg sodium, 46 g carb., 3 g fiber, 23 g pro.

*tip: If you don't have any leftover chicken or turkey, use half of a 2- to 2½-pound whole or cut-up purchased roasted chicken from the supermarket deli, then skin, bone, and chop. Or, poach 12 ounces skinless, boneless chicken breast halves: Place chicken in a skillet with 1½ cups water. Bring to boiling; reduce heat. Simmer, covered, for 12 to 14 minutes or until chicken is tender and no longer pink. Drain; cut into cubes.

The secret ingredient that makes this chowder rich and thick is instant mashed potato flakes. They're a terrific timesaver over peeling, cooking, and mashing a potato.

fresh corn and chicken chowder

start to finish: 30 minutes
makes: 4 servings

12 ounces skinless, boneless chicken breast halves or chicken thighs
4 fresh ears corn
1 32-ounce box reduced-sodium chicken broth
½ cup chopped green sweet pepper (1 small)
1¼ cups instant mashed potato flakes
1 cup milk
Salt
Ground black pepper
Crushed red pepper (optional)

1 In a 4-quart Dutch oven combine chicken, corn, and broth. Bring to boiling; reduce heat. Simmer, covered, about 12 minutes or until chicken is no longer pink. Transfer chicken and corn to a cutting board.

2 Add ¼ cup of the sweet pepper to broth in Dutch oven. Stir in potato flakes and milk. Using two forks, shred chicken. Return chicken to Dutch oven.

3 Using a kitchen towel to hold hot corn, cut kernels from cobs. Add corn kernels to chowder in Dutch oven; heat through. Season with salt and black pepper. Top each serving with 1 tablespoon chopped sweet pepper. If desired, sprinkle with crushed red pepper.

nutrition facts per serving: 269 cal., 3 g total fat (1 g sat. fat), 54 mg chol., 721 mg sodium, 33 g carb., 3 g fiber, 29 g pro.

make-ahead directions: Prepare chowder as directed; let cool. Transfer chowder to an airtight container. Cover and store in the refrigerator for up to 3 days. Reheat chowder in the Dutch oven over medium heat until heated through.

The red-skinned potatoes in this rustic soup are roughly mashed so the soup has a creamy and chunky texture, all at the same time.

country chicken and potato soup

start to finish: 25 minutes
makes: 4 servings

2   14.5-ounce cans reduced-sodium chicken broth
1   20-ounce package refrigerated red-skinned potato wedges
½   cup chopped leek, white part only
2   to 3 cloves garlic, minced
2   cups chopped cooked chicken (10 ounces)
1   tablespoon snipped fresh chives
⅛   teaspoon ground black pepper
1   cup half-and-half, light cream, or milk
Whole fresh chives
Garlic-flavor olive oil* (optional)

1 In a large saucepan combine 1 can of the broth, the potatoes, leek, and garlic. Bring to boiling; reduce heat. Simmer, covered, for 5 minutes. Remove from heat.

2 Using a potato masher, slightly mash potatoes, leaving some potato pieces. Add chicken, snipped chives, and pepper. Stir in the remaining broth and half-and-half; heat through.

3 Top each serving with whole chives and, if desired, a few drops of garlic-flavor oil.

nutrition facts per serving: 319 cal., 12 g total fat (6 g sat. fat), 85 mg chol., 707 mg sodium, 23 g carb., 4 g fiber, 28 g pro.

*tip: To make your own garlic-flavor olive oil, in a small skillet heat 2 tablespoons olive oil over medium heat. Add 1 clove garlic, minced; cook and stir until garlic begins to brown. Remove from heat. Strain to remove garlic. Discard any unused oil (do not store).

kitchen tip: Leeks look like oversized green onions. But while the leek and the scallion are related, they are not one and the same. Leeks are also related to garlic, and they have a milder flavor than other onions. To clean, cut off the root end and remove the dark green leaves, leaving the white and light green stalk. Cut leeks in half lengthwise and run under cool water between the layers to wash out any dirt or grit.

Serve this refined chili with warmed tortillas. Tightly wrap tortillas in aluminum foil and place in a 350°F oven for 10 minutes or until warm and pliable.

white bean chicken chili

start to finish: 25 minutes
makes: 6 servings

1 tablespoon olive oil
1 cup chopped onion (1 large)
1¾ pounds chicken breast tenderloins, cut into quarters
3 cloves garlic, minced
1 1.5-ounce packet taco seasoning mix
1 cup water
1 15.5-ounce can cannellini beans (white kidney beans) rinsed and drained
1 13.75-ounce can artichoke hearts, drained and cut into quarters
1 cup chopped tomatoes (2 medium)
1 tablespoon snipped fresh cilantro (optional)

1 In a very large skillet heat oil over medium-high heat. Add onion; cook for 3 to 5 minutes or until tender. Add chicken, garlic, and ½ teaspoon of the taco seasoning mix; cook about 5 minutes or until the chicken is no longer pink.

2 Stir the water and the remaining taco seasoning into the chicken mixture. Bring to boiling. Add beans, artichoke hearts, and tomatoes. Return to boiling; reduce heat. Simmer, uncovered, for 5 minutes. Ladle into bowls. If desired, sprinkle with cilantro.

nutrition facts per serving: 289 cal., 4 g total fat (1 g sat. fat), 77 mg chol., 1039 mg sodium, 24 g carb., 4 g fiber, 36 g pro.

Crispy tortilla strips top this veggie-packed Mexican-style soup.

turkey tortilla soup

start to finish: 20 minutes
makes: 6 servings

2 tablespoons canola oil
3 6-inch corn tortillas, cut into strips
2 14.5-ounce cans reduced-sodium chicken broth
1 cup chunky salsa*
2 cups cubed cooked turkey, chicken, pork, or beef (10 ounces)
2 cups coarsely chopped zucchini (2 small)
   Light sour cream (optional)
   Snipped fresh cilantro (optional)
   Lime wedges (optional)

1 In a large skillet heat oil over medium heat. Add tortilla strips; cook about 3 minutes or until crisp and golden brown, tossing occasionally with tongs. Use the tongs to remove tortilla strips from skillet; drain on paper towels.

2 Meanwhile, in a large saucepan combine broth and salsa. Bring to boiling over medium-high heat. Stir in turkey and zucchini; heat through.

3 Ladle soup into bowls. If desired, top with sour cream and cilantro. Serve with tortilla strips. If desired, serve with lime wedges.

*tip: Read the nutritional facts on the labels of the salsas available at your grocery store and choose the salsa that's lowest in sodium.

nutrition facts per serving: 173 cal., 7 g total fat (1 g sat. fat), 35 mg chol., 614 mg sodium, 10 g carb., 2 g fiber, 17 g pro.

This soup is a favorite for a simple post-Thanksgiving meal when you have leftover bird and are looking for creative ways to use it. If your family can't eat all of the leftovers at once, freeze the meat in 2-cup portions and use it over the next few months instead of the next few days.

turkey and rice soup

start to finish: 30 minutes
makes: 6 servings

2   14.5-ounce cans
    reduced-sodium
    chicken broth
1½ cups water
1   teaspoon snipped
    fresh rosemary or
    ¼ teaspoon dried
    rosemary, crushed
¼   teaspoon black
    pepper
½   cup thinly sliced
    carrot
    (1 medium)
½   cup thinly sliced
    celery
    (1 stalk)
⅓   cup thinly sliced
    onion
    (1 small)
1   cup instant brown
    rice
1   cup frozen cut green
    beans
2   cups chopped cooked
    turkey or chicken
    breast (10 ounces)
1   14.5-ounce can
    no-added-salt
    diced tomatoes,
    undrained

1 In a large saucepan or Dutch oven combine broth, the water, fresh or dried rosemary, and pepper. Add carrot, celery, and onion. Bring to boiling.

2 Stir in uncooked rice and frozen green beans. Return to boiling; reduce heat. Cover and simmer for 10 to 12 minutes or until vegetables are tender.

3 Stir in turkey and tomatoes; heat through.

nutrition facts per serving: 143 cal., 1 g total fat (0 g sat. fat), 39 mg chol., 384 mg sodium, 16 g carb., 3 g fiber, 18 g pro.

make-ahead directions: Prepare soup through Step 2. Thoroughly chill the mixture. Stir in the cooked turkey and tomatoes. Ladle into airtight containers and store in refrigerator for up to 3 days. Place soup in large saucepan or Dutch oven; cook over medium heat until heated through.

Cioppino is an Italian fisherman's stew that originated on the docks of San Francisco. It's made with different combinations of fish and shellfish, depending on the cook—but always with tomatoes.

easy cioppino

start to finish: 30 minutes
makes: 8 servings

2   pounds fresh or
     frozen skinless
     salmon, cod, and/or
     sea scallops
3   tablespoons olive oil
2   fennel bulbs, trimmed
     and thinly sliced
4   cloves garlic, minced
3   cups coarsely
     chopped tomatoes
     (3 large)
1   14- to 15-ounce can
     fish stock or chicken
     broth
2   teaspoons snipped
     fresh oregano or
     1 teaspoon dried
     oregano, crushed
½   teaspoon anise seeds,
     crushed (optional)
     Salt
     Freshly ground black
     pepper
     Fennel fronds or
     shredded fresh basil
     (optional)

1 Thaw fish and/or scallops, if frozen. Rinse fish and/or scallops; pat dry with paper towels. If using fish, cut into 2-inch pieces; set aside.

2 In a 4- to 6-quart Dutch oven heat oil over medium heat. Add sliced fennel; cook about 10 minutes or until tender, stirring occasionally. Add garlic; cook and stir for 1 minute more.

3 Add tomatoes, fish stock, dried oregano (if using), and, if desired, anise seeds to fennel mixture in Dutch oven. Bring to boiling. Stir in fish and/or scallops. Return to boiling; reduce heat. Simmer, uncovered, for 6 to 8 minutes or until fish flakes easily when tested with a fork and scallops are opaque.

4 Season with salt and pepper. Stir in fresh oregano (if using). If desired, top individual servings with fennel fronds.

nutrition facts per serving: 178 cal., 6 g total fat (1 g sat. fat), 49 mg chol., 169 mg sodium, 9 g carb., 3 g fiber, 22 g pro.

A bowl of this creamy pink soup, served with crusty bread and a green salad, makes a meal. A cup of it is an elegant starter to a formal dinner.

fast shrimp bisque

start to finish: 25 minutes
makes: 4 servings

12   ounces fresh or
      frozen medium
      shrimp in shells
2   cups water
1   cup thinly sliced
      celery (2 stalks)
2   teaspoons reduced-
      sodium Old Bay
      Seasoning or other
      reduced-sodium
      seafood seasoning
1   12-ounce can
      evaporated milk
1   cup milk
2   tablespoons all-
      purpose flour
1½   teaspoons anchovy
      paste or 1 or
      2 anchovies, finely
      chopped
      Old Bay Seasoning
      or other seafood
      seasoning (optional)

1 Thaw shrimp, if frozen. In a 4-quart Dutch oven combine shrimp, the water, celery, and the 2 teaspoons Old Bay Seasoning. Bring to boiling; reduce heat. Simmer, uncovered, for 5 to 8 minutes or until shrimp shells turn pink and shrimp are opaque. Using a slotted spoon or tongs, remove shrimp; set aside to cool.

2 In a medium bowl whisk together evaporated milk, milk, flour, and anchovy paste; stir into liquid in Dutch oven. Cook, uncovered, over medium heat for 10 minutes, stirring occasionally.

3 Peel shrimp. Chop about half of the shrimp. Add chopped shrimp to soup; cook for 1 to 2 minutes or until heated through. Ladle soup into bowls. Top with the remaining shrimp. If desired, pass additional Old Bay Seasoning.

nutrition facts per serving: 212 cal., 8 g total fat (4 g sat. fat), 177 mg chol., 811 mg sodium, 16 g carb.,17 g pro.

This cooling soup is very similar to gazpacho—with the addition of cooked shrimp to make it heartier.

shrimp cocktail soup

start to finish: 30 minutes
makes: 6 servings

3 cups peeled, seeded, and chopped ripe tomatoes (6 medium)
1¾ cups peeled, seeded, and chopped cucumber (1 medium)
½ cup finely chopped green sweet pepper (1 small)
⅓ cup finely chopped red onion (1 small)
2 cloves garlic, minced
2 cups tomato juice
1 14.5-ounce can reduced-sodium chicken broth
¼ cup red wine vinegar
2 tablespoons snipped fresh basil or 2 teaspoons dried basil, crushed
½ teaspoon salt
¼ to ½ teaspoon bottled hot pepper sauce
¼ teaspoon ground black pepper
12 ounces chopped, peeled, and deveined cooked shrimp
Lime wedges (optional)

1 In a very large bowl combine tomatoes, cucumber, sweet pepper, red onion, and garlic. Stir in tomato juice, broth, vinegar, basil, salt, hot pepper sauce, and black pepper. Stir in shrimp.

2 Ladle soup into bowls. If desired, serve with lime wedges.

nutrition facts per serving: 109 cal., 1 g total fat (0 g sat. fat), 111 mg chol., 734 mg sodium, 11 g carb., 2 g fiber, 16 g pro.

make-ahead directions: Prepare as directed except do not add shrimp. Cover soup and chill for up to 24 hours. Before serving, stir in shrimp.

246

soups & stews
no cook

248

Italians love the combination of pasta and beans in soup. The most famous is pasta e fagioli (literally, "pasta and beans").

minestrone

start to finish: 20 minutes
makes: 4 servings

1   28-ounce can diced
     tomatoes with
     Italian herbs,
     undrained
2   cups water
1   14- to 15-ounce can
     garbanzo beans
     (chickpeas), rinsed
     and drained
1   cup dried rigatoni or
     penne pasta
1   cup low-sodium
     vegetable broth
½   cup chopped yellow
     sweet pepper
     (1 medium)
2   teaspoons dried
     Italian seasoning,
     crushed, or
     1 teaspoon each
     dried basil and
     garlic powder
2   to 3 cups baby
     spinach
     Shaved Parmesan
     and/or fresh basil
     (optional)

1 In a 4-quart Dutch oven combine tomatoes, the water, garbanzo beans, pasta, broth, sweet pepper, and Italian seasoning. Bring to boiling; reduce heat. Cook, covered, for 10 minutes or just until pasta is barely tender, stirring occasionally.

2 Stir spinach into soup. Ladle into bowls. If desired, top with Parmesan cheese and/or fresh basil.

nutrition facts per serving: 234 cal., 2 g total fat (0 g sat. fat), 0 mg chol., 759 mg sodium, 46 g carb., 7 g fiber, 10 g pro.

tip: For a heartier version of this soup, substitute browned Italian sausage or cut-up chicken for the garbanzo beans. Vary the greens by swapping chopped fresh chard or kale for the spinach.

Stir in some cubed tofu with the frozen vegetables to make this soup heartier, if you like.

curried vegetable soup

start to finish: 20 minutes
makes: 4 servings

3   cups cauliflower
     florets
1   14.5-ounce can
     vegetable broth
1   14-ounce can
     unsweetened
     coconut milk
¼   cup snipped fresh
     cilantro
1   tablespoon curry
     powder
¼   teaspoon salt
2   cups frozen
     baby peas and
     vegetables blend
     Crushed red pepper
     (optional)
     Snipped fresh cilantro
     (optional)
1   recipe Curry Pita
     Crisps (optional)

1 In a 4-quart Dutch oven combine cauliflower, broth, coconut milk, the ¼ cup cilantro, the curry powder, and salt. Bring to boiling; reduce heat. Simmer, covered, about 10 minutes or until cauliflower is tender. Stir in frozen vegetables; heat through.

2 Ladle soup into bowls. If desired, sprinkle with crushed red pepper and additional cilantro and serve with Curry Pita Crisps.

nutrition facts per serving: 138 cal., 6 g total fat (4 g sat. fat), 0 mg chol., 620 mg sodium, 19 g carb., 4 g fiber, 3 g pro.

Curry Pita Crisps: Preheat broiler. Cut 2 pita bread rounds into wedges. Brush both sides of wedges with 1 tablespoon olive oil; place on a large baking sheet. Sprinkle with ¼ teaspoon curry powder. Broil 3 to 4 inches from heat about 4 minutes or until golden, turning once.

In Italian cooking, the term "Florentine" refers to dishes that contain spinach. The story goes that Catherine de Medici introduced spinach to the court of France, and—to honor her roots—dubbed anything containing spinach, "Florentine."

tortellini florentine soup

start to finish: 30 minutes
makes: 6 servings

1   9-ounce package refrigerated 3-cheese tortellini
2   14.5-ounce cans reduced-sodium chicken or vegetable broth
1   10-ounce container refrigerated light Alfredo pasta sauce
2   cups shredded deli-roasted chicken (10 ounces)
½   cup oil-packed dried tomato strips, drained
3   cups lightly packed packaged fresh baby spinach
1   ounce Parmesan cheese, shaved or shredded (optional)

1 In a 4-quart Dutch oven cook tortellini according to package directions. Drain and set aside.

2 In the same Dutch oven combine broth and Alfredo sauce. Stir in chicken and tomato strips. Bring to boiling; reduce heat. Simmer, uncovered, for 5 minutes.

3 Add cooked tortellini and spinach to chicken mixture; cook for 1 to 2 minutes or until heated through and spinach is wilted. Serve in bowls. If desired, top with Parmesan cheese.

nutrition facts per serving: 286 cal., 15 g total fat (6 g sat. fat), 77 mg chol., 1094 mg sodium, 21 g carb., 1 g fiber, 20 g pro.

To save time, you can use frozen chopped sweet peppers. You can buy them, but you can also stock up when fresh peppers are on sale and chop and freeze your own. Frozen chopped peppers work perfectly in soups such as this one.

pepper and basil tortellini soup

start to finish: 20 minutes
makes: 4 servings

1   14.5-ounce can Italian-style stewed tomatoes, undrained
1   14.5-ounce can reduced-sodium chicken or vegetable broth
1¼ cups water
1   9-ounce package refrigerated three-cheese tortellini
1½ cups chopped red and/or yellow sweet peppers (2 medium)
⅓   cup snipped fresh basil
    Grated Parmesan cheese (optional)

1 In a large saucepan combine tomatoes, chicken broth, and the water; bring to boiling. Add tortellini and sweet peppers. Return to boiling; reduce heat. Simmer, covered, about 7 minutes or until tortellini is tender. Stir in basil. If desired, sprinkle Parmesan cheese over individual servings.

nutrition facts per serving: 245 cal., 5 g total fat (2 g sat. fat), 30 mg chol., 816 mg sodium, 40 g carb., 3 g fiber, 13 g pro.

Top bowls of this soup with freshly grated Pecorino Romano or Parmesan cheese, if you like.

tuscan bean soup

start to finish: 20 minutes
makes: 4 servings

3 tablespoons olive oil
1 cup packaged peeled fresh baby carrots, coarsely chopped
⅓ cup chopped onion (1 small)
1 32-ounce carton reduced-sodium chicken broth
2 15-ounce cans cannellini beans (white kidney beans), rinsed and drained
2 to 3 teaspoons dried Italian seasoning, crushed
1 5-ounce package fresh baby spinach
Freshly cracked black pepper
Crisp breadsticks (optional)

1 In a 4-quart Dutch oven heat 1 tablespoon of the oil over medium-high heat. Add carrots and onion; cook and stir for 3 minutes. Add broth, beans, and Italian seasoning; bring to boiling. Mash beans slightly with a potato masher; reduce heat. Simmer, uncovered, for 8 minutes, stirring occasionally.

2 Meanwhile, in a large skillet heat the remaining 2 tablespoons oil over medium-high heat. Add spinach; cook for 1 to 2 minutes or just until wilted, tossing constantly with tongs. Remove from heat.

3 Ladle soup into bowls. Top with spinach and sprinkle with pepper. If desired, serve with crisp breadsticks.

nutrition facts per serving: 254 cal., 11 g total fat (2 g sat. fat), 0 mg chol., 919 mg sodium, 36 g carb., 12 g fiber, 16 g pro.

Serve this light and refreshing soup with bread or pita and hummus to bulk up the meal a bit.

garden vegetable gazpacho

start to finish: 20 minutes
makes: 4 servings

1 In a large bowl combine tomatoes, sweet pepper, green onions, basil, and garlic. Stir in tomato juice, chicken broth, lemon juice, pepper, salt, and hot pepper sauce.

2 To serve, ladle soup into chilled soup bowls or mugs. If desired, garnish with basil leaves.

nutrition facts per serving: 41 cal., 1 g total fat (0 g sat. fat), 0 mg chol., 162 mg sodium, 9 g carb., 2 g fiber, 2 g pro.

2¼ cups chopped, peeled
    tomatoes
    (3 medium)
½ cup chopped yellow
    or green sweet
    pepper
¼ cup thinly sliced
    green onions (2)
1 tablespoon snipped
    fresh basil or
    ½ teaspoon dried
    basil, crushed
1 clove garlic, minced
1 5.5-ounce can
    reduced-sodium
    tomato juice
½ cup reduced-sodium
    chicken broth or
    vegetable broth
1 tablespoon lemon
    juice
    Dash freshly ground
    black pepper
⅛ teaspoon salt
    Several dashes
    bottled hot pepper
    sauce
    Fresh basil leaves
    (optional)

make-ahead directions: Prepare as directed. Cover and chill for up to 24 hours.

Spring garlic is the immature bulbs of regular garlic. Also called green garlic, spring garlic has a much milder flavor than mature garlic—which is why this recipe calls for four cloves of regular garlic or 1 to 2 bulbs of spring garlic.

hearty garlic and snap pea soup

start to finish: 30 minutes
makes: 4 servings

2   tablespoons olive oil
4   cloves garlic, or 1 to
     2 bulbs spring
     garlic, chopped
¼   cup chopped onion
1   pound Yukon gold
     potatoes, quartered
2   14.5-ounce cans
     reduced-sodium
     chicken broth or
     vegetable broth
1¾   cups water
1   medium fennel bulb,
     thinly slivered
     (fronds reserved)
1½   cups sugar snap
     peas, trimmed
½   teaspoon salt
¼   teaspoon ground
     black pepper
1   tablespoon fresh
     snipped fennel
     fronds
     Plain yogurt
     (optional)
     Olive oil (optional)

1 In a large saucepan heat the 2 tablespoons oil over medium heat. Add garlic; cook for 1 minute. Add onion; cook until tender. Add potatoes, chicken broth, and the water. Bring to boiling; reduce heat. Simmer, covered, for 15 to 18 minutes or until potatoes are tender. Cool slightly.

2 Using a food processor or blender, puree soup in batches until smooth. Return to saucepan. Add fennel and peas. Bring to boiling; reduce heat. Simmer, uncovered, for 3 minutes.

3 Stir in salt and pepper. Ladle soup into bowls. Sprinkle with fennel fronds. If desired, serve with yogurt and drizzle with additional oil.

nutrition facts per serving: 102 cal., 3 g total fat (0 g sat. fat), 0 mg chol., 404 mg sodium, 15 g carb., 3 g fiber, 3 g pro.

soups & **stews**

If you have an immersion blender, use it to puree this creamy soup right in the pot rather than transferring it to a blender or food processor to do the job.

cream of fennel and potato soup

start to finish: 30 minutes
makes: 4 servings

1	tablespoon olive oil
3	cups chopped fennel (1½ pounds)
¾	cup chopped yellow onion
1	clove garlic, minced
2½	cups reduced-sodium chicken broth
8	ounces yellow-flesh potatoes, peeled and sliced
¾	cup fat-free milk
¼	teaspoon dried thyme, crushed
8	ounces uncooked bulk turkey Italian sausage
1½	teaspoons lemon juice
	Slivered green onions (optional)

1 In a large saucepan heat oil over medium heat. Add fennel, yellow onion, and garlic; cook for 5 to 6 minutes or until fennel and onion are tender, stirring occasionally. Add broth, potatoes, milk, and thyme. Bring to boiling; reduce heat. Simmer, covered, for 10 to 15 minutes or until potatoes are tender. Cool slightly.

2 Meanwhile, in a medium nonstick skillet cook sausage over medium heat until brown, using a wooden spoon to break up sausage as it cooks; drain off fat.

3 Transfer potato mixture, half at a time, to a food processor or blender. Cover and process or blend until smooth. Return pureed mixture to saucepan. Stir in sausage and lemon juice; heat through.

4 Ladle soup into serving bowls. If desired, sprinkle with green onions.

nutrition facts per serving: 254 cal., 9 g total fat (2 g sat. fat), 39 mg chol., 831 mg sodium, 29 g carb., 7 g fiber, 17 g pro.

shrimp pasta diavolo

pasta &
noo

10

Bring some fun to the table! Saucy takes on Italian, American, and Asian favorites feature toothsome noodles mingling with vegetables, herbs, meats, and seafood to make a meal everyone will enjoy.

dles

This deconstructed lasagna has all of the same elements of traditional layered lasagna—ruffled and ribbony noodles, meat, cheese, and tomato sauce—but it can be on the table in 30 minutes or less.

quick skillet lasagna

start to finish: 30 minutes
makes: 6 servings

3   cups dried mafalda (mini lasagna) noodles (6 ounces)
12 ounces lean ground beef or bulk pork sausage
1   26- to 27¾-ounce jar tomato-based pasta sauce
1½ cups shredded part-skim mozzarella cheese (6 ounces)
¼   cup grated Parmesan cheese (1 ounce)

1 Cook pasta according to package directions; drain.

2 Meanwhile, in a large nonstick skillet cook meat over medium-high heat until brown, using a wooden spoon to break up meat as it cooks; drain off fat. Remove meat from skillet; set aside. Wipe skillet with paper towels.

3 Spread about half of the cooked pasta into the skillet. Cover with half of the pasta sauce. Spoon meat over sauce. Sprinkle with 1 cup of the mozzarella cheese. Top with remaining pasta and sauce. Sprinkle the remaining ½ cup mozzarella and the Parmesan cheese over top.

4 Cook, covered, over medium heat for 5 to 7 minutes or until heated through and cheese melts. Remove skillet from heat and let stand, covered, for 1 minute.

nutrition facts per serving: 358 cal., 14 g total fat (6 g sat. fat), 57 mg chol., 784 mg sodium, 32 g carb., 3 g fiber, 25 g pro.

nutrition note: Buying lean ground beef is a first line of defense against consuming too much fat. You can reduce the amount of fat in your food even more by cooking and then rinsing ground meats such as ground beef and sausage in a colander under hot running tap water. Just be sure it is completely drained before proceeding with the recipe.

Orange marmalade provides the sweet and cider vinegar kicks in the sour in this quick-to-cook Asian-style noodle dish.

sweet-and-sour pork lo mein

start to finish: 20 minutes
makes: 4 servings

1   9-ounce package
    refrigerated
    linguine
2   tablespoons canola
    oil
1½ cups packaged
    julienned or
    shredded fresh
    carrot
1   large onion, cut into
    thin wedges
12 ounces boneless pork
    loin, trimmed of fat
    and cut into thin
    strips
⅓   cup orange
    marmalade
¼   cup cider vinegar
    Salt
    Ground black pepper
    Chopped peanuts
    (optional)

1 If desired, snip linguine into 2- to 3-inch lengths. Cook linguini according to package directions; drain.

2 Meanwhile, in a large skillet heat 1 tablespoon of the oil over medium-high heat. Add carrot and onion; cook and stir about 4 minutes or just until onion is tender. Remove vegetables from skillet. Add the remaining 1 tablespoon oil and the pork to skillet; cook and stir for 3 to 4 minutes or until pork is no longer pink. Return vegetables to skillet.

3 Add drained linguini, marmalade, and vinegar to pork mixture in skillet; toss to mix. Heat through. Season with salt and pepper. If desired, sprinkle with chopped peanuts.

nutrition facts per serving: 452 cal., 12 g total fat (3 g sat. fat), 121 mg chol., 252 mg sodium, 60 g carb., 4 g fiber, 27 g pro.

Sage, pumpkin, and pork make this the perfect meal for a cool fall night.

sage-fried pork and pumpkin noodle bowls

start to finish: 30 minutes
makes: 4 servings

1   pound pork loin, trimmed of fat and cut into ½-inch slices
3   tablespoons reduced-sodium soy sauce
     Ground black pepper
8   ounces dried whole wheat linguine
1   small red onion, cut into thin wedges
1   tablespoon olive oil
12   fresh sage leaves
1   cup water
1   cup canned pumpkin
2   cloves garlic, minced, or ½ teaspoon garlic powder
¼   cup crumbled blue cheese (1 ounce) (optional)

1 Brush pork with some of the soy sauce; sprinkle with pepper; set aside. Cook linguine according to package directions, adding the onion for the last 5 minutes of cooking. Drain.

2 Meanwhile, in a very large skillet heat oil over medium-high heat. Add sage leaves; cook about 1 minute or until crisp. Using a slotted spoon, remove sage leaves from skillet; drain on paper towels.

3 Add pork slices to skillet; cook about 4 minutes or until golden on the outside, slightly pink inside, and juices run clear (160°F), turning once halfway through cooking. Remove pork from skillet. Cover and keep warm.

4 Add the water, ¼ cup of the pumpkin, the remaining soy sauce, and the garlic to skillet. Bring to boiling. Cook, uncovered, for 1 to 2 minutes or until slightly reduced. Add pasta mixture to skillet; heat through.

5 Divide pasta mixture among four bowls. Top pasta with pork and, if desired, blue cheese.

6 Return skillet to heat; add the remaining ¾ cup pumpkin. Heat through. Spoon over pasta. Garnish with sage leaves.

nutrition facts per serving: 414 cal., 9 g total fat (2 g sat. fat), 71 mg chol., 645 mg sodium, 51 g carb., 2 g fiber, 34 g pro.

Traditional Spaghetti alla Carbonara made with bacon and whole eggs usually runs nearly 600 calories and 30 grams of fat for a 1-cup serving. This version offers a significant savings on both counts—with no sacrifice in flavor.

spaghetti alla carbonara

start to finish: 30 minutes
makes: 6 servings

6 ounces dried multigrain spaghetti
3 ounces thinly sliced pancetta
1 medium yellow or red sweet pepper, seeded and cut into bite-size strips
½ cup chopped onion (1 medium)
4 cloves garlic, minced
⅓ cup dry white wine
¾ cup fat-free half-and-half
½ cup refrigerated egg product
3 ounces grated Pecorino Romano cheese
Freshly ground black pepper
Fresh Italian (flat-leaf) parsley sprigs (optional)

1 Cook spaghetti according to package directions; drain and keep warm.

2 Meanwhile, remove and discard some of the fat from the pancetta. Coarsely chop pancetta. In a large nonstick skillet cook pancetta over medium heat until brown. Remove pancetta and drain on paper towels, reserving drippings in skillet. Add sweet pepper and onion to the drippings; cook over medium heat for 8 to 10 minutes or until very tender, stirring occasionally. Add garlic; cook and stir for 30 seconds.

3 Remove skillet from heat. Add wine; return skillet to heat. Cook for 2 to 4 minutes or until most of the wine is evaporated. Add half-and-half. Bring just to boiling, stirring constantly. Add pancetta and cooked spaghetti; toss to coat. Remove from heat. Add egg product and half of the Pecorino Romano cheese; quickly toss to coat.

4 Divide spaghetti among serving plates. Sprinkle with the remaining cheese and black pepper. If desired, garnish with parsley.

nutrition facts per serving: 391 cal., 14 g total fat (6 g sat. fat), 32 mg chol., 504 mg sodium, 40 g carb., 4 g fiber, 23 g pro.

nutrition note: As the name suggests, multigrain pasta is made from several types of grain. It is higher in fiber and lower in carbohydrates than traditional white-flour pasta. Some brands of multigrain pasta also include ground flaxseed and legumes, which can boost protein content. Read the label to be sure.

Bucatini, also called perciatelli, is a long, thick tubular pasta that is similar to spaghetti but larger in scale.

bucatini and bacon

start to finish: 25 minutes
makes: 4 servings

8   ounces dried bucatini or fusilli pasta
3   cups fresh baby spinach
1   28-ounce can whole peeled tomatoes with basil, undrained
6   slices bacon, crisp-cooked, drained, and crumbled
3   cloves garlic, minced
½   cup freshly grated Pecorino Romano cheese
    Salt
    Freshly ground black pepper
    Freshly grated Pecorino Romano cheese (optional)

1 In a Dutch oven cook pasta according to package directions; drain. Return pasta to hot Dutch oven. Stir in spinach; cover Dutch oven.

2 Meanwhile, drain tomatoes, reserving liquid. Snip the tomatoes into bite-size pieces. In a medium saucepan add snipped tomatoes, bacon, and garlic. Bring to boiling; reduce heat. Simmer, uncovered, for 10 minutes, stirring occasionally.

3 Add tomato mixture to pasta mixture; cook until heated through, tossing gently to coat pasta and adding some of the reserved tomato liquid if mixture is dry. Stir in the ½ cup Pecorino Romano cheese. Season with salt and pepper. If desired, sprinkle each serving with additional cheese.

nutrition facts per serving: 355 cal., 9 g total fat (4 g sat. fat), 24 mg chol., 845 mg sodium, 51 g carb., 4 g fiber, 17 g pro.

*Fresh acorn squash cooks
perfectly in the microwave
in just 7 to 10 minutes.
Pureed and flavored with
chicken broth and sage, it
makes a creamy bed for the
chicken and gnocchi.*

chicken
and gnocchi with squash

start to finish: 20 minutes
makes: 4 servings

1   1-pound package
    shelf-stable potato
    gnocchi
1   small acorn squash,
    halved and seeded
2   tablespoons water
14 to 16 ounces chicken
    breast tenderloins
    Salt
    Ground black pepper
1   tablespoon canola oil
¾   cup chicken broth
1   tablespoon snipped
    fresh sage
2   tablespoons milk
    Tiny whole sage
    leaves (optional)
    Grated nutmeg
    (optional)

1 Prepare gnocchi according to package
directions; drain. Cover and keep warm.

2 Meanwhile, place squash, cut sides down,
in a microwave-safe baking dish; add the
water. Cover with vented clear plastic wrap.
Microwave on 100 percent power (high) for 7 to
10 minutes, rearranging squash once. Let stand,
covered, for 5 minutes.

3 Sprinkle chicken with salt and pepper. In a
large skillet heat oil over medium-high heat.
Add chicken; cook for 6 to 8 minutes or until no
longer pink. Remove chicken from skillet; keep
warm.

4 Scrape flesh from squash into a medium
bowl. Mash with a potato masher or beat
with an electric mixer on low speed. Transfer
mashed squash to hot skillet; stir in broth and
the 1 tablespoon sage. Bring to boiling; simmer
for 1 minute. Stir in milk. Spoon mashed squash
into serving bowls. Top with chicken and
gnocchi. If desired, top with sage leaves and
sprinkle with nutmeg.

nutrition facts per serving: 366 cal., 6 g total fat (1 g sat.
fat), 59 mg chol., 796 mg sodium, 50 g carb., 4 g fiber, 29 g pro.

Broccolini is similar to broccoli but has smaller florets and longer, thinner stalks.

chicken and pasta in peanut sauce

start to finish: 20 minutes
makes: 4 servings

264

6   ounces dried thin spaghetti
1   bunch broccolini, cut into 2-inch lengths
1   red sweet pepper, cut into bite-size strips
1   pound skinless, boneless chicken breast halves
    Salt
    Ground black pepper
1   tablespoon olive oil
½   cup bottled peanut sauce
    Crushed red pepper (optional)

1 In a Dutch oven cook spaghetti according to package directions, adding broccolini and sweet pepper during the last 2 minutes of cooking; drain. Return pasta and vegetables to the Dutch oven; set aside.

2 Meanwhile, halve chicken breasts horizontally.* Lightly sprinkle chicken with salt and black pepper. In a very large skillet heat oil over medium-high heat. Add chicken; cook about 4 minutes or until chicken is no longer pink (170°F), turning once. Transfer chicken to a cutting board. Slice chicken; add to pasta and vegetables. Heat through. Add peanut sauce. If desired, pass crushed red pepper.

nutrition facts per serving: 427 cal., 13 g total fat (2 g sat. fat), 47 mg chol., 659 mg sodium, 49 g carb., 4 g fiber, 28 g pro.

*tip: The safest way to cut the chicken breasts in half horizontally is to lay a breast flat on the work surface. Place one hand firmly on top of the chicken, pressing down lightly to hold it steady. Use the other hand to hold the knife horizontally and cut through the meat.

Reserve some of the pasta cooking water to loosen the sauce, if necessary, after you've stirred everything together.

chicken and sweet pepper linguine alfredo

start to finish: 25 minutes
makes: 4 servings

6 ounces dried whole wheat linguine
2 teaspoons canola oil
1 medium red sweet pepper, cut into thin strips
2 medium zucchini and/or yellow summer squash, halved lengthwise and sliced (about 2½ cups)
8 ounces packaged chicken stir-fry strips*
1 10-ounce container refrigerated light Alfredo pasta sauce
⅓ cup finely shredded Parmesan, Pecorino Romano, or Asiago cheese (optional)
2 teaspoons snipped fresh thyme
⅛ teaspoon freshly ground black pepper

1 Break linguine in half. Cook linguine according to package directions; drain. Return to hot pan. Cover and keep warm.

2 Meanwhile, heat 1 teaspoon of the oil in a large skillet over medium-high heat. Add sweet pepper; cook and stir for 2 minutes. Add zucchini; cook and stir for 2 to 3 minutes more or until vegetables are crisp-tender. Remove from skillet.

3 Add the remaining 1 teaspoon oil to skillet. Add chicken; cook and stir for 2 to 3 minutes or until no longer pink. Return vegetables to skillet. Stir in Alfredo sauce; heat through.

4 Add chicken-vegetable mixture, Parmesan cheese (if desired), and thyme to cooked linguine; toss gently to coat. Sprinkle with black pepper.

nutrition facts per serving: 364 cal., 12 g total fat (5 g sat. fat), 54 mg chol., 485 mg sodium, 43 g carb., 5 g fiber, 24 g pro.

*tip: If you prefer, cut skinless, boneless chicken breast halves into thin strips.

Real risotto can take 35 to 40 minutes just in stirring time. This "pastafied" version takes just 15 minutes.

chicken with greek orzo risotto

start to finish: 25 minutes
makes: 4 servings

4   skinless, boneless
    chicken breast
    halves (about
    1¼ pounds total)
    Salt
    Ground black pepper
2   tablespoons olive oil
3   cups reduced-sodium
    chicken broth
2   cloves garlic, minced
1   cup dried orzo pasta
    (rosamarina)
¾   cup quartered cherry
    tomatoes
½   cup crumbled feta
    cheese (2 ounces)
¼   cup sliced pitted ripe
    olives
1   tablespoon snipped
    fresh oregano

1 Lightly sprinkle chicken with salt and pepper. In a very large skillet heat 1 tablespoon of the oil over medium heat. Add chicken; cook for 8 to 12 minutes or until chicken is no longer pink (170°F), turning once.

2 Meanwhile, for risotto, in a medium saucepan bring broth and garlic to boiling; reduce heat and simmer. In a large saucepan heat the remaining 1 tablespoon oil over medium heat. Add orzo; cook and stir for 1 minute. Slowly add ½ cup of the hot broth to orzo, stirring constantly. Continue to cook and stir over medium heat until broth is absorbed. Continue adding broth, ½ cup at a time, stirring constantly until broth is absorbed and mixture is creamy. (This should take about 15 minutes.) Remove from heat.

3 Stir tomatoes, feta cheese, olives, and oregano into risotto. Serve chicken with risotto.

nutrition facts per serving: 451 cal., 14 g total fat (4 g sat. fat), 99 mg chol., 952 mg sodium, 35 g carb., 2 g fiber, 44 g pro.

kitchen tip: To keep fresh herbs such as oregano, parsley, and basil fresh longer, wrap them in a moist paper towel and store in a plastic bag in the refrigerator.

Most Asian-style noodle dishes rely on peanut butter as a base for the creamy, sweet, and spicy sauce. This twist uses almond butter instead.

almond noodle bowl

start to finish: 30 minutes
makes: 5 servings

1 teaspoon toasted sesame oil
4 cloves garlic, minced
¼ teaspoon crushed red pepper (optional)
¼ cup almond butter
¼ cup canned unsweetened light coconut milk
1 tablespoon lime juice
1 tablespoon reduced-sodium soy sauce
½ teaspoon ground ginger
4 ounces dried whole grain spaghetti
1 tablespoon olive oil
1 pound skinless, boneless chicken breast halves, cut into 1-inch pieces
1 16-ounce package frozen stir-fry vegetables
2 tablespoons water
¼ cup fresh cilantro leaves
2 tablespoons chopped dry roasted whole almonds (optional)

1 For sauce, in a small skillet heat sesame oil over medium heat. Add garlic and, if desired, crushed red pepper; cook and stir about 1 minute or until garlic starts to brown. Stir in almond butter until melted. Stir in coconut milk, lime juice, soy sauce, and ginger; set aside.

2 Cook spaghetti according to package directions; drain.

3 Meanwhile, in a large skillet heat olive oil over medium-high heat. Add chicken; cook and stir for 4 to 5 minutes or until no longer pink. Stir in vegetables and the water; cook, covered, about 5 minutes or until vegetables are crisp-tender, stirring occasionally. Stir in sauce and spaghetti. Sprinkle with cilantro and, if desired, almonds.

nutrition facts per serving: 338 cal., 14 g total fat (2 g sat. fat), 58 mg chol., 282 mg sodium, 26 g carb., 5 g fiber, 26 g pro.

The grape tomatoes are just barely warmed at the end of the cooking time. The heat brings out their juiciness but they retain their shape and add texture to the dish.

pasta with chicken, spinach, tomatoes, and feta

start to finish: 35 minutes
makes: 6 servings

4 ounces dried whole grain penne pasta
Nonstick cooking spray
1¼ pounds skinless, boneless chicken breast halves
3 tablespoons canola oil or olive oil
2 tablespoons red wine vinegar
1 teaspoon finely shredded orange peel
2 tablespoons orange juice
1 tablespoon honey
1 tablespoon Dijon-style mustard
½ teaspoon salt
¼ teaspoon ground black pepper
1 teaspoon canola oil or olive oil
3 cups grape tomatoes, halved
4 cloves garlic, minced
10 ounces fresh baby spinach
¾ cup crumbled feta cheese or goat cheese (chèvre) (3 ounces)

1 Cook pasta according to package directions; drain.

2 Meanwhile, lightly coat the rack of an indoor electric grill* with cooking spray. Preheat grill. Place chicken on grill rack. If using a grill with a cover, close lid. Grill until chicken is no longer pink (170°F). For a covered grill, allow about 6 minutes. For an uncovered grill, allow 12 to 15 minutes, turning once halfway. Cut chicken into bite-size pieces.

3 For dressing, in a small bowl whisk together the 3 tablespoons oil, vinegar, orange peel, orange juice, honey, mustard, salt, and pepper; set aside.

4 In a 5- to 6-quart Dutch oven heat the 1 teaspoon oil over medium-high heat. Add tomatoes and garlic; cook for 1 minute, stirring frequently. Stir in cooked pasta and chicken; remove from heat.

5 Gradually add spinach and dressing to chicken mixture, tossing gently until spinach is slightly wilted. Transfer mixture to a serving bowl. Sprinkle with feta cheese.

nutrition facts per serving: 320 cal., 14 g total fat (3 g sat. fat), 73 mg chol., 538 mg sodium, 23 g carb., 4 g fiber, 26 g pro.

*tip: To cook chicken in a grill pan, place each chicken breast half between two pieces of plastic wrap. Using the flat side of a meat mallet, pound chicken lightly until about ½ inch thick. Remove plastic wrap. Coat a grill pan with nonstick cooking spray; heat pan over medium-high heat. Add chicken; cook for 10 to 12 minutes or until no longer pink (170°F), turning once.

With artichokes, garlic, Kalamata olives, tomatoes, mozzarella, and basil, this has all of the elements of a standard-bearing Italian pasta dish that nearly everyone will love.

italian penne

start to finish: 30 minutes
makes: 4 servings

3   ounces dried whole
    grain penne pasta
    (1 cup)
    Nonstick cooking
    spray
⅓   cup chopped onion
    (1 small)
2   cloves garlic, minced
1   14.5-ounce can
    no-salt-added
    diced tomatoes,
    undrained
1¼ cups chopped roma
    tomatoes
1   14-ounce can
    quartered
    artichokes, drained
    and halved
1   cup chopped cooked
    chicken breast
    (5 ounces)
¼   cup Kalamata olives,
    sliced
⅛   teaspoon salt
⅛   teaspoon freshly
    ground black
    pepper
2   ounces fresh
    mozzarella cheese,
    coarsely chopped
2   tablespoons fresh
    basil leaves

1 Cook pasta according to package directions; drain and set aside.

2 Lightly coat a large saucepan with cooking spray; heat saucepan over medium heat. Add onion; cook about 3 minutes or just until tender. Add garlic; cook for 1 minute more. Stir in tomatoes, artichokes, chicken, and olives. Cook and stir about 5 minutes or until heated through.

3 Stir cooked pasta into the tomato mixture, tossing gently to mix well. Heat through. Sprinkle with salt and pepper. Top with fresh mozzarella cheese and basil.

nutrition facts per serving: 256 cal., 6 g total fat (2 g sat. fat), 40 mg chol., 614 mg sodium, 30 g carb., 6 g fiber, 19 g pro.

If you'd like, you can add more heat to this dish with a little crushed red pepper stirred in with the peanut sauce—or sprinkled on top at serving time.

peanut-sauced shrimp and pasta

start to finish: 20 minutes
makes: 4 servings

12 ounces fresh or
    frozen peeled and
    deveined medium
    shrimp
½ of a 14-ounce
    package dried
    medium rice
    noodles
1 tablespoon canola oil
12 ounces fresh
    asparagus spears,
    trimmed and cut
    into 2-inch pieces
    (3 cups)
1 large red and/
    or yellow sweet
    pepper, cut into
    ¾-inch pieces
    (1 cup)
½ cup bottled peanut
    sauce

1 Thaw shrimp, if frozen. Rinse shrimp; pat dry with paper towels.

2 Place noodles in a large bowl. Bring 4 cups water to boiling; pour boiling water over noodles in bowl. Let stand for 10 minutes.

3 Meanwhile, in a large skillet heat oil over medium-high heat. Add shrimp, asparagus, and sweet pepper; cook and stir for 3 to 5 minutes or until shrimp are opaque. Add peanut sauce; heat through.

4 Drain noodles. Divide noodles among shallow serving bowls, using a fork to twist noodles into nests. Top with shrimp mixture.

nutrition facts per serving: 396 cal., 9 g total fat (2 g sat. fat), 129 mg chol., 642 mg sodium, 55 g carb., 5 g fiber, 21 g pro.

Cornstarch helps thicken the broth-based sauce without adding butter or cream.

rotini with shrimp and spinach

start to finish: 20 minutes
makes: 4 servings

12 ounces fresh or
     frozen peeled and
     deveined medium
     shrimp
6 ounces dried rotini or
     other pasta
1 tablespoon olive oil
3 cloves garlic, minced
1 cup chicken broth
1 tablespoon
     cornstarch
1 teaspoon dried basil,
     crushed
1 teaspoon dried
     oregano, crushed
4 cups fresh baby
     spinach or torn
     spinach
     Finely shredded
     Parmesan cheese
     (optional)

1 Thaw shrimp, if frozen. In a large pot cook pasta according to package directions; drain. Return pasta to pot. Cover and keep warm.

2 Meanwhile, rinse shrimp; pat dry with paper towels. In a large skillet heat oil over medium-high heat. Add garlic; cook and stir for 15 seconds. Add shrimp; cook and stir for 2 to 3 minutes or until shrimp are opaque. Remove from skillet.

3 In a small bowl combine broth, cornstarch, basil, and oregano. Add mixture to skillet; cook and stir until thickened and bubbly. Add spinach; cook and stir for 1 to 2 minutes more or just until spinach starts to wilt. Return shrimp to skillet.

4 Add shrimp mixture to cooked pasta; toss gently to combine. If desired, sprinkle each serving with Parmesan cheese.

nutrition facts per serving: 333 cal., 7 g total fat (1 g sat. fat), 136 mg chol., 422 mg sodium, 39 g carb., 3 g fiber, 25 g pro.

Keeping the tails on the shrimp looks prettier, but it does make eating it a little more difficult. In most cases, it's best to cut the tails off when the shrimp is being incorporated into a dish.

shrimp and winter greens with pasta

start to finish: 25 minutes
makes: 4 servings

12 ounces fresh or frozen peeled and deveined shrimp, with tails if desired
6   ounces dried multigrain or whole grain rotini or penne pasta
1   tablespoon olive oil
4   cloves garlic, thinly sliced
½   teaspoon ground black pepper
4   cups coarsely chopped fresh kale and/or Swiss chard
1   14.5-ounce can no-salt-added diced tomatoes with basil, garlic, and oregano, undrained
1   8-ounce can no-salt-added tomato sauce
⅓   cup pitted Kalamata olives, halved
¼   cup shredded Parmesan cheese (1 ounce)

1 Thaw shrimp, if frozen. Cook pasta according to package directions; drain.

2 Meanwhile, rinse shrimp; pat dry with paper towels. In a very large nonstick skillet heat oil over medium-high heat. Add shrimp and garlic; cook for 3 to 4 minutes or until shrimp are opaque, stirring occasionally. (If shrimp or garlic brown too quickly, reduce heat to medium.) Sprinkle with ¼ teaspoon of the pepper; toss to coat. Remove shrimp and garlic from skillet.

3 Add kale to the same skillet; cook and stir for 3 to 4 minutes or just until tender. Stir in tomatoes, tomato sauce, olives, the remaining ¼ teaspoon pepper, cooked pasta, and shrimp mixture. Cook and stir for 2 to 3 minutes or until heated through.

4 Divide shrimp mixture among serving plates. Sprinkle with Parmesan cheese.

nutrition facts per serving: 377 cal., 9 g total fat (1 g sat. fat), 112 mg chol., 771 mg sodium, 53 g carb., 15 g fiber, 23 g pro.

Use a lemon reamer or juicer to maximize the amount of juice you get from the lemon, rather than just squeezing it with your hands.

lemon shrimp and pasta

start to finish: 25 minutes
makes: 4 servings

12 ounces frozen peeled
    and deveined
    medium shrimp,
    thawed
1 lemon
8 ounces dried
    fettucine
2 tablespoons olive oil
3 to 4 cloves garlic,
    thinly sliced
6 cups fresh baby
    spinach
½ teaspoon dried Italian
    seasoning, crushed
    Salt
    Freshly ground black
    pepper
    Fresh dill (optional)

1 Rinse shrimp; pat dry with paper towels. Finely shred 1 teaspoon peel from the lemon. Juice the lemon over a bowl; set aside peel and juice. Cook pasta according to package directions; drain.

2 Meanwhile, in a very large skillet heat oil over medium heat. Add garlic; cook for 1 minute. Add shrimp; cook for 3 to 4 minutes or until shrimp are opaque, turning frequently. Add spinach and cooked pasta; toss just until spinach begins to wilt. Stir in Italian seasoning, lemon peel, and 2 tablespoons of the lemon juice. Season with salt and pepper. If desired, top with fresh dill. Serve at once.

nutrition facts per serving: 359 cal., 9 g total fat (1 g sat. fat), 107 mg chol., 696 mg sodium, 50 g carb., 5 g fiber, 21 g pro.

tip: Another time, substitute bite-size pieces of deli-roasted chicken for the shrimp. For a peppery bite, replace half the spinach with arugula.

"Diavolo" means "devil" in Italian and refers to the presence of hot chiles in a dish. In this case, the heat comes from crushed red pepper.

shrimp pasta diavolo

start to finish: 20 minutes
makes: 4 servings

12 ounces medium fresh shrimp, peeled and deveined
8 ounces dried linguine
2 tablespoons olive oil
1 medium onion, cut into thin wedges
3 cloves garlic, minced
¼ teaspoon crushed red pepper
1 14.5-ounce can diced tomatoes, undrained
2 cups fresh baby spinach
½ cup torn fresh basil
½ cup finely shredded Parmesan cheese (2 ounces) (optional)

1 Rinse shrimp; pat dry with paper towels. In a large pot cook linguine according to package directions. Drain pasta; set aside.

2 Meanwhile, in a large skillet heat oil over medium-high heat. Add onion, garlic, and crushed red pepper; cook until tender. Stir in tomatoes. Bring to boiling; reduce heat. Simmer, uncovered, for 3 minutes. Add shrimp to skillet; simmer, covered, for 3 minutes or until shrimp are opaque.

3 Stir in spinach and basil. Serve over cooked pasta. If desired, top each serving with Parmesan cheese.

nutrition facts per serving: 367 cal., 9 g total fat (1 g sat. fat), 107 mg chol., 702 mg sodium, 51 g carb., 4 g fiber, 21 g pro.

A generous helping of meaty shiitake and cremini or button mushrooms not only add flavor and texture to this dish but also bulk it up.

shrimp and mushroom pasta

start to finish: 30 minutes
makes: 4 servings

12 ounces fresh or frozen medium shrimp in shells
6 ounces dried whole grain angel hair pasta or spaghetti
1 tablespoon olive oil
8 ounces fresh shiitake mushrooms, stemmed and chopped
8 ounces fresh cremini or button mushrooms, sliced
2 cloves garlic, minced
1 14.5-ounce can no-salt-added diced tomatoes, undrained
2 teaspoons snipped fresh oregano
¼ teaspoon freshly ground black pepper
¼ teaspoon salt
   Fresh oregano sprigs or snipped fresh parsley (optional)

1 Thaw shrimp, if frozen. Peel and devein shrimp, leaving tails intact (if desired). Rinse shrimp; pat dry with paper towels. Set aside.

2 Cook pasta according to package directions; drain. Return pasta to hot pan. Cover and keep warm.

3 Meanwhile, for sauce, in a very large nonstick skillet heat oil over medium-high heat. Add mushrooms and garlic; cook and stir for 4 minutes. Stir in tomatoes, the snipped oregano, pepper, and salt. Bring to boiling; reduce heat. Simmer, uncovered, for 5 to 10 minutes or until thickened. Stir in shrimp. Cook, covered, about 2 minutes more or until shrimp are opaque.

4 Serve shrimp mixture over hot cooked pasta. If desired, garnish with oregano sprigs.

nutrition facts per serving: 322 cal., 6 g total fat (1 g sat. fat), 129 mg chol., 338 mg sodium, 39 g carb., 6 g fiber, 29 g pro.

Scallops are quickly seared and served warm from the pan on top of a cool noodle salad for an interesting contrast in textures, tastes, and temperatures.

seared scallops with noodle salad

start to finish: 30 minutes
makes: 4 servings

12 fresh or frozen sea scallops (about 18 ounces total)
4 ounces dried brown rice fettuccine or banh pho (Vietnamese wide rice noodles)
¼ cup orange juice
2 tablespoons rice vinegar
2 tablespoons toasted sesame oil
1 teaspoon finely shredded lime peel
1 teaspoon grated fresh ginger
½ teaspoon salt
1½ cups chopped fresh spinach leaves
1 cup chopped cucumber
⅔ cup coarsely shredded daikon or thinly sliced radishes
¼ teaspoon ground black pepper
Nonstick cooking spray
2 tablespoons sesame seeds, toasted*

1 Thaw scallops, if frozen. Cook fettuccine according to package directions; drain. Rinse with cold water; drain again.

2 In a large bowl combine orange juice, vinegar, sesame oil, lime peel, ginger, and ¼ teaspoon of the salt. Add cooked fettuccine, spinach, cucumber, and daikon; toss gently to coat. Set aside.

3 Rinse scallops; pat dry with paper towels. Sprinkle with the remaining ¼ teaspoon salt and the pepper.

4 Coat a large nonstick skillet with cooking spray; heat skillet over medium-high heat. Add scallops; cook for 3 to 5 minutes or until scallops are opaque, turning once. Serve scallops with fettuccine mixture. Sprinkle with sesame seeds.

nutrition facts per serving: 297 cal., 10 g total fat (2 g sat. fat), 31 mg chol., 817 mg sodium, 31 g carb., 2 g fiber, 19 g pro.

✽tip: To toast sesame seeds, scatter them in a dry small skillet and heat over medium heat just until golden. Stir frequently so they don't burn.

Except for the broccoli raab, nearly all of these ingredients store well in the pantry or refrigerator for a satisfying last-minute pasta meal. Serve with a glass of chilled white wine.

pasta with broccoli raab and clams

start to finish: 25 minutes
makes: 6 servings

278

12 ounces dried pasta
2 tablespoons olive oil
1 pound broccoli raab, trimmed and cut into 2-inch pieces, or 3 cups broccoli florets
3 cloves garlic, sliced
1 13-ounce can whole baby clams
¼ cup butter
½ cup dry white wine
½ teaspoon crushed red pepper
¼ teaspoon ground black pepper
¼ cup grated Parmesan cheese

1 Cook pasta according to package directions; drain. Return pasta to hot pan. Cover and keep warm.

2 Meanwhile, in a very large skillet heat oil over medium-high heat. Add broccoli raab and garlic; cook for 5 minutes, stirring occasionally. Stir in undrained clams and butter. Cook over medium heat until butter is melted.

3 Stir in wine, crushed red pepper, and black pepper. Bring just to boiling; reduce heat. Simmer, uncovered, about 2 minutes or until mixture is slightly reduced.

4 Serve broccoli raab mixture over cooked pasta. Sprinkle each serving with Parmesan cheese.

nutrition facts per serving: 433 cal., 15 g total fat (6 g sat. fat), 68 mg chol., 467 mg sodium, 57 g carb., 4 g fiber, 21 g pro.

One of the nicest things about roma tomatoes—also called plum tomatoes—is that they taste fairly good most of the year, even when tomatoes are not in season. They are especially good for making quick homemade sauces.

pasta puttanesca

start to finish: 30 minutes
makes: 4 servings

6 ounces dried thin spaghetti
2 tablespoons olive oil
1 clove garlic, thinly sliced
2 cups peeled and chopped roma tomatoes (6 medium)
½ cup coarsely chopped pitted Kalamata or ripe olives
4 to 5 anchovy fillets, chopped
1 teaspoon drained capers, chopped
½ teaspoon ground black pepper
¼ to ½ teaspoon crushed red pepper
¼ cup snipped fresh Italian (flat-leaf) parsley

1 Cook spaghetti according to package directions; drain. Return spaghetti to hot pan. Cover and keep warm.

2 Meanwhile, for sauce, in a large skillet heat oil over medium heat. Add garlic to skillet; cook for 30 seconds. Stir in tomatoes, olives, anchovies, capers, black pepper, and crushed red pepper. Bring just to boiling; reduce heat. Simmer, uncovered, for 5 to 7 minutes or until slightly thickened, stirring occasionally.

3 Serve sauce over cooked spaghetti. Sprinkle with parsley.

nutrition facts per serving: 265 cal., 10 g total fat (1 g sat. fat), 3 mg chol., 323 mg sodium, 37 g carb., 3 g fiber, 8 g pro.

Tamarind is a fruit native to Asia and Mexico that provides the sour element in much of Thai cooking. Look for it in Asian or Indian markets.

tofu pad thai

start to finish: 30 minutes
makes: 4 servings

5 ounces dried brown rice fettuccine

3 tablespoons rice vinegar

3 tablespoons packed brown sugar

2 tablespoons Asian chile bean sauce

2 tablespoons fish sauce or reduced-sodium soy sauce

1 tablespoon tamarind pulp concentrate

3 cloves garlic, minced
Nonstick cooking spray

1 egg, lightly beaten

1 tablespoon canola oil

3 cups coarsely shredded napa cabbage

1 cup packaged julienned fresh carrots

4 green onions, cut into 1-inch pieces

½ to 1 fresh Thai chile pepper, cut into thin strips (see tip, page 318)

1 18-ounce package firm, tub-style tofu (fresh bean curd), drained and cut into ½-inch slices

¼ cup unsalted dry roasted peanuts

2 tablespoons snipped fresh cilantro
Lime wedges

1 Cook fettuccine according to package directions, except cook for 2 minutes less than the suggested time; drain. Rinse with cold water; drain again.

2 Meanwhile, for sauce, in a small bowl combine vinegar, brown sugar, chile bean sauce, fish sauce, tamarind, and garlic; set aside.

3 Coat a wok or large nonstick skillet with nonstick cooking spray; heat wok over medium heat. Add egg. Immediately begin stirring gently but continuously until egg resembles small pieces of cooked egg surrounded by liquid egg. Stop stirring; cook for 20 to 30 seconds or until egg is set. Turn egg over; cook for 20 to 30 seconds more or until egg is cooked through. Transfer egg to a cutting board; set aside.

4 Add 1 teaspoon of the oil to wok. Add cabbage, carrots, green onions, and chile pepper; cook and stir over medium-high heat for 2 to 3 minutes or until vegetables are crisp-tender. Remove vegetables from wok.

5 Add the remaining 2 teaspoons oil to wok. Add tofu; cook for 4 to 5 minutes or until tofu is light brown, turning occasionally. Remove tofu from wok. Add sauce and cooked fettuccine; cook and stir for 2 to 3 minutes or until fettuccine is tender but still firm. Return vegetables and tofu to wok; cook for 1 to 2 minutes or until heated through, gently stirring occasionally. Cut egg into thin slices; gently stir into fettuccine mixture.

6 Divide pad thai among serving plates. Sprinkle with peanuts and cilantro. Serve with lime wedges.

nutrition facts per serving: 389 cal., 14 g total fat (2 g sat. fat), 47 mg chol., 1000 mg sodium, 50 g carb., 4 g fiber, 16 g pro.

If you are shunning meat but are in the mood for carbs, this is your dish. The protein is provided by cannellini beans and the finished pasta gets a topping of crusty homemade croutons.

rigatoni with broccoli, beans, and basil

start to finish: 25 minutes
makes: 4 servings

8   ounces dried rigatoni (about 3½ cups)

2   cups broccoli florets

1   19-ounce can cannellini beans (white kidney beans), rinsed and drained

2   teaspoons bottled minced garlic

4   tablespoons olive oil

¼   cup snipped fresh basil

½   teaspoon salt

2   slices bread, cut into small cubes

¼   teaspoon crushed red pepper

    Snipped fresh basil (optional)

1 In a large pot cook pasta according to package directions, adding broccoli for the last 5 minutes of cooking. Drain, reserving ¾ cup of the pasta water. Return pasta and broccoli to pot; keep warm.

2 Meanwhile, in a large bowl combine beans, garlic, and 3 tablespoons of the oil. Mash about half of the bean mixture. Stir in the basil, salt, and the reserved pasta water. Stir bean mixture into pasta and broccoli in pot. Cover and keep warm.

3 For croutons, in a large skillet heat the remaining 1 tablespoon oil over medium heat. Add bread cubes and crushed red pepper; cook and stir for 1 to 2 minutes until crisp. Top pasta with croutons and, if desired, additional basil.

nutrition facts per serving: 456 cal., 15 g total fat (2 g sat. fat), 0 mg chol., 601 mg sodium, 70 g carb., 9 g fiber, 17 g pro.

The reserved pasta cooking water helps moisten the salad without the addition of extra oil and—if the water is still hot—also helps to slightly wilt the pasta.

greek spinach pasta salad with feta and beans

start to finish: 25 minutes
makes: 6 servings

12   ounces dried cavatappi or farfalle pasta

1   15-ounce can Great Northern beans, rinsed and drained

1   5- to 6-ounce package fresh baby spinach

1   cup crumbled feta cheese (4 ounces)

¼   cup dried tomatoes (not oil-packed), snipped

¼   cup chopped green onions (2)

1   teaspoon finely shredded lemon peel

2   tablespoons lemon juice

2   tablespoons olive oil

1   tablespoon snipped fresh oregano

1   tablespoon snipped fresh lemon thyme or thyme

½   teaspoon kosher salt

½   teaspoon freshly ground black pepper

2   cloves garlic, minced
    Shaved Parmesan cheese (optional)

1 Cook pasta according to package directions. Drain pasta, reserving ¼ cup of the cooking water.

2 Meanwhile, in a large serving bowl combine beans, spinach, feta cheese, tomatoes, green onions, lemon peel, lemon juice, oil, oregano, thyme, salt, pepper, and garlic.

3 Toss pasta and the reserved pasta water with spinach mixture. Serve warm or at room temperature. If desired, top with shaved Parmesan cheese.

nutrition facts per serving: 408 cal., 10 g total fat (4 g sat. fat), 19 mg chol., 487 mg sodium, 62 g carb., 6 g fiber, 17 g pro.

Double this recipe and take it to your next potluck. Bring it on a big beautiful platter—it's sure to be a hit!

penne salad with green beans and gorgonzola

start to finish: 30 minutes
makes: 4 servings

283

6 ounces dried penne, ziti, elbow macaroni, or other short pasta

8 ounces fresh green beans, trimmed and bias-sliced into 1-inch pieces, or one 9-ounce package frozen Italian green beans, thawed

⅓ cup fat-free Italian salad dressing

1 tablespoon snipped fresh tarragon or ½ teaspoon dried tarragon, crushed

½ teaspoon freshly ground black pepper

2 cups torn radicchio or 1 cup finely shredded red cabbage

4 cups fresh spinach leaves, cleaned, trimmed, and shredded

½ cup crumbled Gorgonzola cheese (2 ounces)

1 In a large pot cook pasta according to package directions, adding fresh green beans to pasta the last 5 to 7 minutes of cooking. (Or, add frozen and thawed beans the last 3 to 4 minutes.) Rinse pasta and beans well under cold running water; drain thoroughly.

2 In a large bowl combine Italian dressing, tarragon, and pepper. Add pasta mixture and radicchio; toss gently to coat. Serve on a bed of shredded spinach and top with the Gorgonzola cheese.

nutrition facts per serving: 258 cal., 6 g total fat (4 g sat. fat), 12 mg chol., 534 mg sodium, 40 g carb., 4 g fiber, 12 g pro.

The peppery arugula is a welcome addition to this dish of pillowy gnocchi tossed with cream and sweet corn.

gnocchi, sweet corn, and arugula in cream sauce

start to finish: 20 minutes
makes: 4 servings

1   pound shelf-stable
      potato gnocchi

2   fresh small ears
      sweet corn or
      2 cups frozen whole
      kernel corn

¾   cup fat-free half-and-
      half or milk

3   ounces reduced-
      fat cream cheese
      (Neufchâtel), cut up

½   teaspoon garlic
      powder

½   teaspoon dried basil
      or oregano, crushed

¼   teaspoon salt

¼   teaspoon ground
      black pepper

5   cups torn fresh
      arugula
      Crushed red pepper
      (optional)
      Dried basil or oregano
      (optional)

1 In a large pot cook gnocchi according to package directions, adding corn the last 5 minutes of cooking time. Using tongs, transfer ears of corn (if using) to cutting board. Drain gnocchi and corn kernels (if using), reserving ¼ cup of the pasta water. Do not rinse.

2 Meanwhile, for cream sauce, in a medium saucepan combine half-and-half, cream cheese, garlic powder, the ½ teaspoon basil, salt, and pepper. Cook over medium heat for 5 minutes, stirring frequently. Stir in the reserved pasta water.

3 Return cooked pasta to pot. Pour cream sauce over pasta; heat through if necessary. Stir in arugula. Cut corn from cobs; add to pasta. Serve in bowls. If desired, sprinkle with crushed red pepper and additional dried basil or oregano.

nutrition facts per serving: 292 cal., 6 g total fat (3 g sat. fat), 18 mg chol., 797 mg sodium, 52 g carb., 1 g fiber, 9 g pro.

tip: If you like, replace the corn with 1 cup chopped red sweet pepper and add 12 ounces cooked shrimp after tossing gnocchi with the cream sauce.

Just the smallest amount of sugar softens the acidity in the flash-cooked fresh tomato sauce. The garlic-basil toast is a healthier take on traditional fat-saturated garlic bread.

linguine in fresh tomato sauce with garlic-basil toast

start to finish: 20 minutes
makes: 4 servings

285

10 ounces dried linguini
3 tablespoons olive oil
6 cloves garlic, minced, or 1 tablespoon bottled minced garlic
2 English muffins, split
¾ cup fresh basil, chopped
2 cups cherry or grape tomatoes, halved
½ cup chicken broth or pasta water
1 teaspoon sugar
Salt
Freshly ground black pepper
½ cup halved, pitted Kalamata olives (optional)
Grated Parmesan cheese and/or fresh basil (optional)

1 Preheat broiler. Cook pasta according to package directions. Drain; set aside.

2 Meanwhile, for garlic-basil toasts, in a medium bowl combine 1 tablespoon of the oil and about one-third of the minced garlic; brush on cut sides of muffins. Place muffins on baking sheet. Broil 3 to 4 inches from heat for 2 to 3 minutes or until golden. Sprinkle 1 tablespoon of the chopped basil over muffins; set aside.

3 In a large saucepan heat the remaining 2 tablespoons oil over medium-high heat. Add tomatoes, the remaining basil, and the remaining garlic; cook for 2 minutes. Add broth and sugar; cook for 3 to 4 minutes or until tomatoes soften. Season with salt and pepper. Stir in pasta and, if desired, olives; heat through.

4 Serve garlic-basil toasts with pasta. If desired, top pasta with Parmesan cheese and additional fresh basil.

nutrition facts per serving: 450 cal., 12 g total fat (2 g sat. fat), 1 mg chol., 403 mg sodium, 72 g carb., 3 g fiber, 12 g pro.

Meaty portobello mushrooms stand in for the meat in this vegetarian pasta dish. Even the most dedicated carnivores won't miss it.

farfalle with mushrooms and spinach

start to finish: 20 minutes
makes: 4 servings

6 ounces dried farfalle pasta
1 tablespoon olive oil
1 cup sliced portobello or other fresh mushrooms
½ cup chopped onion (1 medium)
2 cloves garlic, minced
4 cups thinly sliced fresh spinach
1 teaspoon snipped fresh thyme
⅛ teaspoon ground black pepper
2 tablespoons shredded Parmesan cheese

1 Cook pasta according to package directions; drain.

2 Meanwhile, in a large skillet heat oil over medium heat. Add mushrooms, onion, and garlic; cook and stir for 2 to 3 minutes or until mushrooms are nearly tender.

3 Stir in spinach, thyme, and pepper. Cook for 1 minute or until heated through and spinach is slightly wilted. Stir in cooked pasta; toss gently to mix. Sprinkle with Parmesan cheese.

nutrition facts per serving: 219 cal., 5 g total fat (1 g sat. fat), 2 mg chol., 86 mg sodium, 35 g carb., 4 g fiber, 9 g pro.

Substitute thinly sliced zucchini for the yellow summer squash, if you like. Or better yet, use a blend of both kinds of squash.

ravioli with garden vegetables

start to finish: 25 minutes
makes: 4 servings

1 9-ounce package refrigerated cheese-filled ravioli or tortellini
2 teaspoons olive oil or canola oil
2 cloves garlic, minced
1¼ cups thinly sliced yellow summer squash (1 medium)
1 15-ounce can garbanzo beans (chickpeas), rinsed and drained
4 roma tomatoes, quartered
2 teaspoons snipped fresh thyme or ½ teaspoon dried thyme, crushed
¼ teaspoon ground black pepper
4 cups shredded fresh spinach
Olive oil or canola oil (optional)
Grated Parmesan cheese (optional)

1 Cook ravioli according to package directions; drain.

2 Meanwhile, in a large skillet heat the 2 teaspoons oil over medium-high heat. Add garlic; cook and stir for 30 seconds. Add squash, garbanzo beans, tomatoes, thyme, and pepper; cook and stir for 4 to 5 minutes or until squash is crisp-tender and mixture is heated through.

3 Add ravioli to vegetable mixture. Toss lightly to mix. Arrange spinach on four serving plates; top with ravioli mixture. If desired, drizzle with a little additional oil and/or sprinkle with Parmesan cheese.

nutrition facts per serving: 304 cal., 7 g total fat (2 g sat. fat), 25 mg chol., 688 mg sodium, 48 g carb., 7 g fiber, 15 g pro.

Serve this rich-tasting stroganoff with steamed green beans.

smoky mushroom stroganoff

start to finish: 20 minutes
makes: 4 servings

1   8.8-ounce package
    dried pappardelle
    (wide egg noodles)
1   tablespoon olive oil
1½ pounds sliced fresh
    mushrooms, such
    as button, cremini,
    and/or shiitake
2   cloves garlic, minced
1   8-ounce carton light
    sour cream
2   tablespoons all-
    purpose flour
1½ teaspoons smoked
    paprika
¼   teaspoon ground
    black pepper
1   cup vegetable broth
    Snipped fresh Italian
    (flat-leaf) parsley
    (optional)

1 Cook noodles according to package directions; drain and keep warm.

2 In a very large skillet heat oil over medium-high heat. Add mushrooms and garlic; cook for 5 to 8 minutes or until tender, stirring occasionally. (Reduce heat if mushrooms brown too quickly.) Using a slotted spoon transfer mushroom mixture to a bowl. Cover and keep warm.

3 For sauce, in a medium bowl stir together sour cream, flour, paprika, and black pepper. Stir in broth until smooth. Add to skillet; cook and stir until thickened and bubbly. Cook and stir for 1 minute more. Serve sauce and mushroom mixture over noodles. If desired, sprinkle with parsley.

nutrition facts per serving: 407 cal., 13 g total fat (5 g sat. fat), 72 mg chol., 443 mg sodium, 59 g carb., 4 g fiber, 17 g pro.

Cooking the lemon peel softens it and heightens the flavors of the aromatic oils contained in the peel. Combined with basil, the flavor and scent of this lively flavored pasta transports you directly to the Mediterranean.

lemon-basil pasta

start to finish: 25 minutes
makes: 4 servings

10   ounces dried linguine or desired pasta
1   19-ounce can cannellini beans (white kidney beans), rinsed and drained
3   tablespoons olive oil
2   teaspoons finely shredded lemon peel
2   tablespoons lemon juice
1   cup packed fresh basil leaves
    Salt
    Ground black pepper
    Small fresh basil leaves (optional)

1 In a large pot cook pasta according to package directions, adding beans for the last 2 minutes of cooking time. Drain, reserving ½ cup of the cooking liquid.

2 Meanwhile, in a small skillet heat 2 teaspoons of the oil over medium heat. Add lemon peel to skillet; cook about 1 minute or until lightly brown and tender, stirring frequently.

3 In a food processor combine cooked lemon peel, the remaining 2 tablespoons oil, lemon juice, the 1 cup basil, and salt and pepper to taste. Cover and process until smooth. Add the reserved cooking liquid, 1 tablespoon at a time, until desired consistency, processing mixture after every addition.

4 To serve, toss hot cooked pasta mixture with lemon-basil mixture. If desired, garnish with additional small basil leaves.

nutrition facts per serving: 452 cal., 10 g total fat (1 g sat. fat), 0 mg chol., 648 mg sodium, 75 g carb., 9 g fiber, 18 g pro.

middle eastern bulgur-spinach salad

grains &
legu

11

Earthy ingredients such as brown rice, quinoa, farro, and barley—plus a rainbow of beans—take on the starring role in these tasty, high-fiber dishes.

mes

If you don't have garbanzo beans, any type of white bean—Great Northern, cannellini, or navy beans—will work equally well in this warm grain-and-legume salad with a confetti of corn, beets, basil, and parsley.

quinoa toss with garbanzo beans and herbs

start to finish: 25 minutes
makes: 8 servings

1   cup quinoa
2   cups chicken broth or
      vegetable broth
2   fresh ears corn or
      1 cup frozen corn,
      thawed
1   15-ounce can
      garbanzo beans
      (chickpeas), rinsed
      and drained
½   cup crumbled feta
      cheese (2 ounces)
¼   cup finely chopped
      sweet onion
3   tablespoons snipped
      fresh basil
2   tablespoons snipped
      fresh Italian (flat-
      leaf) parsley
¼   cup olive oil
2   tablespoons lemon
      juice
½   teaspoon salt
½   teaspoon ground
      black pepper
1   cup diced, cooked
      beets
      Romaine leaves

1 Rinse quinoa in a fine mesh sieve under cold running water; drain. In a medium saucepan bring broth to boiling. Add quinoa. Return to boiling; reduce heat. Simmer, covered, for 15 minutes or until broth is absorbed. Remove from heat; set aside to cool.

2 Meanwhile cut corn from cobs. In a large bowl combine quinoa, corn, garbanzo beans, feta cheese, onion, basil, and parsley.

3 For dressing, in a small bowl whisk together oil, lemon juice, salt, and pepper. Add to quinoa mixture; toss to coat.

4 Stir in beets. Line bowls with romaine lettuce; top with quinoa mixture and serve immediately.

nutrition facts per serving: 270 cal., 11 g total fat (2 g sat. fat), 7 mg chol., 665 mg sodium, 37 g carb., 6 g fiber, 9 g pro.

nutrition note: Not only is quinoa a complete protein, it's also loaded with riboflavin, which helps your body's cells produce energy and fuel for your brain.

make ahead directions: Prepare recipe through Step 3. Cover and chill up to 24 hours. Let stand at room temperature for 30 minutes before serving. Right before serving, stir in beets and proceed with Step 4.

Smoky sweet pepper blend is a commercially available ground spice blend of dried tomatoes, sweet peppers, smoked paprika, onion, garlic, and salt.

quinoa and red bean burritos

prep: 15 minutes   bake: 12 minutes at 350°F
makes: 8 burritos

1 cup quinoa
2 cups water
2 teaspoons smoky sweet pepper blend
1 15-ounce can red kidney beans, rinsed, drained, and slightly mashed
1½ cups purchased salsa
   Nonstick cooking spray
8 7- or 8-inch whole wheat tortillas
1 cup shredded Mexican-style four-cheese blend
   Purchased salsa (optional)

1 Rinse quinoa; drain. In a medium saucepan bring the water to boiling. Slowly add quinoa and pepper blend to boiling water. Return to boiling; reduce heat. Simmer, covered, about 15 minutes. Drain if necessary. Stir in beans and 1 cup of the salsa.

2 Meanwhile preheat oven to 350°F. Lightly coat large baking sheet with cooking spray.

3 Wrap tortillas in paper towels. Microwave on 100 percent power (high) for 45 seconds or until softened. Place ½ cup of the quinoa mixture in the center of each tortilla. Fold bottom edge of each tortilla up and over filling. Fold opposite sides in and over filling. Roll up from bottoms. Place on prepared baking sheet. Lightly coat burritos with cooking spray. Top burritos with the remaining ½ cup salsa and the cheese.

4 Bake burritos about 12 minutes or until heated through and cheese melts. If desired, serve with additional salsa.

nutrition facts per burrito: 315 cal., 8 g total fat (4 g sat. fat), 13 mg chol., 734 mg sodium, 47 g carb., 8 g fiber, 14 g pro.

kitchen tip: Rinsing quinoa before cooking it is an important step. The seeds are coated with a naturally occurring substance that has a bit of a bitter taste, to keep insects from eating the seeds. While most quinoa is rinsed before it's packaged, it certainly doesn't hurt to give it a rinse and a drain with very fine-mesh strainer before using it.

Farro is a chewy grain favored by Italian cooks that is a relative of wheat. It is available pearled and semi-pearled. Opt for the semi-pearled variety, as it has more of the bran intact—and hence, has more fiber.

creamy farro-smothered portobellos

start to finish: 30 minutes
makes: 6 servings

3 cups reduced-sodium vegetable broth
1 cup semi-pearled farro
6 5-inch fresh portobello mushrooms, stems and gills removed
Nonstick cooking spray
2 cups coarsely chopped fresh Swiss chard leaves
¼ cup snipped dried tomatoes (not oil-pack)
2 teaspoons snipped fresh thyme or ½ teaspoon dried thyme, crushed
4 ounces semisoft goat cheese (chèvre), cut up
¼ cup finely shredded or shaved Parmesan cheese (1 ounce)
¼ cup sliced green onion tops
Freshly ground black pepper

1 In a medium saucepan bring broth to boiling; slowly stir in farro. Return to boiling; reduce heat. Simmer, covered, for 15 minutes.

2 Meanwhile, lightly coat both sides of mushrooms with cooking spray. Preheat a grill pan over medium heat. Add mushrooms; cook for 8 to 10 minutes or until tender, turning once.

3 Stir Swiss chard, dried tomatoes, and thyme into farro. Cook, covered, for 5 to 10 minutes more or until farro is tender. Remove from heat. Stir in goat cheese until melted.

4 To serve, place mushrooms, stemmed sides up, on a serving platter. Spoon farro mixture into mushrooms. Sprinkle with Parmesan cheese, green onion tops, and pepper.

nutrition facts per serving: 215 cal., 6 g total fat (4 g sat. fat), 12 mg chol., 482 mg sodium, 28 g carb., 3 g fiber, 12 g pro.

Creamy cubes of avocado provide a nice buttery bite amidst the crunch and chewiness of the farro, shredded carrot, pistachio nuts, and dried tomatoes. The colorful mélange is dressed with a quick vinaigrette and served in butterhead lettuce leaves.

farro white bean cups

start to finish: 25 minutes
makes: 4 servings

295

1 15-ounce can cannellini beans (white kidney beans), rinsed and drained
1 cup packaged, precooked plain farro, such as Archer Farms brand, or packaged cooked whole grain brown rice
½ cup matchstick-size carrot strips
¼ cup coarsely chopped salted dry-roasted pistachio nuts
3 tablespoons oil-pack dried tomatoes, drained and chopped
3 tablespoons chopped red onion
1 avocado, halved, seeded, and peeled
2 tablespoons lime juice
1 teaspoon olive oil
1 clove garlic, minced
¼ teaspoon salt
¼ teaspoon dried Italian seasoning, crushed
8 large butterhead (Boston or Bibb) lettuce leaves

1 In a medium bowl combine cannellini beans, farro, carrot, pistachio nuts, tomatoes, and onion. Cube the avocado and toss with the lime juice. Add the avocado to the bean mixture; toss gently.

2 In a small bowl whisk together oil, garlic, salt, and Italian seasoning. Drizzle over bean mixture. Toss gently to combine.

3 Spoon about ½ cup of the bean mixture onto each lettuce leaf.

nutrition facts per serving: 277 cal., 11 g total fat (1 g sat. fat), 0 mg chol., 463 mg sodium, 36 g carb., 10 g fiber, 10 g pro.

*Looking for a quick, cheap, and tasty meal everyone will love?
Topped with melty cheese, this complete-protein combo fills the bill.*

quick rice and red beans

start to finish: 25 minutes
makes: 8 servings

1 tablespoon olive oil or canola oil
½ cup chopped onion (1 medium)
1 14-ounce package instant brown rice (2 cups)
1 cup water
2 15-ounce cans kidney beans or black beans, rinsed and drained
2 14.5-ounce cans Italian-style stewed tomatoes, cut up
¼ teaspoon crushed red pepper (optional)
1 cup shredded Monterey Jack cheese or cheddar cheese (4 ounces)
¼ cup snipped fresh cilantro

1 In a large saucepan heat oil over medium heat. Add onion; cook until tender. Add rice and the water. Stir in beans, tomatoes, and, if desired, crushed red pepper. Bring to boiling; reduce heat. Simmer, covered, for 10 minutes. Remove from heat.

2 Stir in half of the Monterey Jack cheese and the cilantro. Let stand, covered, for 5 minutes. Top with the remaining cheese.

nutrition facts per serving: 376 cal., 8 g total fat (3 g sat. fat), 13 mg chol., 479 mg sodium, 67 g carb., 10 g fiber, 17 g pro.

nutrition note: When possible, try to incorporate more plant-based proteins into your diet. Swapping beans for red meat saves money, fat, and calories.

Substitute shelled edamame for the baby lima beans, if you like.

vegetable curry

prep: 10 minutes   cook: 8 minutes
makes: 4 servings

1 16-ounce package
   frozen baby lima
   beans
½ cup water
1 15-ounce can tomato
   sauce with garlic
   and onion
1½ teaspoons curry
   powder
2 8.8-ounce pouches
   cooked Spanish-
   style rice
¼ cup sliced green
   onions (2) or
   snipped fresh
   cilantro
   Olive oil (optional)

1 In a medium saucepan combine lima beans
and the water. Bring to boiling; reduce heat.
Simmer, covered, for 5 minutes. Stir in tomato
sauce and curry powder; return to boiling.
Reduce heat. Simmer, covered, for 3 minutes.

2 Meanwhile, microwave rice following
package directions. Spoon rice on one side
of 4 plates; spoon bean mixture alongside rice.
Sprinkle with green onions. If desired, drizzle
with oil.

nutrition facts per serving: 385 cal., 3 g total fat (0 g
sat. fat), 0 mg chol., 939 mg sodium, 72 g carb., 9 g fiber, 14 g pro.

Nuts and cheese provide the protein in these peppers stuffed with dried fruit and grains, instead of the usual ground meat.

peppers stuffed with cinnamon bulgur

start to finish: 30 minutes
makes: 4 servings

1¾	cups water
½	cup shredded carrot
¼	cup chopped onion
1	teaspoon instant vegetable or chicken bouillon granules
⅛	teaspoon salt
1	3-inch stick cinnamon or dash ground cinnamon
¾	cup bulgur
⅓	cup dried cranberries or raisins
2	large or 4 small sweet peppers,* any color
¾	cup shredded Muenster, brick, or mozzarella cheese (12 ounces)
½	cup water
2	tablespoons sliced almonds or chopped pecans, toasted**

1 In a large skillet stir together the 1¾ cups water, carrot, onion, bouillon granules, salt, and cinnamon. Bring to boiling; reduce heat. Simmer, covered, for 5 minutes. Stir in uncooked bulgur and cranberries. Remove from heat. Cover and let stand for 5 minutes. If using stick cinnamon, remove from the bulgur mixture. Drain off excess liquid.

2 Meanwhile, halve the sweet peppers lengthwise, removing the seeds and membranes.

3 Stir Muenster cheese into bulgur mixture; spoon bulgur mixture into sweet pepper halves. Place sweet pepper halves in skillet. Add the ½ cup water. Bring to boiling; reduce heat. Simmer, covered, for 5 to 10 minutes or until sweet peppers are crisp-tender and bulgur mixture is heated through. Sprinkle with nuts.

nutrition facts per serving: 250 cal., 9 g total fat (4 g sat. fat), 20 mg chol., 432 mg sodium, 35 g carb., 8 g fiber, 10 g pro.

*tip: Four large poblano peppers may be substituted for the sweet peppers. Prepare as directed above.

**tip: To toast nuts, spread them in a shallow baking pan. Bake in a 350°F oven for 5 to 10 minutes or until light brown, shaking pan once or twice. Watch carefully so the nuts don't burn.

Bulgur is an ideal multitasker's ingredient. While it's softening and absorbing water, you can be prepping the rest of the recipe—or reading the mail, feeding the dog, or folding a load of laundry.

middle eastern bulgur-spinach salad

start to finish: 30 minutes

makes: 4 servings

1	cup bulgur
1	cup boiling water
½	cup plain yogurt
¼	cup bottled red wine vinaigrette salad dressing
2	tablespoons snipped fresh parsley
½	teaspoon ground cumin
6	cups torn fresh spinach
1	15-ounce can garbanzo beans (chickpeas), rinsed and drained
1	cup coarsely chopped apple
½	of a medium red onion, thinly sliced and separated into rings
3	tablespoons raisins (optional)

1 In a medium bowl combine uncooked bulgur and the boiling water. Let stand about 10 minutes or until bulgur has absorbed all the water. Cool for 15 minutes.

2 Meanwhile, for dressing, in a small bowl stir together yogurt, vinaigrette salad dressing, parsley, and cumin.

3 In a large bowl combine bulgur, spinach, garbanzo beans, apple, onion, and, if desired, raisins. Pour dressing over salad. Toss lightly to coat.

nutrition facts per serving: 340 cal., 11 g total fat (2 g sat. fat), 2 mg chol., 673 mg sodium, 53 g carb., 16 g fiber, 13 g pro.

make-ahead directions: Prepare salad as directed except do not add spinach. Cover and chill for up to 24 hours. Add spinach and toss to serve.

If you can't find young fresh pea pods, sugar snap peas make a fine substitute in this recipe.

spiced bulgur with beef and mango

start to finish: 30 minutes
makes: 4 servings

1   cup reduced-sodium chicken broth
⅔   cup bulgur
½   teaspoon ground cumin
¼   teaspoon ground coriander
⅛   teaspoon ground cinnamon
⅛   teaspoon cayenne pepper
1   clove garlic, minced
6   ounces lower-sodium deli roast beef, cut into thin strips
½   of a medium mango, peeled and coarsely chopped
½   cup fresh pea pods, halved crosswise
¼   cup sliced green onions (2)
¼   cup snipped fresh cilantro
¼   cup unsalted peanuts, chopped (optional)

1 In a 1½-quart microwave-safe casserole combine broth, uncooked bulgur, cumin, coriander, cinnamon, cayenne pepper, and garlic. Microwave, covered, on 100 percent power (high) about 4 minutes or until mixture is boiling. Remove from microwave. Let stand about 20 minutes or until bulgur is tender. Drain, if necessary.

2 Divide bulgur mixture among four serving bowls. Top with beef, mango, pea pods, green onions, cilantro, and, if desired, peanuts.

nutrition facts per serving: 164 cal., 2 g total fat (1 g sat. fat), 26 mg chol., 421 mg sodium, 25 g carb., 5 g fiber, 13 g pro.

Draining the tomatoes before stuffing them helps retain their beautiful, globular shape.

spinach-tabbouleh-stuffed tomato

prep: 15 minutes stand: 15 minutes
makes: 6 servings

1   cup water
¾   cup bulgur
6   medium tomatoes
½   cup light mayonnaise
1   tablespoon lemon juice
¼   teaspoon bottled hot pepper sauce
1   5-ounce package fresh baby spinach, coarsely chopped
2   tablespoons snipped fresh mint
½   teaspoon salt
3   tablespoons pine nuts, toasted*

1 In a medium saucepan bring the 1 cup water to boiling. Slowly add uncooked bulgur; stir and remove from heat. Let stand for 15 minutes or until most of the liquid is absorbed.

2 Meanwhile, slice ¼ inch from top of each tomato. Using a spoon, scoop out insides of tomatoes, being careful not to break shells. Drain tomatoes upside down on a plate lined with paper towels.

3 For dressing, in a small bowl stir together mayonnaise, lemon juice, and hot pepper sauce. Set dressing aside.

4 In a large bowl combine bulgur, spinach, mint, and salt. Stir in dressing. Fill each tomato shell with ½ cup of bulgur mixture. Sprinkle with nuts. Serve immediately.

nutrition facts per serving: 148 cal., 4 g total fat (0 g sat. fat), 0 mg chol., 413 mg sodium, 26 g carb., 5 g fiber, 5 g pro.

*tip: To toast nuts, spread them in a shallow baking pan. Bake in a 350°F oven for 5 to 10 minutes or until light brown, shaking pan once or twice. Watch carefully so the nuts don't burn.

This hearty Middle Eastern–style salad is equally delicious served warm, room temperature, or even chilled. It's just the thing for a hot summer night.

tabbouleh with edamame and feta

start to finish: 25 minutes
makes: 6 servings

2½ cups water
1¼ cups bulgur
¼ cup lemon juice
3 tablespoons purchased basil pesto
2 cups fresh or thawed frozen shelled sweet soybeans (edamame)
2 cups cherry tomatoes, cut up
⅓ cup crumbled feta cheese
⅓ cup thinly sliced green onion
2 tablespoons snipped fresh parsley
¼ teaspoon ground black pepper
Fresh parsley sprigs (optional)

1 In a medium saucepan bring the water to boiling; add uncooked bulgur. Return to boiling; reduce heat. Simmer, covered, about 15 minutes or until most of the liquid is absorbed. Remove from heat. Transfer to a large bowl.

2 In a small bowl whisk together lemon juice and pesto; add to bulgur. Stir in soybeans, tomatoes, feta cheese, green onion, the 2 tablespoons parsley, and pepper. Toss gently to combine. If desired, garnish with parsley sprigs.

nutrition facts per serving: 320 cal., 13 g total fat (2 g sat. fat), 8 mg chol., 175 mg sodium, 37 g carb., 10 g fiber, 18 g pro.

make-ahead directions: Prepare as directed. Cover and chill for up to 4 hours.

Chewy barley in a creamy sauce studded with fresh vegetables and cannellini beans is a nourishing vegetarian main dish. To mix it up, heartier barley stands in for rice in this recipe.

risotto-style barley and vegetables

start to finish: 30 minutes
makes: 4 servings

2   tablespoons olive oil
1   cup quick-cooking barley
½   cup finely chopped onion (1 medium)
1   clove garlic, minced
2½ cups reduced-sodium chicken broth or vegetable broth
8   ounces fresh asparagus spears, trimmed and cut into 1-inch pieces
1   cup shredded carrots (2 medium)
1   15- to 16-ounce can cannellini beans (white kidney beans) or pinto beans, rinsed and drained
½   cup finely shredded Asiago or Parmesan cheese (2 ounces)
¼   cup snipped fresh basil
    Ground black pepper

1 In a 3-quart saucepan heat oil over medium heat. Add barley, onion, and garlic; cook and stir for 3 to 5 minutes or until onion is tender and barley is golden.

2 Meanwhile, in a 1½-quart saucepan bring broth to simmering. Slowly add ¾ cup of the broth to the barley mixture, stirring constantly. Continue to cook and stir over medium heat until liquid is absorbed. Add another ½ cup of the broth, stirring constantly. Continue to cook and stir until liquid is absorbed. Add remaining broth, about ½ cup at a time, stirring constantly until liquid is almost all absorbed but is still creamy. (This should take about 12 minutes.) Add asparagus and carrots to saucepan. Reduce heat and cook, covered, about 5 minutes or until barley and vegetables are tender. Stir in beans, Asiago cheese, and basil; heat through. Season with pepper.

nutrition facts per serving: 348 cal., 10 g total fat (3 g sat. fat), 7 mg chol., 764 mg sodium, 50 g carb., 11 g fiber, 17 g pro.

Not counting the olive oil, there are just four ingredients in this tasty tofu dish. Starting with a flavored couscous mix gives you a leg up on both prep time and taste.

mediterranean couscous with tofu

start to finish: 15 minutes
makes: 4 servings

305

1   5.7-ounce package curry-flavored or roasted garlic and olive oil–flavored couscous mix
½   of a 12- to 16-ounce package extra-firm tofu (fresh bean curd), well drained
1   tablespoon olive oil
½   cup sliced pitted ripe olives or sliced pitted Greek black olives
½   cup crumbled feta cheese or finely shredded Parmesan cheese (2 ounces)

1 Prepare couscous according to package directions, except omit oil. Meanwhile, cut tofu into ½-inch cubes. Pat tofu dry with paper towels.

2 In a large skillet heat oil over medium-high heat. Add tofu; cook and stir for 5 to 7 minutes or until tofu is browned. Stir tofu and olives into couscous. Transfer to a serving dish. Top with feta cheese.

nutrition facts per serving: 259 cal., 10 g total fat (4 g sat. fat), 17 mg chol., 763 mg sodium, 33 g carb., 3 g fiber, 11 g pro.

grains & legumes

There is no appreciable loss of either fiber or nutrient content by using instant brown rice instead of regular brown rice—and you save lots of time.

chicken, brown rice, and vegetable skillet

start to finish: 30 minutes
makes: 5 servings

2 tablespoons dried porcini mushrooms
2 teaspoons olive oil
½ cup chopped onion (1 medium)
½ cup sliced celery (1 stalk)
½ cup bite-size strips red or green sweet pepper
1 14.5-ounce can reduced-sodium chicken broth
1½ cups instant brown rice
4 medium carrots, cut into matchstick-size strips
2 cups chopped cooked skinless chicken breast (10 ounces)
1 13.75- to 14-ounce can artichoke hearts, drained and halved
1 teaspoon poultry seasoning
½ teaspoon garlic-and-herb salt-free seasoning blend
¼ teaspoon garlic powder
¼ teaspoon salt
¼ teaspoon ground black pepper

1 Place mushrooms in a small bowl; add enough boiling water to cover. Let stand for 5 minutes. Drain well; snip mushrooms and set aside.

2 In a very large skillet heat oil over medium heat. Add onion, celery, and sweet pepper; cook about 4 minutes or until tender, stirring occasionally.

3 Add broth and mushrooms to skillet. Bring to boiling. Stir in uncooked rice. Return to boiling; reduce heat. Simmer, covered, for 5 minutes. Stir in carrots. Cook, covered, for 5 minutes more. Stir in chicken, artichokes, poultry seasoning, seasoning blend, garlic powder, salt, and black pepper. Heat through.

nutrition facts per serving: 290 cal., 5 g total fat (1 g sat. fat), 48 mg chol., 661 mg sodium, 39 g carb., 6 g fiber, 23 g pro.

Oven-baked stuffed peppers can take up to 1 hour to cook. These meatless microwave beauties take only 12 minutes total cooking time.

bean and rice stuffed peppers

start to finish: 30 minutes
makes: 4 servings

4   large yellow, red, and/or green sweet peppers
3   tablespoons water
1   15-ounce can no-salt-added black beans, rinsed and drained
1   15-ounce can no-salt-added whole kernel corn, drained
1   14.5-ounce can diced tomatoes, undrained
1   8.8-ounce pouch cooked whole grain brown rice, heated according to package directions
½   cup purchased salsa
½   teaspoon ground cumin or chili powder

1 Cut off tops of sweet peppers; remove cores and stems, hollowing out the peppers. Arrange peppers in a 2-quart microwave-safe square baking dish. Pour the water around peppers.

2 Microwave peppers, uncovered, on 100 percent power (high) about 8 minutes or just until peppers are starting to soften.

3 Meanwhile, in a medium bowl stir together black beans, corn, tomatoes, rice, salsa, and cumin.

4 Divide bean mixture evenly among peppers. Microwave, uncovered, on 100 percent power (high) about 4 minutes more or until filling is heated through and peppers are tender.

nutrition facts per serving: 362 cal., 3 g total fat (0 g sat. fat), 0 mg chol., 327 mg sodium, 76 g carb., 12 g fiber, 13 g pro.

An onion and a can of chili beans with gravy provides all of the flavoring you need in the rice and bean mixture that tops these crunchy tostadas.

rice and bean tostadas

prep: 20 minutes bake: 5 minutes at 350°F
makes: 8 tostadas

1½   cups water
1½   cups quick-cooking
       brown rice
 ½   cup chopped onion
       (1 medium)
  1   15-ounce can chili
       beans with chili
       gravy
  1   8-ounce can whole
       kernel corn, drained
  8   purchased tostada
       shells
  3   cups shredded
       lettuce
 ½   cup shredded
       cheddar cheese
       (2 ounces)
  1   cup quartered cherry
       tomatoes

1 Preheat oven to 350°F. In a large saucepan bring the water to boiling. Stir in rice and onion. Return to boiling; reduce heat. Simmer, covered, for 5 minutes. Remove from heat; stir. Cover and let stand for 5 minutes. Stir undrained chili beans and corn into rice mixture. Heat through.

2 Meanwhile, place tostada shells on a baking sheet. Bake for 5 minutes or until heated through.

3 To assemble, place 2 tostada shells on each dinner plate. Top tostadas with shredded lettuce and the rice-bean mixture. Sprinkle with cheddar cheese and top with tomatoes.

nutrition facts per 2 tostadas: 438 cal., 12 g total fat (4 g sat. fat), 15 mg chol., 621 mg sodium, 70 g carb., 11 g fiber, 15 g pro.

Prepared ketchup is high in sugar. The only sugar in the Easy Ketchup that accompanies these veggie sliders is the natural sugar from the fresh tomatoes.

mini veggie burgers with easy ketchup

prep: 20 minutes   cook: 8 minutes

makes: 8 mini burgers

1 19-ounce can cannellini beans (white kidney beans), rinsed and drained
1½ cups soft bread crumbs
¼ cup shredded carrot
¼ cup finely chopped onion
1 egg
2 tablespoons snipped fresh parsley
1 tablespoon olive oil
¼ teaspoon salt
¼ teaspoon ground black pepper
2 tablespoons olive oil
1 cup packed fresh baby spinach
16 slices from a small whole wheat baguette
¼ cup Easy Ketchup
    Thinly sliced red onion (optional)

1 In a medium bowl mash beans with a fork or potato masher. Stir in half of the bread crumbs, the carrot, chopped onion, egg, half of the parsley, the 1 tablespoon oil, the salt, and pepper. Place the remaining bread crumbs and parsley in a shallow dish; stir to combine.

2 Shape bean mixture into eight round patties (mixture will be soft). Dip both sides of each patty into bread crumb mixture in dish, carefully turning to coat.

3 In a large skillet heat the 2 tablespoons oil over medium heat. Add patties; cook for 6 to 8 minutes or until browned and an instant-read thermometer inserted near the center registers 160°F, turning once halfway through cooking.

4 Arrange spinach on 8 of the bread slices; place bean burgers on top. Top with Easy Ketchup and, if desired, sliced onion. Top with remaining bread slices.

nutrition facts per mini burgers: 174 cal., 7 g total fat (1 g sat. fat), 23 mg chol., 376 mg sodium, 24 g carb., 5 g fiber, 8 g pro.

Easy Ketchup: Place one 14.5-ounce can diced tomatoes, undrained, in a food processor or blender. Cover and process or blend to desired consistency. Pour into a medium bowl; stir in 2 tablespoons snipped fresh basil. Season with salt and ground black pepper. Store ketchup in a covered container in the refrigerator for up to 3 days.

Adding the broccoli the last few minutes of cooking time is an efficient way to get a pasta-and-vegetables dish together fast— and with just one pot to wash.

broccoli and bean linguine

start to finish: 25 minutes
makes: 4 servings

6   ounces dried linguine
3   cups broccoli florets
1   15-ounce can
     cannellini beans
     (white kidney
     beans), rinsed and
     drained
1   10-ounce container
     refrigerated light
     Alfredo sauce
3   cloves garlic, minced
½   cup croutons,
     coarsely crushed
¼   teaspoon crushed red
     pepper
     Olive oil

1 Cook pasta according to package directions, adding broccoli the last 3 to 4 minutes of cooking; drain, reserving ½ cup of the pasta water. Return pasta mixture to pan; keep warm.

2 Meanwhile, for sauce, in a food processor or blender combine beans, Alfredo sauce, garlic, and the reserved pasta water. Cover and process or blend until nearly smooth. Transfer to a small saucepan; heat through over medium heat, stirring frequently.

3 Spoon sauce onto serving plates. Top with pasta mixture, crushed croutons, crushed red pepper, and a drizzle of oil.

nutrition facts per serving: 402 cal., 12 g total fat (5 g sat. fat), 18 mg chol., 659 mg sodium, 60 g carb., 8 g fiber, 19 g pro.

Garam ("hot") masala ("spices") is an Indian blend of spices that varies from cook to cook, but that usually contains black and white pepper, cloves, cinnamon, cumin, and cardamom. The name doesn't refer to heat or spiciness but rather the intensity of the flavors and the warming effect it has on the body.

indian lentils and rice

start to finish: 20 minutes
makes: 4 servings

1 tablespoon vegetable oil
½ cup chopped onion (1 medium)
2 teaspoons garam masala
2 cups bite-size cauliflower florets
½ cup bias-sliced carrot (1 medium)
1 cup water
1 17.3-ounce package refrigerated steamed lentils* or one 15-ounce can lentils, rinsed and drained
1 8.8-ounce pouch cooked long grain rice
1 cup frozen peas
⅓ cup golden raisins
  Salt
  Freshly ground black pepper

1 In a very large skillet heat oil over medium heat. Add onion and garam masala; cook about 5 minutes or until onion is tender. Add cauliflower, carrot, and the water. Bring to boiling; reduce heat. Simmer, covered, about 5 minutes or until tender.

2 Stir in lentils, rice, peas, and raisins. Cook and stir until heated through and water is absorbed. Season with salt and pepper.

nutrition facts per serving: 373 cal., 6 g total fat (0 g sat. fat), 0 mg chol., 510 mg sodium, 65 g carb., 14 g fiber, 17 g pro.

*tip: If refrigerated steamed lentils are not available, in a large saucepan combine 8 ounces dry lentils and 2½ cups water. Bring to boiling; reduce heat. Simmer, covered, about 30 minutes or until tender.

Red lentils are the quickest-cooking of all types of lentils. They break down into a creamy consistency fairly easily, which makes them a good choice for topping tostadas.

lentil and veggie tostadas

start to finish: 25 minutes
makes: 4 tostadas

1¾   cups water
¾   cup dry red lentils,
     rinsed and drained
¼   cup chopped onion
1   to 2 tablespoons
     snipped fresh
     cilantro
1   clove garlic, minced
½   teaspoon salt
½   teaspoon ground
     cumin
4   tostada shells
2   cups chopped fresh
     vegetables (such
     as broccoli, tomato,
     zucchini, and/or
     yellow summer
     squash)
¾   cup shredded
     reduced-fat
     Monterey Jack
     cheese (3 ounces)

1 In a medium saucepan stir together the water, lentils, onion, cilantro, garlic, salt, and cumin. Bring to boiling; reduce heat. Simmer, covered, for 12 to 15 minutes or until lentils are tender and most of the liquid is absorbed. Use a fork to mash the cooked lentils.

2 Preheat broiler. Spread the lentil mixture on tostada shells; top with the vegetables and Monterey Jack cheese. Place on a large baking sheet. Broil tostadas 3 to 4 inches from the heat about 2 minutes or until cheese is melted.

nutrition facts per tostada: 269 cal., 9 g total fat (3 g sat. fat), 16 mg chol., 595 mg sodium, 34 g carb., 8 g fiber, 16 g pro.

Freshly crushed cumin seeds are highly aromatic, and toasting them in oil in a skillet makes them even more so. Crush the seeds using a mortar and pestle or in a small bag with a rolling pin.

red lentil rice

start to finish: 30 minutes
makes: 6 servings

1   tablespoon olive oil
½   cup chopped onion
     (1 medium)
1   teaspoon cumin
     seeds, crushed
½   teaspoon salt
⅛   teaspoon cayenne
     pepper
2   cloves garlic, minced
1⅓   cups uncooked
     basmati rice or long
     grain rice
2   14.5-ounce cans
     chicken broth
½   cup water
1   cup frozen peas
½   cup dry red lentils,
     rinsed and drained
¼   cup snipped fresh
     mint
1   teaspoon garam
     masala
1   recipe Yogurt Raita

1 In a 4-quart Dutch oven heat oil over medium-high heat. Add onion, cumin seeds, salt, cayenne pepper, and garlic; cook and stir for 2 minutes. Add rice; cook and stir for 1 minute more. Carefully add broth and the water. Bring to boiling; reduce heat. Simmer, covered, for 10 minutes.

2 Stir peas and lentils into onion mixture. Return to boiling; reduce heat. Simmer, covered, for 8 to 10 minutes more or until lentils are just tender. Remove Dutch oven from heat; stir in mint and garam masala. Let stand, covered, for 5 minutes before serving. Serve topped with Yogurt Raita.

nutrition facts per serving: 274 cal., 3 g total fat (1 g sat. fat), 3 mg chol., 827 mg sodium, 50 g carb., 4 g fiber, 10 g pro.

Yogurt Raita: In a medium bowl stir together one 6-ounce carton plain yogurt, ¾ cup chopped seeded cucumber, ½ cup chopped seeded tomato, 1 tablespoon snipped fresh mint, ⅛ teaspoon salt, and dash ground black pepper.

12

Get fired up for dinner with these flame-kissed dishes that offer the fun of cooking outdoors all year round in just 30 minutes or less.

grill

tomato-topped lamb chops and rice

ing

Serve these Asian-style kabobs on a bed of hot cooked rice, if you like.

five-spice beef kabobs

start to finish: 20 minutes
makes: 4 servings

1 pound beef flank
    steak or boneless
    beef sirloin
2 tablespoons reduced-
    sodium soy sauce
1 to 1½ teaspoons
    five-spice powder
1 6-ounce carton plain
    Greek yogurt
1 tablespoon snipped
    fresh mint leaves
2 small limes
    Fresh mint leaves

1 Trim fat from beef. Thinly slice beef across grain. If necessary, flatten slices with palm of hand or meat mallet to ¼-inch thickness. In a medium bowl combine beef, soy sauce, and five-spice powder; toss to coat beef. Thread beef on skewers.*

2 For charcoal or gas grill, grill kabobs on rack of covered grill directly over medium heat for 4 to 6 minutes or to desired doneness, turning once.

3 Meanwhile, in small bowl combine yogurt and the 1 tablespoon snipped mint. From one lime, finely shred 1 teaspoon peel. Juice the lime. Stir peel and 1 tablespoon juice into yogurt. Cut remaining lime in wedges.

4 Serve kabobs with yogurt sauce and lime wedges. Top with additional fresh mint.

nutrition facts per serving: 213 cal., 8 g total fat (3 g sat. fat), 74 mg chol., 366 mg sodium, 5 g carb., 1 g fiber, 29 g pro.

tip: To serve with fresh carrot ribbons, use a vegetable peeler to make thin ribbons. Toss with a squeeze of lime juice and lightly sprinkle with five-spice powder.

*tip: If using wooden skewers, soak in enough water to cover for at least 1 hour before using.

Barbecued Beef Kabobs: Prepare as directed except substitute bottled barbecue sauce for the soy sauce, chili powder for the five-spice powder, sour cream for the yogurt, and cilantro for mint.

The substantial texture of pineapple makes it ideal for grilling. The fruit holds its shape when cooked and the sugars caramelize into beautiful grill marks.

grilled pork and pineapple

start to finish: 20 minutes
makes: 4 servings

4   boneless pork top loin chops, cut ¾ inch thick (about 1¼ pounds total)
¼   teaspoon salt
¼   teaspoon ground black pepper
1   purchased peeled and cored fresh pineapple
3   tablespoons orange marmalade
½   cup plain yogurt
¼   cup coarsely chopped roasted, lightly salted cashews
   Fresh thyme sprigs (optional)

1 Trim fat from pork chops. Sprinkle both sides of chops with the salt and pepper. Cut pineapple crosswise into ½-inch slices; set aside.

2 For a charcoal or gas grill, place chops on the grill rack directly over medium heat. Grill, uncovered, for 4 minutes. Turn; add pineapple to grill. Brush chops and pineapple with 1 tablespoon of the marmalade. Grill for 3 to 5 minutes more or until chops are done (160°F) and pineapple has light grill marks, turning pineapple once. Let chops rest for 3 minutes.

3 Arrange pineapple and chops on serving plates. Combine yogurt and remaining 2 tablespoons of marmalade. Spoon yogurt mixture over chops and pineapple; sprinkle with cashews. If desired, garnish with fresh thyme.

nutrition facts per serving: 317 cal., 7 g total fat (1 g sat. fat), 80 mg chol., 313 mg sodium, 29 g carb., 2 g fiber, 35 g pro.

Pork is often paired with fruit—most commonly pineapple, peaches, oranges, apples, plums, and pears—because the natural sweetness of the meat seems to take to it especially well.

grilled pork chops with chile rub and chutney

start to finish: 30 minutes
makes: 4 servings

1 tablespoon olive oil
1 medium sweet onion such as Vidalia or Walla Walla, thinly sliced
½ teaspoon cumin seeds
¼ teaspoon sea salt
4 pork loin chops,* cut ¾ inch thick (about 2 pounds total)
1 large chipotle pepper in adobo sauce, finely chopped**
2 oranges, peeled, seeded, and sectioned
¼ cup orange juice

1 In a large skillet heat oil over medium heat. Add onion, cumin seeds, and sea salt; cook for 12 to 15 minutes or until onion is tender and golden brown, stirring occasionally.

2 Meanwhile, trim fat from pork chops. Rub chopped chipotle pepper onto chops.

3 For a charcoal or gas grill, grill chops on the rack of a covered grill directly over medium heat for 11 to 14 minutes or until pork is slightly pink in the center (160°F), turning once.

4 Add orange sections and orange juice to onion mixture. Bring to boiling; reduce heat. Simmer, uncovered, for 5 minutes, stirring occasionally. Serve over grilled pork chops.

nutrition facts per serving: 289 cal., 14 g total fat (4 g sat. fat), 78 mg chol., 207 mg sodium, 16 g carb., 3 g fiber, 25 g pro.

*tip: If using pork chops that have not been injected with a sodium solution, sprinkle chops with ¼ teaspoon sea salt before grilling.

**tip: Because hot chile peppers contain volatile oils that can burn your skin and eyes, avoid direct contact with chiles as much as possible. When working with chile peppers, wear plastic or rubber gloves. If your bare hands do touch the chile peppers, wash your hands and fingernails well with soap and water when you are done.

Chipotle chiles are dried, smoked jalapeño peppers. Their sweet, spicy, and smoky flavor has become a favorite in salsas, rubs, and sauces.

pork chops and squash

start to finish: 20 minutes
makes: 4 servings

4   pork rib chops, cut
     ¾ inch thick
4   small zucchini and/
     or yellow summer
     squash, halved
     lengthwise
1   tablespoon olive oil
     Salt
     Ground black pepper
1   orange, peeled,
     sectioned, and
     chopped
½   cup chipotle salsa

1 Trim fat from pork chops. Brush chops and zucchini lightly with the olive oil and sprinkle with salt and pepper.

2 For a charcoal or gas grill, place chops and zucchini, cut sides down, on the rack of a covered grill directly over medium heat. Grill squash for 6 to 8 minutes or until tender; grill chops for 11 to 13 minutes or until slightly pink in center (160°F), turning once.

3 Meanwhile, in a small bowl stir together orange and salsa. Cut squash into bite-size pieces; place squash and chops on a serving platter. Serve with salsa mixture.

nutrition facts per serving: 252 cal., 9 g total fat (2 g sat. fat), 94 mg chol., 395 mg sodium, 10 g carb., 2 g fiber, 32 g pro.

Here's how to quickly prep a sweet pepper for eating or cooking: Stand it on its end and cut down close to the center core on all four "sides" of the pepper. You'll be left with a membrane, seeds, and stem you can toss—and four clean and neat pieces of sweet pepper for slicing or dicing.

pork chops and pineapple with chili slaw

start to finish: 20 minutes
makes: 4 servings

8 boneless top loin pork chops, cut ½ inch thick (1½ pounds total)
  Salt
1½ teaspoons chili powder
½ of a cored fresh pineapple, sliced
3 tablespoons cider vinegar
2 tablespoons orange juice
2 tablespoons olive oil
1 tablespoon sugar
⅓ of a small green cabbage, cored and sliced (about 5 cups)
½ of a red onion, thinly sliced
1 small red sweet pepper, cut in strips
  Salt
  Freshly ground black pepper

1 Trim fat from chops. Sprinkle chops with salt and 1 teaspoon of the chili powder. For charcoal or gas grill, grill chops and pineapple on the rack of a covered grill directly over medium heat for 6 to 8 minutes, or until chops are done (160°F), turning once.

2 Meanwhile, for chili slaw, in large bowl whisk together vinegar, juice, oil, sugar, and the remaining ½ teaspoon chili powder. Add cabbage, onion, and sweet pepper; toss to mix. Season with salt and pepper. Serve chops with pineapple and slaw.

nutrition facts per serving: 357 cal., 12 g total fat (3 g sat. fat), 112 mg chol., 392 mg sodium, 20 g carb., 4 g fiber, 40 g pro.

kitchen tip: Here's a sweet way to use up the other half of the pineapple from this recipe: Place the remaining pineapple slices on the grill and cook until caramelized, turning once. If you like, grill some other fruit, such as sliced peaches or nectarines, alongside the pineapple. Cut an angel food cake into thick slices; grill both sides until lightly toasted. Top toasted cake slices with grilled fruit and a dollop of frozen whipped topping, thawed, or a scoop of frozen vanilla yogurt. Dessert is done!

The fusion taco craze has resulted in nearly every flavor profile represented in a tortilla. These Japanese-style tacos are fresh, light, and cheese-free—with a nose-clearing shot of wasabi.

pork-wasabi tacos

prep: 15 minutes **grill:** 12 minutes
makes: 6 tacos

1   1½-pound pork tenderloin, cut into 1-inch pieces
⅓   cup hoisin sauce
6   flatbreads or flour tortillas
1   to 2 teaspoons prepared wasabi paste
2   tablespoons water
2   tablespoons canola oil
½   teaspoon white wine vinegar
½   teaspoon sugar
¼   of a head napa cabbage, shredded
2   carrots, shredded
½   English cucumber, thinly sliced

1 Thread pork on skewers.* Brush with hoisin sauce. For charcoal or gas grill, grill pork on the rack of a covered grill directly over medium heat for 12 to 14 minutes or until no pink remains (160°F), turning once. Add flatbreads the last 1 minute of grilling time, turning once to heat through.

2 Meanwhile, for wasabi oil, in a small bowl whisk together wasabi paste, the water, oil, vinegar, and sugar.

3 Serve pork and vegetables on flatbreads. Drizzle with wasabi oil. Serve immediately.

nutrition facts per taco: 447 cal., 13 g total fat (5 g sat. fat), 89 mg chol., 470 mg sodium, 50 g carb., 2 g fiber, 31 g pro.

✳ tip: If using wooden skewers, soak in enough water to cover for at least 1 hour before using.

It's not a necessity, but the bourbon does add just a hint of smoky molasses flavor to these homemade pork-sausage patties.

fennel and pork sausage with grape relish

prep: 15 minutes grill: 14 minutes
makes: 4 servings

1 egg, lightly beaten
1 tablespoon bourbon (optional)
½ cup quick-cooking rolled oats
1 tablespoon fennel seeds, crushed
1 teaspoon finely shredded lemon peel
1 teaspoon paprika
½ teaspoon salt
½ teaspoon ground black pepper
1 clove garlic, minced
1 pound lean ground pork
1½ cups red seedless grapes, halved
1 cup coarsely chopped fennel (1 medium bulb)
1 tablespoon butter
2 tablespoons balsamic vinegar
4 slices bread, toasted (optional)
¼ cup snipped fresh parsley

1 In a large bowl combine the egg and, if desired, bourbon. Stir in rolled oats, fennel seeds, lemon peel, paprika, salt, pepper, and garlic. Add ground pork; mix well. Shape the pork mixture into four ¾-inch-thick patties; set aside.

2 Fold a 36×18-inch piece of heavy foil in half to make a double thickness of foil that measures 18×18 inches. Place the grapes, fennel, butter, and vinegar in the center of the foil. Sprinkle with additional salt and pepper. Bring up 2 opposite edges of foil and seal with a double fold. Fold remaining edges to completely enclose the grape mixture, leaving space for steam to build.

3 For a charcoal or gas grill, place pork patties and foil packet on grill rack over medium heat. Grill, covered, for 14 to 16 minutes or until no pink remains in the patties (160°F),* turning once.

4 If desired, serve pork burgers on bread. Carefully open packet and spoon grape mixture over the grilled patties. Sprinkle with the fresh parsley.

nutrition facts per serving: 284 cal., 14 g total fat (5 g sat. fat), 106 mg chol., 409 mg sodium, 23 g carb., 7 g fiber, 18 g pro.

*tip: The internal color of a burger is not a reliable doneness indicator. A beef or pork patty cooked to 160°F is safe, regardless of color. To check the doneness of a patty, insert an instant-read thermometer through the side of the patty to a depth of 2 to 3 inches.

This recipe is so simple but lamb chops are special enough to make it an ideal entrée for casual entertaining. For dessert, serve frozen Greek yogurt drizzled with honey and topped with fresh fruit and toasted slivered almonds.

tomato-topped lamb chops and rice

start to finish: 20 minutes
makes: 4 servings

8   lamb loin chops, cut
      1 inch thick
      Salt
      Ground black pepper
1   8.8-ounce pouch
      cooked long grain
      rice
4   roma tomatoes, cut
      up
4   green onions, cut into
      1-inch pieces
1   tablespoon snipped
      fresh oregano
1   tablespoon balsamic
      vinegar

1 Trim fat from chops. Sprinkle chops with salt and pepper. For a charcoal or gas grill, grill chops on the rack of a covered grill directly over medium heat for 12 to 14 minutes for medium-rare (145°F) or 15 to 17 minutes for medium (160°F), turning once halfway through grilling time.

2 Meanwhile, heat rice in the microwave oven according to package directions. In a food processor combine tomatoes, green onions, and oregano. Cover and process with on/off pulses until coarsely chopped. Transfer to a small bowl; stir in balsamic vinegar. Season with additional salt and pepper.

3 Divide rice among four dinner plates; top with chops. Serve with tomato mixture.

nutrition facts per serving: 273 cal., 7 g total fat (2 g sat. fat), 70 mg chol., 153 mg sodium, 26 g carb., 3 g fiber, 25 g pro.

Peaches are at peak season in August, which is the perfect time to make this colorful dish.

chicken and peaches with green beans and orzo

start to finish: 30 minutes
makes: 6 servings

8 ounces dried orzo (rosamarina) (1⅓ cups)
8 ounces green beans, trimmed (about 2½ cups)
2 medium peaches, cut into wedges
1 pound chicken breast tenderloins
2 tablespoons olive oil
¼ teaspoon salt
¼ teaspoon ground black pepper
2 to 4 ounces herb-flavor feta cheese (garlic and herb or peppercorn), crumbled
Fresh thyme (optional)

1 In a large saucepan or Dutch oven cook orzo according to package directions. Add green beans for the last 5 minutes of cooking time. Drain; do not rinse. Remove green beans and set aside.

2 Meanwhile, lightly brush peaches, then chicken with some of the oil, sprinkle with the ¼ teaspoon salt and the ¼ teaspoon pepper.

3 For a charcoal or gas grill, grill chicken and peaches on the rack of a covered grill directly over medium heat for 4 to 6 minutes or until chicken is no longer pink and peaches are tender.

4 In a large bowl combine orzo, feta cheese, and the remaining oil; gently toss to mix. Season with additional salt and pepper.

5 Divide green beans among four serving plates. Top with orzo mixture, chicken, and peaches. If desired, garnish with fresh thyme.

nutrition facts per serving: 323 cal., 9 g total fat (4 g sat. fat), 55 mg chol., 296 mg sodium, 36 g carb., 3 g fiber, 24 g pro.

Here's a nifty, no-mess trick for husking corn: Cut off the stalk end about 1 inch above the last row of kernels. Place the corn in the microwave and cook on high for 2 to 4 minutes. Remove corn from the microwave and hold at the top. Gently shake and squeeze the cob; it should slide right out of the husk—clean as a whistle.

grilled chicken and creamy corn

prep: 15 minutes   **grill:** 12 minutes
makes: 4 servings

2   tablespoons olive oil
1   teaspoon smoked
    paprika
3   fresh ears corn, husks
    and silks removed
4   skinless, boneless
    chicken breast
    halves (1 to 1¼
    pounds total)
¼   teaspoon salt
⅛   teaspoon ground
    black pepper
⅓   cup light sour cream
    Fat-free milk
¼   cup shredded fresh
    basil

1 In small bowl combine oil and paprika. Brush corn and chicken with oil mixture. Sprinkle with the ¼ teaspoon salt and the ⅛ teaspoon pepper. For a charcoal or gas grill, place corn and chicken on rack directly over medium heat. Grill, covered, for 12 to 15 minutes or until chicken is no longer pink (170°F), turning once.

2 On a cutting board, place an ear of corn, pointed tip down. While holding corn firmly at stem end to keep in place, use a sharp knife to cut corn from cob, leaving some corn in planks; rotate cob as needed to cut corn from all sides. Repeat with remaining ears. (Use a kitchen towel to grip, if necessary.) Transfer corn to a medium bowl; stir in sour cream. Stir in milk to desired creaminess. Slice chicken breasts. Serve with corn and sprinkle with shredded basil.

nutrition facts per serving: 267 cal., 11 g total fat (2 g sat. fat), 71 mg chol., 228 mg sodium, 15 g carb., 2 g fiber, 29 g pro.

Brush the apricot glaze on just during the last 3 minutes of grilling, as directed. If you try to brush it sooner, it will likely burn due to the high sugar content.

apricot chicken kabobs

prep: 20 minutes   **grill:** 8 minutes
makes: 4 servings

1   pound skinless, boneless chicken breast halves, cut into 1-inch pieces
1½   teaspoons Jamaican jerk seasoning
1   cup fresh sugar snap peas or snow pea pods, strings and tips removed
1   cup fresh or canned pineapple cubes
1   medium red sweet pepper, seeded and cut into 1-inch pieces
¼   cup apricot spreadable fruit

1 Sprinkle chicken with about half of the jerk seasoning; toss gently to coat. Cut any large pea pods in half crosswise.

2 Alternately thread chicken, sugar snap peas, pineapple, and sweet pepper onto skewers,* leaving about ¼ inch between pieces.

3 For sauce, in a small saucepan combine spreadable fruit and the remaining jerk seasoning. Cook and stir just until spreadable fruit is melted; set aside.

4 For a charcoal or gas grill, grill kabobs on the rack of a covered grill directly over medium heat for 8 to 12 minutes or until chicken is no longer pink and vegetables are crisp-tender, turning once and brushing occasionally with sauce during the last 3 minutes of grilling.

nutrition facts per serving: 199 cal., 2 g total fat (0 g sat. fat), 66 mg chol., 173 mg sodium, 20 g carb., 2 g fiber, 27 g pro.

*tip: If using wooden skewers, soak in enough water to cover for at least 1 hour before using.

This sauce is very similar to chimichurri, an herb sauce that is as commonly served in Argentina (mostly with its famous grilled steaks) as ketchup is served here. Try it on grilled beef, pork, and fish as well.

lemon and herb sauced chicken

prep: 15 minutes **grill:** 12 minutes
makes: 4 servings

4   skinless, boneless chicken breast halves (1 to 1¼ pounds total)
3   tablespoons canola oil
½   teaspoon salt
¼   teaspoon ground black pepper
12 ounces fresh young green beans
1   tablespoon water
¾   cup fresh Italian (flat-leaf) parsley
1   tablespoon cider vinegar
2   cloves garlic, halved
¼   teaspoon crushed red pepper
1   lemon

1 Brush chicken with 1 tablespoon of the oil; sprinkle with ¼ teaspoon of the salt and the black pepper. For a charcoal or gas grill, place chicken on the rack of a grill directly over medium heat. Grill, covered, for 12 to 15 minutes or until no longer pink (170°F), turning once.

2 In a 1½-quart microwave-safe baking dish combine green beans and the water. Cover loosely with plastic wrap. Microwave on 100 percent power (high) for 3 minutes; drain.

3 For herb sauce, in a small food processor combine parsley, the remaining 2 tablespoons oil, the remaining ¼ teaspoon salt, the vinegar, garlic, and crushed red pepper. Cover and process until nearly smooth. Finely shred peel from the lemon. Cut lemon in half. Serve chicken and green beans with herb sauce. Garnish with lemon peel. Squeeze lemon juice over all.

nutrition facts per serving: 281 cal., 12 g total fat (2 g sat. fat), 82 mg chol., 376 mg sodium, 8 g carb., 3 g fiber, 35 g pro.

Ground turkey breast is extremely lean—and that's a good thing—but be careful not to overcook and dry it out. (But be sure the patties register 165°F internally before serving.)

grilled turkey gyros

prep: 20 minutes **grill:** 6 minutes
makes: 4 gyros

1 recipe Cucumber-
    Yogurt Sauce
1 egg, lightly beaten
12 ounces uncooked
    ground turkey
    breast
¼ cup finely chopped
    onion
1 tablespoon fine dry
    bread crumbs
2 cloves garlic, minced
1 teaspoon ground
    coriander
½ teaspoon ground
    cumin
⅛ teaspoon salt
⅛ teaspoon ground
    black pepper
1 tablespoon olive oil
4 whole wheat pita
    bread rounds
1 cup thinly sliced
    cucumber
1 cup diced tomato
2 tablespoons snipped
    fresh Italian (flat-
    leaf) parsley

1 Prepare Cucumber-Yogurt Sauce. For patties, in a large bowl combine egg, turkey, onion, bread crumbs, garlic, coriander, cumin, salt, and pepper. Shape mixture into 12 patties, flattening each to about ½-inch thickness. Brush all sides of the patties with oil. Wrap pita bread rounds in foil.

2 For a charcoal or gas grill, grill patties and foil-wrapped pita bread on the greased rack of a covered grill directly over medium heat about 6 minutes or until an instant-read thermometer inserted into each patty registers 165°F* and pitas are heated through, turning once halfway through grilling.

3 Place three patties on each pita bread round. Top with cucumber slices, tomato, and parsley. Drizzle with Cucumber-Yogurt Sauce. Fold pitas around fillings; secure with toothpicks.

nutrition facts per gyro: 332 cal., 9 g total fat (1 g sat. fat), 95 mg chol., 560 mg sodium, 37 g carb., 6 g fiber, 31 g pro.

＊tip: The internal color of a burger is not a reliable doneness indicator. A chicken or turkey patty cooked to 165°F is safe, regardless of color. To measure the doneness of a patty, insert an instant-read thermometer through the side to the center of the patty.

Cucumber-Yogurt Sauce: In a small bowl combine ⅓ cup plain fat-free yogurt; ¼ cup shredded, seeded cucumber; 1 tablespoon tahini (sesame seed paste); 2 cloves garlic, minced; and ⅛ teaspoon salt. Cover and chill for at least 20 minutes.

You can remove the pit from an avocado in two ways: Firmly strike it with the cutting edge of a chef's knife, then gently twist with the knife and pop the pit out. Or, you can gently insert a spoon underneath the pit and pop it out that way.

tex-mex turkey patties

prep: 20 minutes   **grill:** 10 minutes
makes: 2 servings

8   ounces uncooked ground turkey breast or lean ground beef
¼   cup purchased salsa
¼   teaspoon ground cumin
⅛   teaspoon ground black pepper
    Dash salt
1   small sweet onion (such as Vidalia or Walla Walla), thinly sliced
½   of a medium red sweet pepper, cut into thin strips
1   teaspoon canola oil
2   tostada shells
¼   of a medium avocado, seeded, peeled, and sliced or chopped

1 In a medium bowl combine ground turkey, salsa, cumin, black pepper, and salt; mix well. Shape turkey mixture into two ½-inch-thick patties.

2 Fold a 24×12-inch piece of heavy foil in half to make a 12-inch square. Place onion and sweet pepper in the center of foil; drizzle with oil. Bring up two opposite edges of foil; seal with a double fold. Fold the remaining ends to completely enclose vegetables, leaving space for steam to build.

3 For a charcoal or gas grill, grill patties and vegetable packet on the rack of a covered grill directly over medium heat for 10 to 13 minutes or until patties are done (165°F for turkey, 160°F for beef) and vegetables are tender, turning patties and packet once.

4 Serve burgers on tostada shells. Carefully open vegetable packet. Top patties with vegetables and avocado.

nutrition facts per serving: 285 cal., 10 g total fat (1 g sat. fat), 55 mg chol., 430 mg sodium, 20 g carb., 5 g fiber, 29 g pro.

The salsa is also delicious as an appetizer with tortillas chips, for those who like their salsa sweet and hot.

salmon with cilantro-pineapple salsa

prep: 20 minutes grill: 8 minutes
makes: 4 servings

1 pound fresh or frozen skinless salmon fillet, about 1 inch thick

2 cups coarsely chopped fresh pineapple

½ cup chopped red or green sweet pepper

¼ cup finely chopped red onion

3 tablespoons lime juice

1 small fresh jalapeño chile pepper, seeded and finely chopped*

2 tablespoons snipped fresh cilantro or parsley

½ teaspoon finely shredded lime peel

½ teaspoon chili powder

¼ teaspoon salt
Dash cayenne pepper
Lime wedges (optional)
Torn lettuce (optional)

1 Thaw fish, if frozen. Rinse fish; pat dry with paper towels. For salsa, in a medium bowl combine pineapple, sweet pepper, red onion, 2 tablespoons of the lime juice, the chile pepper, and 1 tablespoon of the cilantro; set aside.

2 In a small bowl combine lime peel, the remaining 1 tablespoon lime juice, the remaining 1 tablespoon cilantro, the chili powder, salt, and cayenne pepper. Brush on both sides of fish.

3 Generously grease a wire grill basket. Place fish in grill basket, tucking under any thin edges for an even thickness. Place fish in grill basket on the rack of a grill directly over medium heat. Grill, covered, for 8 to 12 minutes or just until fish flakes easily when tested with a fork, carefully turning once.

4 To serve, cut fish into four serving-size pieces; top with salsa. If desired, serve with lime wedges and lettuce.

nutrition facts per serving: 257 cal., 12 g total fat (2 g sat. fat), 66 mg chol., 219 mg sodium, 13 g carb., 2 g fiber, 23 g pro.

*tip: Because chile peppers contain volatile oils that can burn your skin and eyes, avoid direct contact with them as much as possible. When working with chile peppers, wear plastic or rubber gloves. If your bare hands do touch the peppers, wash your hands and nails well with soap and warm water.

Ancho chiles are ripened and dried poblano chiles—the deep green pepper used in cheese-stuffed and deep-fried chiles relleños. As the poblano ripens, it gets redder and hotter. The deep red ancho chile powder infuses the fish and veggies with a warm (but not hot), slightly sweet chile flavor.

grilled tuna steaks and vegetables

prep: 15 minutes   **grill:** 8 minutes
makes: 4 servings

4 5-ounce fresh or frozen tuna steaks, cut 1 inch thick
2 tablespoons canola oil
2 tablespoons lime juice
½ teaspoon ground ancho chile pepper or chili powder
¼ teaspoon ground cumin
1 clove garlic, minced
¼ teaspoon salt
1 large zucchini, trimmed and halved lengthwise
1 large red sweet pepper, seeded and quartered
2 ¼-inch slices red onion
2 tablespoons coarsely chopped walnuts, toasted*
   Fresh cilantro (optional)
   Lime wedges (optional)

1 Thaw fish, if frozen. Rinse fish; pat dry with paper towels. In a small bowl whisk together oil, lime juice, ancho chile pepper, cumin, garlic, and salt. Brush about half of the oil mixture onto both sides of each zucchini half, pepper quarter, and onion slice. Brush the remaining oil mixture on the tuna.

2 For a charcoal or gas grill, place fish and vegetables on the greased rack of a covered grill directly over medium heat. Grill, covered, for 8 to 12 minutes or until fish flakes easily when tested with a fork and vegetables are crisp-tender, gently turning fish and vegetables once.

3 Cut zucchini pieces in half and then cut into thick lengthwise slices. Cut pepper quarters into thick lengthwise slices. Using tongs, separate onion slices into rings.

4 To serve, place vegetables on plates. Top with tuna and nuts. If desired, garnish with cilantro and pass lime wedges.

nutrition facts per serving: 265 cal., 11 g total fat (1 g sat. fat), 63 mg chol., 209 mg sodium, 7 g carb., 2 g fiber, 35 g pro.

＊tip: To toast nuts, spread them in a shallow baking pan. Bake in a 350°F oven for 5 to 10 minutes or until light brown, shaking pan once or twice. Watch carefully so the nuts don't burn.

The bright, sweet flavor of red pepper is a lovely complement to the meaty, buttery taste of the cod in this Mediterranean-style fish dish.

grilled cod with red pepper sauce

prep: 25 minutes   **grill:** 4 to 6 minutes per ½-inch thickness
makes: 4 servings

4 to 6 fresh or frozen skinless cod fillets (4 ounces each)
1 tablespoon olive oil
1¼ cups chopped red sweet pepper (1 large)
1 cup chopped, seeded, peeled tomatoes (2 medium)
2 tablespoons white wine vinegar
¼ teaspoon salt
Dash cayenne pepper
1 tablespoon olive oil
1 tablespoon snipped fresh basil or oregano or ½ teaspoon dried basil or oregano, crushed
Red and/or yellow cherry tomatoes (optional)
Fresh basil or oregano sprigs (optional)

1 Thaw fish, if frozen. Rinse fish; pat dry with paper towels. Measure thickness of fish; set aside.

2 For sauce, in a small skillet heat 1 tablespoon oil over medium heat. Add sweet pepper; cook for 3 to 5 minutes or until tender, stirring occasionally. Stir in chopped tomatoes, 1 tablespoon of the vinegar, the salt, and cayenne pepper. Cook about 5 minutes or until tomatoes are softened, stirring occasionally. Cool slightly. Transfer mixture to a food processor or blender. Cover and process or blend until smooth. Return sauce to skillet. Cover and keep warm.

3 In a small bowl stir together the remaining 1 tablespoon vinegar, 1 tablespoon oil, and snipped basil; brush over both sides of fish. Place fish in a greased grill basket, tucking under any thin edges.

4 For a charcoal or gas grill, grill fish in basket on the rack of a covered grill directly over medium heat until fish flakes easily when tested with a fork, turning basket once. Allow 4 to 6 minutes per ½-inch thickness of fish.

5 Serve fish with sauce. If desired, serve with cherry tomatoes and fresh basil sprigs.

nutrition facts per serving: 194 cal., 8 g total fat (1 g sat. fat), 41 mg chol., 223 mg sodium, 4 g carb., 1 g fiber, 26 g pro.

If you have frozen fish fillets in individually wrapped packages, you can quickly and safely thaw them from a solid state. Place the wrapped fillets in a bowl of cool water. They will be thawed in just about 30 minutes.

grilled fish tacos

prep: 25 minutes **grill:** 4 minutes
makes: 12 tacos

1 pound fresh or frozen
  skinless cod, sole,
  or flounder fillets,
  about ½ inch thick
1 tablespoon lemon
  juice
1 tablespoon olive oil
1 teaspoon chili
  powder
½ teaspoon ground
  cumin
¾ teaspoon salt
¼ teaspoon ground
  black pepper
1 cup chopped fresh
  pineapple
¼ cup chopped red
  sweet pepper
¼ cup chopped red
  onion
2 tablespoons snipped
  fresh cilantro
1 fresh serrano or
  jalapeño chile
  pepper, seeded and
  finely chopped*
1 teaspoon finely
  shredded lemon
  peel
12 7- to 8-inch fat-free
  flour tortillas

1 Thaw fish, if frozen. Rinse fish; pat dry with paper towels. Arrange fish in a 2-quart square baking dish; set aside. For marinade, in a small bowl whisk together lemon juice, oil, chili powder, cumin, ¼ teaspoon of the salt, and the black pepper. Pour marinade over fish; turn fish to coat with marinade. Cover and marinate in the refrigerator for 15 minutes.

2 Meanwhile, for salsa, in a medium bowl stir together pineapple, sweet pepper, onion, cilantro, chile pepper, lemon peel, and the remaining ½ teaspoon salt. Set salsa aside.

3 Stack tortillas and wrap in foil; set aside.

4 Drain fish, discarding any marinade. For a charcoal or gas grill, place fish and tortilla packet on the greased rack of a grill directly over medium heat. Grill, covered, for 4 to 6 minutes or until fish flakes easily when tested with a fork and tortillas are warmed, turning tortilla packet once halfway through grilling.

5 Transfer fish to a cutting board. Cut or flake fish into 1-inch pieces. Serve fish in warmed tortillas topped with salsa.

nutrition facts per 2 tacos: 305 cal., 3 g total fat (0 g sat. fat), 33 mg chol., 823 mg sodium, 49 g carb., 0 g fiber, 18 g pro.

*tip: Because chile peppers contain volatile oils that can burn your skin and eyes, avoid direct contact with them as much as possible. When working with chile peppers, wear plastic or rubber gloves. If your bare hands do touch the peppers, wash your hands and nails well with soap and warm water.

Prepared corn relish is the fast ticket to a delicious succotash salad—just stir in cooked lima beans and baby spinach.

catfish with summer succotash salad

start to finish: 20 minutes
makes: 4 servings

4 4- to 6-ounce fresh or
   frozen catfish fillets,
   about ½ inch thick
2 cups frozen lima
   beans
   Olive oil
   Garlic salt
   Ground black pepper
1 cup purchased corn
   relish
1 cup fresh baby
   spinach

1 Thaw fish, if frozen. Cook lima beans according to package directions. Drain in colander; rinse under cold water to cool. Set lima beans aside.

2 Meanwhile, rinse fish; pat dry with paper towels. Brush fish with oil; sprinkle with garlic salt and pepper. Place fish in a well-greased grill basket. For a charcoal or gas grill, place grill basket on the rack of a covered grill directly over medium heat. Grill for 6 to 9 minutes or until fish flakes easily when tested with a fork, turning basket once. Place fish on a serving platter or four serving plates.

3 For succotash salad, in a large bowl toss together cooled lima beans, corn relish, and spinach. Serve with fish.

nutrition facts per serving: 372 cal., 12 g total fat (3 g sat. fat), 53 mg chol., 509 mg sodium, 41 g carb., 5 g fiber, 24 g pro.

kitchen tip: A grill basket is a handy tool to have if you grill a lot of fish—particularly thinner, more delicate fillets such as catfish, tilapia, and trout. A grill basket allows you to turn the fish while cooking without having it stick to the grill or break.

Using a grill wok (with holes) is a great way to cook smaller ingredients—such as shrimp and chopped vegetables—over an open flame and reap all of the delicious, smoky benefits that offers.

cajun shrimp stir-fry in a grill wok

prep: 20 minutes **grill:** 6 minutes
makes: 4 servings

12   ounces fresh or
        frozen peeled and
        deveined medium
        shrimp
 2   tablespoons canola
        oil
 2   cups red and/
        or yellow sweet
        pepper strips
        (2 medium)
 1   cup thin onion
        wedges
 1   cup broccoli florets or
        zucchini chunks
 1   teaspoon Cajun
        seasoning
        Nonstick cooking
        spray
 ¼   cup chopped pecans,
        toasted*
 1   tablespoon snipped
        fresh parsley
        Lime wedges
        (optional)

1 Thaw shrimp, if frozen. Rinse shrimp; pat dry with paper towels. In a medium bowl combine shrimp and 1 tablespoon of the oil; toss gently to coat. Set aside.

2 In a large bowl combine sweet pepper, onion, broccoli, and Cajun seasoning. Drizzle with the remaining 1 tablespoon oil; toss gently to coat.

3 Lightly coat a grill wok with cooking spray. For a charcoal grill, place grill wok on the rack of an uncovered grill directly over medium-hot coals. Heat wok for 5 minutes. Carefully add shrimp; grill for 2 to 3 minutes or until shrimp begin to brown, stirring occasionally. Add vegetable mixture; grill and stir for 4 to 6 minutes or until shrimp are opaque and vegetables are tender. (For a gas grill, preheat grill. Reduce heat to medium-high. Place grill wok on grill rack directly over heat. Cover and heat wok, then grill as above.)

4 Sprinkle shrimp mixture with pecans and parsley. If desired, serve with lime wedges.

nutrition facts per serving: 249 cal., 14 g total fat (1 g sat. fat), 129 mg chol., 185 mg sodium, 13 g carb., 4 g fiber, 20 g pro.

nutrition note: Many Cajun seasonings are high in sodium. If you are watching your salt intake, read the label carefully or choose a reduced-salt or no-salt-added version.

*tip: To toast nuts, spread them in a shallow baking pan. Bake in a 350°F oven for 5 to 10 minutes or until light brown, shaking pan once or twice. Watch carefully so the nuts don't burn.

Give the tequila-lime marinade and slaw dressing a smoky flavor by substituting sweet smoked paprika for the regular paprika, if you like.

grilled drunken shrimp and scallop skewers

start to finish: 30 minutes
makes: 6 servings

20 large fresh or frozen sea scallops (about 1¾ pounds total)
20 large fresh or frozen shrimp (about 12 ounces total)
¼ cup tequila
¼ cup lime juice
¼ cup olive oil
2 tablespoons snipped fresh oregano
2 teaspoons sugar
2 teaspoons salt
4 cloves garlic, sliced
½ teaspoon paprika
1 to 1¼ pounds jicama, peeled and cut into bite-size strips (about 4 cups)
1 medium avocado, halved, seeded, peeled, and thinly sliced
½ cup fresh cilantro leaves
Salt
Ground black pepper
Lime wedges

1 Thaw scallops and shrimp, if frozen. Peel and devein shrimp. Rinse scallops and shrimp with cold water; pat dry with paper towels. Place scallops and shrimp in a large resealable plastic bag set in a shallow dish; set aside.

2 In a small bowl stir together tequila, lime juice, olive oil, oregano, sugar, the 2 tesaspoons salt, the garlic, and paprika. Set aside ½ cup of the tequila mixture to use in the jicama slaw. Pour the remaining tequila mixture over the scallops and shrimp. Seal bag; turn to coat scallops and shrimp. Marinate at room temperature for 15 minutes, turning bag occasionally.

3 Meanwhile, for the jicama slaw, in a medium bowl combine jicama, avocado, and cilantro. Pour the reserved ½ cup tequila mixture over jicama mixture. Toss to combine. Season to taste with salt and pepper. Cover and chill until serving time.

4 Drain scallops and shrimp; discard marinade. On six long skewers,* alternately thread scallops and shrimp, leaving ¼ inch between pieces. For a charcoal or gas grill, place skewers on the rack of a covered grill directly over medium-high heat. Grill for 8 to 10 minutes or until scallops and shrimp are opaque, turning once halfway through grilling. Serve skewers with jicama slaw and lime wedges.

nutrition facts per serving: 261 cal., 9 g total fat (1 g sat. fat), 103 mg chol., 1323 mg sodium, 17 g carb., 6 g fiber, 25 g pro.

∗tip: If using wooden skewers, soak in enough water to cover for at least 1 hour before using.

A 20-minute marinating time is perfectly fine for fish or shellfish. Too much longer, and the acid in the marinade—whether citrus juice, wine, or vinegar—begins to "cook" the fish.

shrimp tacos with lime slaw

prep: 25 minutes   grill: 5 minutes
makes: 12 tacos

1   pound fresh or
    frozen medium
    shrimp, peeled and
    deveined
1   tablespoon olive oil
1   teaspoon ground
    cumin
½   teaspoon chili
    powder
½   teaspoon salt
3   cloves garlic, minced
1   lime
3   cups shredded red
    cabbage
½   cup sour cream
1   teaspoon finely
    chopped canned
    chipotle pepper in
    adobo sauce
12 6-inch corn tortillas
    Fresh cilantro
    (optional)
    Lime wedges
    (optional)

1 Thaw shrimp, if frozen. Rinse shrimp; pat dry with paper towels. In a resealable plastic bag combine oil, cumin, chili powder, ¼ teaspoon of the salt, and the garlic; add shrimp. Seal bag and turn to coat shrimp; chill for 20 minutes.

2 Meanwhile, finely shred peel from lime; juice lime. For lime slaw, in a large bowl combine the lime peel, lime juice, cabbage, and the remaining ¼ teaspoon salt; set aside. In a small bowl combine sour cream and chipotle pepper; set aside.

3 Wrap tortillas in foil. Thread shrimp on 10-inch metal skewers.*

4 For a charcoal or gas grill, place shrimp skewers and tortilla packet on grill rack directly over medium heat. Grill, covered, for 5 to 8 minutes or until shrimp are opaque and tortillas are heated through, turning once.

5 Carefully open tortilla packet. Remove shrimp from skewers. To serve, spread tortillas with sour cream mixture. Top with lime slaw and shrimp. If desired, sprinkle with cilantro and pass lime wedges.

nutrition facts per 2 tacos: 135 cal., 4 g total fat (1 g sat. fat), 62 mg chol., 198 mg sodium, 15 g carb., 2 g fiber, 9 g pro.

*** tip:** If using wooden skewers, soak in enough water to cover for at least 1 hour before using.

If you'd like, substitute creamy, spreadable goat cheese for the feta cheese on these sandwiches. After grilling the rolls, simply spread the cheese on the toasted sides of the tops and bottoms of the bread. Layer the veggies on the bottoms, and add the roll tops.

grilled veggie sandwiches

start to finish: 30 minutes
makes: 4 sandwiches

2 tablespoons olive oil
4 ciabatta rolls or other hearty rolls, split
1 lemon, halved and seeded
1 tablespoon balsamic vinegar
3 small zucchini and/ or yellow summer squash, cut lengthwise into ¼-inch-thick slices
1 small red onion, cut into ¼-inch-thick slices
   Salt
   Ground black pepper
½ cup crumbled feta cheese (2 ounces)
   Fresh mint leaves (optional)

1 Lightly brush 1 tablespoon of the oil on cut sides of rolls and the cut sides of lemon halves; set aside. In a small bowl combine the remaining 1 tablespoon oil and the vinegar. Brush zucchini and onion slices with some of the oil-vinegar mixture; sprinkle with salt and pepper.

2 For a charcoal or gas grill, place vegetables and lemon on the rack of a covered grill directly over medium-high heat for 4 to 6 minutes or until tender, turning once. Add rolls, cut sides down, during last 3 minutes of grilling.

3 Arrange vegetables on roll bottoms. Top with feta cheese and, if desired, mint. Drizzle with remaining oil-vinegar mixture. Squeeze juice from lemon over all. Add roll tops.

nutrition facts per sandwich: 294 cal., 11 g total fat (3 g sat. fat), 13 mg chol., 684 mg sodium, 41 g carb., 4 g fiber, 10 g pro.

bacon-wrapped salmon with fruit chutney

.five
ingred

Count down to dinner with these recipes featuring five ingredients or fewer (not counting staples such as salt, pepper, oil, and nonstick cooking spray).

ients

Montreal steak seasoning is an efficient choice for flavoring these steaks. Each shake contains garlic, coriander, black pepper, cayenne, dill seed, and salt.

steak with sweet potato–mango chutney

start to finish: 20 minutes
makes: 4 servings

1 large sweet potato (about 12 ounces), peeled and diced
4 6-ounce boneless beef round steaks, about ¾ inch thick
Salt
Steak seasoning
⅓ cup mango chutney
¼ cup dried cranberries

1 In a medium saucepan bring lightly salted water to boiling. Add sweet potato. Return to boiling; reduce heat. Simmer, covered, for 8 to 10 minutes or until tender. Drain; keep warm.

2 Meanwhile, preheat a large nonstick skillet over medium-high heat. Trim fat from steaks. Sprinkle steaks with salt and steak seasoning. Add meat to skillet; reduce heat to medium. Cook for 8 to 10 minutes or until desired doneness. (If meat browns too quickly, reduce heat to medium low.) Transfer to plates; cover to keep warm.

3 Add potatoes to skillet; cook and stir for 2 minutes. Add chutney and cranberries; heat through. Serve with steaks.

nutrition facts per serving: 344 cal., 5 g total fat (2 g sat. fat), 70 mg chol., 418 mg sodium, 32 g carb., 4 g fiber, 40 g pro.

Flat iron steak (also called top blade steak) is a relatively new cut of beef that has become very popular in the last few years. It is prized for its reasonable price in comparison to its flavor, leanness, and tenderness. Flat iron steak is cut from the shoulder of the animal.

flat iron steak with bbq beans

start to finish: 20 minutes
makes: 4 servings

Nonstick cooking
    spray
2 boneless beef
    shoulder top blade
    (flat iron) steaks,
    halved (1 to 1¼
    pounds total)
2 teaspoons fajita
    seasoning
1 15-ounce can black
    beans, rinsed and
    drained
⅓ cup bottled barbecue
    sauce
2 to 3 tomatoes, sliced
    Pickled jalapeño
    peppers (optional)

1 Lightly coat a grill pan with cooking spray. Preheat grill pan over medium-high heat. Trim fat from steaks. Sprinkle steaks with fajita seasoning. Place steaks on prepared grill pan; cook for 8 to 12 minutes for medium-rare (145°F) or 12 to 15 minutes for medium (160°F), turning steaks twice.

2 Meanwhile, in a microwave-safe medium bowl stir together beans and barbecue sauce. Cover with vented plastic wrap. Microwave on 100 percent power (high) about 3 minutes or until heated through, stirring once.

3 Serve steaks with bean mixture and sliced tomatoes. If desired, garnish with pickled jalapeño slices.

nutrition facts per serving: 272 cal., 8 g total fat (2 g sat. fat), 67 mg chol., 667 mg sodium, 25 g carb., 6 g fiber, 29 g pro.

nutrition note: Do your heart a favor—always rinse and drain canned beans before using. A quick rinse may reduce the sodium content by as much as 40 percent.

Using a package of refrigerated beef pot roast makes these soft tacos superfast to put together. Top them with your favorite salsa.

mexican beef and tortillas

start to finish: 20 minutes
makes: 4 servings

8   6-inch corn tortillas
1   17-ounce package refrigerated beef pot roast with juices
1   14.5-ounce can diced tomatoes with green chiles
1   green sweet pepper, cut into strips
1   lime, cut into wedges
    Light sour cream (optional)
    Fresh cilantro sprigs (optional)

1 Wrap tortillas in paper towels. Microwave on 100 percent power (high) for 45 to 60 seconds or until warm. Cover; set aside.

2 Microwave beef according to package directions. Meanwhile, place undrained tomatoes in small saucepan; heat through.

3 Remove meat, reserving juices. Cut into slices. Serve meat on warmed tortillas with tomatoes and green pepper strips. Drizzle reserved juices. Pass lime wedges and, if desired, sour cream and cilantro.

nutrition facts per serving: 319 cal., 10 g total fat (5 g sat. fat), 64 mg chol., 857 mg sodium, 34 g carb., 5 g fiber, 27 g pro.

nutrition note: Corn tortillas have between 25 percent and 50 percent fewer calories and 50 percent less fat and sodium than flour tortillas of the same kind.

Green onions are an underappreciated ingredient. Sprinkled on top of finished food, they add delightful flavor and texture.

spicy beef-noodle bowl

start to finish: 20 minutes
makes: 4 servings

1   tablespoon vegetable
       oil
1   pound boneless
       beef sirloin steak,
       trimmed of fat and
       cut in thin strips
2   14.5-ounce cans
       50 percent less
       sodium beef broth
⅓   cup bottled peanut
       sauce
1½   cups medium egg
       noodles (3 ounces)
2   cups broccoli florets
¼   cup bias-sliced green
       onions (optional)

1 In a 4-quart Dutch oven heat oil over medium-high heat. Add beef; cook until brown.

2 Carefully add broth and peanut sauce; bring to boiling. Stir in noodles; reduce heat. Simmer, uncovered, for 4 minutes, stirring occasionally to separate noodles. Add broccoli; return to boiling. Reduce heat. Simmer, uncovered, for 3 to 4 minutes more or just until noodles are tender, stirring occasionally.

3 Divide beef and noodle mixture among four bowls. If desired, top with green onions.

nutrition facts per serving: 316 cal., 12 g total fat (3 g sat. fat), 60 mg chol., 762 mg sodium, 18 g carb., 2 g fiber, 31 g pro.

Yes, you can have meat loaf on a busy Monday night—when it's already prepared. Make it special by layering it on toasted Italian bread with eggplant and tomato sauce.

meat loaf open-facers

start to finish: 20 minutes
makes: 4 open-face sandwiches

4   ½-inch slices
    eggplant
1   tablespoon olive oil
    Salt
    Ground black pepper
1   15-ounce package
    refrigerated meat
    loaf with tomato
    sauce
½   cup no-salt-added
    tomato sauce
4   1-inch diagonal
    slices Italian bread,
    toasted
¼   cup finely shredded
    Parmesan cheese
    (optional)

1 Preheat broiler. Brush both sides of eggplant slices with oil. Sprinkle with salt and pepper. Place eggplant slices on the unheated rack of broiler pan. Broil 3 to 4 inches from heat for 4 to 6 minutes or until browned, turning once.

2 Slice meat loaf. In a large skillet arrange meat loaf slices in a single layer. Pour tomato sauce over slices. Cook, covered, over medium-high heat about 6 minutes or until heated through.

3 To assemble sandwiches, divide meat loaf slices among bread slices. Top with eggplant slices, any remaining sauce, and, if desired, Parmesan cheese.

nutrition facts per open-face sandwich: 304 cal., 13 g total fat (4 g sat. fat), 45 mg chol., 1042 mg sodium, 29 g carb., 3 g fiber, 17 g pro.

Pierogi, a Polish specialty, get the Mediterranean treatment in this dish flavored with balsamic vinegar and rosemary.

balsamic pork and dumplings

start to finish: 30 minutes
makes: 4 servings

1   16.9-ounce package frozen potato-and-onion-filled pierogi (potato dumplings)
12 ounces fresh green and/or wax beans, trimmed (3 cups)
1   1-pound pork tenderloin
    Salt
    Ground black pepper
2   tablespoons olive oil
½   cup balsamic vinegar
2   teaspoons snipped fresh rosemary (optional)

1 In a large saucepan cook pierogi and beans in boiling water according to pierogi package directions. Drain pierogi and beans; divide among serving plates.

2 Meanwhile, slice pork into ½-inch slices. Using your hands, gently flatten pork slices to ¼-inch thickness; lightly sprinkle with salt and pepper. In a large skillet heat oil over medium heat. Add pork; cook for 4 to 6 minutes or until no pink remains, turning once. Transfer pork to the plates with pierogi and beans.

3 Drain fat from skillet. Add balsamic vinegar to hot skillet; cook, uncovered, about 1 minute or until reduced by half. Drizzle over pork, pierogi, and beans. If desired, sprinkle with rosemary.

nutrition facts per serving: 419 cal., 11 g total fat (2 g sat. fat), 79 mg chol., 636 mg sodium, 47 g carb., 4 g fiber, 30 g pro.

Add a side of lightly buttered egg noodles or spaetzle to round out the menu.

pork medallions with lemon-dill green beans

start to finish: 20 minutes

makes: 4 servings

1   1- to 1½-pound honey-mustard marinated pork tenderloin
1   tablespoon butter
1   9-ounce package frozen French-cut green beans, thawed
1   teaspoon dried dill
1   teaspoon lemon juice

1 Cut pork tenderloin into ¼-inch slices. In a very large skillet melt butter over medium heat. Add pork; cook for 4 to 6 minutes or until juices run clear, turning once. Remove meat from skillet; reserve drippings. Keep warm.

2 Add green beans and dill to drippings in skillet; cook and stir for 3 to 4 minutes or until beans are tender. Stir in lemon juice. Transfer beans to a serving platter. Arrange pork slices alongside beans.

nutrition facts per serving: 189 cal., 8 g total fat (4 g sat. fat), 53 mg chol., 531 mg sodium, 8 g carb., 2 g fiber, 21 g pro.

Making the pork into medallions—very thin slices of meat—allows it to cook in just about 6 minutes.

pork with sweet cherry sauce

start to finish: 20 minutes
makes: 4 servings

1½ **pounds pork tenderloin**
Salt
Ground black pepper
Nonstick cooking spray
¾ **cup cranberry juice or apple juice**
2 **teaspoons spicy brown mustard**
1 **teaspoon cornstarch**
1 **cup sweet cherries (such as Rainier or Bing), halved and pitted, or 1 cup frozen unsweetened pitted dark sweet cherries, thawed**

1 Cut pork crosswise into 1-inch slices. Place each slice between 2 pieces of plastic wrap. With the heel of your hand, press each slice into a ½-inch medallion. Discard plastic wrap. Sprinkle lightly with salt and pepper.

2 Coat a large nonstick skillet with cooking spray; heat skillet over medium-high heat. Add pork slices; cook about 6 minutes or until meat is slightly pink in center and juices run clear, turning once. Transfer to a serving platter; cover to keep warm.

3 For sauce, in a small bowl stir together cranberry juice, mustard, and cornstarch. Add cranberry juice mixture to skillet; cook and stir until thickened and bubbly. Cook and stir for 2 minutes more. Stir cherries into cranberry mixture in skillet. Serve sauce over meat.

nutrition facts per serving: 197 cal., 5 g total fat (2 g sat. fat), 81 mg chol., 127 mg sodium, 12 g carb., 0 g fiber, 26 g pro.

This is a quick take on Wiener Schnitzel, the Austrian dish that consists of breaded and fried scallops of veal. Serve the meat with lemon wedges for squeezing, if you like.

breaded pork with cabbage and kale

start to finish: 30 minutes
makes: 4 servings

1¼ pounds center cut
    pork loin, trimmed
    of fat and cut into
    4 slices
2   cups corn bread
    stuffing mix,
    crushed
2   tablespoons olive oil
2   cups sliced red
    cabbage
6   cups coarsely
    chopped kale
⅓   cup balsamic vinegar
    Salt
    Ground black pepper

1 Preheat oven to 250°F. Place each pork slice between two pieces of plastic wrap. Using the flat side of a meat mallet, lightly pound pork to ¼-inch thickness. Place stuffing mix in shallow dish; coat pork with stuffing mix.

2 In a very large skillet heat 1 tablespoon of the oil over medium-high heat. Add two of the pork slices; cook for 4 to 6 minutes or until golden and cooked through, turning once. Transfer to a baking sheet; keep warm in oven. Repeat with the remaining oil and pork.

3 Wipe skillet. Add cabbage; cook and stir until cabbage is crisp-tender. Add kale and vinegar; cook just until wilted. Lightly sprinkle with salt and pepper. Serve pork with cabbage mixture.

nutrition facts per serving: 394 cal., 14 g total fat (2 g sat. fat), 78 mg chol., 769 mg sodium, 35 g carb., 4 g fiber, 32 g pro.

Clean fresh mushrooms by wiping them with a damp paper towel, then trim the bottoms of the stems. Never run mushrooms under water or soak them in water—they will get waterlogged and soggy.

chicken and lemon-broccoli alfredo

start to finish: 20 minutes
makes: 4 servings

351

4   small skinless,
    boneless chicken
    breast halves
    Salt
    Ground black pepper
1   tablespoon olive or
    canola oil
8   ounces fresh
    mushrooms, halved
1   lemon
3   cups fresh broccoli
    florets
1   10-ounce container
    refrigerated light
    Alfredo pasta sauce

1 Sprinkle chicken with salt and pepper. In a large skillet heat oil over medium-high heat. Add chicken and mushrooms; cook about 4 minutes or until browned, turning chicken once.

2 Meanwhile, finely shred 2 teaspoons peel from the lemon; set peel aside. Slice lemon. Add lemon slices and broccoli to skillet; cook, covered, about 8 minutes or until chicken is no longer pink (170°F).

3 Place chicken and vegetables on plates. Add Alfredo sauce to skillet; heat through. Spoon sauce over chicken; sprinkle with lemon peel and additional pepper.

nutrition facts per serving: 295 cal., 12 g total fat (5 g sat. fat), 91 mg chol., 705 mg sodium, 16 g carb., 4 g fiber, 35 g pro.

When searing or stir-frying meat, be sure to pat it as dry as possible with clean paper towels before adding to the pan to prevent spattering when it hits the hot oil.

jamaican pork stir-fry

start to finish: 20 minutes
makes: 4 servings

352

1   tablespoon canola oil
1   16-ounce package
    frozen stir-fry
    vegetables (carrots,
    snow peas,
    mushrooms, and
    onions)
12 ounces pork strips for
    stir-frying*
2   to 3 teaspoons
    Jamaican jerk
    seasoning
½   cup bottled plum
    sauce
    Soy sauce (optional)
    Peanuts (optional)
2   cups hot cooked rice
    or pasta

1 In a wok or large skillet heat oil over medium-high heat. Add frozen vegetables; cook and stir for 5 to 7 minutes or until vegetables are crisp-tender. Remove vegetables from wok.

2 Trim fat from pork if necessary. Toss pork with jerk seasoning; add to wok. Add more oil if necessary; cook and stir for 2 to 5 minutes or until pork is no longer pink.

3 Add plum sauce to wok; return vegetables. Gently toss to coat; heat through. If desired, season with soy sauce and sprinkle with peanuts. Serve over rice.

nutrition facts per serving: 357 cal., 9 g total fat (2 g sat. fat), 54 mg chol., 405 mg sodium, 45 g carb., 2 g fiber, 22 g pro.

*tip: If your supermarket doesn't sell pork strips, cut your own from trimmed pork loin roast or boneless chops.

The intense flavor of pure maple syrup is called for here. It's one of just a few flavoring ingredients in this very simple dish.

maple-glazed chicken with sweet potatoes

start to finish: 25 minutes
makes: 4 servings

1   24-ounce package
    refrigerated mashed
    sweet potatoes
1   pound chicken breast
    tenderloins
2   teaspoons steak
    grilling seasoning
    blend, such as
    Montreal
2   tablespoons butter
¼   cup maple syrup
½   cup sliced green
    onions (about 4)

1 Prepare sweet potatoes in microwave oven according to package directions.

2 Meanwhile, lightly coat chicken with steak seasoning. In large skillet melt butter over medium-high heat. Add chicken; cook for 5 to 6 minutes until no longer pink (170°F), turning once. Remove chicken from skillet; cover to keep warm. Stir maple syrup into hot skillet; cook for 2 minutes. Stir in green onions.

3 Divide chicken and potatoes among 4 plates. Drizzle with maple syrup mixture.

nutrition facts per serving: 384 cal., 7 g total fat (4 g sat. fat), 81 mg chol., 505 mg sodium, 50 g carb., 6 g fiber, 30 g pro.

Mango fans will appreciate their favorite fruit's appearance in three forms in this dish—cubes of fresh fruit, in chutney, and in a mango-blend fruit drink.

triple-mango chicken

start to finish: 20 minutes
makes: 4 servings

1 tablespoon olive oil
4 small skinless, boneless chicken breast halves
1 mango, seeded, peeled, and cubed
½ cup mango-blend fruit drink*
¼ cup mango chutney
2 medium zucchini, thinly sliced lengthwise
¼ cup water
Salt
Ground black pepper

1 In very large skillet heat oil over medium-high heat; reduce to medium. Add chicken; cook 6 minutes and turn. Add mango cubes, mango drink, and chutney; cook for 4 to 6 minutes or until chicken is no longer pink, stirring occasionally.

2 Meanwhile, in a microwave-safe 2-quart square baking dish place zucchini and the water. Cover with vented plastic wrap. Microwave on 100 percent power (high) for 2 to 3 minutes or until zucchini is crisp-tender, stirring once; drain. Place chicken on top of zucchini. Sprinkle with salt and pepper.

nutrition facts per serving: 274 cal., 9 g total fat (1 g sat. fat), 66 mg chol., 277 mg sodium, 22 g carb., 2 g fiber, 28 g pro.

*tip: Mango nectar, carrot juice, or orange juice may be substituted for the mango-blend drink.

Use one sweet pepper of each color—red and orange—for the most vibrant color.

chicken-pineapple fajitas

prep: 15 minutes   bake: 10 minutes at 350°F
makes: 8 fajitas

8   6-inch flour tortillas
    Nonstick cooking
       spray
4   1-inch slices peeled
       fresh pineapple
       (about half of a
       whole pineapple)
1   pound skinless,
       boneless chicken
       breast halves
2   small red or orange
       sweet peppers,
       seeded and cut into
       strips
2   teaspoons Jamaican
       jerk seasoning
⅛   teaspoon ground
       black pepper
1   tablespoon canola oil
    Fresh cilantro
       (optional)
    Lime wedges
       (optional)

1 Preheat oven to 350°F. Wrap tortillas in foil and heat about 10 minutes or until heated through. Meanwhile, coat a very large nonstick skillet with cooking spray; heat skillet over medium heat. Add pineapple slices; cook for 4 to 6 minutes or until browned, turning once. Remove pineapple from skillet.

2 Cut chicken into strips. In a large bowl toss together chicken, sweet peppers, jerk seasoning, and black pepper. Add oil to hot skillet. Increase heat to medium-high. Add chicken mixture to skillet; cook and stir for 4 to 6 minutes or until chicken is no longer pink.

3 Chop pineapple, removing core if necessary. Top tortillas with chicken mixture, pineapple, and, if desired, cilantro. Roll up tortillas. If desired, serve with lime wedges.

nutrition facts per 2 fajitas: 393 cal., 10 g total fat (2 g sat. fat), 66 mg chol., 633 mg sodium, 43 g carb., 4 g fiber, 32 g pro.

Cook an extra turkey tenderloin or two, while you are at it, to slice and serve on sandwiches during the week. Made from fresh turkey breast, it doesn't have the sodium, fillers, or preservatives of deli meat.

turkey tenderloin with bean and corn salsa

start to finish: 20 minutes
makes: 4 servings

356

2 turkey breast tenderloins (about 1 pound total)
Salt
Ground black pepper
¼ cup red jalapeño chile pepper jelly
1¼ cups purchased black bean and corn salsa
2 tablespoons fresh cilantro leaves

1 Preheat broiler. Split each turkey breast tenderloin in half horizontally. Place turkey on the unheated rack of a broiler pan. Sprinkle with salt and pepper. Broil 4 to 5 inches from heat for 5 minutes.

2 Meanwhile, in a small saucepan melt jelly over low heat. Remove 2 tablespoons of the jelly. Turn turkey; spoon the 2 tablespoons jelly evenly over turkey. Broil for 4 to 6 minutes more or until tender and no longer pink (170°F).

3 Transfer turkey to a serving plate. Spoon remaining jelly over turkey. Cover and keep warm. In a small saucepan heat salsa. Spoon salsa over turkey. Sprinkle with cilantro.

nutrition facts per serving: 196 cal., 2 g total fat (1 g sat. fat), 66 mg chol., 377 mg sodium, 16 g carb., 1 g fiber, 27 g pro.

kitchen tip: Keep cilantro fresh by snipping off the ends and placing the bunch in a glass of water. Cover loosely with a plastic bag and refrigerate for up to 1 week. Leftover cilantro can be used in your favorite Mexican and Thai dishes.

Center cut bacon is leaner than regular bacon—by about 30 percent. It's cut closer to the bone, so it's less fatty than standard strips.

bacon-wrapped salmon with fruit chutney

start to finish: 20 minutes
makes: 4 servings

4   4-ounce fresh or
     frozen skinless
     salmon fillets, about
     ½ inch thick
8   slices center cut
     bacon
     Salt
     Ground black pepper
1   teaspoon olive oil
½   cup fresh or frozen
     cranberries,
     coarsely chopped
⅓   cup apricot jam
1   teaspoon fresh thyme
     (optional)

1 Thaw fish, if frozen. Line a microwave-safe plate with paper towels. Place 4 slices of the bacon on the plate. Microwave on 100 percent power (high) for 1½ minutes. Repeat with the remaining 4 slices bacon.

2 Rinse salmon; pat dry with paper towels. Lightly sprinkle with salt and pepper. Wrap two bacon slices around each fillet. In a very large skillet heat oil over medium-high heat. Add salmon, bacon seam sides down; cook for 3 minutes. Turn salmon; cook for 3 to 5 minutes more or until bacon is crisp and salmon flakes easily when tested with a fork.

3 For chutney, in a small saucepan combine cranberries and jam. Cook over medium heat until heated through, stirring occsionally. Serve salmon with chutney. If desired, garnish with thyme.

nutrition facts per serving: 341 cal., 15 g total fat (4 g sat. fat), 80 mg chol., 706 mg sodium, 20 g carb., 1 g fiber, 28 g pro.

Use any kind of salsa you like in these smoky fish tacos. Fire-roasted varieties—both red and green—benefit from having their elements cooked over smoke and flame before being pureed into salsa.

chipotle salmon tacos

prep: 10 minutes   bake: 18 minutes at 450°F
makes: 8 tacos

1¼ pounds fresh or
     frozen salmon fillets
     with skin
  1 canned chipotle
     pepper in adobo
     sauce, seeded and
     chopped*
  ¼ teaspoon salt
  8 purchased taco shells
  1 11-ounce can whole
     kernel corn with
     sweet peppers
  1 cup purchased salsa

1 Thaw fish, if frozen. Preheat oven to 450°F. Rinse fish; pat dry with paper towels. Place salmon, skin sides down, in a 2-quart rectangular baking dish. Mix chipotle pepper with 1 tablespoon adobo sauce from can. Spread chipotle mixture over salmon; sprinkle with the salt.

2 Bake about 18 minutes or until fish flakes easily when tested with a fork. Place taco shells in oven for 3 minutes or until warm.

3 Meanwhile, place corn in a small saucepan. Bring to boiling; reduce heat. Simmer, covered, about 3 minutes or until heated through; keep warm.

4 To serve, lift salmon from skin; use a fork to break salmon into pieces. Divide salmon and corn among taco shells. Serve with salsa.

nutrition facts per 2 tacos: 349 cal., 10 g total fat (2 g sat. fat), 66 mg chol., 1079 mg sodium, 31 g carb., 5 g fiber, 32 g pro.

∗tip: Because hot chile peppers, contain volatile oils that can burn your skin and eyes, avoid direct contact with chiles as much as possible. When working with chile peppers, wear plastic or rubber gloves. If your bare hands do touch chile peppers, wash your hands well with soap and warm water.

If you happen to have some leftover cooked green beans, add them to this salad for a touch of authenticity.

crispy potato and tuna salad

start to finish: 20 minutes
makes: 4 servings

1 tablespoon butter
2 cups refrigerated red potato wedges
6 cups packaged mixed salad greens
3 3-ounce packages Wild Planet Albacore Tuna Pouch
1 cup cherry tomatoes
⅓ to ½ cup bottled roasted garlic vinaigrette salad dressing
Salt
Freshly ground black pepper

1 In a large skillet melt butter over medium heat. Add potatoes; cook, covered, about 15 minutes or until golden, stirring occasionally.

2 Meanwhile, place greens on plates. Top with tuna, tomatoes, and potatoes. Drizzle with vinaigrette. Sprinkle with salt and pepper.

nutrition facts per serving: 269 cal., 11 g total fat (1 g sat. fat), 31 mg chol., 426 mg sodium, 15 g carb., 4 g fiber, 26 g pro.

If you can find fresh shrimp that is already peeled and deveined, it is a terrific timesaver. It may cost a little bit more, but it will trim minutes off of your prep time.

grilled shrimp and pineapple kabobs

prep: 20 minutes   grill: 8 minutes
makes: 4 servings

1   pound fresh or frozen
     jumbo shrimp in
     shells
½   of a fresh pineapple
6   tablespoons orange
     marmalade
½   cup water
1   tablespoon reduced-
     sodium soy sauce
1   8.8-ounce pouch
     cooked long grain
     rice
¼   cup snipped fresh
     cilantro (optional)

1 Thaw shrimp, if frozen. Peel and devein shrimp. Rinse shrimp; pat dry with paper towels. Thread shrimp onto four skewers.* Cut pineapple crosswise into four slices; core, if desired. Cut each slice into quarters to make 16 small wedges. Thread onto four additional skewers. For sauce, in a small saucepan combine 4 tablespoons of the marmalade, the water, and soy sauce. Brush some of the marmalade–soy sauce mixture onto shrimp and pineapple.

2 For a charcoal or gas grill, place skewers on the rack of a grill directly over medium heat. Grill, covered, for 8 to 10 minutes or until shrimp are opaque and pineapple is heated through, turning once. Remove skewers from heat; keep warm.

3 Return remaining sauce to saucepan; bring to a rolling boil. Heat rice according to package directions. Transfer rice to a serving bowl; stir in the remaining 2 tablespoons marmalade and, if desired, the cilantro.

4 Serve skewers with rice and the marmalade–soy sauce mixture.

nutrition facts per serving: 257 cal., 2 g total fat (0 g sat. fat), 107 mg chol., 642 mg sodium, 47 g carb., 1 g fiber, 14 g pro.

*tip: If using wooden skewers, soak in enough water to cover for at least 1 hour before using.

The microwave is the true hero in preparing this vegetarian dish. It's proof positive that you can use it for more than just reheating leftovers or making popcorn—it can help you turn out a delicious and healthful meal in just minutes.

rice and sweet pepper bowl

start to finish: 30 minutes
makes: 4 servings

4   medium green and/or red sweet peppers
2   tablespoons water
1   8.8-ounce pouch cooked Spanish-style rice
1   14.5-ounce can stewed tomatoes, undrained
4   1-ounce slices Monterey Jack cheese with jalapeño peppers
1   ounce Parmesan cheese, shaved
1   tablespoon olive oil
    Fresh oregano (optional)

1 Quarter peppers; remove stems, seeds, and ribs. Place pepper quarters in a 2-quart square microwave-safe baking dish. Add the water. Cover with parchment or waxed paper. Microwave on 100 percent power (high) about 4 minutes or until crisp-tender, turning dish once if no turntable. Remove peppers from dish; drain and set aside.

2 Microwave rice according to package directions. Drain tomatoes, reserving 2 tablespoons of the liquid. In the baking dish layer half the peppers (cut sides up), the rice, drained tomatoes, Monterey Jack cheese, and the remaining peppers (cut sides down). Drizzle with reserved tomato liquid. Cover with parchment or waxed paper. Microwave on 100 percent power (high) for 5 to 6 minutes or until heated through, turning once. Let stand for 5 minutes.

3 To serve, top with Parmesan cheese and a drizzle of olive oil. If desired, garnish with oregano.

nutrition facts per serving: 304 cal., 15 g total fat (7 g sat. fat), 32 mg chol., 835 mg sodium, 31 g carb., 4 g fiber, 12 g pro.

If you can't find baby pattypan squash—which are sometimes hard to come by—thick slices of yellow summer squash work just fine.

ravioli with spinach pesto

start to finish: 20 minutes
makes: 4 servings

1   9-ounce package refrigerated four-cheese ravioli or tortellini
12   ounces baby pattypan squash, halved, or yellow summer squash, halved lengthwise and sliced ½ inch thick
3½   cups fresh baby spinach
½   cup torn fresh basil
¼   cup bottled Caesar Parmesan vinaigrette salad dressing
2   tablespoons water
    Shaved Parmesan cheese (optional)

1 In a large saucepan cook ravioli according to package directions, adding squash the last 2 minutes of cooking; drain.

2 Meanwhile, for pesto, in a blender combine spinach, basil, salad dressing, and the water. Cover and blend until smooth, stopping to scrape down sides as needed.

3 Toss ravioli and squash with pesto. If desired, top with shaved Parmesan cheese.

nutrition facts per serving: 218 cal., 6 g total fat (2 g sat. fat), 27 mg chol., 525 mg sodium, 31 g carb., 3 g fiber, 11 g pro.

spicy skillet pork chops

make-ahead
me

14

A little time spent in the kitchen today yields a delicious meal tomorrow—or a few months from now. These recipes require no more than 30 minutes initial prep time—and no more than 30 minutes to get table-ready.

als

This is a potluck-perfect casserole you can make the night before you have to take it. Just bake for 30 minutes, sprinkle with cheese and cilantro, and serve!

bean-and-beef enchilada casserole

prep: 25 minutes bake: 35 minutes at 350°F chill: overnight
makes: 6 servings

Nonstick cooking
   spray
8   ounces lean ground
   beef
½   cup chopped onion
   (1 medium)
1   teaspoon chili
   powder
½   teaspoon ground
   cumin
1   15-ounce can no-salt-
   added pinto beans,
   rinsed and drained
1   4-ounce can diced
   green chiles,
   undrained
1   8-ounce carton light
   sour cream
2   tablespoons all-
   purpose flour
¼   teaspoon garlic
   powder
8   6-inch corn tortillas
1   10-ounce can
   enchilada sauce
1   cup reduced-fat
   shredded cheddar
   cheese (4 ounces)
   Snipped fresh cilantro
   (optional)

1 Lightly coat a 2-quart rectangular baking dish with cooking spray; set aside. In a large skillet cook ground beef and onion over medium-high heat until meat is brown and onion is tender, using a wooden spoon to break up meat as it cooks. Drain off fat. Stir chili powder and cumin into the meat mixture in skillet. Stir pinto beans and chiles into meat mixture in skillet. Remove from heat.

2 In a small bowl stir together sour cream, flour, and garlic powder; set aside.

3 Place half of the tortillas in bottom of the prepared baking dish, overlapping as necessary. Top evenly with half of the meat mixture. Spoon half of the sour cream mixture over meat mixture in small mounds; spread to an even layer. Top with half of the enchilada sauce. Repeat layers.

4 Cover baking dish with plastic wrap. Chill in the refrigerator overnight.

To Serve

5 Preheat oven to 350°F. Remove plastic wrap; cover with foil. Bake about 30 minutes or until heated through. Sprinkle with cheddar cheese. Bake, uncovered, about 5 minutes more or until cheese is melted. If desired, sprinkle with cilantro.

nutrition facts per serving: 333 cal., 12 g total fat (6 g sat. fat), 47 mg chol., 484 mg sodium, 35 g carb., 6 g fiber, 21 g pro.

Espresso powder gives the rub for this steak an intense, earthy flavor. Get it ready to grill between 2 hours and 24 hours ahead.

coffee and smoked paprika–rubbed steak with buttermilk dressing

prep: 25 minutes chill: 2 hours to 24 hours broil: 17 minutes
stand: 5 minutes makes: 4 servings

1	1-pound beef flank steak
1	tablespoon packed brown sugar
1½	teaspoons instant espresso coffee powder
¾	teaspoon sweet smoked paprika
½	teaspoon garlic powder
½	teaspoon salt
⅛	teaspoon freshly ground black pepper
1	medium zucchini, cut into 1-inch pieces
16	cherry tomatoes
12	to 16 fresh whole mushrooms
1	recipe Buttermilk Dressing

1 Trim fat from steak. Score both sides of steak in a diamond pattern by making shallow diagonal cuts at 1-inch intervals. In a small bowl combine brown sugar, espresso powder, paprika, garlic powder, salt, and pepper. Sprinkle evenly over both sides of steak; rub in with your fingers.

2 In a large saucepan bring a large amount of water to boiling. Add zucchini to boiling water; cook for 2 minutes. Drain zucchini. Thread tomatoes, mushrooms, and zucchini onto eight skewers.* Cover and chill both steak and skewers for 2 to 24 hours.

To Serve

3 Preheat broiler. Place steak on the unheated rack of a broiler pan. Broil 3 to 4 inches from heat for 17 to 21 minutes or until medium doneness (160°F), turning once. Add skewers to the broiler pan for the last 7 to 8 minutes of broiling or just until vegetables are tender, turning once. Transfer steak to a cutting board. Let stand for 5 minutes.

4 Thinly slice steak across the grain. Serve steak with vegetables and Buttermilk Dressing.

nutrition facts per serving: 256 cal., 11 g total fat (4 g sat. fat), 43 mg chol., 535 mg sodium, 12 g carb., 2 g fiber, 27 g pro.

Buttermilk Dressing: In a small bowl whisk together 2 tablespoons low-fat buttermilk, 2 tablespoons light mayonnaise, 1 tablespoon snipped fresh chives (optional), 1 teaspoon cider vinegar, 1 teaspoon Dijon-style mustard, ¼ teaspoon sugar, ⅛ teaspoon garlic powder, ⅛ teaspoon salt, and ⅛ teaspoon ground black pepper.

*tip: If using wooden skewers, soak in enough water to cover for at least 1 hour before using.

kitchen tip: If you can't find smoked paprika, use 1 teaspoon regular paprika and ½ teaspoon ground cumin instead.

These lean beef burgers are packed with veggies, inside and out.

veggie-filled hamburgers

prep: 25 minutes   freeze: up to 3 months   grill: 11 minutes
makes: 4 servings

2   tablespoons fat-free
      milk
½   cup finely shredded
      carrot (1 medium)
¼   cup thinly sliced
      green onions (2)
¼   cup soft whole wheat
      bread crumbs
¼   teaspoon garlic salt
¼   teaspoon dried Italian
      seasoning, crushed
      Dash ground black
      pepper
12   ounces lean ground
      beef or uncooked
      ground turkey
      breast or chicken
      breast
4   whole wheat
      hamburger buns,
      split and toasted
      Curry Mustard
      (optional)
4   lettuce leaves
4   to 8 slices tomato
½   cup sliced zucchini

1 In a medium bowl stir together milk, carrot, green onions, bread crumbs, garlic salt, Italian seasoning, and pepper. Add the ground meat; mix well. Divide the mixture into four portions. Shape each portion into a ½-inch-thick patty.

2 Place patties in a single layer in a freezer container. Seal, label, and freeze for up to 3 months.

To Serve

3 To serve, thaw patties in the refrigerator overnight. For a charcoal or gas grill, place patties on the grill rack directly over medium heat. Grill, covered, for 11 to 14 minutes or until an instant-read thermometer inserted into the side of each patty registers 160°F* for beef or 165°F for turkey or chicken, turning once.

4 If desired, spread bottoms of buns with Curry Mustard. Layer patties with lettuce leaves, tomato, and zucchini. Add bun tops.

nutrition facts per serving: 254 cal., 6 g total fat (2 g sat. fat), 53 mg chol., 359 mg sodium, 27 g carb., 3 g fiber, 24 g pro.

kitchen tip: If you like your condiments spicy, try using hot curry powder in the curry mustard—and add up to 1 teaspoon, if you like.

*tip: The internal color of a burger is not a reliable doneness indicator. A beef or pork patty cooked to 160°F is safe, regardless of color. To measure the doneness of a patty, insert an instant-read thermometer through the side of the patty to a depth of 2 to 3 inches.

Curry Mustard: In a small bowl stir together ⅓ cup Dijon-style mustard and ½ teaspoon curry powder.

The filling for these burritos is half beef and half bean, which helps lower the fat and calories—and increase the fiber.

beef-bean burritos

prep: 25 minutes   chill: up to 24 hours   bake: 30 minutes at 350°F
makes: 8 burritos

Nonstick cooking spray
8 8-inch flour tortillas
8 ounces lean ground beef
1 cup chopped onion (1 large)
2 cloves garlic, minced
1 15-ounce can black beans or pinto beans, rinsed and drained
½ cup salsa
2 teaspoons chili powder
Several dashes bottled hot pepper sauce
1 cup shredded cheddar cheese (4 ounces)
1½ cups shredded fresh spinach
1½ cups shredded lettuce
Salsa (optional)
Light sour cream (optional)

1 Preheat oven to 350°F. Line a 15×10×1-inch baking pan with foil. Lightly coat foil with cooking spray; set aside. Stack tortillas; wrap in foil. Bake for 10 minutes to soften. Meanwhile, for filling, in a large skillet cook ground beef, onion, and garlic until meat is brown and onion is tender, using a wooden spoon to break up meat as it cooks. Drain off fat. Stir beans, the ½ cup salsa, the chili powder, and hot pepper sauce into meat mixture in skillet.

2 Spoon about ½ cup of the filling onto each tortilla and top with 1 tablespoon of the cheddar cheese. Fold bottom edge up and over filling, just until covered. Fold in opposite sides. Roll up, tucking in sides. Secure with wooden toothpicks. Arrange tortillas, seam sides down, in prepared baking pan.

3 Cover baking pan with plastic wrap; cover with foil. Chill in the refrigerator overnight.

To Serve

4 Preheat oven to 350°F. Remove plastic wrap; cover with foil. Bake for 30 to 40 minutes or until heated through. Sprinkle with the ½ cup remaining cheddar cheese. Bake, uncovered, about 5 minutes more or until cheese is melted. Serve burritos on a bed of spinach and lettuce. If desired, serve with additional salsa and sour cream.

nutrition facts per 2 burritos: 300 cal., 11 g total fat (4 g sat. fat), 33 mg chol., 539 mg sodium, 36 g carb., 3 g fiber, 17 g pro.

*This hearty soup can be stored in the refrigerator for up to 3 days—
or frozen for up to 2 months—so it truly can be ready when you are.*

kansas city steak soup

prep: 30 minutes chill: up to 3 days freeze: up to 2 months
heat: 30 minutes makes: 6 servings

1½ pounds lean ground
       beef
1   cup chopped onion
       (1 large)
1   cup sliced celery
       (2 stalks)
2   14.5-ounce cans
       50 percent less
       sodium beef broth
1   28-ounce can
       diced tomatoes,
       undrained
1   10-ounce package
       frozen mixed
       vegetables
2   tablespoons steak
       sauce
2   teaspoons
       Worcestershire
       sauce
¼   teaspoon salt
¼   teaspoon ground
       black pepper
¼   cup all-purpose flour
       Snipped fresh Italian
       (flat-leaf) parsley

1 In a large Dutch oven cook ground beef, onion, and celery over medium-high heat until meat is brown and vegetables are tender, using a wooden spoon to break up meat as it cooks. Drain off fat.

2 Stir in 1 can of the broth, the tomatoes, frozen vegetables, steak sauce, Worcestershire sauce, salt, and pepper into meat mixture in Dutch oven. Bring to boiling; reduce heat. Simmer, covered, for 20 minutes.

3 In a medium bowl whisk together the remaining can of broth and flour; stir into mixture in Dutch oven. Cook over medium-high heat until thickened and bubbly. Cook and stir for 1 minute more.

4 Cool soup slightly. Transfer soup to airtight containers. Cover and chill for up to 3 days. (Or transfer to freezer containers. Seal and freeze for up to 2 months.)

To Serve

5 If frozen, thaw soup in the refrigerator for 24 to 48 hours. Transfer chilled or thawed soup to a large Dutch oven. Cook over medium heat about 30 minutes or until heated through, stirring occasionally.

6 Ladle soup into soup bowls; sprinkle with parsley.

nutrition facts per serving: 306 cal., 12 g total fat (5 g sat. fat), 74 mg chol., 747 mg sodium, 21 g carb., 4 g fiber, 27 g pro.

This is big-batch cooking. One recipe yields 8 servings that can be divided and frozen to be at the ready any way you want—two 4-serving containers or four 2-serving containers.

spicy skillet pork chops

prep: 30 minutes cook: 20 minutes freeze: up to 3 months
makes: two 4-serving containers

3   cups frozen whole
    kernel corn
2   10-ounce cans
    chopped tomatoes
    and green chiles,
    undrained
1   teaspoon ground
    cumin
½   teaspoon bottled hot
    pepper sauce
4   cloves garlic, minced
8   boneless pork loin
    chops, cut ¾ inch
    thick (about 1½
    pounds total)
1   teaspoon chili
    powder
1   tablespoon canola oil
2   medium onions, cut
    into thin wedges
    Light sour cream
    (optional)

1 In a medium bowl combine frozen corn, undrained tomatoes, cumin, hot pepper sauce, and garlic; set aside.

2 Trim fat from chops. Sprinkle chili powder over all sides of the chops. In a very large nonstick skillet heat oil over medium-high heat. Add chops; cook about 4 minutes or until brown, turning once. Remove chops from skillet, reserving drippings.

3 Reduce heat to medium. Add onions to skillet; cook and stir for 3 minutes. Stir corn mixture into onion mixture in skillet. Place chops on corn mixture. Bring to boiling; reduce heat. Simmer, covered, for 10 to 12 minutes or until pork is slightly pink (145°F). Allow chops to rest for at least 3 minutes.

4 Remove skillet from heat; cool slightly. Divide chops and corn mixture between two large freezer containers. Seal, label, and freeze for up to 3 months.

To Serve

5 Thaw one container in the refrigerator for 24 to 48 hours. Transfer mixture to a large skillet. Cook, covered, over medium-low heat until heated through. If desired, top with sour cream.

nutrition facts per serving: 330 cal., 11 g total fat (3 g sat. fat), 93 mg chol., 360 mg sodium, 18 g carb., 2 g fiber, 40 g pro.

The Sweet and Spicy Rub is a natural on pork as well as chicken.

chicken noodle toss with greens

prep: 30 minutes   bake: 18 minutes at 400°F   freeze: up to 4 months
makes: 4 servings

2   skinless boneless chicken breast halves
1   teaspoon canola oil
1   tablespoon Sweet and Spicy Rub
6   ounces medium rice sticks (noodles)
4   cups boiling water
1   tablespoon olive oil
2   tablespoons lime juice
2   tablespoons soy sauce
2   tablespoons sliced green onion (1)
1   cup arugula leaves
½   cup packed basil leaves
¼   cup lightly packed cilantro leaves
     Crushed red pepper (optional)

1 Preheat oven to 400°F. Brush chicken breasts with canola oil. Sprinkle 1 tablespoon Sweet and Spicy Rub over chicken; rub into chicken. Place chicken in a shallow baking dish. Bake for 18 to 20 minutes or until chicken is tender and no longer pink (170°F). Let cool. Place chicken in a freezer container or freezer bag. Seal, label, and freeze for up to 4 months.

To Serve

2 Thaw chicken overnight in the refrigerator. Cut or shred chicken into bite-size pieces.

3 Place noodles in a large bowl. Add the boiling water. Let stand for 10 minutes or until tender; drain.

4 Meanwhile, in a large skillet heat olive oil over medium-high heat. Add chicken. Reduce heat to medium. Cook and stir for 2 minutes or until heated through. Remove from heat. Stir in lime juice, soy sauce, and green onion.

5 In a large bowl toss together chicken mixture and noodles. Add arugula, basil, and cilantro; toss to combine. If desired, sprinkle with crushed red pepper.

nutrition facts per serving: 297 cal., 6 g total fat (1 g sat. fat), 41 mg chol., 727 mg sodium, 39 g carb., 2 g fiber, 20 g pro.

Sweet and Spicy Rub: In a small bowl stir together ¼ cup packed brown sugar, 2 tablespoons paprika, 1 teaspoon salt, 2 teaspoons ground coriander, 1 teaspoon ground black pepper, and ½ teaspoon cayenne pepper. Transfer to an airtight container. Cover and store at room temperature for up to 2 weeks.

Having these delicious, delicately flavored dumplings in the freezer is like having money in the bank!

spicy chicken pot stickers with ginger and green onion dipping sauce

prep: 30 minutes freeze: up to 2 months cook: 5 minutes
makes: 4 servings

8 ounces uncooked ground chicken breast
¼ cup canned whole or sliced water chestnuts, drained and chopped
2 tablespoons finely chopped green onion (1)
2 tablespoons snipped fresh cilantro
1 tablespoon reduced-sodium soy sauce
1 teaspoon grated fresh ginger
1 clove garlic, minced
¼ teaspoon crushed red pepper
1 egg white
1 tablespoon water
20 wonton wrappers
1 recipe Ginger and Green Onion Dipping Sauce
1 tablespoon canola oil
½ cup water

1 Lightly flour a baking sheet; set aside. For filling, in a large bowl combine chicken, water chestnuts, green onion, cilantro, soy sauce, ginger, garlic, and crushed red pepper.

2 In a small bowl lightly beat together egg white and the 1 tablespoon water. Spoon about 1 tablespoon of the filling into the center of each wonton wrapper. Brush edges with egg white mixture. Fold wrappers in half across filling, bringing opposite corners together. Pleat edges and press to seal. Arrange pot stickers on prepared baking sheet. Keep filled pot stickers covered while filling remaining wrappers.

3 Loosely cover the pot stickers with plastic wrap and freeze about 3 hours or until completely frozen. Transfer pot stickers to a resealable plastic freezer bag. Seal, label, and freeze for up to 2 months. Place Ginger and Green Onion Dipping Sauce in a resealable plastic freezer bag. Seal, label, and freeze for up to 2 months.

To Serve

4 In a very large nonstick skillet heat oil over medium-high heat. Arrange frozen pot stickers in the skillet so they don't touch. Cook for 2 to 3 minutes or until nicely browned on the bottom. Carefully add the ½ cup water to the skillet. Cover; reduce heat. Cook for 3 to 5 minutes more or until tender and filling is cooked through.

5 While pot stickers are cooking, place the freezer bag with the sauce on a microwave-safe plate. Microwave on 50 percent power (medium) about 30 seconds or until thawed. Transfer to a serving bowl. Serve sauce with the pot stickers.

Ginger and Green Onion Dipping Sauce: In a small bowl combine ¼ cup reduced-sodium soy sauce, ¼ cup rice vinegar, 3 tablespoons chopped green onions, 2 teaspoons grated fresh ginger, ½ teaspoon sugar, and ¼ teaspoon toasted sesame oil.

nutrition facts per serving: 244 cal., 5 g total fat (1 g sat. fat), 36 mg chol., 974 mg sodium, 30 g carb., 1 g fiber, 20 g pro.

These freeze beautifully, and you can take out as many or as few as you want at a time.

turkey-spinach calzones

prep: 30 minutes bake: 18 minutes at 375°F freeze: up to 3 months
makes: 8 calzones

3   cups chopped cooked turkey breast or chicken breast (about 1 pound)
2½ cups chopped fresh spinach
1½ cups shredded pizza cheese (6 ounces)
½   cup pizza sauce
2   13.8-ounce package refrigerated pizza dough (each for 1 crust)
    Fat-free milk
    Grated Parmesan or Romano cheese (optional)
    Pizza sauce, warmed (optional)

1 Preheat oven to 375°F. In a large bowl, combine turkey, spinach, pizza cheese, and the ½ cup pizza sauce. On a lightly floured surface, roll out one package of the pizza dough to a 12-inch square. Cut into four 6-inch squares.

2 Place about ⅔ cup of the turkey mixture on half of each square, spreading to within about ½ inch of edge. Moisten edges of dough with water and fold over, forming a triangle or rectangle. Pinch or press with a fork to seal edges. Prick tops of calzones with a fork; brush with milk. Place on a baking sheet. Repeat with remaining dough and turkey mixture. If desired, sprinkle tops of calzones with grated Parmesan cheese.

3 Bake about 18 minutes or until golden. Transfer calzones to wire rack; cool. Transfer calzones to an ungreased baking sheet. Cover loosely and freeze until firm. Transfer to resealable freezer bags or airtight freezer containers. Seal, label, and freeze for up to 3 months.

To Serve

4 Thaw calzones overnight in the refrigerator. Preheat oven to 350°F. Lightly grease a baking sheet. Unwrap calzones and place on prepared baking sheet. Bake, uncovered, for 12 to 15 minutes or until heated through. If desired, serve with warmed pizza sauce.

nutrition facts per calzone: 300 cal., 8 g total fat (4 g sat. fat), 62 mg chol., 415 mg sodium, 28 g carb., 2 g fiber, 27 g pro.

*Come home on a hot summer night to this cool and fresh salad
waiting in the refrigerator.*

pork and noodle salad

prep: 20 minutes   chill: 2 hours to 24 hours
makes: 4 servings

4   ounces dried Chinese
      egg noodles or fine
      noodles, broken in
      half
¾   pound fresh
      asparagus, trimmed
      and cut into 2-inch-
      long pieces, or
      one 10-ounce
      package frozen cut
      asparagus
2   carrots, cut into thin
      strips
8   ounces cooked lean
      pork, cut into thin
      strips
1   recipe Soy-Sesame
      Vinaigrette
      Sliced green onions
      (optional)
      Sesame seeds
      (optional)

1 Cook pasta according to package directions;
    drain.

2 If using fresh asparagus, cook in a covered
    saucepan in a small amount of boiling
lightly salted water for 4 to 6 minutes or until
crisp-tender. (Or, if using frozen asparagus, cook
according to package directions.) Drain well.

3 In a large bowl combine noodles, asparagus,
    carrots, and pork. Cover and chill in the
refrigerator for 2 to 24 hours.

To Serve

4 Pour Soy-Sesame Vinaigrette over salad; toss
    gently to coat. If desired, sprinkle salad with
green onions and sesame seeds.

nutrition facts per serving: 328 cal., 12 g total fat
(3 g sat. fat), 76 mg chol., 974 mg sodium, 31 g carb., 2 g fiber,
24 g pro.

Soy-Sesame Vinaigrette: In a 1-cup
screw-top jar combine ¼ cup reduced-
sodium soy sauce, 2 tablespoons rice
vinegar or cider vinegar, 1 tablespoon
canola oil, 1 tablespoon honey, and
1 teaspoon toasted sesame oil. Cover and
shake well to mix. Chill for 2 to 24 hours.

The Avocado-Lime Dressing tastes creamy and rich without the addition of mayonnaise or any additional fat of any kind.

orzo chicken salad with avocado-lime dressing

prep: 30 minutes   chill: 2 hours to 24 hours
makes: 4 servings

⅔ cup dried whole wheat or regular orzo pasta (rosamarina)
1   cup fresh or frozen whole kernel corn
2   cups shredded or chopped cooked chicken breast (about 10 ounces)
1   cup grape tomatoes, halved
¼ cup snipped fresh cilantro
½ cup crumbled reduced-fat feta cheese (2 ounces)
1   recipe Avocado-Lime Dressing

1 In a medium saucepan cook orzo according to package directions, adding corn for the last 1 minute of cooking; drain. Rinse with cold water; drain again.

2 In a large bowl combine orzo mixture, chicken, tomatoes, and cilantro. Sprinkle with feta cheese. Cover and chill for 2 to 24 hours.

To Serve

3 Divide chicken mixture among individual salad bowls or plates. Stir dressing and drizzle over salads.

nutrition facts per serving: 321 cal., 10 g total fat (3 g sat. fat), 65 mg chol., 439 mg sodium, 30 g carb., 7 g fiber, 30 g pro.

Avocado-Lime Dressing:
In a blender or food processor combine 1 small avocado, seeded, peeled, and cut up; ⅓ cup water; ½ teaspoon finely shredded lime peel; ¼ cup lime juice; 4 cloves garlic, minced; ½ teaspoon crushed red pepper; and ¼ teaspoon salt. Cover and blend or process until smooth. Transfer dressing to a small bowl. Cover and chill for 2 to 24 hours.

The chicken mixture—including the tomatoes—would be delicious tossed with hot cooked pasta as well.

savory chicken salad

prep: 10 minutes   cook: 10 minutes   freeze: up to 3 months
makes: 4 servings

1   2- to 2¼-pound purchased roasted chicken
1   tablespoon olive oil
1   pound sliced fresh mushrooms
⅓   cup dried tomato pesto
3   tablespoons white or regular balsamic vinegar
½   cup grape tomatoes
1   5-ounce package mixed salad greens (about 8 cups)
    Shaved Parmesan cheese (optional)

1 Remove and chop enough meat from the chicken to make 2 cups. (Save any remaining chicken for another use.)

2 In a large skillet heat oil over medium heat. Add mushrooms; cook about 10 minutes or until tender, stirring occasionally. Remove from heat. Stir in tomato pesto and vinegar. Add chicken; stir gently to combine.

3 Transfer to a freezer container. Seal, label, and freeze for up to 3 months.

To Serve

4 Thaw chicken mixture in refrigerator for 24 to 48 hours. Stir tomatoes into chicken mixture. Line a platter with salad greens and top with chicken mixture. If desired, top with shaved Parmesan cheese.

nutrition facts per serving: 264 cal., 12 g total fat (3 g sat. fat), 61 mg chol., 216 mg sodium, 12 g carb., 3 g fiber, 29 g pro.

This molded salad is perfect for a company-special lunch—and you can make it the night before serving.

chopped salmon salad

prep: 30 minutes   chill: 2 hours to 24 hours
makes: 4 servings

Nonstick cooking
   spray
¾ cup flaked smoked
   salmon
¼ cup thinly sliced
   green onions (2)
½ cup coarsely chopped
   yellow sweet
   pepper
1⅓ cups chopped seeded
   tomatoes
¼ cup chopped onion
2 cups coarsely
   chopped cucumber
   (1 large)
2 teaspoons small
   capers, drained
1 recipe Lemon
   Vinaigrette

1 Coat four 6-ounce coffee cups with cooking spray. Equally divide and layer ingredients in each cup in the following order: salmon, green onions, sweet pepper, tomatoes, onion, and cucumber. Cover tops with plastic wrap and firmly press mixture into cups with a soup can or similar object slightly smaller than diameter of cup. Cover and chill for 2 to 24 hours.

To Serve

2 Invert salads onto 4 serving plates; carefully lift off cups. Sprinkle salads with capers and drizzle with Lemon Vinaigrette.

nutrition facts per serving: 137 cal., 9 g total fat (1 g sat. fat), 8 mg chol., 445 mg sodium, 8 g carb., 2 g fiber, 8 g pro.

Lemon Vinaigrette:
In a screw-top jar
combine 2 tablespoons
olive oil, 2 teaspoons
finely shredded lemon
peel, 2 tablespoons
lemon juice, ½ teaspoon
sugar, ¼ teaspoon salt,
and several dashes
bottled hot pepper
sauce. Shake well before
serving.

Plums are in season from May through October. Look for smooth, unblemished skin and flesh that yields slightly when pressed. The dusty-white bloom you see on some plums is perfectly natural—it's the sign of a mature fruit.

shrimp and rice noodle salad

prep: 20 minutes   chill: 2 hours to 24 hours
makes: 2 servings

6   ounces fresh or
    frozen peeled,
    cooked small
    shrimp
3   ounces dried rice
    noodles
2   medium plums, sliced
½   cup fresh snow pea
    pods, trimmed and
    halved diagonally
½   cup coarsely
    shredded carrot
    (1 medium)
¼   cup coarsely snipped
    fresh cilantro
½   of a small fresh
    serrano chile
    pepper, thinly
    sliced*
¼   cup bottled light
    Asian salad
    dressing
2   tablespoons unsalted
    dry roasted
    peanuts, coarsely
    chopped
    Crushed red pepper

1 Thaw shrimp, if frozen. Cook noodles according to package directions; drain.

2 Meanwhile, in a medium bowl combine shrimp, plums, pea pods, carrot, cilantro, and chile pepper. Gently stir in noodles. Drizzle with salad dressing; toss gently to coat. Cover and chill for 2 to 24 hours.

To Serve

3 Divide salad between two salad plates. Sprinkle with peanuts and crushed red pepper.

nutrition facts per serving: 137 cal., 9 g total fat (1 g sat. fat), 8 mg chol., 445 mg sodium, 8 g carb., 2 g fiber, 8 g pro.

✳ tip: Because chile peppers contain volatile oils that can burn your skin and eyes, avoid direct contact with them as much as possible. When working with chile peppers, wear plastic or rubber gloves. If your bare hands do touch the peppers, wash your hands and nails well with soap and warm water.

For a change of pace, serve this salad with the crisp lentil crackers called papadum in place of the pitas. You'll find them at any Indian market. Toast them lightly over an open flame before eating: Hold them with tongs over a burner on your stove.

indian garbanzo bean salad with pitas

prep: 25 minutes   chill: 2 hours to 24 hours
makes: 6 servings

2   15-ounce cans garbanzo beans (chickpeas), rinsed and drained
3   cups chopped roma tomatoes (about 1 pound)
1   medium cucumber, halved lengthwise and thinly sliced
1   cup shredded carrots (2 medium)
½   of a medium red onion, very thinly sliced
2   teaspoons finely shredded lemon peel
¼   cup lemon juice
3   tablespoons olive oil
1   teaspoon ground cumin
1   teaspoon curry powder
½   teaspoon salt
¼   teaspoon ground black pepper
1   cup plain low-fat yogurt
3   pita bread rounds, cut into wedges*

1 In a large bowl combine garbanzo beans, tomatoes, cucumber, carrots, and red onion.

2 For dressing, in a screw-top jar combine lemon peel, lemon juice, oil, cumin, curry powder, salt, and pepper. Cover and shake well.

3 Pour dressing over bean mixture; toss gently to coat. Cover and chill for 2 to 24 hours.

To Serve

4 Divide salad among six serving plates or bowls. Serve with yogurt and pita wedges.

nutrition facts per serving: 295 cal., 9 g total fat (1 g sat. fat), 2 mg chol., 905 mg sodium, 49 g carb., 8 g fiber, 14 g pro.

✳ tip: If desired, before cutting into wedges, grill pita bread on an indoor or outdoor grill over medium heat until warm and toasted. Transfer to a cutting board and cut into wedges.

Before serving, give this salad a good stir, as the dressing and juices from the vegetables tend to settle at the bottom of the bowl.

farro and pine nut tabbouleh

prep: 25 minutes   cook: 30 minutes   chill: 2 hours to 12 hours
makes: 4 servings

1   cup farro,* rinsed and drained
1   tablespoon pine nuts
2   tablespoons olive oil
1   teaspoon finely shredded lemon peel
2   tablespoons lemon juice
1   clove garlic, minced
½   teaspoon salt
⅛   teaspoon ground black pepper
1   cup coarsely chopped tomato (1 large)
½   of a medium cucumber, halved lengthwise, seeded, and sliced
⅓   cup snipped fresh parsley
⅓   cup snipped fresh cilantro
⅓   cup snipped fresh mint
¼   cup chopped red onion
    Crumbled feta cheese (optional)
    Lemon wedges

1 In a large saucepan bring a large amount of lightly salted water to boiling. Stir in farro; reduce heat. Simmer, uncovered, about 30 minutes or until tender, stirring occasionally. Drain and cool.

2 Meanwhile, heat a small dry skillet over medium-low heat. Add pine nuts; cook for 2 to 3 minutes or until toasted, shaking skillet frequently to ensure even browning. (Pine nuts can burn quickly, so watch them closely.) Remove from skillet. Let cool.

3 For dressing, in a small bowl whisk together oil, lemon peel, lemon juice, garlic, salt, and pepper.

4 In a large bowl combine farro, pine nuts, tomato, cucumber, parsley, cilantro, mint, and red onion. Pour dressing over farro mixture; stir gently to combine. Cover and chill for 2 to 12 hours.

To Serve

5 Divide tabbouleh among serving plates. If desired, sprinkle with feta cheese. Serve with lemon wedges.

nutrition facts per serving: 272 cal., 9 g total fat (1 g sat. fat), 0 mg chol., 329 mg sodium, 41 g carb., 5 g fiber, 9 g pro.

*tip: Farro is an ancient Italian wheat grain. If you can't find it at your local grocery store, substitute cooked barley or coarse-ground bulgur.

The Fresh Tomato Sauce is a good basic sauce that can be used on pasta, baked or grilled chicken breasts—even on pizza.

white beans and couscous with fresh tomato sauce

prep: 25 minutes   chill: 8 hours to 24 hours
makes: 4 servings

1¼   cups boiling or very hot water
1   cup whole wheat couscous
1   teaspoon olive oil
½   teaspoon salt
½   teaspoon ground black pepper
1   15-ounce can no-salt-added cannellini beans (white kidney), rinsed and drained
¼   cup crumbled feta cheese (1 ounce)
2   tablespoons pine nuts or chopped walnuts, toasted*
2   tablespoons snipped fresh basil
1   recipe Fresh Tomato Sauce

1 In a large bowl or saucepan combine the boiling water, couscous, oil, salt, and pepper. Cover and let stand for 5 minutes. Fluff couscous with a fork. Stir in beans, feta cheese, pine nuts, and basil. Cover and chill for 8 to 24 hours.

To Serve

2 Divide salad among serving plates; serve salad with Fresh Tomato Sauce.

nutrition facts per serving: 406 cal., 14 g total fat (3 g sat. fat), 8 mg chol., 729 mg sodium, 58 g carb., 12 g fiber, 15 g pro.

✳tip: To toast nuts, spread them in a shallow baking pan. Bake in a 350°F oven for 5 to 10 minutes or until light brown, shaking pan once or twice. Watch carefully so the nuts don't burn.

Fresh Tomato Sauce:
In a medium bowl combine 1¼ pounds tomatoes (4 medium), peeled, cored, and chopped; ½ cup chopped fresh basil; 2 tablespoons olive oil; 2 cloves garlic, minced; ½ teaspoon salt; and ½ teaspoon ground black pepper. Cover and chill for 8 to 24 hours.

sauteed green beans with shallot crisps

sid

15

Round out the menu with this
collection of salads, breads,
and vegetable side dishes.

es

Truly a different way to serve asparagus, this is a lovely presentation of a favorite spring vegetable.

fresh asparagus ribbon salad

start to finish: 30 minutes
makes: 6 servings

1   pound thick green, purple, or white asparagus (about 14 spears)
2   cloves garlic, peeled
½   teaspoon kosher salt
½   cup sour cream
⅓   cup olive oil
3   to 4 tablespoons lemon juice
½   cup snipped fresh Italian (flat-leaf) parsley
¼   cup snipped fresh chives
1   tablespoon milk (optional)
   Ground black pepper
1   head Bibb lettuce, torn (6 cups)
½   English (seedless) cucumber, thinly sliced
3   radishes, very thinly sliced

make-ahead directions:
Prepare dressing as directed. Use within 3 days. Stir well before serving.

1 Remove scales from asparagus spears.* Using a vegetable peeler, peel thin "ribbons" from the spears.** Place ribbons in a medium bowl of ice water; set aside.

2 Meanwhile, to make garlic paste, on a cutting board finely chop the garlic. Sprinkle with coarse salt. Holding a large flat chef's knife at a slight angle, blade almost flat with cutting board, mash and rub the salt into the garlic.

3 For dressing, in a large bowl whisk together the garlic paste, sour cream, oil, and lemon juice. Stir in parsley and chives. If desired, thin with milk. Season with pepper.

4 Drain asparagus ribbons and pat dry (or spin in a salad spinner). On a platter arrange lettuce, asparagus ribbons and tips, cucumber slices, and radish slices. Drizzle with dressing. Cover and chill any remaining dressing for up to 3 days. Stir dressing well before serving.

nutrition facts per serving: 73 cal., 6 g total fat (1 g sat. fat), 3 mg chol., 73 mg sodium, 4 g carb., 2 g fiber, 2 g pro.

*tip: The dark triangular leaves or scales on asparagus spears can be especially tough on thick spears. To remove them, use a paring knife to peel them off. Discard the scales.

**tip: Thin asparagus ribbons are easy to cut using a sharp vegetable peeler on thick asparagus spears. Trim the asparagus, then lay it flat on a work surface. Beginning from the stem or bottom end, peel toward the tips. Either take care to avoid snapping off the tender tips with the peeler, or deliberately break off the tips to toss in the salad with the ribbons.

Serve this crisp and refreshing salad with roast pork. Use a combination of red and green apples for the most eye-catching color.

apple-onion salad

start to finish: 15 minutes
makes: 4 servings

2 medium tart green and/or red apples, cored
1 tablespoon lemon juice
1 tablespoon olive oil
1 tablespoon honey
¼ teaspoon salt
½ of a small red onion, sliced

1 Slice apples; set aside.

2 In a medium bowl whisk together lemon juice, oil, honey, and salt. Add apple and onion slices; toss gently to coat.

nutrition facts per serving: 98 cal., 4 g total fat (0 g sat. fat), 0 mg chol., 147 mg sodium, 18 g carb., 2 g fiber, 0 g pro.

You might not be able to find yellow carrots at your supermarket, but they have become popular at farmer's markets and in the baskets delivered by your local CSA (Community Supported Agriculture).

carrot ribbon salad

start to finish: 20 minutes
makes: 4 servings

1 tablespoon drained juice from can of pitted ripe olives or lemon juice
1 tablespoon olive oil
⅛ teaspoon salt
⅛ teaspoon ground black pepper
4 orange and/or yellow carrots
⅓ cup sliced green onions

1 For dressing, in a medium bowl whisk together drained juice from can of pitted ripe olives or lemon juice, oil, salt, and pepper; set aside.

2 Using a vegetable peeler, peel carrots lengthwise to make long strips or coarsely shred. Add carrots and green onion to dressing; toss to coat.

nutrition facts per serving: 58 cal., 4 g total fat (0 g sat. fat), 0 mg chol., 116 mg sodium, 7 g carb., 2 g fiber, 1 g pro.

The only chopping required to make this salad is the mincing of a single garlic clove. Just arrange the lettuce on a platter, blitz the dressing in the blender and drizzle it over the leaves, then sprinkle a little cayenne and cheese on top—and it's done!

hearts of romaine with creamy feta dressing

start to finish: 15 minutes
makes: 12 servings

3   hearts of romaine lettuce
¼   cup water
¼   cup olive oil
2   tablespoons lemon juice
1   tablespoon red wine vinegar
½   cup crumbled feta cheese (2 ounces)
1   teaspoon dried oregano, crushed
1   clove garlic, minced
¼   teaspoon sea salt
¼   teaspoon cayenne pepper
¼   cup crumbled feta cheese (1 ounce)

1 Cut each heart of romaine in half lengthwise. Arrange romaine on a serving platter.

2 For dressing, in a food processor or blender combine the water, oil, lemon juice, vinegar, the ½ cup feta cheese, oregano, garlic, and salt. Cover and process or blend until smooth.

3 Drizzle dressing over romaine; sprinkle with cayenne pepper. Top with the ¼ cup feta cheese. To serve, cut romaine halves crosswise into quarters.

nutrition facts per serving: 65 cal., 6 g total fat (2 g sat. fat), 6 mg chol., 130 mg sodium, 2 g carb., 1 g fiber, 1 g pro.

This is a taste of summer in a bowl: fresh sweet corn, cucumber, sweet pepper, tomatoes, chiles, and herbs, dressed in a whisper-light, oil-free vinaigrette.

fresh corn salad

start to finish: 30 minutes
makes: 8 servings

½ cup cider vinegar
¼ to ⅓ cup sugar
1 teaspoon kosher salt
½ teaspoon coarsely ground black pepper
4 ears fresh corn
½ cup finely chopped red onion (1 medium)
½ cup chopped, seeded cucumber
½ cup chopped red and/or orange sweet pepper
½ cup halved or quartered cherry or pear tomatoes
3 tablespoons chopped fresh Italian (flat-leaf) parsley
1 tablespoon chopped fresh basil
1 tablespoon fresh jalapeño pepper, seeded and finely chopped*
½ teaspoon kosher salt (optional)
1 to 2 cups small arugula leaves

1 For dressing, in a small bowl whisk together vinegar, sugar, the 1 teaspoon kosher salt, and black pepper until sugar is dissolved. Let dressing stand while preparing salad.

2 For salad, cut corn kernels from cobs. In a large bowl toss corn, onion, cucumber, sweet pepper, tomatoes, parsley, basil, and chile pepper. If desired, sprinkle with the ½ teaspoon salt. Pour dressing over salad; toss to coat. Stir in arugula.

nutrition facts per serving: 77 cal., 1 g total fat (0 g sat. fat), 0 mg chol., 356 mg sodium, 17 g carb., 2 g fiber, 2 g pro.

★tip: Because hot chile peppers, contain volatile oils that can burn your skin and eyes, avoid direct contact with chiles as much as possible. When working with chile peppers, wear plastic or rubber gloves. If your bare hands do touch chile peppers, wash your hands well with soap and warm water.

This autumnal slaw made with cabbage, apples, cranberries, and pecans is particularly good with pork or chicken.

harvest slaw

start to finish: 30 minutes
makes: 12 servings

3   tablespoons olive oil
2   garlic cloves, coarsely
      chopped
2   teaspoons caraway
      seeds, lightly
      crushed
¼   cup cider vinegar
1   tablespoon honey
      Salt
      Ground black pepper
4   cups finely shredded
      red and/or green
      cabbage
2   red apples, cored and
      thinly sliced
½   cup dried cranberries
½   cup pecan halves,
      toasted*
2   tablespoons cilantro
      or Italian (flat leaf)
      parsley leaves

1 In a large skillet heat oil over medium heat. Add garlic and caraway seeds; cook and stir for 1 minute. Whisk in vinegar and honey. Heat and stir just until mixture comes to simmering. Remove from heat. Season with salt and pepper.

2 In a large bowl toss together cabbage, apples, cranberries, and pecans. Pour dressing over slaw; toss to combine. Sprinkle with cilantro.

nutrition facts per serving: 108 cal., 7 g total fat (1 g sat. fat), 0 mg chol., 56 mg sodium, 13 g carb., 2 g fiber, 1 g pro.

★ tip: To toast nuts, spread them in a shallow baking pan. Bake in a 350°F oven for 5 to 10 minutes or until light brown, shaking pan once or twice. Watch carefully so the nuts don't burn.

Try this tequila-and-lime-infused slaw with grilled fish.

spicy ginger-carrot slaw

start to finish: 25 minutes
make: 8 servings

1   small head napa
      cabbage, core
      removed, shredded
2   medium red sweet
      peppers, cut into
      bite-size strips
4   to 6 medium carrots,
      shredded
1   pink grapefruit,
      sectioned
4   green onions, thinly
      sliced
1   recipe Lime Dressing

1 In a large glass bowl layer cabbage, sweet peppers, carrots, and grapefruit.

2 Just before serving, add green onions. Add about half of the dressing; toss. Pass the remaining dressing.

nutrition facts per serving: 118 cal., 7 g total fat (1 g sat. fat), 0 mg chol., 31 mg sodium, 11 g carb., 3 g fiber, 2 g pro.

make-ahead directions: Prepare slaw as directed in Step 1. Cover and chill for up to 24 hours. Prepare dressing and continue as directed in Step 2.

Lime Dressing: In a small screw-top jar combine ¼ cup olive oil; 2 to 4 tablespoons tequila; ½-inch piece fresh ginger, peeled and finely chopped; 1 teaspoon finely shredded lime peel; 2 tablespoons lime juice; and ½ teaspoon crushed red pepper. Cover and shake to combine. If desired, let stand at room temperature for 1 hour; shake again before using.

The tanginess of the blue cheese complements the sweetness of the fruits beautifully in this vinaigrette-dressed slaw. Make it in late summer, when peaches are at their peak.

peach and blackberry slaw

start to finish: 30 minutes
makes: 6 servings

¼ cup white wine vinegar
¼ cup olive oil
1 tablespoon snipped fresh chives, basil, and/or tarragon
1 teaspoon sugar
Salt
Ground black pepper
1 small head cabbage
3 fresh peaches
½ pint blackberries
2 ounces blue cheese, coarsely crumbled (optional)
Snipped fresh chives, Italian (flat-leaf) parsley, basil, and/or tarragon (optional)

1 For dressing, in a small bowl whisk together vinegar, oil, the 1 tablespoon chives, and sugar. Season with salt and pepper; set aside.

2 Shred cabbage and place in a large bowl. Halve, pit, and thinly slice peaches; add to bowl with cabbage. Gently toss to combine. Drizzle with half of the dressing; toss to coat. Top with blackberries and, if desired, blue cheese. If desired, sprinkle with additional chives. Pass the remaining dressing.

nutrition facts per serving: 151 cal., 9 g total fat (1 g sat. fat), 0 mg chol., 116 mg sodium, 16 g carb., 5 g fiber, 2 g pro.

The three vegetables in this side dish are barely cooked, then plunged into ice water to stop the cooking. The process helps them retain their gorgeous green color and crisp texture. It's best served at room temperature.

asparagus, haricots verts, and snow peas

prep: 20 minutes stand: 10 minutes
makes: 6 to 8 servings

6   cups water
8   ounces fresh snow
    pea pods, trimmed
    (2½ cups)
8   ounces fresh
    haricots verts
    or green beans,
    trimmed and cut
    into 2-inch pieces
    (2 cups)
8   ounces fresh
    asparagus spears,
    trimmed and cut
    into 2-inch pieces
    (1¼ cups)
⅓   cup bottled fat-
    free raspberry
    vinaigrette salad
    dressing
½   teaspoon Jamaican
    jerk seasoning
1   tablespoon white
    sesame seeds,
    toasted*

1 In a large saucepan bring the water to boiling. Add snow peas, haricots verts, and asparagus. Return to boiling. Boil gently, uncovered, for 2 minutes. Immediately remove vegetables from boiling water with a slotted spoon; plunge into a large bowl half-filled with ice water. Let stand 10 minutes. Drain vegetables well; pat dry. Transfer vegetables to the large bowl.

2 In a small bowl combine salad dressing and Jamaican jerk seasoning; pour over vegetables, tossing to coat. Transfer vegetables to a serving platter; sprinkle with sesame seeds.

nutrition facts per serving: 59 cal., 1 g total fat (0 g sat. fat), 0 mg chol., 109 mg sodium, 11 g carb., 3 g fiber, 3 g pro.

*tip: To toast sesame seeds, scatter them in a dry small skillet and heat over medium heat just until golden. Stir frequently so they don't burn.

As simple as it is, this is a lovely side dish for Thanksgiving—in place of the heavy green bean casserole that's traditionally served on so many holiday tables.

sauteed green beans with shallot crisps

start to finish: 30 minutes
makes: 8 servings

⅓ cup canola oil
5 to 6 shallots, thinly
   sliced (½ cup)
2 pounds green beans,
   trimmed
1 tablespoon butter
1 tablespoon olive oil
   Salt
   Freshly ground black
   pepper

make-ahead directions:
Shallot crisps may be prepared
up to 2 hours ahead.

1 For shallot crisps, in 6-inch skillet heat oil over medium-high heat.* Using a slotted spoon, add half the shallots. Fry for 3 to 4 minutes or until crisp and dark golden brown. Remove from oil; drain on paper towels. Repeat with remaining shallots; set aside.

2 Meanwhile, in large pot cook beans, covered, in enough boiling water to cover for 6 to 8 minutes or until crisp-tender. Drain and plunge into a bowl half-filled with ice water to cool quickly. Drain well.

3 Heat a very large skillet over medium-high heat. Add butter and oil, swirling to coat skillet. Add beans; cook about 5 minutes or until beans are heated through, stirring frequently. Season with salt and pepper. Transfer to a serving bowl and top with shallot crisps.

nutrition facts per serving: 100 cal., 7 g total fat (2 g sat. fat), 4 mg chol., 18 mg sodium, 10 g carb., 4 g fiber, 2 g pro.

*tip: Test oil by adding 1 shallot slice to oil. When oil sizzles without spattering and shallot is golden, the oil is ready.

When we think of cooking methods for vegetables, boiling, steaming, and roasting come to mind—but broiling? It actually gives the vegetables lovely charring and flavor.

broiled bok choy with miso sauce

prep: 20 minutes   broil: 13 minutes
makes: 4 servings

Nonstick cooking
   spray
4   teaspoons olive oil
6   baby bok choy (about
      1 pound), halved
      lengthwise
4   ounces fresh shiitake
      mushrooms,
      stemmed and
      halved lengthwise
2   tablespoons orange
      juice
2   tablespoons sweet
      rice wine (mirin)
1   tablespoon red miso
      paste
1   tablespoon honey
2   teaspoons grated
      fresh ginger
2   teaspoons finely
      shredded orange
      peel
1   to 2 teaspoons Asian
      chili sauce (Sriracha
      sauce)
   Orange slice,
      quartered (optional)

1 Preheat broiler. Coat a 15×10×1-inch baking pan with cooking spray; drizzle pan with 2 teaspoons of the oil. Add bok choy and mushrooms to pan; stir and toss to coat vegetables with oil.

2 For sauce, in a small bowl whisk together the remaining 2 teaspoons oil, the orange juice, rice wine, miso paste, honey, ginger, orange peel, and chili sauce; set aside.

3 Broil vegetables about 6 inches from the heat for 6 minutes. Turn bok choy over. Broil for 7 to 8 minutes more or until bok choy leaves are slightly charred and stems are crisp-tender.

4 Transfer bok choy and mushrooms to a serving platter. If desired, garnish sauce with orange pieces. Drizzle sauce over vegetables.

nutrition facts per serving: 108 cal., 5 g total fat (1 g sat. fat), 0 mg chol., 327 mg sodium, 15 g carb., 2 g fiber, 3 g pro.

Even those who profess to hate Brussels sprouts will be charmed by this simple preparation that involves caramelizing the sprouts in a skillet (which sweetens and crisps them), then splashing them with fresh lemon.

caramelized brussels sprouts with lemon

start to finish: 20 minutes
makes: 6 servings

¼ cup extra-virgin olive
    oil
4 cups Brussels
    sprouts, rinsed,
    trimmed, and
    halved lengthwise
    (4 cups)
    Salt
    Freshly ground black
    pepper
2 tablespoons water
1 tablespoon lemon
    juice

1 In a very large nonstick skillet heat 3 tablespoons of the oil over medium heat. Arrange sprouts in a single layer, cut sides down. Drizzle with the remaining 1 tablespoon oil; sprinkle with salt and pepper. Cook, covered, for 3 minutes. Remove lid and sprinkle sprouts with the water. Cook, covered, for 2 minutes more. Sprouts should just be beginning to caramelize and, when pierced with a fork, slightly tender.

2 Remove lid and increase heat slightly. When cut sides are well caramelized and golden brown, toss Brussels sprouts in pan; drizzle with lemon juice.

nutrition facts per serving: 106 cal., 9 g total fat (1 g sat. fat), 0 mg chol., 209 mg sodium, 6 g carb., 2 g fiber, 2 g pro.

kitchen tip: Fresh Brussels sprouts don't store particularly well. Use them within 3 days of purchasing for the best possible flavor and texture. Store unwashed and untrimmed in an airtight container in the refrigerator. Wash and trim right before use.

The homemade croutons give this dish of soft, braised cabbage a pleasing crunch.

braised cabbage with spicy croutons

prep: 10 minutes cook: 18 minutes
makes: 6 servings

2   tablespoons olive oil
1   tablespoon butter
⅓ of a 12-ounce
     baguette, torn into
     coarse crumbs
     (2 cups)
¼ teaspoon garlic
     powder
¼ teaspoon crushed red
     pepper
1   small head green
     cabbage, cut into
     6 wedges
     Salt
     Ground black pepper
½ cup water
     Snipped fresh Italian
     (flat-leaf) parsley
     Lemon wedges

1 For croutons, in a very large skillet heat 1 tablespoon of the oil and the butter over medium-high heat. Add bread, garlic powder, and crushed red pepper; cook and stir for 3 to 5 minutes or until golden brown. Remove croutons from skillet with slotted spoon; cool in a single layer on paper towels.

2 Add cabbage to the skillet, overlapping wedges if necessary. Sprinkle with salt and black pepper. Add the water; bring to boiling. Reduce heat; simmer, covered, about 15 minutes or until tender.

3 Place cabbage on a platter; drizzle the remaining 1 tablespoon olive oil over cabbage. Sprinkle with croutons and parsley; serve with lemon wedges.

nutrition facts per serving: 141 cal., 7 g total fat (2 g sat. fat), 5 mg chol., 254 mg sodium, 19 g carb., 4 g fiber, 4 g pro.

Serve this super-healthy Asian-style side with grilled salmon and steamed brown rice.

sesame kale and edamame

start to finish: 25 minutes
makes: 4 servings

½ cup frozen shelled sweet soybeans (edamame)
1 bunch kale (about 12 ounces)
1 large red sweet pepper, seeded and cut into bite-size strips
2 tablespoons reduced-sodium soy sauce
1 tablespoon sweet rice wine (mirin)
2 teaspoons grated fresh ginger
2 teaspoons toasted sesame oil
1 teaspoon sesame seeds, toasted*

1 In a small saucepan cook edamame in enough boiling water to cover for 3 to 4 minutes or until tender; drain and set aside. Remove and discard thick stems from kale. Chop or tear leaves into bite-size pieces (you should have about 8 cups).

2 In a 4-quart Dutch oven cook kale and sweet pepper in boiling water for 30 seconds. Drain and plunge into a bowl half-filled with ice water for 1 minute. Drain well; dry kale mixture using salad spinner or pat dry with paper towels.

3 Place kale mixture in a shallow serving bowl. In a small bowl combine soy sauce, rice wine, ginger, and sesame oil. Drizzle soy mixture over kale mixture. Sprinkle with sesame seeds. Serve immediately or cover and chill for up to 2 hours.

nutrition facts per serving: 111 cal., 4 g total fat (1 g sat. fat), 0 mg chol., 359 mg sodium, 15 g carb., 3 g fiber, 6 g pro.

*tip: To toast sesame seeds, scatter them in a dry small skillet and heat over medium heat just until golden. Stir frequently so they don't burn.

nutrition note: Dark, leafy greens such as kale, collard greens, mustard greens, and Swiss chard are nutritional powerhouses. They are all great sources of magnesium, a key mineral in maintaining a healthy heart rhythm, muscle function, and bone health.

The natural sweetness of peas is enhanced with honey—and spiked with head-clearing wasabi—in this fun dish.

honey-wasabi mashed peas

prep: 10 minutes cook: 10 minutes
makes: 6 servings

1 14- to 16-ounce
   package frozen
   peas
2 tablespoons honey
2 tablespoons lemon
   juice or rice vinegar
1 teaspoon prepared
   wasabi paste
1 small clove garlic,
   minced
¼ teaspoon salt
¼ teaspoon ground
   black pepper
   Lemon slices
   (optional)
   Watercress (optional)

1 In a medium saucepan combine peas with enough water to cover. Bring to boiling; reduce heat. Simmer, uncovered, for 7 minutes or until very tender; drain.

2 Stir honey, lemon juice, wasabi paste, garlic, salt, and pepper into peas in saucepan. Cook for 3 minutes. Mash peas slightly with a potato masher or fork just until coarsely mashed. If desired, top with lemon slices and watercress.

nutrition facts per serving: 76 cal., 0 g total fat (0 g sat. fat), 0 mg chol., 178 mg sodium, 15 g carb., 3 g fiber, 4 g pro.

Fat is flavor, they say, but it doesn't have to be. Mashing potatoes with mustard gives them loads of great flavor without resorting to adding a lot of butter.

mustard-chive mashed potatoes

prep: 10 minutes cook: 20 minutes
makes: 8 servings

1½ pounds round red potatoes, scrubbed and cut into 2-inch pieces

⅓ cup fat-free milk

⅓ cup light sour cream

2 tablespoons Dijon-style mustard

⅛ teaspoon salt

¼ cup snipped fresh chives or green onion tops

1 In a covered large saucepan cook potatoes in enough boiling water to cover for 20 to 25 minutes or until tender. Drain potatoes in a colander.

2 Add milk to the same saucepan; heat just to boiling over medium heat. Add drained potatoes, sour cream, mustard, and salt. Remove from heat.

3 Coarsely mash mixture with a potato masher. Stir in chives.

nutrition facts per serving: 78 cal., 1 g total fat (1 g sat. fat), 3 mg chol., 141 mg sodium, 15 g carb., 1 g fiber, 2 g pro.

Sneak some antioxidant beta-carotene and vitamin A into your mashed potatoes with the addition of pumpkin puree. It also gives them a beautiful golden color on the plate.

pumpkin mashed potatoes

prep: 10 minutes   cook: 20 minutes
makes: 4 servings

1 pound medium baking potatoes, peeled and quartered
2 cloves garlic, peeled
1 cup canned pumpkin
2 tablespoons reduced-fat cream cheese (Neufchâtel)
1 tablespoon butter or tub-style vegetable oil spread
⅛ teaspoon ground sage
¼ teaspoon salt
¼ teaspoon ground black pepper
¼ cup fat-free milk
1 recipe Miniature Pumpkin Bowls (optional)
Fresh sage leaves (optional)

1 In a covered large saucepan, cook potatoes and garlic in enough boiling water to cover for 20 to 25 minutes or until potatoes are tender; drain and transfer to a mixing bowl. Mash with a potato masher or beat with an electric mixer on low speed until nearly smooth. Beat in canned pumpkin, cream cheese, butter, ground sage, salt, and pepper. Gradually add milk, beating until light and fluffy. Return to saucepan; heat through.

2 If desired, spoon mashed potatoes into Miniature Pumpkin Bowls and garnish with sage leaves and pumpkin tops.

nutrition facts per serving: 138 cal., 5 g total fat (3 g sat. fat), 13 mg chol., 209 mg sodium, 22 g carb., 3 g fiber, 4 g pro.

Miniature Pumpkin Bowls: Preheat oven to 325°F. Cut off ½ inch from the tops of 4 miniature pumpkins (6 to 8 ounces each); set aside tops. Using a spoon, scoop out seeds and membranes and discard. Place pumpkins, cut sides down, on a baking sheet. Bake for 20 to 25 minutes or just until pumpkins are easily pierced with a fork.

Larger portions of this veggie and noodle side dish could be served as a main dish.

brussels sprouts and noodle stir-fry with cilantro and almonds

start to finish: 30 minutes
makes: 8 servings

3   ounces dried whole wheat thin spaghetti
2   tablespoons olive oil
1   cup thinly sliced red onion
3   cloves garlic, minced
12 ounces Brussels sprouts, trimmed and thinly sliced or shredded
1   tablespoon grated fresh ginger
¼   to ½ teaspoon crushed red pepper
½   cup reduced-sodium chicken broth
2   tablespoons reduced-sodium soy sauce
½   cup shredded carrot (1 medium)
⅓   cup snipped fresh cilantro
3   tablespoons slivered almonds, toasted*

1 Break spaghetti into 1-inch pieces. Cook spaghetti according to package directions; drain. Return spaghetti to hot pan. Cover and keep warm.

2 Heat oil in a large skillet over medium-high heat. Add onion and garlic; cook and stir for 1 minute. Add Brussels sprouts, ginger, and crushed red pepper; cook and stir for 1 minute. Add broth and soy sauce; cook about 2 minutes more or until liquid is almost evaporated, stirring occasionally. Remove from heat.

3 Stir in cooked spaghetti, carrot, and cilantro. Before serving, sprinkle with almonds.

nutrition facts per serving: 115 cal., 5 g total fat (1 g sat. fat), 0 mg chol., 196 mg sodium, 15 g carb., 3 g fiber, 4 g pro.

✳ tip: To toast nuts, spread them in a shallow baking pan. Bake in a 350°F oven for 5 to 10 minutes or until light brown, shaking pan once or twice. Watch carefully so the nuts don't burn.

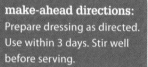

make-ahead directions:
Prepare dressing as directed. Use within 3 days. Stir well before serving.

Dark, leafy greens of all stripes are all the rage right now. Try collard greens—a Southern favorite—without the traditional bacon-fat braising.

collard greens with lemon, farro, and feta

start to finish: 30 minutes
makes: 6 servings

1 bunch collard greens, mustard greens, or Swiss chard (about 12 ounces)
½ cup semi-pearled farro
1 tablespoon olive oil
4 cloves garlic, minced
½ teaspoon salt
1 tablespoon finely shredded lemon peel
1 tablespoon lemon juice
½ cup crumbled reduced-fat feta cheese (2 ounces)
¼ cup snipped fresh Italian (flat-leaf) parsley
Lemon wedges (optional)

1 Remove and discard thick stems from collard greens. Chop leaves into bite-size pieces (you should have about 8 cups). In a Dutch oven cook collard greens in boiling water about 7 minutes or until tender. Using a slotted spoon, plunge greens into a bowl half-filled with ice water for 1 minute. Drain and set aside.

2 Stir farro into the boiling water. Cook about 10 minutes or until tender. Drain in a colander.

3 In the same Dutch oven heat oil over medium-high heat. Add garlic; cook and stir about 2 minutes or until golden. Stir in collard greens, farro, and salt; heat through. Stir in lemon peel and lemon juice.

4 Sprinkle greens with feta cheese and parsley. If desired, serve with lemon wedges.

nutrition facts per serving: 115 cal., 4 g total fat (1 g sat. fat), 3 mg chol., 368 mg sodium, 14 g carb., 3 g fiber, 6 g pro.

nutrition note: Farro (pronounced FAHR-oh) is an ancient, nonhybrid wheat variety often served at upscale Italian restaurants. Semi-pearled farro is a good compromise between pearled farro, which has more of the nutrient-rich bran stripped away, and whole farro, which takes longer to cook.

These scones are a cinch to make. They're quickly mixed, rolled into an 8-inch square and then cut into smaller squares, and baked.

crisp cornmeal scones

prep: 15 minutes bake: 12 minutes at 425°F
makes: 16 to 25 scones

2 cups all-purpose flour
1 cup yellow cornmeal
2 tablespoons granulated sugar
1½ teaspoons baking powder
½ teaspoon salt
½ cup cold butter, coarsely shredded* or cubed
1 cup buttermilk
Buttermilk
Coarse sugar

1 Preheat oven to 425°F. In large bowl whisk together flour, cornmeal, sugar, baking powder, and salt.

2 Add shredded butter to flour mixture; toss to distribute. (Or cut cubed butter into flour mixture with pastry blender until it resembles coarse crumbs). Make well in center of flour mixture. Add the 1 cup buttermilk; stir with spoon until moistened. Do not overmix. (If dough appears dry, add 1 to 2 tablespoons additional buttermilk.)

3 Turn dough out onto floured surface. Gently knead by lifting and folding dough, 4 or 5 times, giving a quarter turn after each knead. Roll into an 8-inch square, about ¾ inch thick. Cut into 1½- to 2-inch squares. Place squares 1 inch apart on ungreased baking sheet. Brush with buttermilk; sprinkle with coarse sugar. Bake for 12 to 15 minutes or until lightly browned; cool scones on a rack. Serve warm.

nutrition facts per scone: 155 cal., 6 g total fat (4 g sat. fat), 16 mg chol., 165 mg sodium, 24 g carb., 1 g fiber, 3 g pro.

*tip: To shred butter, freeze the butter for 15 minutes. Using a grater, coarsely shred the cold butter. Toss into flour mixture or chill, loosely covered, until needed.

The goat cheese in these elegant scones serves as both the fat that creates flakiness and the flavor that makes the scones delicious. Serve them with roast beef or chicken.

goat cheese and onion scones

prep: 15 minutes bake: 15 minutes at 400°F
makes: 12 scones

2 cups all-purpose flour
2 tablespoons finely chopped green onion (1)
2 teaspoons baking powder
¼ teaspoon baking soda
¼ teaspoon salt
¼ teaspoon freshly ground black pepper
1 egg, beaten
4 ounces semisoft goat cheese (chèvre), crumbled or cut into small cubes
½ cup buttermilk or fat-free sour milk*

1 Preheat oven to 400°F. In a medium bowl combine flour, green onion, baking powder, baking soda, salt, and pepper. Make a well in the center of flour mixture; set aside.

2 In a small bowl stir together the egg, goat cheese, and buttermilk. Add egg mixture all at once to flour mixture. Using a fork, stir just until moistened.

3 Turn dough out onto a lightly floured surface. Knead dough by folding and gently pressing dough for 10 to 12 strokes or until dough is nearly smooth. Divide dough in half. Pat or lightly roll half of the dough into a 5-inch circle. Cut into 6 wedges. Repeat with remaining dough. Place wedges 1 inch apart on an ungreased baking sheet.

4 Bake for 15 to 18 minutes or until golden. Serve warm.

nutrition facts per scone: 106 cal., 3 g total fat (2 g sat. fat), 22 mg chol., 193 mg sodium, 15 g carb., 1 g fiber, 5 g pro.

*tip: To make ½ cup fat-free sour milk, place 1½ teaspoons lemon juice or vinegar in a glass measuring cup. Add enough milk to make ½ cup total liquid; stir. Let mixture stand for 5 minutes before using.

Start with a tube of refrigerated pizza dough, and you can have freshly baked yeast bread on the table in 30 minutes or less.

pumpkin seed breadsticks

prep: 15 minutes   bake: 8 minutes per batch at 425°F
makes: 24 breadsticks

1   13.8-ounce
    refrigerated pizza
    dough
1   egg, lightly beaten
1   to 3 tablespoons
    shelled pumpkin
    seeds, poppy seeds,
    flaxseeds, plain
    sesame seeds,
    and/or black
    sesame seeds
    Coarse salt or salt

1 Preheat oven to 425°F. Lightly grease two large baking sheets. Unroll pizza dough on a lightly floured surface. Using your hands, shape dough into a 12×9-inch rectangle. Brush the dough with some of the egg. Sprinkle with seeds and lightly sprinkle with salt. Use a floured long knife or floured pizza cutter to cut dough crosswise into ¼- to ½-inch-wide strips.

2 Place strips on prepared baking sheets. Bake one sheet at a time for 8 to 10 minutes or until golden brown. Cool on wire racks.

nutrition facts per breadstick: 39 cal., 1 g total fat (0 g sat. fat), 9 mg chol., 75 mg sodium, 6 g carb., 0 g fiber, 1 g pro.

These crunchy seeded biscuits are delicious with dinner—or baked for Sunday brunch and served with marmalade and a cup of hot tea.

three-seed biscuit squares

prep: 15 minutes   bake: 10 minutes at 450°F
makes: 9 biscuits

1   cup all-purpose flour
½   cup whole wheat flour or white whole wheat flour
2   teaspoons baking powder
¼   teaspoon cream of tartar
¼   teaspoon salt
¼   cup tub-style vegetable oil spread, chilled
2   tablespoons butter
½   cup plus 1 tablespoon fat-free milk
1   egg white, beaten
2   teaspoons sesame seeds
1   teaspoon cumin seeds
1   teaspoon poppy seeds
    Low-sugar orange marmalade or low-sugar fruit spread (optional)

1 Preheat oven to 450°F. In a medium bowl stir together flours, baking powder, cream of tartar, and salt. Using a pastry blender, cut in vegetable oil spread and butter until mixture resembles coarse crumbs. Make a well in the center of the flour mixture. Add milk all at once; stir just until dough clings together.

2 Turn dough out onto a lightly floured surface. Knead by folding and gently pressing dough for four to six strokes or until nearly smooth. Pat or lightly roll dough into a 7×7-inch square. Brush with egg white and sprinkle dough with sesame seeds, cumin seeds, and poppy seeds. Press seeds in lightly with your fingers.

3 Cut dough into nine squares. Place squares 1 inch apart on an ungreased baking sheet. Bake for 10 to 12 minutes or until golden brown. Serve warm. If desired, serve with marmalade or fruit spread.

nutrition facts per biscuit: 148 cal., 8 g total fat (3 g sat. fat), 7 mg chol., 211 mg sodium, 17 g carb., 1 g fiber, 4 g pro.

16

Indulge in these extra-special appetizers, entrées, sides, and desserts to celebrate a special occasion—without overtime in the kitchen or overindulging in unhealthy foods.

entertaining & special occas

coconut hot chocolate

ions

Be sure to buy the shelled edamame to make this creamy green dip.

edamame-lemongrass hummus

start to finish: 25 minutes
makes: 10 servings

2   green onions
1   10-ounce package
     frozen sweet
     soybeans
     (edamame) (2 cups)
½   cup fresh Italian (flat-
     leaf) parsley sprigs
½   cup water
2   tablespoons lemon
     juice
1   tablespoon chopped
     fresh lemongrass or
     ½ teaspoon finely
     shredded lemon
     peel
1   tablespoon canola oil
2   cloves garlic,
     quartered
1   teaspoon finely
     chopped fresh
     ginger or
     ¼ teaspoon
     ground ginger
¾   teaspoon salt
¼   teaspoon crushed red
     pepper (optional)
40 Belgian endive leaves
     and/or 10 cups
     assorted dippers,
     such as radishes,
     red sweet pepper
     strips, Belgian
     endive leaves, and/
     or peeled jicama
     sticks

1 Thinly slice green onions, keeping green tops separate from white bottoms; set aside. Cook edamame according to package directions, except omit salt. Drain; rinse with cold water. Drain again.

2 In food processor combine white parts of green onions, cooked edamame, parsley, the water, lemon juice, lemongrass, oil, garlic, ginger, salt, and, if desired, crushed red pepper. Cover and process until nearly smooth. Stir in green onion tops. Serve with vegetable dippers.

nutrition facts per ¼ cup hummus + 4 endive leaves: 51 cal., 3 g total fat (0 g sat. fat), 0 mg chol., 180 mg sodium, 4 g carb., 2 g fiber, 3 g pro.

make-ahead directions: Prepare as directed, except cover and store in the refrigerator for up to 24 hours.

The crisp wonton cups are made by lightly coating wonton skins with cooking spray, then molding them into a muffin tin and baking until golden brown. No frying necessary!

sweet potato wontons

prep: 20 minutes bake: 10 minutes at 350°F
makes: 24 wontons

24   wonton wrappers
     Nonstick cooking
        spray
 3   tablespoons mango
        chutney
 2   tablespoons canola
        oil
⅓   cup finely chopped
        onion (1 small)
 2   teaspoons curry
        powder
 1   teaspoon minced
        fresh ginger
 1   clove garlic, minced
 1   tablespoon all-
        purpose flour
1½   cups chopped cooked
        sweet potato*
⅓   cup half-and-half
     Carrots, cut into thin
        bite-size strips and
        sautéed (optional)

1 Preheat oven to 350°F. Lightly coat wonton wrappers with cooking spray. Press wrappers, sprayed sides down, into twenty-four 1¾-inch muffin cups, pleating as necessary. Bake about 10 minutes or until golden brown.

2 Meanwhile, cut up any large pieces of fruit in chutney; set aside. In a large heavy skillet heat the canola oil over medium heat. Add onion, curry powder, ginger, and garlic; cook until onion is tender. Stir in flour. Stir in cooked sweet potato, half-and-half, and chutney. Cook and stir until thickened. Cook and stir for 1 minute more.

3 Spoon sweet potato mixture into wonton shells. If desired, sprinkle with carrot strips. Serve immediately.

nutrition facts per 2 wontons: 61 cal., 2 g total fat (0 g sat. fat), 2 mg chol., 69 mg sodium, 10 g carb., 1 g fiber, 1 g pro.

*tip: For cooked sweet potato, peel and cut one 10- to 12-ounce sweet potato into thirds. In a covered small saucepan cook potato in boiling lightly salted water about 20 minutes or just until tender. Drain and chop.

Whirl roasted vegetables in a food processor to make this chunky dip. A splash of vinegar and hot pepper sauce provides extra zip.

roasted vegetable caviar with toasted pita chips

prep: 10 minutes   roast: 25 minutes at 450°F
makes: about 2 cups dip (32 1-tablespoon servings)

414

1 Place tomatoes, sweet pepper, onion, summer squash or zucchini, carrot, and garlic in a 15×10×1-inch baking pan. Drizzle olive oil over vegetables; stir to coat. Roast, uncovered, in a 450°F oven for 25 minutes, stirring once, or until vegetables are tender. Remove from oven; let cool.

2 Transfer vegetable mixture to a food processor. Cover and process with several on/off pulses until coarsely chopped. Stir in vinegar, salt, and hot pepper sauce. Serve with Toasted Pita Chips.

nutrition facts per 1 tablespoon: 29 cal., 1 g total fat (0 g sat. fat), 0 mg chol., 54 mg sodium, 4 g carb., 0 g fiber, 1 g pro.

3   medium plum tomatoes, halved
1   small yellow or red sweet pepper, stemmed, halved, and seeded
1   small onion, quartered
1   small summer squash or zucchini, halved lengthwise
1   small carrot, halved lengthwise
2   cloves garlic, peeled and halved
1   tablespoon olive oil
4   teaspoons red wine vinegar
1/4   teaspoon salt
1/4   teaspoon bottled hot pepper sauce
1   recipe Toasted Pita Chips

make-ahead directions: Up to 1 week ahead, prepare Toasted Pita Chips. Store in an airtight container until serving time.

Toasted Pita Chips: Split 3 pita bread rounds in half horizontally. Melt 3 tablespoons margarine or butter; lightly brush the split side of each pita bread half with melted margarine or butter. Cut each half into six wedges. Arrange in a single layer on a baking sheet. Bake in a 350°F oven for 10 to 15 minutes or until crisp; let cool.
makes: 36 pita chips

To toast the bread for these bruschetta, lay the slices in a single layer on a rimmed baking pan. Bake in a 350°F oven for about 15 minutes or until lightly golden, turning once about halfway through baking time. Cool completely before using.

fennel-mushroom bruschetta

prep: 10 minutes   cook: 12 minutes
makes: 24 bruschetta

1   tablespoon butter
1   small fennel bulb, thinly sliced
¼   of a medium sweet onion, chopped
1   8-ounce package sliced fresh mushrooms
2   cloves garlic, minced
2   tablespoons white wine or 1½ tablespoons reduced-sodium chicken broth plus 1½ teaspoons white wine vinegar
1   cup arugula
1   tablespoon reduced-sodium soy sauce
12 ounces whole wheat baguette-style French bread, cut into 24 thin slices, toasted
    Snipped fennel fronds (optional)

1 In a large skillet melt butter over medium heat. Add fennel and onion; cook and stir about 5 minutes or until vegetables just begin to soften. Add mushrooms and garlic; cook and stir for 3 to 5 minutes more or until vegetables are crisp-tender. Remove from heat. Carefully add wine to skillet. Return to heat. Cook and stir until nearly all of the liquid has evaporated, making sure to scrape up any browned bits from the bottom of the pan.

2 Remove pan from heat. Stir in arugula and soy sauce. Spoon about 1 tablespoon mushroom mixture over each toasted baguette slice. If desired, garnish with fennel fronds.

nutrition facts per 2 bruschetta: 93 cal., 2 g total fat (1 g sat. fat), 3 mg chol., 185 mg sodium, 15 g carb., 2 g fiber, 3 g pro.

If you choose to use persimmons, make sure they are in season—which is in the fall. Fuyu persimmons have a mild, pumpkin-like flavor. Buy them when they are hard and let them ripen a couple of days at room temperature. They should be more orange than yellow when eaten—and just the slightest bit soft to the touch.

goat cheese and tomato bites

start to finish: 15 minutes
makes: 12 appetizers

4   roma tomatoes or
    4 small firm but ripe
    Fuyu persimmons
4   ounces semisoft goat
    cheese (chèvre), cut
    into
    12 slices
2   tablespoons honey
2   tablespoons coarsely
    chopped walnuts,
    toasted* (optional)
¼   to ½ teaspoon freshly
    ground black
    pepper

1 Trim ends off tomatoes and discard. Cut each tomato into 3 slices. Place slices on a serving platter. Top each with a slice of goat cheese. Drizzle with honey and sprinkle with walnuts (if desired) and pepper.

nutrition facts per appetizer: 58 cal., 4 g total fat (2 g sat. fat), 7 mg chol., 50 mg sodium, 4 g carb., 0 g fiber, 2 g pro.

✱tip: To toast nuts, spread them in a shallow baking pan. Bake in a 350°F oven for 5 to 10 minutes or until light brown, shaking pan once or twice. Watch carefully so the nuts don't burn.

When made with jalapeños, these crisp peppers stuffed with cream cheese are like a healthier, unfried version of the popular jalapeño poppers.

creamy stuffed peppers

start to finish: 20 minutes
makes: 6 servings

12   miniature sweet peppers and/or fresh jalapeño chile peppers*
1   8-ounce package reduced-fat cream cheese (Neufchâtel), softened
¼   cup thinly sliced green onions (2)
½   to 1 canned chipotle chile pepper in adobo sauce, finely chopped*
⅛   teaspoon salt
⅛   teaspoon ground black pepper
1   small tomato, seeded and chopped
Very thin strips fresh jalapeño chile pepper* (optional)

1 Cut the sweet peppers in half lengthwise. Remove seeds and ribs; set aside.

2 In a medium bowl stir together cream cheese, green onions, chipotle pepper, salt, and black pepper. Gently stir in the tomato.

3 To serve, spoon the cream cheese mixture into the pepper halves. If desired, top with very thin strips jalapeño pepper.

nutrition facts per 4 stuffed pepper halves:
111 cal., 9 g total fat (5 g sat. fat), 28 mg chol., 184 mg sodium, 5 g carb., 1 g fiber, 4 g pro.

*tip: Because chile peppers contain volatile oils that can burn your skin and eyes, avoid direct contact with them as much as possible. When working with chile peppers, wear plastic or rubber gloves. If your bare hands do touch the peppers, wash your hands and nails well with soap and warm water.

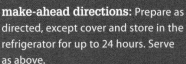

make-ahead directions: Prepare as directed, except cover and store in the refrigerator for up to 24 hours. Serve as above.

The sweet and spicy smell of this simmering on the stove is warm and welcoming during the holiday season.

hot cranberry toddy

start to finish: 20 minutes
makes: 12 servings

1   48-ounce bottle low-calorie cranberry juice (6 cups)
2   cups water
¼   cup lemon juice
3   1-inch-long strips lemon peel (set aside)
1   3-inch stick cinnamon
½   teaspoon whole cloves
⅓   cup bourbon, rum, or orange juice
    Fresh lemon slices (optional)
    Stick cinnamon (optional)

1 In a 4-quart saucepan or Dutch oven combine cranberry juice, the water, and lemon juice.

2 For spice bag, place lemon peel, the 3-inch stick cinnamon, and the cloves in the center of a double-thick 6-inch square of 100 percent cotton cheesecloth. Bring the corners together; tie with clean kitchen string. Add to juice mixture.

3 Bring just to boiling; reduce heat. Simmer, covered, for 10 minutes. Discard spice bag. Stir bourbon into juice mixture. If desired, garnish servings with lemon slices and additional stick cinnamon.

nutrition facts per 6-ounce serving: 38 cal., 0 g total fat (0 g sat. fat), 0 mg chol., 5 mg sodium, 6 g carb., 0 g fiber, 0 g pro.

Made with light coconut milk instead of regular milk, this fabulous hot chocolate is a drinkable dessert!

coconut hot chocolate

start to finish: 20 minutes
makes: 6 servings

419

⅓ cup unsweetened cocoa powder

⅓ cup sugar

2½ cups water

1 13- to 14-ounce can unsweetened light coconut milk

⅓ cup coconut-flavor or light rum (optional)

Frozen light whipped dessert topping, thawed (optional)

Toasted coconut (optional)

Cinnamon sticks (optional)

1 In a medium saucepan whisk together cocoa powder and sugar. Gradually whisk in water. Bring to boiling over medium heat, whisking to dissolve sugar. Reduce heat. Stir in coconut milk. Heat through but do not boil.

2 If desired, stir in rum. Serve in warm mugs. If desired, add a small spoonful of whipped topping, a sprinkling of toasted coconut, and a cinnamon stick to each drink.

nutrition facts per 5-ounce serving: 91 cal., 4 g total fat (3 g sat. fat), 0 mg chol., 20 mg sodium, 16 g carb., 1 g fiber, 1 g pro.

Just the right hues for the holidays, these grilled lamb chops feature a Cilantro-Mint Sauce and a Cherry-Orange Sauce—one green, one red, one sweet and one savory.

lamb chops with red and green sauces

prep: 20 minutes cook: 12 minutes
makes: 4 servings

Nonstick cooking
  spray
8 lamb loin chops, cut
  1 inch thick (about
  2 pounds total)
½ teaspoon salt
¼ teaspoon ground
  black pepper
1 recipe Cherry-Orange
  Sauce
1 recipe Cilantro-Mint
  Sauce

1 Coat an indoor grill pan with cooking spray. Heat pan over medium heat. Meanwhile, trim fat from lamb chops. Sprinkle chops with the salt and pepper.

2 Place lamb chops on the heated grill pan. Cook for 12 to 14 minutes for medium-rare (145°F) or 15 to 17 minutes for medium (160°F), turning once. Serve lamb chops with Cherry-Orange Sauce and Cilantro-Mint Sauce.

nutrition facts per serving: 335 cal., 11 g total fat (3 g sat. fat), 118 mg chol., 539 mg sodium, 18 g carb., 3 g fiber, 40 g pro.

broiling directions: Preheat broiler. Trim fat from chops. Place chops on the unheated rack of a broiler pan. Sprinkle chops with the salt and pepper. Broil chops 3 to 4 inches from the heat for 8 to 10 minutes for medium-rare (145°F) or 10 to 15 minutes for medium (160°F), turning once halfway. Serve with sauces.

Cilantro-Mint Sauce: In a food processor or blender combine ½ cup lightly packed fresh Italian (flat-leaf) parsley; ½ cup lightly packed fresh cilantro; ½ cup lightly packed fresh mint leaves; 1 tablespoon lemon juice; 1 tablespoon plain lowfat yogurt; 1 tablespoon olive oil; 1 clove garlic, minced; 1/8 teaspoon salt; and 1/8 teaspoon ground black pepper. Cover and process or blend with several on/off pulses until finely chopped but not completely smooth.

Cherry-Orange Sauce: Chop ¾ cup frozen unsweetened pitted dark sweet cherries and place in a small saucepan. Add 1/3 cup orange juice. Bring to boiling over medium heat. Add ¼ cup dried tart cherries, ¼ teaspoon finely shredded orange peel, dash ground cinnamon, and dash salt. Simmer, uncovered, for 6 to 8 minutes or until thickened (the mixture will thicken further after it is removed from the heat). Remove from heat and set aside.

The Spiced Kumquat Chutney is delicious paired with a simple beef or pork roast as well as pan-seared chicken.

chicken with spiced kumquat chutney

prep: 20 minutes   **cook:** 10 minutes
makes: 4 servings

Nonstick cooking
spray
4   medium skinless,
boneless chicken
breast halves (1¼
to 1½ pounds total)
¼   teaspoon salt
⅛   teaspoon ground
black pepper
1   recipe Spiced
Kumquat Chutney
2   tablespoons chopped
pistachio nuts

1 Coat a nonstick grill pan with cooking spray; heat pan over medium-high heat. Sprinkle chicken with the salt and pepper and add to hot pan.

2 Cook for 10 to 12 minutes or until no longer pink (170°F), turning once halfway through cooking. Serve Spiced Kumquat Chutney over chicken. Sprinkle with pistachios.

nutrition facts per serving: 261 cal., 6 g total fat (1 g sat. fat), 82 mg chol., 242 mg sodium, 17 g carb., 3 g fiber, 34 g pro.

kitchen tip: Kumquats belong to the citrus family. They're tiny little orange orbs of sweet-tart flavor that are intended to be eaten whole, skin and all. Like the rest of the citrus family, they are at peak season during the winter months, which makes them a natural feature for holiday entertaining.

Spiced Kumquat Chutney: In a small saucepan heat 2 teaspoons canola oil over medium heat. Add ¼ cup thinly sliced green onions; ¼ teaspoon ground ginger; ¼ teaspoon ground coriander; and ⅛ teaspoon ground cinnamon. Cook and stir for 1 minute. Stir in ½ cup chopped kumquats, ⅓ cup dried cranberries, 3 tablespoons water, 2 tablespoons cider vinegar, and 1 tablespoon sugar. Bring to boiling; reduce heat. Cook, covered, over medium-low heat for 5 minutes, stirring once or twice. Remove from heat and set aside.

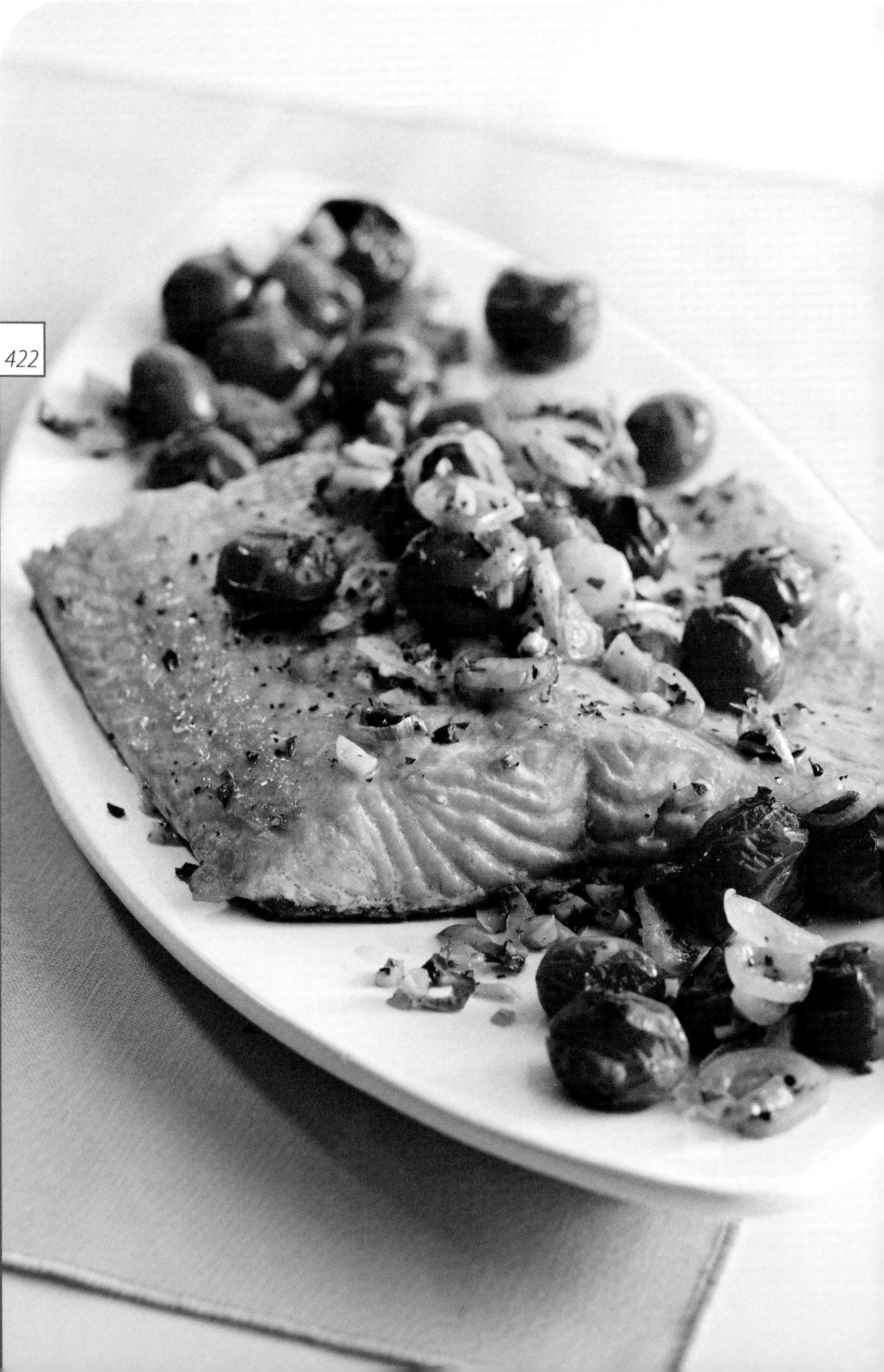

The sweetness and acidity of the roasted tomatoes nicely complements the rich flavor of the salmon. Serve it with a couscous or orzo.

salmon with roasted tomatoes and shallots

prep: 5 minutes roast: 30 minutes at 400°F
makes: 4 servings

1 pound fresh or frozen salmon fillet(s), skinned if desired
  Nonstick cooking spray
4 cups grape tomatoes
½ cup thinly sliced shallots
6 cloves garlic, minced
2 tablespoons snipped fresh oregano or 1½ teaspoons dried oregano, crushed
1 tablespoon olive oil
½ teaspoon salt
½ teaspoon ground black pepper

1 Thaw fish, if frozen. Preheat oven to 400°F. Rinse fish; pat dry with paper towels.

2 Lightly coat a 3-quart baking dish with nonstick cooking spray. In the baking dish combine tomatoes, shallots, garlic, oregano, olive oil, ¼ teaspoon of the salt, and ¼ teaspoon of the pepper. Toss to coat.

3 Roast, uncovered, for 15 minutes. Place salmon, skin side down, on top of the tomato-shallot mixture. Sprinkle salmon with the remaining ¼ teaspoon salt and the remaining ¼ teaspoon pepper. Roast, uncovered, for 15 to 18 minutes or until salmon flakes easily when tested with a fork. Use two large pancake turners to transfer the salmon to a cutting board.

4 If desired, use the turners to lift the salmon meat off the skin and onto a large platter; discard skin. Serve salmon with the tomato-shallot mixture.

nutrition facts per serving: 292 cal., 16 g total fat (3 g sat. fat), 66 mg chol., 273 mg sodium, 12 g carb., 2 g fiber, 25 g pro.

nutrition note: All fat is not created equal. The fat content in this recipe may appear high at first glance, but the recipe really only contains 3 grams of saturated fat. The remainder is the heart-healthy variety. These omega-3 fatty acids help to lower cholesterol.

This crisp-crusted fish, served with a beautiful herbed vegetable salad, is so elegant and easy to do. The fish bakes as you toss together the salad—and a company-worthy dinner is done!

crusted grouper with mint-artichoke salad

prep: 20 minutes   bake: 4 to 6 minutes per ½-inch thickness of fish at 425°F
makes: 4 servings

4   4- to 6-ounce fresh or frozen skinless grouper or cod fillets
½   teaspoon paprika
¼   teaspoon salt
¼   teaspoon ground black pepper
2   slices whole grain bread
2   tablespoons olive oil
2   6- to 6.5-ounce jars marinated artichoke hearts
1   medium red sweet pepper, cut into thin bite-size strips
¼   cup pitted Kalamata olives, coarsely chopped
1   tablespoon snipped fresh mint
1   teaspoon snipped fresh rosemary
1   clove garlic, minced

1 Thaw fish, if frozen. Preheat oven to 425°F. Rinse fish; pat dry with paper towels. Place fish on a lightly greased baking sheet. Measure thickness of fish. In a small bowl combine paprika, salt, and black pepper; sprinkle evenly over fish.

2 Tear bread into large pieces and place in a food processor. Cover and process with several on/off pulses to make very large crumbs. You should have about 1½ cups. Transfer bread to a small bowl. Add oil; toss to coat. Spoon bread crumbs evenly over fish fillets.

3 Bake fish for 4 to 6 minutes per ½-inch thickness or until fish flakes easily when tested with a fork, tenting with foil toward the end of baking time, if needed, to avoid overbrowning.

4 Meanwhile, for salad, drain artichoke hearts reserving 1 tablespoon of the marinade. Coarsely chop artichoke hearts. In a small bowl combine artichoke hearts, reserved marinade, sweet pepper, olives, mint, rosemary, and garlic.

5 To serve, place one fish fillet on each of four serving plates. Divide artichoke salad evenly over fish.

nutrition facts per serving: 280 cal., 14 g total fat (1 g sat. fat), 42 mg chol., 582 mg sodium, 15 g carb., 2 g fiber, 25 g pro.

Watch for lobster-tail sales and stock up. You can occasionally get them for as little as $5 a tail. Tuck the tails away in the freezer to someday make this very special dish for some very special people.

lobster tails with lemon-chamomile sesame sauce

prep: 20 minutes   bake: 10 minutes at 425°F
makes: 4 servings

4   8- to 10-ounce fresh
    or frozen lobster
    tails
⅛   teaspoon salt
⅛   teaspoon ground
    ginger
⅛   teaspoon cayenne
    pepper
1   chamomile tea bag
⅓   cup boiling water
3   tablespoons lemon
    juice
3   tablespoons
    untoasted sesame
    oil
⅛   teaspoon salt

1 Preheat oven to 425°F. Thaw lobster, if frozen. Rinse lobster; pat dry with paper towels. Butterfly tails by using kitchen shears or a sharp knife to cut lengthwise through centers of hard top shells and meat, cutting to, but not through, bottoms of shells. Press shell halves of tails apart with your fingers.

2 Grease an indoor grill pan and heat pan over medium-high heat. Add two of the lobster tails, meat sides down, to the hot pan; cook for 3 to 4 minutes or until browned. Transfer lobster tails to a 15×10×1-inch baking pan, placing them meat sides up. Repeat with remaining two lobster tails.

3 In a small bowl combine the ⅛ teaspoon salt, the ginger, and cayenne pepper. Sprinkle evenly over lobster tails. Bake for 10 to 12 minutes or until lobster meat is opaque.

4 Meanwhile, for sauce, place tea bag in a small mug. Add the boiling water; steep for 3 minutes. Remove tea bag, squeezing bag. In a small bowl whisk together tea, lemon juice, sesame oil, and the ⅛ teaspoon salt. To serve, place a lobster tail on each of four serving plates. Drizzle each tail with about 1 tablespoon of the sauce. Serve remaining sauce in little cups to use for dipping.

nutrition facts per serving: 218 cal., 11 g total fat (2 g sat. fat), 92 mg chol., 630 mg sodium, 3 g carb., 0 g fiber, 26 g pro.

This twist on spinach salad with warm bacon dressing is lovely served with beef roast and popovers fresh from the oven.

warm pancetta and goat cheese spinach salad

start to finish: 25 minutes
makes: 4 servings

2 ounces thinly sliced pancetta, chopped
½ of a small red onion, thinly sliced (about ½ cup)
2 tablespoons white wine vinegar
8 cups packaged fresh baby spinach
1 ounce semisoft goat cheese (chèvre), crumbled

1 In a large skillet cook pancetta and red onion over medium heat about 8 minutes or until pancetta is crisp and onion is just tender, stirring occasionally. Remove pancetta and onion from skillet using a slotted spoon.

2 Stir vinegar into drippings in skillet. Add spinach; cook and toss for 30 to 60 seconds or just until spinach is wilted. Transfer spinach mixture to a serving platter. Top with pancetta mixture and goat cheese. Serve immediately.

nutrition facts per serving: 92 cal., 5 g total fat (3 g sat. fat), 10 mg chol., 191 mg sodium, 5 g carb., 3 g fiber, 6 g pro.

Take your pick of citrus for making this refreshing salad—oranges, tangerines, kumquats—or a combination of all three!

orange, fennel, and olive salad with cranberry vinaigrette

start to finish: 25 minutes
makes: 12 servings

427

1   small fennel bulb, thinly sliced (4 ounces)
6   cups torn mixed salad greens
4   medium navel oranges, peeled and sliced; 6 tangerines, peeled and sliced; and/or 8 kumquats, sliced
1   medium red onion, thinly sliced and separated into rings
½   cup pitted Kalamata olives
1   recipe Cranberry Vinaigrette

1 Place sliced fennel in a medium bowl and pour enough boiling water over fennel to cover. Let stand for 5 minutes; drain. Place greens in a large salad bowl. Arrange fennel, orange slices, onion, and olives on top of the greens. Drizzle Cranberry Vinaigrette over salad. Toss lightly before serving.

nutrition facts per serving: 96 cal., 3 g total fat (0 g sat. fat), 0 mg chol., 123 mg sodium, 15 g carb., 2 g fiber, 1 g pro.

Cranberry Vinaigrette: In a medium saucepan combine 1 cup cranberry juice cocktail, ½ cup dry red wine, and ¼ cup dried cranberries. Bring to boiling; reduce heat. Simmer, uncovered, for 15 minutes or until mixture is reduced to about ⅓ cup; cool slightly. Meanwhile, in a small saucepan cook 2 tablespoons finely chopped shallots in 1 tablespoon olive oil until tender but not brown. In a food processor or blender combine cranberry juice mixture, the shallots, 2 tablespoons orange juice, 1 tablespoon olive oil, 1 tablespoon red wine vinegar, 1 tablespoon honey, 1 teaspoon snipped fresh dill, ¼ teaspoon salt, and ¼ teaspoon ground black pepper. Cover and process or blend until smooth.

Citus fruits are at their peak during the winter months. Grapefruit is amazingly juicy and sweet during this time—a taste of sunshine just when it's needed most!

sweet-tart winter salad

start to finish: 30 minutes
makes: 6 servings

9 cups torn butterhead (Boston or Bibb) lettuce
¼ cup grapefruit juice reserved from sectioning grapefruit
1½ tablespoons olive oil
1 tablespoon honey
¼ teaspoon salt
¼ teaspoon cracked black pepper
2 cups pink grapefruit sections*
6 small shallots, thinly sliced and separated into rings
2 ounces Parmesan cheese, coarsely shredded

1 Divide lettuce among six salad plates; set aside.

2 For dressing, in a medium bowl whisk together ¼ cup reserved grapefruit juice, oil, honey, salt, and pepper. Toss grapefruit sections with dressing; arrange on top of lettuce on salad plates. Top with shallots and Parmesan cheese.

nutrition facts per serving: 139 cal., 6 g total fat (2 g sat. fat), 6 mg chol., 255 mg sodium, 18 g carb., 3 g fiber, 6 g pro.

✱tip: To section grapefruit, work over a bowl to catch juice; cut into the center of the grapefruit, cutting between one section and membrane. Cut along the other side of the section next to the membrane to free the section. Repeat with the remaining sections.

Add a few rings of thinly sliced red onion to this beautiful composed salad, if you like.

avocado-grapefruit salad with jicama

start to finish: 15 minutes
makes: 6 servings

4 cups packaged fresh baby spinach
¼ of a medium jicama, peeled
2 small pink or red grapefruit, peeled,* seeded, and sectioned
1 small avocado, halved, seeded, peeled, and sliced
1 recipe White Wine Vinaigrette

1 Divide spinach among six salad plates. Use a vegetable peeler to make shavings from the jicama. Top the spinach with the jicama, grapefruit, and avocado. Drizzle with White Wine Vinaigrette.

nutrition facts per serving: 97 cal., 5 g total fat (1 g sat. fat), 0 mg chol., 80 mg sodium, 11 g carb., 4 g fiber, 2 g pro.

nutrition note: Extra-virgin avocado oil is similar to extra-virgin olive oil in that it is cold-pressed, which preserves its rich, buttery flavor and an amazing array of nutrients, including lutein for eye health; the powerful antioxidant vitamin E; and heart-healthy monosaturated fats and omega-3 fatty acids, which lower blood cholesterol. Try it on salads or drizzled over cooked vegetables, or cook with it as you would olive oil. It has a very high smoke point, which makes it ideal for stir-frying and sautéeing.

*tip: Cut the peel off the grapefruit using a sharp knife, making sure to remove all the bitter white pith.

White Wine Vinaigrette: In a screw-top jar combine ¼ cup white wine vinegar, 4 teaspoons canola oil or avocado oil, ⅛ teaspoon salt, and dash crushed red pepper or cracked black pepper. Cover and shake well.

There is not an ounce of fat in this soup—if you don't garnish with the optional Apple Crème Fraîche. If you would like a creamy touch on top but don't want to add any fat, try a dollop of fat-free plain Greek yogurt.

creamy carrot soup

start to finish: 30 minutes
makes: 8 servings

4 cups reduced-sodium chicken broth
1 pound carrots, peeled and chopped (2½ cups)
½ cup chopped celery (1 stalk)
¼ cup chopped onion
2 teaspoons finely shredded orange peel
3 tablespoons orange juice
2 to 3 teaspoons chopped peeled ginger
2 cloves garlic, minced
   Apple Crème Fraîche (optional)
   Sautéed Green Onions (optional)
   Fresh rosemary sprigs

1 In large saucepan combine broth, carrots, celery, onion, orange peel, juice, ginger, and garlic. Bring to boiling; reduce heat. Simmer, covered, for 10 to 12 minutes or until vegetables are tender.

2 In a food processor or blender, carefully puree the carrot mixture, half at a time, until it's smooth. Return mixture to saucepan; cook and stir until heated through. Ladle into soup bowls. If desired, garnish with Apple Crème Fraîche, Sautéed Green Onions, and rosemary sprigs.

nutrition facts per serving: 39 cal., 0 g total fat (0 g sat. fat), 0 mg chol., 322 mg sodium, 8 g carb., 2 g fiber, 2 g pro.

Sautéed Green Onions: In a small skillet cook ½ cup chopped green onions in 1 tablespoon toasted sesame oil until tender, but not brown.

Apple Crème Fraîche: In a small bowl combine ¼ cup whipping cream (not ultrapasteurized) and ¼ cup sour cream. Cover and let stand at room temperature for 2 to 5 hours or until mixture thickens. (You can cover and refrigerate the plain crème fraîche for up to 1 week.) Stir ½ cup shredded, unpeeled tart apple and 1 tablespoon snipped fresh cilantro into the crème fraîche.

This gorgeous green soup is a perfect way to start a special meal.

italian spinach soup

start to finish: 30 minutes
makes: 6 servings

2 tablespoons butter
½ cup chopped onion
   (1 medium)
4 cloves garlic, minced
2 teaspoons dried
   Italian seasoning,
   crushed
2 tablespoons dry
   sherry (optional)
2 14.5-ounce cans
   chicken broth*
1 cup chopped, peeled
   potato (1 large)
2 9-ounce packages
   fresh spinach
2 cups watercress,
   tough stems
   removed
2 tomatoes, quartered,
   seeded, and thinly
   sliced
2 ounces Parmesan
   cheese, shaved

1 In a 4-quart Dutch oven heat butter over medium heat until melted. Add onion, garlic, and Italian seasoning; cook about 5 minutes or until onion is tender, stirring occasionally.

2 Carefully add sherry (if desired); cook and stir for 1 minute. Add broth and potato. Bring to boiling; reduce heat. Simmer, covered, about 10 minutes or until potato is tender.

3 Set aside 2 cups of the spinach. Stir the remaining spinach, half at a time, into potato mixture just until wilted. Cook for 5 minutes.

4 Transfer potato mixture, half at a time, to a food processor or blender. Cover and process or blend until smooth. Return pureed mixture to Dutch oven; heat through.

5 Ladle soup into bowls. Top with the reserved 2 cups spinach, the watercress, tomatoes, and Parmesan cheese.

nutrition facts per serving: 151 cal., 7 g total fat (4 g sat. fat), 18 mg chol., 881 mg sodium, 16 g carb., 4 g fiber, 8 g pro.

*tip: You can lower sodium in this recipe by using reduced-sodium chicken broth.

To quickly trim the tops off of the beans, line them up on a cutting board and chop them off with a chef's knife.

haricots verts with herb butter

prep: 15 minutes cook: 5 minutes
makes: 4 servings

2 tablespoons butter, softened
1 tablespoon very finely chopped onion
2 teaspoons snipped fresh tarragon
½ teaspoon finely shredded lemon peel
¼ teaspoon salt
¼ teaspoon ground black pepper
1 clove garlic, minced
12 ounces fresh haricots verts or other thin green beans (4 cups)

1 For herb butter, in a small bowl stir together butter, onion, tarragon, lemon peel, salt, pepper, and garlic. Cover and chill until ready to use.

2 If desired, trim tips off beans. Place a steamer basket in a large skillet. Add water to just below the bottom of basket. Bring water to boiling. Add beans to steamer basket. Cover skillet and steam for 5 to 6 minutes or until beans are crisp-tender; drain.

3 To serve, place green beans on a serving platter. Top with small spoonfuls of the herb butter. Spread butter over beans.

nutrition facts per serving: 80 cal., 6 g total fat (4 g sat. fat), 15 mg chol., 202 mg sodium, 7 g carb., 2 g fiber, 2 g pro.

434

Topped with crispy slices of toasted garlic, this ingeniously cooked broccoli dish will make fans of even the most avowed broccoli-haters.

skillet-browned broccoli with pan-toasted garlic

prep: 15 minutes cook: 15 minutes
makes: 8 servings

3   large broccoli stems with stem end attached
3   tablespoons olive oil
½   teaspoon salt
¼   teaspoon ground black pepper
3   tablespoons thinly sliced garlic cloves

1 Preheat a very large cast-iron skillet over medium heat. Slice broccoli heads lengthwise into 1-inch slices, cutting from the bottom of the stem through the crown to preserve the shape of the broccoli (reserve any florets that fall away for another use). Brush both sides of each broccoli slice with some of the oil and sprinkle with salt and pepper.

2 Place half of the slices in the heated skillet and set a heavy medium skillet on the slices to press them to the cast-iron skillet. Cook over medium heat for 3 to 4 minutes or until well browned. Turn slices and cook for 3 to 4 minutes more or until browned (for more tender broccoli, cook over medium-low heat for 5 to 6 minutes per side). Repeat with the remaining broccoli slices. Transfer to a warm platter. Cover and keep warm.*

3 Drizzle the remaining oil into the hot skillet. Reduce heat to medium low. Add garlic slices; cook and stir garlic about 2 minutes or until the slices are lightly browned. Transfer to a plate lined with paper towels.

4 Arrange broccoli on serving platter. Sprinkle the toasted garlic slices over broccoli.

nutrition facts per serving: 79 cal., 5 g total fat (1 g sat. fat), 0 mg chol., 174 mg sodium, 7 g carb., 2 g fiber, 3 g pro.

* tip: Keep cooked broccoli slices warm in a 300°F oven or cover with foil while the remaining broccoli cooks.

When preparing Brussels sprouts for cooking, just barely trim the stem end off of the sprout—just enough to remove the browned area but not so much that the sprout falls apart. Then cut sprouts in half if directed.

pan-roasted brussels sprouts

start to finish: 30 minutes
makes: 12 servings

2 pounds Brussels sprouts, halved lengthwise
1 tablespoon rice oil or olive oil
7 cloves garlic, minced
2 tablespoons butter
½ of a bunch fresh thyme (about 10 sprigs)
1 large sprig fresh rosemary, halved
2 teaspoons fennel seeds
½ teaspoon salt
1 tablespoon sherry or white wine vinegar

1 In a large saucepan cook Brussels sprouts, uncovered, in enough boiling lightly salted water to cover for 3 minutes; drain well. Pat dry with paper towels.

2 Place a very large heavy skillet or sauté pan over high heat for 1 to 2 minutes. Reduce heat to medium. Add oil and garlic; cook and stir for 2 minutes. Add 1 tablespoon of the butter. Increase heat to medium high; carefully arrange half the sprouts, cut sides down, in the hot skillet. Top with half the thyme, rosemary, fennel seeds, and salt. Cook, uncovered, for 3 to 4 minutes or until the sprouts are well browned. Remove sprouts from pan. Repeat with the remaining 1 tablespoon butter, the sprouts, thyme, rosemary, fennel seeds, and salt.

3 Return all sprouts to skillet along with sherry. Quickly toss to distribute flavors.

nutrition facts per serving: 61 cal., 3 g total fat (1 g sat. fat), 5 mg chol., 128 mg sodium, 7 g carb., 3 g fiber, 3 g pro.

make-ahead directions: Step 1 may be done 1 day ahead. Cover and refrigerate the well-drained Brussels sprouts.

These meaty herbed mushrooms are just the thing to serve with roast beef and mashed potatoes.

pan-roasted mushrooms

prep: 15 minutes cook: 11 minutes
makes: 4 servings

1   tablespoon olive oil
12 ounces fresh
    mushrooms
    (such as cremini,
    stemmed shiitake,
    and/or button),
    halved
½   cup chopped red
    onion
2   cloves garlic, minced
2   tablespoons balsamic
    vinegar
1   tablespoon snipped
    fresh thyme
¼   teaspoon salt
⅛   teaspoon ground
    black pepper

1 In a large skillet heat oil over medium heat. Add mushrooms and onion; cook for 10 to 12 minutes or until tender and golden brown, stirring occasionally. Add garlic; cook and stir for 30 seconds. Remove from heat. Carefully add vinegar, thyme, salt, and pepper. Toss to coat.

nutrition facts per serving: 69 cal., 3 g total fat (0 g sat. fat), 0 mg chol., 153 mg sodium, 7 g carb., 1 g fiber, 2 g pro.

Two of the three cheeses in these velvety whipped potatoes—part-skim ricotta and low-fat cottage cheese—add oodles of creaminess to the dish without a spot of cream.

three-cheese whipped potatoes

start to finish: 30 minutes
makes: 8 servings

437

1½ pounds russet
     potatoes, scrubbed
     and cut into
     1½-inch chunks
⅓ cup part-skim ricotta
     cheese
⅓ cup low-fat cottage
     cheese
⅓ cup crumbled
     Gorgonzola cheese
½ teaspoon dried
     rosemary, crushed
½ teaspoon garlic
     powder
¼ to ½ teaspoon ground
     black pepper
¼ teaspoon salt
 2 green onions, sliced

1 In a covered large saucepan cook potatoes in enough boiling water to cover for 15 to 20 minutes or until tender; drain.

2 Meanwhile, place ricotta cheese and cottage cheese in a food processor or blender. Cover and process or blend until smooth. Transfer mixture to a large bowl; add Gorgonzola cheese, rosemary, garlic powder, pepper, and salt.

3 Immediately add hot cooked potatoes to the cheese mixture. Beat with an electric mixer on low speed for 30 seconds. Beat on high speed for 2 minutes more. Transfer potato mixture to a serving bowl. Sprinkle with sliced green onions.

nutrition facts per serving: 107 cal., 3 g total fat (2 g sat. fat), 8 mg chol., 206 mg sodium, 16 g carb., 2 g fiber, 5 g pro.

White whole wheat flour has the same bran content and nutrients as regular whole wheat flour—it's just a different variety of wheat that is light in color. It is nice for making breads that you want to look elegant and not rustic—but that you also want to retain an element of healthfulness.

two-cheese garlic and herb biscuits

prep: 20 minutes **bake:** 10 minutes at 450°F
makes: 9 biscuits

1 cup all-purpose flour
½ cup white whole wheat flour or whole wheat flour
1 tablespoon snipped fresh basil or 1 teaspoon dried basil, crushed
2 teaspoons baking powder
2 cloves garlic, minced
¼ teaspoon cream of tartar
⅛ teaspoon salt
2 ounces semisoft goat cheese (chèvre) or reduced-fat cream cheese (Neufchâtel)
2 tablespoons butter
¼ cup finely shredded Parmesan cheese (1 ounce)
½ cup fat-free milk

1 Preheat oven to 450°F. In a medium bowl stir together flours, basil, baking powder, garlic, cream of tartar, and salt. Using a pastry blender, cut in goat cheese and butter until mixture resembles coarse crumbs. Stir in 3 tablespoons of the Parmesan cheese. Make a well in the center of the flour mixture. Add milk all at once; stir just until dough clings together.

2 Turn out dough onto a lightly floured surface. Knead by folding and gently pressing dough for four to six strokes or until nearly smooth. Pat or lightly roll dough into an 8×6-inch rectangle.

3 Cut dough into nine rectangles. Sprinkle tops with the remaining 1 tablespoon Parmesan cheese. Place rectangles 1 inch apart on an ungreased baking sheet. Bake for 10 to 12 minutes or until golden brown. Serve warm.

nutrition facts per biscuit: 127 cal., 5 g total fat (3 g sat. fat), 12 mg chol., 171 mg sodium, 17 g carb., 1 g fiber, 5 g pro.

Using some pastry flour in addition to the all-purpose flour in these biscuits makes them extra-tender and flaky.

ginger peach tea biscuits

prep: 20 minutes   **bake:** 12 minutes at 375°F
makes: 12 biscuits

Nonstick cooking
  spray
1   cup all-purpose flour
½   cup whole wheat
      pastry flour or
      whole wheat flour
2   tablespoons sugar
1   tablespoon loose-leaf
      green, white, or
      black tea, crushed
2   teaspoons baking
      powder
1   teaspoon ground
      ginger
¼   teaspoon salt
¼   cup butter
½   cup finely chopped
      dried peaches
1   6-ounce carton plain
      low-fat yogurt
¼   cup refrigerated or
      frozen egg product,
      thawed, or 1 egg,
      lightly beaten

1 Preheat oven to 375°F. Coat a large baking sheet with cooking spray or line with parchment paper; set aside. In a large bowl stir together flours, sugar, tea, baking powder, ginger, and salt. Using a pastry blender, cut in butter until mixture resembles coarse crumbs. Stir in peaches. Make a well in the center of the flour mixture.

2 In a small bowl combine yogurt and egg product. Add yogurt mixture all at once to flour mixture. Using a fork, stir until combined. Drop dough into 12 mounds 2 inches apart on prepared baking sheet.

3 Bake for 12 to 15 minutes or until tops are lightly browned. Transfer biscuits to wire racks; serve warm.

nutrition facts per biscuit: 121 cal., 4 g total fat (3 g sat. fat), 11 mg chol., 157 mg sodium, 18 g carb., 1 g fiber, 3 g pro.

You can fill and seal the ravioli several hours ahead—just spray them lightly with cooking oil and cover with plastic wrap before chilling. Right before serving, remove the plastic wrap, spray again lightly with cooking spray, and proceed with Step 3.

chocolate ravioli

e

start to finish: 30 minutes
makes: 10 ravioli

Nonstick cooking
  spray
½ cup tub-style light
  cream cheese
2 tablespoons sugar
2 ounces milk chocolate
20 square wonton
  wrappers
1 tablespoon pine
  nuts, toasted* and
  coarsely chopped

1 Preheat broiler. Coat a large baking sheet with cooking spray; set aside. For filling, in a small bowl stir together cream cheese and sugar until smooth. Set aside one-fourth of the chocolate. Finely chop the remaining chocolate; stir into cream cheese mixture.

2 Lay 10 of the wonton wrappers on a work surface. Spoon 1 tablespoon filling into the center of each wrapper. Lightly moisten the edges of each wrapper with water. Top each with another wonton wrapper, pressing edges to seal. If desired, use a fluted pastry wheel to trim edges of each square.

3 Place squares on prepared baking sheet. Coat the tops of the squares with cooking spray. Broil 4 to 5 inches from heat about 2 minutes or until golden brown (do not turn).

4 Meanwhile, place the reserved milk chocolate in a small microwave-safe bowl. Microwave on 50 percent power (medium) for 1 minute. Stir until smooth. Drizzle chocolate over warm ravioli; sprinkle with toasted pine nuts.

nutrition facts per ravioli: 116 cal., 4 g total fat (3 g sat. fat), 9 mg chol., 157 mg sodium, 16 g carb., 0 g fiber, 3 g pro.

*tip: To toast nuts, spread them in a shallow baking pan. Bake in a 350°F oven for 5 to 10 minutes or until light brown, shaking pan once or twice. Watch carefully so the nuts don't burn.

If you can't find mini cannoli shells at your supermarket, look at an Italian grocery or specialty-foods store.

cherry-pistachio cannoli

start to finish: 20 minutes
makes: 12 mini cannoli

1 cup light ricotta cheese
½ cup chopped dried cherries
¼ cup chopped roasted pistachio nuts or chopped almonds, toasted*
2 tablespoons honey
¼ teaspoon ground ginger
1 4.8-ounce package mini cannoli shells (12)
1 ounce white baking chocolate, melted

1 For filling, in a medium bowl combine ricotta cheese, cherries, nuts, honey, and ginger.

2 Spoon filling into a pastry bag fitted with large open tip. (Or spoon into a resealable plastic bag; snip off a corner of the bag.) Pipe filling into cannoli shells. Drizzle filled cannoli with white chocolate. Let stand until chocolate is set.

nutrition facts per mini cannoli: 130 cal., 6 g total fat (3 g sat. fat), 10 mg chol., 60 mg sodium, 17 g carb., 1 g fiber, 4 g pro.

*tip: To toast nuts, spread them in a single layer in a shallow baking pan. Bake in a 350°F oven for 5 to 10 minutes or until pieces are golden, stirring once or twice.

Balsamic vinegar might seem like an odd accompaniment to cherries, but its natural combination of sweetness and acidity enhances the flavor of cherries and other fruits as well—especially strawberries and peaches.

cherry-chocolate parfaits

start to finish: 15 minutes
makes: 4 servings

443

⅓ cup balsamic vinegar
1½ ounces dark chocolate and/ or white baking chocolate
1½ cups pitted dark sweet cherries, halved
4 crisp-style lady fingers, coarsely crushed
¾ cup frozen light whipped dessert topping

1 In a small saucepan bring vinegar to boiling over medium heat. Boil gently, uncovered, about 5 minutes or until vinegar is reduced to 2 tablespoons. Cool to room temperature.

2 Meanwhile, use a vegetable peeler to make curls from the chocolate.

3 Spoon half of the cherries evenly into four 6-ounce parfait glasses. Drizzle with half the balsamic vinegar. Top with half of the ladyfingers, half of the whipped topping, and half of the chocolate curls. Repeat layers once. Serve immediately.

nutrition facts per serving: 173 cal., 0 g total fat (4 g sat. fat), 7 mg chol., 14 mg sodium, 29 g carb., 2 g fiber, 2 g pro.

double chocolate brownies

dess

17

There's room for dessert in even a health-conscious diet. Find just the sweet to feed your need in this collection of recipes that weigh in at 250 calories or less per serving.

erts

These crisp croissants substitute phyllo dough with a light dusting of butter-flavored cooking spray for the fat-laden pastry in a traditional croissant.

raspberry strudel croissants

prep: 20 minutes bake: 12 minutes at 375°F
makes: 6 strudels

446

¼ cup frozen red
    raspberries, thawed
    and drained,
    or fresh red
    raspberries
2 tablespoons low-
    sugar red raspberry
    preserves
¼ teaspoon finely
    shredded lemon
    peel
4 sheets frozen phyllo
    dough (14×9-inch
    rectangles), thawed
    Butter-flavor nonstick
    cooking spray
    Powdered sugar and/
    or finely shredded
    lemon peel
    (optional)
    Fresh raspberries
    (optional)

1 In a small bowl combine the ¼ cup raspberries, preserves, and the ¼ teaspoon lemon peel. Using a potato masher or the back of a large spoon, mash berry mixture.

2 Preheat oven to 375°F. Line a baking sheet with parchment paper; set aside. Unfold phyllo dough; place one sheet of the dough on a clean flat surface. (As you work, cover the remaining phyllo dough with plastic wrap to prevent it from drying out.) Lightly coat phyllo sheet with nonstick cooking spray. Place another sheet of the phyllo on top of the first sheet; coat with nonstick cooking spray. Repeat layering with two more sheets, coating each with nonstick cooking spray. You should have a stack of four sheets. Using a pastry wheel or pizza cutter, cut an 8½-inch circle in the dough (discard dough that is cut away to form the circle).

3 Cut circle into six wedges. Spread the raspberry mixture over wedges, leaving a ¼-inch border around the raspberry layer. Starting at the wide end of each wedge, loosely roll toward the point. Place rolls, point sides down, 2 to 3 inches apart on the prepared baking sheet. Lightly coat filled croissants with nonstick cooking spray.

4 Bake for 12 to 14 minutes or until pastry is golden brown. Transfer to a wire rack; let cool. If desired, sprinkle croissants with powdered sugar and/or additional lemon peel. If desired, garnish with additional fresh raspberries.

nutrition facts per strudel: 35 cal., 0 g total fat (0 g sat. fat), 0 mg chol., 30 mg sodium, 8 g carb., 0 g fiber, 1 g pro.

Mascarpone is an Italian triple-cream cheese—so a little goes a long way. If you can't find it, you can substitute regular cream cheese (or even low-fat cream cheese, if you are being really good).

lemon crepes

start to finish: 25 minutes
makes: 10 servings

2½ cups blueberries, raspberries, and/or sliced strawberries
2 to 3 teaspoons honey
¾ cup fat-free milk
½ cup all-purpose flour
1 egg
1 tablespoon canola oil
2 teaspoons sugar
1 teaspoon finely shredded lemon peel
½ cup mascarpone cheese, softened
2 tablespoons honey
Finely shredded lemon peel (optional)

1 In a medium bowl combine berries and the 2 to 3 teaspoons honey; toss gently to combine. Set aside. In a medium bowl combine milk, flour, egg, oil, sugar, and the 1 teaspoon lemon peel; whisk until smooth.

2 Heat a lightly greased medium skillet over medium-high heat; remove from heat. Spoon in 2 tablespoons of the batter; lift and tilt skillet to spread batter evenly. Return to heat; cook for 1 to 2 minutes or until brown on one side only. Invert skillet over paper towels; remove crepe. Repeat with the remaining batter, greasing skillet occasionally. If crepes are browning too quickly, reduce heat to medium.

3 In a small bowl stir together mascarpone cheese and the 2 tablespoons honey. Spread the unbrowned side of each crepe with 1 tablespoon of the cheese mixture; fold crepe into quarters. Serve crepes with berry mixture. If desired, garnish with additional lemon peel.

nutrition facts per 1 crepe + ¼ cup berry mixture: 139 cal., 7 g total fat (3 g sat. fat), 33 mg chol., 22 mg sodium, 17 g carb., 1 g fiber, 4 g pro.

Crystallized or candied ginger adds a bit of heat to the berry filling for these shortcakes.

berry ginger shortcakes

prep: 20 minutes bake: 8 minutes at 425°F
makes: 10 individual shortcakes

Nonstick cooking
    spray
1⅔ cups all-purpose flour
1   tablespoon sugar
2   teaspoons baking
    powder
¼   teaspoon baking soda
3   tablespoons butter
½   cup buttermilk
¼   cup refrigerated or
    frozen egg product,
    thawed, or 1 egg
3   cups fresh berries
    (sliced strawberries,
    blueberries,
    raspberries, and/or
    blackberries)
2   tablespoons
    finely chopped
    crystallized ginger
½   8-ounce container
    frozen fat-free
    whipped dessert
    topping, thawed
¼   cup fat-free dairy
    sour cream

1 Preheat oven to 425°F. Lightly coat a baking sheet with cooking spray; set aside. In a medium bowl stir together flour, sugar, baking powder, and baking soda. Using a pastry blender, cut in butter until the mixture resembles coarse crumbs. Combine buttermilk and egg product. Add to the flour mixture all at once, stirring just until mixture is moistened. On a lightly floured surface pat the dough to ½ inch thickness. Cut the dough with a floured 2½-inch star-shape or heart-shape cookie cutter or a round biscuit cutter, rerolling scraps as necessary. Place shortcakes on prepared baking sheet.

2 Bake for 8 to 10 minutes or until golden. Cool the shortcakes slightly on a wire rack.

3 In a medium bowl combine the berries and the crystallized ginger.

4 To serve, in a small bowl combine the whipped topping and sour cream. Split shortcakes in half. Place bottoms on dessert plates. Divide the berry mixture among bottoms. Top each with some of the whipped topping mixture. Replace the shortcake tops.

nutrition facts per individual shortcake: 166 cal., 4 g total fat (2 g sat. fat), 10 mg chol., 176 mg sodium, 28 g carb., 2 g fiber, 4 g pro.

This yummy dessert couldn't be simpler—just toast slices of purchased angel food cake in a skillet and top with fresh fruit in a warm marmalade glaze. If you'd like, top it with a dollop of frozen whipped topping.

toasted angel food cake with fruit

start to finish: 20 minutes
makes: 4 servings

4 slices purchased or homemade angel food cake
¼ cup orange marmalade
1 orange, peeled and thinly sliced
1 cup sliced fresh strawberries

1 Heat a large nonstick skillet over medium heat. Place angel food cake slices in skillet; cook for 1 to 2 minutes or until lightly toasted, turning once. Place on dessert plates.

2 Place marmalade in a microwave-safe 1-cup measuring cup. Microwave on 100 percent power (high) for 15 to 20 seconds or until melted. If desired, cut orange slices in half crosswise. In a medium bowl combine orange slices, strawberries, and marmalade. Serve fruit over cake slices.

nutrition facts per serving: 150 cal., 0 g total fat (0 g sat. fat), 0 mg chol., 224 mg sodium, 36 g carb., 2 g fiber, 2 g pro.

This old-fashioned dessert never gets old. The smell of it baking envelops your house in both comfort and anticipation—warm gingerbread! Top it with light dessert topping or, for a change of pace, a spoonful of lemon curd.

gingerbread

prep: 10 minutes   bake: 20 minutes at 350°F
makes: 9 servings

Nonstick cooking
  spray
1½ cups all-purpose
  flour
¼ cup sugar
1 teaspoon ground
  ginger
1 teaspoon ground
  cinnamon
½ teaspoon baking
  powder
½ teaspoon baking soda
¼ teaspoon salt
½ cup water
⅓ cup full-flavor
  molasses
3 tablespoons butter,
  melted
2 egg whites
  Frozen light whipped
  dessert topping,
  thawed (optional)

1 Preheat oven to 350°F. Lightly coat an 8×8×2-inch baking pan with nonstick cooking spray; dust lightly with flour. Set aside.

2 In a large mixing bowl combine the 1½ cups flour, the sugar, ginger, cinnamon, baking powder, baking soda, and salt. Add the water, molasses, butter, and egg whites. Beat with an electric mixer on low to medium speed until combined. Beat on high speed for 2 minutes. Spread into prepared pan.

3 Bake about 20 minutes or until a wooden toothpick inserted near the center comes out clean. Cool in the pan on a wire rack for 10 minutes. Remove cake from pan. Serve warm. If desired, top with dessert topping.

nutrition facts per serving: 170 cal., 4 g total fat (2 g sat. fat), 10 mg chol., 193 mg sodium, 30 g carb., 1 g fiber, 3 g pro.

This is one of those recipes that will never fail to please—not anywhere and not anyone. Who doesn't like a gooey, chocolatey brownie? Serve with a glass of cold milk.

double chocolate brownies

prep: 10 minutes bake: 15 minutes at 350°F
makes: 16 brownies

Nonstick cooking
    spray
¼ cup butter
⅔ cup granulated sugar
½ cup cold water
1 teaspoon vanilla
1 cup all-purpose flour
¼ cup unsweetened
    cocoa powder
1 teaspoon baking
    powder
¼ cup miniature
    semisweet
    chocolate pieces
2 teaspoons sifted
    powdered sugar

1 Preheat oven to 350°F. Lightly coat the bottom of a 9×9×2-inch baking pan with cooking spray, being careful not to coat sides of pan.

2 In a medium saucepan melt butter; remove from heat. Stir in granulated sugar, the water, and vanilla. Stir in flour, cocoa powder, and baking powder until combined. Stir in chocolate pieces. Pour batter into prepared pan.

3 Bake for 15 to 18 minutes or until a wooden toothpick inserted near the center comes out clean. Cool on a wire rack. Cut into 16 bars. Sprinkle with the powdered sugar.

nutrition facts per brownie: 113 cal., 4 g total fat (2 g sat. fat), 8 mg chol., 37 mg sodium, 17 g carb., 0 g fiber, 1 g pro.

nutrition note: To reduce fat and calories in your favorite chocolatey baked goods, use 3 tablespoons of cocoa powder with 1 tablespoon canola oil to replace 1 ounce of unsweetened baking chocolate.

If you are less worried about fat and calories on a particular occasion, you can add a thin layer of cream cheese frosting (made with light cream cheese, of course) to these moist blondies.

pumpkin blondies

prep: 10 minutes   bake: 20 minutes at 350°F
makes: 24 bars

Nonstick cooking
    spray
1 cup white whole
    wheat flour
½ cup unbleached all-
    purpose flour
1 tablespoon flaxseed
    meal
1½ teaspoons baking
    powder
½ teaspoon salt
½ teaspoon ground
    cinnamon
¼ teaspoon baking soda
¼ teaspoon ground
    nutmeg
⅛ teaspoon ground
    allspice
⅓ cup canola oil
3 tablespoons butter,
    melted
1 tablespoon molasses
1⅓ cups packed dark
    brown sugar
½ cup canned pumpkin
1 egg
1 egg white
1 teaspoon vanilla
½ cup coarsely chopped
    walnuts

1 Preheat oven to 350°F. Coat a 13×9×2-inch baking pan with cooking spray and parchment paper; set aside. In a medium bowl combine whole wheat flour, all-purpose flour, flaxseed meal, baking powder, salt, cinnamon, baking soda, nutmeg, and allspice; set aside.

2 In a large mixing bowl beat oil, butter, and molasses with an electric mixer on medium speed until combined. Add brown sugar and beat until smooth. Add pumpkin, beating until combined. Beat in egg, egg white, and vanilla until combined. Add flour mixture to sugar mixture, beating just until flour mixture is moistened.

3 Spread batter into prepared pan. Sprinkle with walnuts. Bake for 20 to 22 minutes or until a wooden toothpick inserted near the center comes out clean. Cool completely in pan on a wire rack. Cut into squares.

nutrition facts per bar: 137 cal., 6 g total fat (1 g sat. fat), 13 mg chol., 104 mg sodium, 19 g carb., 1 g fiber, 2 g pro.

nutrition note: To add fiber and protein to brownies, bars, and gingerbread, replace up to half the amount of all-purpose flour with whole wheat flour. For best results use white whole wheat flour, as was done in this recipe. White whole wheat flour has the same fiber content as regular whole wheat flour—it is simply a different variety of wheat that is lighter in color and milder in flavor.

Plumped-up raisins add sweetness, moistness, and texture to these spiced peanut butter–oat chocolate chip cookies.

must-have chocolate chip cookies

prep: 20 minutes   bake: 10 minutes per batch at 350°F
makes: 40 cookies

1   cup raisins
½   cup boiling water
½   cup peanut butter
¼   cup butter, softened
½   cup sugar
½   cup refrigerated or
     frozen egg product,
     thawed
1   teaspoon ground
     cinnamon
1   teaspoon vanilla
½   teaspoon baking soda
½   cup all-purpose flour
1¼   cups regular rolled
     oats
1   cup semisweet
     chocolate pieces or
     chunks

1 Preheat oven to 350°F. In a small bowl combine raisins and the boiling water; set aside.

2 In a large mixing bowl combine peanut butter and butter; beat with an electric mixer on medium speed for 30 seconds. Add sugar, egg product, cinnamon, vanilla, and baking soda. Beat until combined. Add the flour; beat until smooth. Stir in the oats.

3 Drain the raisins; stir raisins and chocolate pieces into oat mixture.

4 Drop dough by rounded teaspoonfuls onto ungreased cookie sheets. Bake about 10 minutes or until lightly browned. Transfer to wire racks; let cool.

nutrition facts per cookie: 87 cal., 4 g total fat (2 g sat. fat), 3 mg chol., 47 mg sodium, 12 g carb., 1 g fiber, 2 g pro.

Make these chocolate-mint cookies especially easy to make: Mix up the dough, then chill overnight. Finish shaping, baking, and filling the next day.

triple chocolate mint sandwich cookies

prep: 20 minutes chill: 1 hour to 24 hours
bake: 6 minutes per batch at 350°F makes: 16 sandwich cookies

½   cup granulated sugar
3   tablespoons canola oil
2   ounces white baking
      chocolate, melted
2   egg whites
¾   teaspoon mint
      flavoring
½   teaspoon butter
      flavoring
1⅓ cups all-purpose flour
½   teaspoon baking
      powder
¼   teaspoon salt
1   tablespoon
      unsweetened cocoa
      powder
½   cup powdered sugar
2   ounces bittersweet
      chocolate, melted
1   to 2 tablespoons water
1   ounce white baking
      chocolate, melted
      (optional)
      Very small fresh mint
      leaves (optional)

1 In a medium bowl combine granulated sugar, oil, the 2 ounces melted white chocolate, the egg whites, mint flavoring, and butter flavoring; stir until well mixed. In a small bowl stir together flour, baking powder, and salt. Add the flour mixture to the egg white mixture; stir just until combined. Cover and chill dough for 1 to 24 hours or until firm enough to roll into balls.

2 Preheat oven to 350°F. Shape dough into ¾-inch balls (1 teaspoon dough each). Place cocoa powder in a small bowl. Roll balls in cocoa powder to coat. Place balls 1½ inches apart on ungreased cookie sheets. Flatten balls with the bottom of a glass to about 1¼-inch-diameter circles.

3 Bake for 6 to 7 minutes or just until edges are firm. Transfer to a wire rack; cool.

4 For chocolate filling, in a small bowl whisk together powdered sugar, melted bittersweet chocolate, and enough of the water to make a smooth spreadable filling. (If mixture seems too thin, allow it to stand a few minutes before using.)

5 Spread the bottoms of half of the cookies with the chocolate filling, using about 1 teaspoon filling on each. Top with the remaining cookies, bottom sides down, to make sandwich cookies.

6 If desired, place the 1 ounce melted white chocolate in a small resealable plastic bag. Seal bag. Using scissors, snip off a very small corner from bag. Drizzle white chocolate over tops of cookies; if desired, place mint leaves on top.

nutrition facts per 2 sandwich cookies: 141 cal., 5 g total fat (2 g sat. fat), 1 mg chol., 63 mg sodium, 22 g carb., 1 g fiber, 2 g pro.

Incorporating applesauce into baked goods is a longstanding health-conscious trick to add moistness and tenderness with a minimal amount of butter or other fat.

whole wheat carrot-raisin cookies

prep: 25 minutes bake: 8 minutes per batch at 375°F
makes: about 36 cookies

½ cup butter, softened
1 cup packed brown sugar
2 teaspoons baking soda
1 teaspoon ground cinnamon
1 teaspoon ground ginger
¼ teaspoon salt
1 egg
¼ cup unsweetened applesauce
1 teaspoon vanilla
2 cups whole wheat flour
1 cup finely shredded carrots (2 medium)
¾ cup raisins
¾ cup finely chopped walnuts

1 Preheat oven to 375°F. In a large bowl beat butter with an electric mixer on medium speed for 30 seconds. Add brown sugar, baking soda, cinnamon, ginger, and salt; beat until combined. Beat in egg, applesauce, and vanilla. Beat in as much of the flour as you can with the mixer. Stir in any remaining flour, the carrots, raisins, and walnuts just until combined.

2 Drop dough by slightly rounded teaspoonfuls 2 inches apart onto ungreased cookie sheets. Bake for 8 to 9 minutes or until edges are firm. Transfer to a wire rack; let cool.

nutrition facts per cookie: 98 cal., 4 g total fat (2 g sat. fat), 13 mg chol., 111 mg sodium, 14 g carb., 1 g fiber, 2 g pro.

kitchen tip: Soften butter by letting is stand at room temperature for 30 to 60 minutes. If you don't have time, pop it in the microwave at 30 percent power for 15 seconds. Check and repeat as necessary.

Either dried cherries or dried cranberries work equally well in this lemony oat cookie.

lemon-cherry oat cookies

prep: 20 minutes bake: 8 minutes per batch at 375°F
makes: about 30 cookies

½ cup tub-style 60 to 70 percent vegetable oil spread
¾ cup packed brown sugar
2 teaspoons baking powder
¼ teaspoon salt
2 egg whites, lightly beaten
1 teaspoon vanilla
1 cup all-purpose flour
1¼ cups quick-cooking oats
¾ cup dried tart cherries, coarsely chopped
1 teaspoon finely shredded lemon peel

1 Preheat oven to 375°F. In a large bowl beat vegetable oil spread with an electric mixer on medium to high speed for 30 seconds. Add brown sugar, baking powder, and salt. Beat until fluffy. Add egg whites and vanilla. Beat until combined. Beat in as much of the flour as you can with the mixer. Using a wooden spoon, stir in any remaining flour, the oats, cherries, and lemon peel.

2 Drop dough by rounded teaspoonfuls onto an ungreased cookie sheet. Bake for 8 to 9 minutes or until edges are lightly browned. Cool on cookie sheet for 1 minute. Transfer cookies to wire rack; let cool.

nutrition facts per cookie: 84 cal., 3 g total fat (0 g sat. fat), 0 mg chol., 80 mg sodium, 15 g carb., 1 g fiber, 1 g pro.

tip: To store cookies, place between sheets of waxed paper in an airtight container. Store at room temperature for 3 days or freeze for up to 3 months.

These cookies are so packed with good things—oats, flaxseed meal, wheat germ, cranberries, and walnuts—you could almost eat them for breakfast.

loaded oatmeal cookies

prep: 25 minutes bake: 9 minutes per batch at 350°F
makes: about 30 cookies

457

¼ cup butter, softened
½ cup packed brown
    sugar
⅓ cup granulated sugar
1 teaspoon ground
    cinnamon
½ teaspoon baking soda
⅛ teaspoon salt
1 egg
1 teaspoon vanilla
¾ cup all-purpose flour
¾ cup rolled oats
¼ cup flaxseed meal
¼ cup wheat germ
2 ounces dark
    chocolate, finely
    chopped
¼ cup dried cranberries
¼ cup chopped walnuts,
    toasted*

1 Preheat oven to 350°F. In a large mixing bowl beat butter with an electric mixer on medium to high speed for 30 seconds. Add brown sugar, granulated sugar, cinnamon, baking soda, and salt. Beat until combined, scraping sides of bowl occasionally. Beat in egg and vanilla until combined. Beat in flour. Stir in rolled oats, flaxseed meal, wheat germ, chocolate, cranberries, and walnuts (dough will be a little crumbly).

2 Drop dough by rounded teaspoonfuls 2 inches apart onto ungreased cookie sheets. Bake for 9 to 11 minutes or until tops are lightly browned. Let cookies cool on cookie sheet for 1 minute. Transfer cookies to wire rack; let cool.

nutrition facts per cookie: 79 cal., 4 g total fat (2 g sat. fat), 11 mg chol., 45 mg sodium, 12 g carb., 1 g fiber, 2 g pro.

*tip: To toast nuts, spread them in a shallow baking pan. Bake in a 350°F oven for 5 to 10 minutes or until light brown, shaking pan once or twice. Watch carefully so the nuts don't burn.

Dark chocolate is lower in fat and higher in antioxidant cacao than milk chocolate—a good reason to indulge (in moderation, of course)!

coconut fruit s'mores

start to finish: 25 minutes
makes: 12 s'mores

4   ounces dark or
    semisweet
    chocolate, chopped
    Nonstick cooking
    spray
3   tablespoons butter,
    melted and cooled
⅓   cup flaked coconut
12 marshmallows
1⅓ cups fresh
    blackberries
24 graham cracker
    squares

1 Preheat broiler. Place chocolate in a small microwave-safe bowl. Microwave on 50 percent power (medium) for 1½ minutes. Let stand for 5 minutes. Stir until smooth. Let cool for 10 minutes.

2 Line a baking sheet with foil; lightly coat with cooking spray.

3 Place melted butter in a shallow bowl; place coconut in another shallow bowl. Roll marshmallows in butter and then coconut. Thread berries and marshmallows on 6-inch skewers* and place on prepared baking sheet. Sprinkle any remaining coconut on marshmallows. Spoon chocolate onto half of the graham crackers and arrange on a platter.

4 Broil skewers 3 to 4 inches from heat for 1 to 1½ minutes or until coconut is lightly browned and marshmallows are puffed, turning once.

5 Immediately top each chocolate-coated graham cracker with a skewer. Use remaining graham cracker to pull marshmallows and berries off skewers and form sandwiches.

nutrition facts per s'more: 150 cal., 9 g total fat (5 g sat. fat), 8 mg chol., 120 mg sodium, 25 g carb., 2 g fiber, 2 g pro.

* tip: If using wooden skewers, soak skewers in enough water to cover for at least 30 minutes before using.

Pine-scented rosemary is the surprise ingredient in these sophisticated s'mores. It's actually lovely with both orange and chocolate.

grown-up s'mores

start to finish: 15 minutes
makes: 6 s'mores

6   graham cracker squares
1   ounce bar dark chocolate, divided into 6 portions
1   teaspoon finely shredded orange peel
1   teaspoon snipped fresh rosemary
    Nonstick cooking spray
6   large marshmallows
6   fresh raspberries

1 Place graham crackers in a single layer on a platter. Top each with a portion of chocolate; set aside. In a small bowl combine orange peel and rosemary; set aside. Lightly coat a long metal skewer with cooking spray. Thread marshmallows on the skewer, leaving a ½-inch space between marshmallows.

2 For a charcoal or gas grill, hold marshmallow skewer just above grill rack directly over medium heat about 2 minutes or until marshmallows are soft and lightly toasted, turning occasionally.

3 Working quickly, use a fork to push one marshmallow onto each chocolate-topped graham cracker. Sprinkle with orange peel mixture and top with raspberries.

nutrition facts per s'more: 91 cal., 3 g total fat (1 g sat. fat), 0 mg chol., 57 mg sodium, 16 g carb., 1 g fiber, 1 g pro.

Kids will love dipping these melty chocolate-and-berry sandwiches in even more chocolate. It doesn't get much better than that!

chocolate-raspberry grillers

start to finish: 18 minutes
makes: 8 servings

461

8   ½-inch-thick slices
      challah or Hawaiian
      sweet bread
2   tablespoons butter,
      melted
4   to 6 ounces
      semisweet
      chocolate, finely
      chopped
1   cup raspberries
1   recipe Warm
      Chocolate Gravy

1 Heat a large heavy nonstick skillet over medium-low heat. Meanwhile, brush one side of each bread slice with some of the melted butter. Place half the bread slices, buttered side down, on a plate. Sprinkle with chocolate and raspberries to within ¼ inch of crusts. Top with remaining bread, buttered sides up.

2 Place two sandwiches in the skillet. Weight with a heavy skillet. Cook over medium-low heat for 6 to 8 minutes or until chocolate is melted and bread is golden brown, turning once. Repeat with remaining sandwiches.

3 Slice in half to serve. Pass Warm Chocolate Gravy for dipping.

nutrition facts per serving: 217 cal., 8 g total fat (5 g sat. fat), 10 mg chol., 180 mg sodium, 34 g carb., 3 g fiber, 4 g pro.

Warm Chocolate Gravy: In a small bowl stir together ¼ cup sugar, 2 tablespoons unsweetened cocoa powder, and 1 tablespoon all-purpose flour; set aside. In a medium saucepan melt 1 tablespoon butter. Stir sugar mixture into melted butter until smooth. Gradually add 1¼ cups milk, stirring constantly. Cook and stir over medium heat until thickened and bubbly; cook and stir for 1 minute more.
makes: 1¼ cups

To toast the coconut, spread in an even layer on a rimmed baking sheet. Bake in a 350°F oven for 5 to 6 minutes, stirring once or twice. Watch it very closely—it will burn in an instant.

chocolate-coconut pudding

start to finish: 30 minutes
makes: 8 servings

1 cup unsweetened light coconut milk
¼ cup unsweetened cocoa powder
2 tablespoons cornstarch
¼ teaspoon salt
1¼ cups unsweetened almond milk
¼ cup packed brown sugar
2 tablespoons granulated sugar
4 ounces semisweet chocolate, chopped
½ teaspoon coconut extract
2 tablespoons unsweetened shredded coconut, toasted

1 In a medium bowl whisk together coconut milk, cocoa powder, cornstarch, and salt; set aside.

2 In a medium saucepan combine almond milk, brown sugar, and granulated sugar. Cook and stir over medium heat just until boiling. Add coconut milk mixture; cook and stir just until mixture returns to boiling. Immediately reduce heat to low. Cook and stir for 2 minutes more. Remove from heat. Add chocolate; let stand for 30 seconds. Add coconut extract; stir until smooth.

3 Spoon ¼ cup of the pudding into each of eight small dessert dishes, mugs, or pots de crème cups. Sprinkle with toasted coconut. Serve warm or chilled.

nutrition facts per serving: 150 cal., 8 g total fat (5 g sat. fat), 0 mg chol., 111 mg sodium, 21 g carb., 2 g fiber, 2 g pro.

Even though it's nice to share, it's even nicer to have your own personal bread pudding.

cherry chocolate bread pudding

prep: 15 minutes   bake: 15 minutes at 350°F
makes: 4 servings

Nonstick cooking
   spray
2   cups firm-textured
   whole-grain bread
   cubes (about
   3 ounces)
3   tablespoons snipped
   dried tart red
   cherries
1   tablespoon toasted
   wheat germ
⅔   cup fat-free milk
¼   cup semisweet
   chocolate pieces
⅓   cup refrigerated or
   frozen egg product,
   thawed
1   teaspoon finely
   shredded orange
   peel
½   teaspoon vanilla
   Frozen light whipped
   dessert topping,
   thawed (optional)
   Unsweetened cocoa
   powder (optional)

1 Preheat the oven to 350°F. Coat four 6-ounce individual soufflé dishes or custard cups with cooking spray. Divide bread cubes, cherries, and wheat germ among the dishes.

2 In a small saucepan combine milk and chocolate. Cook and stir over low heat until the chocolate melts; remove from heat. If necessary, beat with a wire whisk until smooth.

3 In a small bowl gradually stir chocolate mixture into egg product. Stir in orange peel and vanilla. Pour mixture over bread cubes in the dishes. Press lightly with back of spoon to moisten bread.

4 Bake for 15 to 20 minutes or until the tops appear firm and a knife inserted near the centers comes out clean.

5 Serve warm. If desired, serve with whipped topping and sprinkle with cocoa powder.

nutrition facts per serving: 147 cal., 4 g total fat (2 g sat. fat), 1 mg chol., 152 mg sodium, 25 g carb., 3 g fiber, 7 g pro.

make-ahead directions: Prepare as directed through Step 3. Cover and chill for up to 2 hours. Preheat oven to 350°F. Continue as directed in Steps 4 and 5.

If you make these ahead, keep the filling and crusts separate until right before serving time so the crusts don't get soggy.

fruit tarts

start to finish: 20 minutes
makes: 6 tarts

1   cup fresh
    strawberries
½   of an 8-ounce
    package reduced-
    fat cream cheese
    (Neufchâtel),
    softened
1   tablespoon honey
1   4-ounce package (6)
    purchased graham
    cracker crumb tart
    shells
1½ cups assorted fresh
    berries or other
    chopped fruit
    (blueberries, kiwi,
    strawberries, and/
    or raspberries)

1 Mash or puree the 1 cup strawberries until saucy. In a medium bowl stir cream cheese until smooth; gradually blend in mashed berries. Stir in honey. Divide mixture among the tart shells. Top with fresh fruit.

nutrition facts per tart: 207 cal., 9 g total fat (3 g sat. fat), 14 mg chol., 189 mg sodium, 27 g carb., 2 g fiber, 3 g pro.

make-ahead directions: Prepare the cream cheese filling. Cover and chill in the refrigerator for up to 4 hours.

Silken tofu combined with just a little bit of reduced-fat cream cheese creates a light-as-a-cloud mousse that tastes rich but isn't.

key lime mousse

start to finish: 15 minutes
makes: 6 servings

1   12.3-ounce package
    silken-style extra
    firm light tofu (fresh
    bean curd), cut up
½   of an 8-ounce
    package reduced-
    fat cream cheese
    (Neufchâtel), cut
    into cubes and
    softened
3   tablespoons honey
1   teaspoon finely
    shredded Key lime
    or Persian lime peel
1   tablespoon Key lime
    or Persian lime juice
1½ cups frozen light
    whipped dessert
    topping, thawed
    (about ½ of an
    8-ounce container)
1½ cups fresh fruit (such
    as cut-up kiwifruit,
    strawberries,
    blueberries,
    raspberries, and/or
    cut-up mango)
    Honey (optional)

1 In a medium bowl combine tofu, cream cheese, the 3 tablespoons honey, the lime peel, and lime juice. Beat with an electric mixer on medium speed until smooth. Gently fold in whipped dessert topping until combined.

2 Place mousse in bowl and top with fruit or layer mousse and fruit in parfait glasses. If desired, drizzle with additional honey.

nutrition facts per serving: 161 cal., 7 g total fat (4 g sat. fat), 14 mg chol., 121 mg sodium, 18 g carb., 1 g fiber, 6 g pro.

To loosen the peach skins for easy peeling, blanch them: Drop the fruit into a pot of boiling water for 30 seconds to 1 minute, then remove and immediately plunge into a bowl of ice water. The peels will slip right off.

warm spiced peaches

stand: 15 minutes
makes: 4 servings

3 ripe medium peaches, peeled and sliced
1 tablespoon sugar
½ teaspoon ground cinnamon
½ teaspoon finely shredded orange peel
½ teaspoon vanilla
¼ teaspoon ground nutmeg
1 6-ounce carton vanilla yogurt

1 In a medium bowl combine peaches, sugar, cinnamon, orange peel, vanilla, and nutmeg; toss gently to combine. Divide among four 5-ounce individual quiche dishes or 10-ounce custard cups.

2 Place two of the dishes in a microwave oven. Lightly cover with waxed paper. Microwave on 100 percent power (high) for 1 to 1½ minutes or until warm. Repeat with remaining dishes. Serve with yogurt.

nutrition facts per serving: 95 cal., 1 g total fat (0 g sat. fat), 2 mg chol., 28 mg sodium, 20 g carb., 2 g fiber, 3 g pro.

A mix of apples makes this dessert both sweet and tart—as well as red and green.

apple phyllo dessert

prep: 20 minutes bake: 10 minutes at 350°F
makes: 8 servings

Nonstick cooking
   spray
3 tablespoons sugar
1 teaspoon ground
   cinnamon
½ teaspoon ground
   nutmeg
¼ teaspoon ground
   cloves
8 sheets frozen phyllo
   dough (14×9-inch
   rectangles), thawed
⅓ cup butter, melted
3 red cooking apples,
   cored and thinly
   sliced
2 green apples, cored
   and thinly sliced
¼ cup caramel-flavor ice
   cream topping
4 ounces reduced-
   fat cream cheese
   (Neufchâtel)

1 Preheat oven to 350°F. Lightly coat a 2-quart square baking dish with cooking spray; set aside. In a small bowl combine sugar, cinnamon, nutmeg, and cloves. Place 1 sheet of phyllo on a clean dry surface; brush with melted butter and sprinkle with 1 teaspoon of the sugar mixture. Place in prepared baking dish. Repeat with remaining phyllo sheets, melted butter, and sugar mixture staggering phyllo edges as placed in dish.

2 Bake for 10 to 12 minutes or until lightly browned.

3 Meanwhile, place any remaining butter and sugar mixture in a large, nonstick skillet. Add apples and the caramel topping. Bring to boiling; reduce heat. Simmer, covered, about 5 minutes or just until apples are tender. With a slotted spoon, transfer apple slices to prepared crust. Bring remaining mixture in skillet to boiling. Simmer, uncovered, about 2 minutes or until slightly thickened. Place cream cheese in a small bowl; gradually whisk in thickened caramel mixture. Spoon caramel mixture over apples. Cool slightly before serving. Serve in dessert dishes.

nutrition facts per serving: 248 cal., 11 g total fat (7 g sat. fat), 31 mg chol., 187 mg sodium, 36 g carb., 3 g fiber, 3 g pro.

When plain old pudding won't do, try these parfaits flavored in true Rocky Road style with chocolate, peanuts, and marshmallows.

rocky road parfaits

prep: 15 minutes stand: 5 minutes
makes: 4 parfaits

1 4-serving-size package fat-free, sugar-free, reduced-calorie chocolate or chocolate fudge instant pudding mix
2 cups fat-free milk
½ cup frozen light whipped dessert topping, thawed
¼ cup unsalted peanuts, coarsely chopped
¼ cup tiny marshmallows
Chocolate curls (optional)

1 Prepare pudding mix according to package directions using the fat-free milk. Remove ¾ cup of the pudding and place in a small bowl; fold in whipped topping until combined.

2 Divide remaining plain chocolate pudding among four 6-ounce glasses or dessert dishes. Top with dessert topping mixture. Let stand for 5 to 10 minutes or until set.

3 Sprinkle with peanuts and marshmallows just before serving. If desired, garnish with chocolate curls.

nutrition facts per parfait: 162 cal., 6 g total fat (2 g sat. fat), 2 mg chol., 386 mg sodium, 21 g carb., 1 g fiber, 7 g pro.

make-ahead directions: Prepare as directed through Step 2. Cover and chill parfaits for up to 24 hours. Serve as directed in Step 3.

index

471

index

index

index

metric information

The charts on this page provide a guide for converting measurements from the U.S. customary system, which is used throughout this book, to the metric system.

Product Differences

Most of the ingredients called for in the recipes in this book are available in most countries. However, some are known by different names. Here are some common American ingredients and their possible counterparts:

- Sugar (white) is granulated, fine granulated, or castor sugar.
- Powdered sugar is icing sugar.
- All-purpose flour is enriched, bleached, or unbleached white household flour. When self-rising flour is used in place of all-purpose flour in a recipe that calls for leavening, omit the leavening agent (baking soda or baking powder) and salt.
- Light-colored corn syrup is golden syrup.
- Cornstarch is cornflour.
- Baking soda is bicarbonate of soda.
- Vanilla or vanilla extract is vanilla essence.
- Green, red, or yellow sweet peppers are capsicums or bell peppers.
- Golden raisins are sultanas.

Volume and Weight

The United States traditionally uses cup measures for liquid and solid ingredients. The chart, below, shows the approximate imperial and metric equivalents. If you are accustomed to weighing solid ingredients, the following approximate equivalents will be helpful.

- 1 cup butter, castor sugar, or rice = 8 ounces = ½ pound = 250 grams
- 1 cup flour = 4 ounces = ¼ pound = 125 grams
- 1 cup icing sugar = 5 ounces = 150 grams

Canadian and U.S. volume for a cup measure is 8 fluid ounces (237 ml), but the standard metric equivalent is 250 ml.

1 British imperial cup is 10 fluid ounces.

In Australia, 1 tablespoon equals 20 ml, and there are 4 teaspoons in the Australian tablespoon.

Spoon measures are used for smaller amounts of ingredients. Although the size of the tablespoon varies slightly in different countries, for practical purposes and for recipes in this book, a straight substitution is all that's necessary. Measurements made using cups or spoons always should be level unless stated otherwise.

Common Weight Range Replacements

Imperial / U.S.	Metric
½ ounce	15 g
1 ounce	25 g or 30 g
4 ounces (¼ pound)	115 g or 125 g
8 ounces (½ pound)	225 g or 250 g
16 ounces (1 pound)	450 g or 500 g
1¼ pounds	625 g
1½ pounds	750 g
2 pounds or 2¼ pounds	1,000 g or 1 kg

Oven Temperature Equivalents

Fahrenheit Setting	Celsius Setting*	Gas Setting
300°F	150°C	Gas Mark 2 (very low)
325°F	160°C	Gas Mark 3 (low)
350°F	180°C	Gas Mark 4 (moderate)
375°F	190°C	Gas Mark 5 (moderate)
400°F	200°C	Gas Mark 6 (hot)
425°F	220°C	Gas Mark 7 (hot)
450°F	230°C	Gas Mark 8 (very hot)
475°F	240°C	Gas Mark 9 (very hot)
500°F	260°C	Gas Mark 10 (extremely hot)
Broil	Broil	Grill

*Electric and gas ovens may be calibrated using Celsius. However, for an electric oven, increase Celsius setting 10 to 20 degrees when cooking above 160°C. For convection or forced air ovens (gas or electric) lower the temperature setting 25°F/10°C when cooking at all heat levels.

Baking Pan Sizes

Imperial / U.S.	Metric
9×1½-inch round cake pan	22- or 23×4-cm (1.5 L)
9×1½-inch pie plate	22- or 23×4-cm (1 L)
8×8×2-inch square cake pan	20×5-cm (2 L)
9×9×2-inch square cake pan	22- or 23×4.5-cm (2.5 L)
11×7×1½-inch baking pan	28×17×4-cm (2 L)
2-quart rectangular baking pan	30×19×4.5-cm (3 L)
13×9×2-inch baking pan	34×22×4.5-cm (3.5 L)
15×10×1-inch jelly roll pan	40×25×2-cm
9×5×3-inch loaf pan	23×13×8-cm (2 L)
2-quart casserole	2 L

U.S. / Standard Metric Equivalents

⅛ teaspoon = 0.5 ml	
¼ teaspoon = 1 ml	
½ teaspoon = 2 ml	
1 teaspoon = 5 ml	
1 tablespoon = 15 ml	
2 tablespoons = 25 ml	
¼ cup = 2 fluid ounces = 50 ml	
⅓ cup = 3 fluid ounces = 75 ml	
½ cup = 4 fluid ounces = 125 ml	
⅔ cup = 5 fluid ounces = 150 ml	
¾ cup = 6 fluid ounces = 175 ml	
1 cup = 8 fluid ounces = 250 ml	
2 cups = 1 pint = 500 ml	
1 quart = 1 liter	

emergency **substitutions**

If you don't have:	Substitute:
Bacon, 1 slice, crisp-cooked, crumbled	1 tablespoon cooked bacon pieces
Baking powder, 1 teaspoon	½ teaspoon cream of tartar plus ¼ teaspoon baking soda
Balsamic vinegar, 1 tablespoon	1 tablespoon cider vinegar or red wine vinegar plus ½ teaspoon sugar
Bread crumbs, fine dry, ¼ cup	¾ cup soft bread crumbs, or ¼ cup cracker crumbs, or ¼ cup cornflake crumbs
Broth, beef or chicken, 1 cup	1 teaspoon or 1 cube instant beef or chicken bouillon plus 1 cup hot water
Buttermilk, 1 cup	1 tablespoon lemon juice or vinegar plus enough milk to make 1 cup (let stand 5 minutes before using) or 1 cup plain yogurt
Cornstarch, 1 tablespoon (for thickening)	2 tablespoons all-purpose flour
Egg, 1 whole	¼ cup refrigerated or frozen egg product, thawed
Garlic, 1 clove	½ teaspoon bottled minced garlic or ⅛ teaspoon garlic powder
Ginger, grated fresh, 1 teaspoon	¼ teaspoon ground ginger
Half-and-half or light cream, 1 cup	1 tablespoon melted butter or margarine plus enough whole milk to make 1 cup
Mustard, dry, 1 teaspoon	1 tablespoon prepared (in cooked mixtures)
Mustard, yellow, 1 tablespoon	½ teaspoon dry mustard plus 2 teaspoons vinegar
Onion, chopped, ½ cup	2 tablespoons dried minced onion or ½ teaspoon onion powder
Sour cream, dairy, 1 cup	1 cup plain yogurt or 1 cup light sour cream
Sugar, brown, 1 cup packed	1 cup granulated sugar plus 2 tablespoons molasses
Sugar, granulated, 1 cup	1 cup packed brown sugar or 2 cups sifted powdered sugar
Tomato juice, 1 cup	½ cup tomato sauce plus ½ cup water
Tomato sauce, 2 cups	¾ cup tomato paste plus 1 cup water
Wine, red, 1 cup	1 cup beef or chicken broth or cranberry juice in savory recipes; cranberry juice in dessert recipes
Wine, white, 1 cup	1 cup chicken broth in savory recipes; apple juice or white grape juice in dessert recipes

seasoning

If you don't have:	Substitute:
Apple pie spice, 1 teaspoon	½ teaspoon ground cinnamon, ¼ teaspoon ground nutmeg, ⅛ teaspoon ground allspice, and dash ground cloves or ginger
Cajun seasoning, 1 tablespoon	½ teaspoon white pepper, ½ teaspoon garlic powder, ½ teaspoon onion powder, ½ teaspoon cayenne pepper, ½ teaspoon paprika, and ½ teaspoon black pepper
Fajita seasoning, 1 tablespoon	1½ teaspoons ground cumin, ½ teaspoon dried oregano, crushed, ¼ teaspoon salt, ¼ teaspoon cayenne pepper, ¼ teaspoon black pepper, ⅛ teaspoon garlic powder, and ⅛ teaspoon onion powder
Herbs, snipped fresh, 1 tablespoon	½ to 1 teaspoon dried herb, crushed, or ½ teaspoon ground herb
Thai seasoning, 1 tablespoon	1 teaspoon ground coriander plus 1 teaspoon crushed red pepper, ¼ teaspoon salt, ¼ teaspoon ground ginger, ¼ teaspoon garlic powder, and ¼ teaspoon onion powder